HOLLYWOOD

WINNERS & LOSERS

HOLLYWOOD

WINNERS & LOSERS

A TO Z

by Mark Thise

Limelight Editions
An Imprint of Hal Leonard Corporation
New York

Published in 2008 by Limelight Editions
An Imprint of Hal Leonard Corporation
19 West 21st Street, New York, NY 10010

Printed in the United States of America

Interior design and composition
by Leigh McLellan Design

Library of Congress Cataloging-in-Publication Data
is available upon request.

ISBN 978-0-87910-351-4

www.limelighteditions.com

*To my wife, children and family
whose unwavering support and
encouragement enabled me to stay the
course and make this effort a reality.
My sincerest thanks.*

CONTENTS

INTRODUCTION

It's Saturday night, it's snowing and you are burrowed in ready to watch the all-time classic *Casablanca*. With popcorn and a drink close by you fire up your DVD player and vicariously set yourself into the lives of those desperate souls searching for a way out of the city. This all-time classic not only starred the great actors Humphrey Bogart and Ingrid Bergman but many veteran character actors. You start to wonder—were Peter Lorre, Sidney Greenstreet, Claude Rains, Paul Henreid, S.Z. Sakall or Conrad Viedt ever nominated for an Oscar? Where do you look? How would you find out without pausing the movie, running to your computer, getting on the Internet, finding the appropriate web site…

This scenario has repeated itself to me countless times. That is why I have written this easy reference book, for all of those movie mavens like myself who want the answers NOW. I have included date of birth and death, real name, cause of death, "best remembered for roles," major awards and mini-biographies mainly consisting of little known facts. What actor was nominated in five consecutive decades? Who enlisted in the Army four times during WWII and was turned down classified 4-F every time? What actress was a championship archer? Who fought Jack Johnson to a draw? These are just a few of the little known tid-bits you'll learn while reading the Hollywood Winners and Losers. In addition you'll be able to look up who won or was nominated for an Oscar in any given year. I have also included more little known facts to titillate your curiosity.

This book is dedicated to all of those thespians who didn't quite make the Oscar podium. They certainly had their day in the sun—over the years many went on to great careers, others faded into obscurity, most of them are long forgotten. However, among the thousands of actors and actresses who appeared on the silver screen they were honored by their peers as the best in that given year. I felt it was time to recognize these actors and give them the kudos that they deserve. Let us never forget their great performances.

HOW TO USE THIS BOOK

All nominated actors in every category—Best Actor, Best Actress, Best Supporting Actor, and Best Supporting Actress—are listed alphabetically, followed by their nominated roles. (BA) indicates Best Actor, (BSA) Best Supporting Actors. You may also see Best Director (BD) or Best Screenplay (BS). Winners are indicated by a **star** (★) next to the title of the film, no star means they did not win the award that year. The winners' names and films are also listed.

The **spotlight icon** (✎) means "best remembered for" and is generally the name of their most famous role; the **magnifying glass icon** (🔍) indicates their mini-biography and some little known facts.

Following is a list of other awards they have won. See the next page for a complete list of abbreviations.

Have fun!

Baldwin, Alec

2003-(BSA) *The Cooler*
   Winner: Tim Robbins, *Mystic River*
▪ Born *Alexander Rae Baldwin III* on 4/3/58 in Massapequa, NY.
✎ Insulting motivator manager in *Glengarry Glen Ross*
🔍 Graduated from George Washington University. Received an Honorary Doctorate of Letters from Montclair State University. Originally studied to be a lawyer. Taken to court for assaulting a paparazzi newsman who was staking out his house for a quick picture. He was acquitted. Once married to Kim Basinger. Loves Cuban cigars and is a vegetarian.
Major Awards: Obie, NBR

Bates, Kathy

★ 1990-(BA) *Misery*
1998-(BSA) *Primary Colors*
   Winner: Judi Dench, *Shakespeare in Love*
2002-(BSA) *About Schmidt*
   Winner: Catherine Zeta-Jones, *Chicago*
▪ Born 6/28/48 in Memphis, TN
✎ Annie Wilkes in *Misery* (#17 on AFI's Villain List)
🔍 Graduated from Southern Methodist University. Once worked in the New York Museum of Modern Art as a cashier in their gift shop. Since her first success on Broadway, she has owned and operated a very lucrative Talking Books audiocassette company. Lived with her future husband Tony Campisi for 12 years before they got married. They were divorced six years later.
Major Awards: Obie, GG, SAG, NBR

Award Abbreviations

AFI	American Film Institute
BAFTA	British Academy of Film and Television Arts
BIFF	Berlin International Film Festival (German Oscar)
BSFC	Boston Society of Film Critics
BW	Western Heritage-Bronze Wrangler
CAN	Cannes Film Festival Award
CB DeMille	Cecil B. DeMille
César	César (French Oscar)
DDA	David Di Donatello (Italian Oscar)
DG	Directors Guild
Emmy	Emmy
Grammy	Grammy
GG	Golden Globe
Goya	Goya (Spanish Oscar)
ISA	Independent Spirit Award
KCFCC	Kansas City Film Critics Circle
LAFC	Los Angeles Film Critics
LAFC/LA	Los Angeles Film Critic Life Achievement
NBR	National Board of Review
NSFC	National Society of Film Critics
NYFC	New York Film Critics
Obie	Obie
Peabody	Peabody
PC	People's Choice
PUL	Pulitzer Prize For Drama
SAG	Screen Actors Guild
SAT	Saturn (Best Performance in Sci-Fi film)
Tony	Tony
VFF	Venice Film Festival
WFCA	Women in Film Crystal Award
WOF	Walk of Fame

HOLLYWOOD

WINNERS & LOSERS

Abraham, F. Murray

★ 1984-(BA) *Amadeus*
▧ Born 10/24/39 in Pittsburgh, PA
✔ Mozart rival Salieri in nominated role
✎ Graduated from the University of Texas. When not acting, Mr. Abraham is a professor of theater at Brooklyn College. Once did Fruit of the Loom commercials. Past history and common sense has indicated that winning the Oscar leads to better parts, but this has oddly not been the case with this talented actor. The Italian government awarded him the Premio Italianienel Mondo for distinguished Italian immigrants.
Major Awards: Oscar, GG, LAFC, Obie, KCFCC

Adams, Amy

2005-(BSA) *Junebug*
    Winner: Rachel Weisz, *The Constant Gardner*
▧ Born 8/20/74 in Vicenza, Italy
✔ Ashley in nominated role
✎ Her father had a career in the military and moving was a part of life. Grew up in Castle Rock, CO, and then moved to Minneapolis, MN. Brought up in a Mormon household. She has six brothers and sisters. Worked in a Hooters restaurant but quit soon after she turned 18 and they made her wear their signature skimpy outfits.
Major Awards: NSFC, ISA, Sundance

Adams, Nick

1963-(BSA) *Twilight of Honor*
    Winner: Melvyn Douglas, *Hud*
▧ Born *Nicholas Adamschock* 7/10/31 in Nanticoke, PA. Died 2/7/68 of a drug overdose.
✔ Johnny Yuma in western TV series.
✎ Graduated from St. Peters College. Served in the U.S. Coast Guard during the Korean War. He was a good friend of James Dean. Took Dean's passing very hard and was arrested nine times for speeding in one year following Dean's death. He

dubbed his friend's voice in one uncompleted scene from his movie *Giant*. Studied karate with Elvis Presley. He spent over $8,000 advertising for an Oscar win and was devastated when he lost. His best friend was actor Robert Conrad.

Adjani, Isabelle

1975-(BA) *The Story of Adele H*
    Winner: Louise Fletcher, *One Flew over the Cuckoo's Nest*
1989-(BA) *Camille Claudel*
    Winner: Jessica Tandy, *Driving Miss Daisy*
▧ Born 6/27/55 in Paris, France.
✔ Victor Hugo's tormented daughter in *The Story of Adele H*
✎ Made her film debut at age 14. She was featured on the cover of *Time* magazine at the age of 22 without having made one picture in the U.S. Only French actress to win four César Awards, the equivalent of the Oscar. Fluent in English and German. Recorded a million-selling record in 1983. On the Cannes jury in 1987. At age 19 she was the youngest person nominated for Best Actress, until Keisha Castle-Hughes in 2002.
Major Awards: NBR, NYFC, NSFC, César, Cannes, DDA, BIFF, MWFF

Affleck, Ben

★ 1997-(Best Writing for the Screen) *Good Will Hunting*
▧ Born 8/15/72 in Berkeley, CA
✔ Matt Damon's pal in *Good Will Hunting*
✎ Friends with Matt Damon since childhood. Wrote *Good Will Hunting* out of frustration from not landing any acting jobs. Sold script for $600,000. Owns several vintage arcade games. Speaks French, Spanish, and Arabic. Once gave Jennifer Lopez a $3.2 million engagement ring. He won the 2004 California state Poker Championship, a $356,000 prize. Went all in and married actress Jennifer Garner.
Major Awards: Oscar, NBR, GG, SAG

Aghdashloo, Shohreh

2003-(BSA) *House of Sand and Fog*
   Winner: Renée Zellweger, *Cold Mountain*
▫ Born 1952 in Tehran, Iran
✵ Nadi in nominated role.
⚲ Living under the Ayatollah Khomeini's tyranni-
cal rule, she decided to leave her husband and Iran
behind and escaped to London. She got a degree
in international relations and almost had a career in
journalism. First Iranian actress to be nominated
for an Oscar. She elected to have rhinoplasty. At
the age of 36 did her first nude scene.
Major Awards: LAFC, NYFC, ISA

Aherne, Brian

1939-(BSA) *Juarez*
   Winner: Thomas Mitchell, *Stagecoach*
▫ Born 5/2/02 in Kings Norton, Worchester,
   England. Died 2/6/86 of heart failure.
✵ Emperor Maximillian in nominated role.
⚲ Made his stage debut at the age of eight doing a
pantomime act with Sir Noel Coward. Graduated
from Malvern College majoring in architecture.
Had his pilot's license and his own airplane. Got
his wife Joan Fontaine interested in flying, and she
got her license too. He wrote his autobiography *A
Proper Job* in 1969. He was once brother-in-law of
Olivia de Havilland.
Major Awards: WOF

Aiello, Danny

1989-(BSA) *Do the Right Thing*
   Winner: Denzel Washington, *Glory*
▫ Born 6/20/33 in New York, NY
✵ Sal, pizza parlor owner, in nominated role.
⚲ After graduation he dummied up his ID and
joined the Army—he was stationed in Germany for
three years. Mr. Aiello has worked as a bus driver,
labor official, nightclub bouncer, pool hustler, and
according to him, an occasional thief. Voted the
youngest union president of the local bus transit
union. Uncle to New York Yankee's sportscaster
Michael Kay.
Major Awards: LAFC, NBR

Aimee, Anouk

1966-(BA) *A Man and a Woman*
   Winner: Elizabeth Taylor, *Who's Afraid of
   Virginia Woolf?*
▫ Born *Francoise Sorya (Dreyfus)* 4/27/32 in
   Paris, France.
✵ Anne Gauthier in nominated role.
⚲ She made her stage debut when she was 14. She
was married to five-times-nominated actor Albert
Finney. Chosen by *Empire* magazine as one of the
100 sexiest stars in film. After a 27-year break, re-
turned to American films in 1994, in Robert Altman's
Ready to Wear. Bypassed an opportunity to make it
big in America and elected to stay in France.
Major Awards: GG, Cannes, BAFTA, César,
BIFF

Albert, Eddie

1953-(BSA) *Roman Holiday*
   Winner: Frank Sinatra, *From Here to Eternity*
1972-(BSA) *Heartbreak Kid*
   Winner: Joel Grey, *Cabaret*
▫ Born *Edward Albert Heimberger* 4/22/08 in
   Rock Island, IL. Died 5/26/05 of pneumonia
   and Alzheimer's.
✵ Starring as Mr. Douglas with Eva Gabor in
   TV series *Green Acres.*
⚲ In between going to college and singing on a
Minnesota radio show, he was a trapeze artist in
the circus. Serving in the Navy during WW II, he
saved the lives of 70 marines during the Battle of
Tarawa and was awarded the Bronze Star. He was
a tireless conservationist, crusading for endangered
species, healthful food, and pollution cleanups.
Major Awards: NSFC, WOF

Albertson, Jack

★ 1968-(BSA) *The Subject Was Roses*

▦ Born 6/16/07 in Lynn, MA. Died 11/25/81 of cancer.

⚕ The "man" in TV comedy series *Chico and the Man*.

⚲ He was a high school dropout. He headed for NY and was so poor he slept on the subway for a nickel a night in the winter, and in Central Park in the summer. In his younger days as a vaudeville dancer, Albertson suffered stage fright so bad that he thought audiences were looking at his feet. Won the Triple Crown of acting. His last request was that he be cremated and his ashes spread to the sea.

Major Awards: Oscar, Tony, Emmy, DD, WOF

Alda, Alan

2004-(BSA) *The Aviator*
    Winner: Morgan Freeman, *Million Dollar Baby*

▦ Born 1/28/36 in New York, NY.

⚕ Hawkeye Pierce in long running TV series *M*A*S*H**

⚲ Graduated from Fordham University. Contracted polio as a young child and almost died. Was an officer in the Army Reserves and also worked as a cab driver and a gas station clown. Only person to win an Emmy in writing, directing, and acting. Has been nominated an incredible 16 times for an Emmy. Only actor to appear in every episode of *M*A*S*H**. Married to his wife Arlene for 48 years.

Major Awards: GG, DGA, NBR, NYFC, Emmy (4), PC*

Alejandro, Norma

1987-(BSA) *Gaby—A True Story*
    Winner: Olympia Dukakis, *Moonstruck*

▦ Born *Norma Aleandro Robelo* on 12/6/36 in Buenos Aires, Argentina.

⚕ Devoted servant in nominated role.

⚲ Made her stage debut at age 12. She is the third generation of her family to be a thespian. An ardent political activist, she was declared an enemy of the state by Argentina's Military Junta and, amid death threats, she fled to Uruguay then to Spain. She is also a playwright, director, and writer of poems and short stories.

Major Awards: NYFC, Cannes, DDA

Alexander, Jane

1970-(BA) *The Great White Hope*
    Winner: Glenda Jackson, *Women in Love*
1976-(BSA) *All the President's Men*
    Winner: Beatrice Straight, *Network*
1979-(BSA) *Kramer vs. Kramer*
    Winner: Meryl Streep, *Kramer vs. Kramer*
1983-(BSA) *Testament*
    Winner: Shirley MacLaine, *Terms of Endearment*

▦ Born *Jane Quigley* 10/28/39 in Boston, MA.

⚕ Strong mother in *Testament*

⚲ After a year at Edinburgh, she hitchhiked all over Europe. She was once the chair for the National Endowment of the Arts, but resigned after four years of battling conservative opponents. Received an honorary degree from Smith College and was the commencement speaker for Duke University's Class of 1996. Her grandfather, Daniel Quigley, was the personal physician to Buffalo Bill Cody. Nominated five times for a Tony.

Major Awards: Emmy, Tony, Obie, BW, WFCA

Allen, Joan

1995-(BSA) *Nixon*
    Winner: Miro Sorvino, *Mighty Aphrodite*
1996-(BSA) *The Crucible*
    Winner: Juliette Binoche, *The English Patient*
2000-(BA) *The Contender*
    Winner: Julia Roberts, *Erin Brockovich*

▦ Born 7/20/56 in Rochelle, IL

⚕ Pat Nixon in nominated role.

⚲ She was so shy as a child that they thought she had a psychological disorder. She was voted the most likely to succeed in her high school. Graduated from Eastern

Illinois University. She was a founding member of Chicago's famous Steppenwolf Theater. Worked as a secretary to an educational film company.
Major Awards: Tony, NSFC, LAFC, SATURN, KCFCC

Allen, Woody

★ 1977-(BA) *Annie Hall*
    Winner: Richard Dreyfuss, *The Goodbye Girl*
★ 1977-(Best Director) *Annie Hall*
★ 1977-(Best Writer) *Annie Hall*
1978-(BD) *Interiors*
1978-(BW) *Interiors*
1980-(BW) *Manhattan*
1984-(BD) *Broadway Danny Rose*
1984-(BW) *Broadway Danny Rose*
1985-(BW) *Purple Rose of Cairo*
1986-(BD) *Hannah and Her Sisters*
★ 1986-(Best Writer) *Hannah and Her Sisters*
1987-(BW) *Radio Days*
1990-(BD) *Crimes and Misdemeanors*
1990-(BW) *Crimes and Misdemeanors*
1991-(BW) *Alice*
1993-(BW) *Husbands and Wives*
1994-(BD) *Bullets over Broadway*
1995-(BW) *Mighty Aphrodite*
1996-(BW) *Deconstructing Harry*
2005-(BW) *Matchpoint*
▦ Born *Allen Stewart Konigsberg* on 12/1/35 in Brooklyn, NY.
✐ Standup comedian on early TV variety shows, neurotic leading man in many of his own films.
♞ Flunked out of New York University and joined NBC's Writer's Program. Separated from Mia Farrow following his admission of falling in love with her underage adopted daughter Soon-Yi Previn. Woody's daily regimen would put a drill sergeant to task: Rises at 6:00 am, two hours of clarinet practice, one hour of tennis, twelve hours of writing. For years led his Dixieland band at Michael's Pub in New York, now plays at Café Carlyle. Speaks French fluently. Has been nominated for 136 awards, more than Chaplin, Keaton, and Harold Lloyd combined.
Major Awards: Oscar, NYFC, NSFC, BAFTA, BIFF, VFF, BSFC, César, Goya, ISA, KCFCC, LAFC, NBR, WGA

Allgood, Sara

1941-(BSA) *How Green Was My Valley*
    Winner: Mary Astor, *The Great Lie*
▦ Born 10/1/1883 in Dublin, Ireland. Died 9/13/50 of a heart attack.
✐ Mother Morgan in nominated role.
♞ Started her acting career in her native Ireland. On stage, at the revered Abbey Theater, she received rave accolades from poet W. B. Yeats, who was a friend of the family. Her only daughter died during the great influenza epidemic in 1917. She became a U.S. citizen in 1945.
Major Awards: NBR

Ameche, Don

★ 1985-(BSA) *Cocoon*
▦ Born *Dominic Felix Amici* on 5/31/08 in Kenosha, WI. Died 12/6/93 of prostate cancer.
✐ Alexander Graham Bell in *The Story of Alexander Graham Bell*.
♞ Studied law at Wisconsin, Marquette, Georgetown, and Columbia Universities. Before movies was on Broadway and vaudeville, and was a popular radio announcer. Inducted into the Radio Hall of Fame in 1992. Once worked as a circus ringmaster. His cousin was All-American Heisman Trophy winner and Baltimore Colts fullback Alan "The Horse" Ameche.
Major Awards: Oscar, VFF, WOF

Anderson, Dame Judith

1940-(BSA) *Rebecca*
    Winner: Jane Darwell, *The Grapes of Wrath*
▦ Born Frances Margaret Anderson on 2/10/1898 in Adelaide, Australia. Died 1/3/92 of pneumonia.
✐ Mrs. Danvers in nominated role. (#31 on AFI's Villain List).

In 1960 she was named Dame Commander of the British Empire. She was a favorite of the great conductor Arturo Tuscanni—he was so enthralled with her performances that on one occasion he almost tumbled out of his box seat while applauding. Only actress to win two Emmys for playing the same character, Lady Macbeth, in two separate television productions. Starred on the stage for over 30 years and made her final film appearance at age 87.
Major Awards: Emmy, BW

Andrews, Julie

★ 1964-(BA) *Mary Poppins*
1965-(BA) *The Sound of Music*
   Winner: Julie Christie, *Darling*
1982-(BA) *Victor/Victoria*
   Winner: Meryl Streep, *Sophie's Choice*
   Born *Julie Elizabeth Welles* on 10/1/35 in Walton-On-Thames, England.
Mary Poppins
At the age of 13 she was the youngest soloist to ever appear in the *Royal Variety Show*. Her pristine image was a tad tarnished when she shed her top in the movie *S.O.B.* She sued Mt. Sinai Hospital for a botched throat surgery and won a $30 million settlement. She is one of the few singers who have perfect pitch. She also has a rose named after her. Despite her clean cut image she once stated "I don't want to be thought of as wholesome."
Major Awards: Oscar, GG, Emmy, WOF, DDA, BAFTA, KCFCC, SAG Life Achievement

Ann-Margret

1971-(BSA) *Carnal Knowledge*
   Winner: Cloris Leachman, *The Last Picture Show*
1975-(BSA) *Tommy*
   Winner: Louise Fletcher, *One Flew Over the Cuckoo's Nest*
   Born *Ann-Margret Olsen* on 4/28/41 in Valsjobyn, Sweden.
Vegas nightclub performances, starring with Elvis Presley in *Viva Las Vegas*

Attended Northwestern University. Discovered by George Burns who put her in his Las Vegas act. She appeared in Ted Mack's *Amateur Hour* in 1957. In 1972, while performing at Lake Tahoe, she took a near fatal fall off a 22-foot stage, and extensive facial plastic surgery had to be performed. Had a special friendship with Elvis Presley, and he would send her flowers for every one of her stage appearances. Broke her shoulder in a motorcycle accident in 2000. Speaks Swedish fluently.
Major Awards: GG, WFCA, WOF

Archer, Anne

1987-(BSA) *Fatal Attraction*
   Winner: Olympia Dukakis, *Moonstruck*
   Born 8/25/47 in Los Angeles, CA
Beth Gallagher, the wife suffering the infidelities of her husband in *Fatal Attraction*
Graduated from Claremont College, majoring in drama. She was voted Miss Golden Globe in 1971. Anne is the daughter of Marjorie Lord, who played Danny Thomas's wife on the popular '50s sitcom *Make Room for Daddy*. Once did a TV commercial for Chevy Bronco. She is the international spokeswoman for Applied Scholastic International, a front group for the Church of Scientology.
Major Awards: GG, VFF

Arden, Eve

1945-(BSA) *Mildred Pierce*
   Winner: Anne Revere-*National Velvet*
   Born *Eunice Quedens* on 4/30/21 in Mill Valley, CA. Died 11/12/90 of cardiac arrest.
English teacher in '50s sitcom *Our Miss Brooks*
Dropped out of high school to make her stage debut at age 16. After starring in her first two films she changed her name to Eve Arden after two cosmetics she was using, " Evening in Arms" and "Elizabeth Arden." Inducted into the Radio Hall of Fame in 1995. She was known for her wry sense of humor and her hilarious wisecracks.
Major Awards: Emmy, WOF

Arkin, Alan

1966-(BA) *The Russians Are Coming! The Russians Are Coming!*
　　Winner: Paul Scofield-*A Man for All Seasons*
1968, (BA) *The Heart Is a Lonely Hunter*
　　Winner: Cliff Robertson-*Charly*
★ 2006-(BSA) *Little Miss Sunshine*
▨ Born 3/26/34 in New York, NY
✇ Yossarian in *Catch 22*
✎ He has been a director and has written several children's books. In addition he is a producer, singer, composer, and teacher. He was a member of the Terriers, a Calypso group with the hit "Banana Boat Song." He is only one of six actors to be nominated for an Oscar in his first movie. He is a founding member of the Second City Improv. Nominated four times for an Emmy.
Major Awards: GG, Tony, Obie, NYFC, BSFC

Arliss, George

★ 1929/30-(BA) *Disraeli*
1929/30, (BA) *The Green Goddess*
▨ Born *George Augustus Andrews* on 4/10/1868 in London, England. Died 2/5/46 of a bronchial ailment.
✇ Benjamin Disraeli in nominated role.
✎ Retiring in 1937 he spent the rest of his life writing two autobiographies and caring for his blind actress wife, Florence Montgomery. First British actor to win an Oscar. Once described as the world's greatest living actor—by himself—while under oath during a court appearance.
Major Awards: Oscar, WOF

Arthur, Jean

1943-(BA) *The More the Merrier*
　　Winner: Jennifer Jones, *The Song of Bernadette*
▨ Born *Gladys Georgianna-Greene* on 10/17/05 in Plattsburg, NY. Died 6/19/91 of heart failure.
✇ Saunders in *Mr. Smith Goes to Washington*
✎ She was an extreme introvert and suffered from a crippling inferiority complex. Before each scene she would cry, whine, and throw up. Auditioned for the part of Scarlet O'Hara in *Gone with the Wind*. She was Frank Capra's favorite actress. Although she always suffered stage fright, years later she taught at Vassar and the North Carolina School of Arts.
Major Awards: WOF

Ashcroft, Dame Peggy

★ 1984-(BSA) *A Passage to India*
▨ Born 12/22/07 in Croydon, England. Died 6/14/91 of a stroke.
✇ Barbie Batchelor on PBS TV series *The Jewel in the Crown*
✎ Considered one of England's greatest stage actors. Played Desdemona to Paul Robeson's Othello in the '40s. First British actress to have a theater named after while still alive, the Ashcroft in her home town. She was named Commander of the British Empire (CBE) in 1951. Made Dame by Queen Elizabeth in 1956. She is the oldest Best Supporting Actress winner at age 77 years, 3 months. Touché to the elderly!
Major Awards: Oscar, NBR, NYFC, LAFC, GG, VFF, BAFTA, BSFC, KCFCC

Astaire, Fred

★ 1949-Honorary Oscar
1974-(BSA) *The Towering Inferno*
　　Winner: Robert DeNiro, *The Godfather, Part II*
▨ Born *Frederick Austerlitz* on 5/10/1899 in Omaha, NE. Died 9/25/87 of pneumonia.
✇ Dancing with Ginger Rogers
✎ Mother enrolled him in dance school when he was four, and he was on the vaudeville circuit at the age of seven. Thanks to all of the dancing routines, he lost 14 pounds while filming *Holiday Inn*. He was addicted to the soap operas *As the World Turns* and *The Guiding Light*. He had his legs insured by Lloyds of London for one million dollars.
Major Awards: AFI's Life Achievement Award, Emmy, GG, CBD, BAFTA, DDA, WOF

Astor, Mary

★ 1941-(BSA) *The Great Lie*
▦ Born *Lucille Vasconsellos Langhanke* on 5/3/06 in Quincy, IL. Died 10/5/87 of a heart attack.
🖉 Bridget O'Shaughnessy, the femme fatale in *The Maltese Falcon*
🔍 Her German father entered her in a beauty contest when she was 14, which launched her career in show business. Adversity seemed to dog her—her husband died in a plane crash, she suffered bouts of alcoholism and an abortion, and she attempted suicide on several occasions. She also wrote two autobiographies and a children's book. Appeared in over 123 movies.
Major Awards: Oscar, NBR , WOF

Attenborough, Sir Richard

★ 1982-(Best Director) *Gandhi*
★ 1982-(Best Picture/Producer) *Gandhi*
▦ Born 8/29/23 in Cambridge, England
🖉 John Hammond in *Jurassic Park*
🔍 The producer, director, actor started his career at age 12 playing the harmonica and singing. He was in the RAF during WW II. He was appointed CBE in 1967 and was knighted by the Queen in 1976. He gave the eulogy at the funeral of his close friend, Sir John Mills. Tragically, his daughter, his daughter's mother-in-law, and his granddaughter died while vacationing in Phuket, Thailand when the South Asian tsunami hit in 2005. President of the Royal Academy of Dramatic Art (RADA) since 1997.
Major Awards: Oscar, BAFTA, DDA, DGA, GG

Auer, Mischa

1936-(BSA) *My Man Godfrey*
　　Winner: Walter Brennan, *Come and Get It*
▦ Born *Mischa Ounskowski* on 11/17/05 in St. Petersburg, Russia. Died 3/5/67 of a heart attack.
🖉 Carlo the starving artist in the nominated role.
🔍 He adopted his pseudonym from his maternal grandfather, famed Russian violinist Leopold Auer.

His father died in the Russo-Japanese War, and his mother died of typhus. Immigrated to America with his grandfather. He spoke six languages fluently: Russian, English, Italian, French, German, and Spanish. He was accomplished on the piano and violin.

Avery, Margaret

1985-(BSA) *The Color Purple*
　　Winner: Anjelica Houston-*Prizzi's Honor*
▦ Born in Mangum, Oklahoma
🖉 Whoopi Goldberg's long-time friend in *The Color Purple*
🔍 Graduated from San Francisco State University. Tina Turner turned down the role in *The Color Purple*, which gave her a lucky break. Steven Spielberg hired her because he had directed her in a commercial years back and she had left a seemingly indelible impression. Made her TV debut in the movie *Something Evil*, again directed by Steven Spielberg.

Akroyd, Dan

1989-(BSA) *Driving Miss Daisy*
　　Winner: Denzel Washington, *Glory*
▦ Born 7/1/50 in Ontario, Canada
🖉 Elwood Blues, one half of the Blues Brothers with John Belushi
🔍 Studied at a Catholic Seminary from which he got the boot. Was a surveyor, nightclub manager, and train brakeman. Received an Honorary Doctorate from Carlton University. His right eye is blue and his left eye is brown. He was born with syndactylism—in other words he has webbed toes. He's a police wonk and collects badges, and he also has an extensive collection of books on the supernatural. Once engaged to Carrie Fisher.
Major Awards: Emmy, WOF

Ayres, Lew

1948-(BA) *Johnny Belinda*
　　Winner: Laurence Olivier, *Hamlet*

■ Born *Lewis Ayre* on 12/28/08 in Minneapolis, MN. Died 12/30/96 from complications of a coma.

〆 *Dr. Kildare* on the MGM series.

🖊 Attended the University of Arizona but ended up dropping out. Played the banjo, piano, and guitar in nightclubs. When WW II broke out, Ayres declared himself a conscientious objector thus alienating himself from the movie-going public. He volunteered for non-combat medical service. Under intense fire he won three battle stars thus proving to the public that he never was a coward. Had an affair with Jane Wyman, which led to her divorce from Ronald Reagan.

Major Awards: NBR, WOF

Bacall, Lauren

1996-(BSA) *The Mirror Has Two Faces*
   Winner: Juliette Binoche, *The English Patient*
■ Born *Betty Perske* on 9/16/24 in Bronx, NY.
〆 Various roles with husband Humphrey Bogart.
🖊 She once modeled for Montgomery Ward department stores. Discovered by producer Howard Hawks's wife Nancy. Bogie recognized her grit and he said, "Saw your test, I think we'll have fun working together, kid," but they didn't hit it off when they first met. Sick of the roles she was getting, she eventually bought out her contract with Warner Bros. One of her hobbies is collecting beer mugs. Crowned Miss Greenwich Village in 1942. Cousin to former Israeli Prime Minister Shimon Perez. Once engaged to Frank Sinatra.

Major Awards: Tony, DD, GG, SAG, BIFF, NBR, WOF

Baddeley, Hermoine

1959-(BSA) *Room at the Top*
   Winner: Shelly Winters, *The Dairy of Anne Frank*
■ Born *Hermoine Clinton Baddeley* on 11/13/05 in Broseley, England. Died 8/19/86 of a stroke.
〆 The maid in *Mary Poppins*.

🖊 She appeared on stage at the age of 16 with none other than Noel Coward. Good friends with renowned playwright George Bernard Shaw. He liked her performances so much that he suggested she change her last name to "Goodeley." A descendant of revolutionary war British general Sir Henry Clinton.

Major Awards: GG

Badham, Mary

1962-(BSA) *To Kill a Mockingbird*
   Winner: Patty Duke, *The Miracle Worker*
■ Born 10/7/52 in Birmingham, AL.
〆 Scout in *To Kill a Mockingbird*
🖊 Her father was a retired Army officer and past president of Bessemer Steel. She had no previous acting experience before her Oscar-nominated role. She is currently an art restorer and college testing coordinator working out of her home. At the time, the youngest actress, age nine, to be nominated. Years later she still called Gregory Peck "Atticus." She is in high demand as a speaker, talking about *To Kill a Mockingbird*.

Bainter, Faye

1938-(BA) *White Banner*
   Winner: Bette Davis, *Jezebel*
★ 1938-(BSA) *Jezebel*
1961-(BSA) *The Children's Hour*
   Winner: Rita Moreno, *West Side Story*
■ Born 12/7/1891 in Los Angeles, CA.
   Died 4/16/68 of pneumonia.
〆 Mrs. Tilford in *The Children's Hour*
🖊 Mrs. Bainter is buried in Arlington National Cemetery, alongside her husband Lt. Commander Reginald Venable. She is the first actor to be nominated for both awards in the same year. Her double nominations prompted changes in the academy rules.

Major Awards: Oscar, WOF

Baker, Carroll

1956-(BA) *Baby Doll*
    Winner: Ingrid Bergman, *Anastasia*
▪ Born *Karolina Piekarski* on 5/28/35 in Johnstown, PA
🖋 Eve Prescott in *How the West Was Won*
🔍 Her father was a traveling salesman. She was once a magician's assistant. She was a nightclub dancer to earn tuition for the Actors Studio. In 1964 while filming *Mr. Moses* in Africa, a Masai chieftain was so enthralled with her that he offered 150 cows, 200 goats and sheep, plus $750 for her. She was Miss Florida Fruit and Vegetable in 1949.
Major Awards: GG, WOF

Baldwin, Alec

2003-(BSA) *The Cooler*
    Winner: Tim Robbins, *Mystic River*
▪ Born *Alexander Rae Baldwin III* on 4/3/58 in Massapequa, NY
🖋 Insulting motivator manager in *Glengarry Glen Ross*
🔍 Graduated from George Washington University. Received an Honorary Doctorate of Letters from Montclair State University. Originally studied to be a lawyer. Taken to court for assaulting a paparazzi newsman who was staking out his house for a quick picture. He was acquitted. Once married to Kim Basinger. Loves Cuban cigars and is a vegetarian.
Major Awards: Obie, NBR

Balsam, Martin

★ 1965-(BSA) *A Thousand Clowns*
▪ Born 11/4/19 in Bronx, NY. Died 1996 of a heart attack.
🖋 Detective Milton Arbogast in *Psycho*
🔍 He served with the U.S. Army Combat Engineers during WW II. One of the first students to attend the Lee Strasberg's Actors Studio. Auditioned for the voice of HAL in *2001: A Space Odyssey*. Director Kubrick turned him down, stating his voice wasn't malevolent enough. Once brother-in-law to Dick Van Dyke and ex-uncle of George Clooney. Studied Kung Fu. For years after *Psycho*, fans would ask if he hurt himself in the fall down the stairs.
Major Awards: Tony, NBR, Obie

Bancroft, Anne

★ 1962-(BA) *The Miracle Worker*
1964-(BA) *The Pumpkin Eater*
    Winner: Julie Andrews, *Mary Poppins*
1967-(BA) *The Graduate*
    Winner: Katharine Hepburn, *Guess Who's Coming To Dinner?*
1977-(BA) *The Turning Point*
    Winner: Diane Keaton, *Annie Hall*
1985-(BA) *Agnes of God*
    Winner, Geraldine Page, *The Trip to Bountiful*
▪ Born *Anne Marie Italiano* on 9/17/31 in Bronx, NY. Died 6/6/05 of uterine cancer.
🖋 Mrs. Robinson in *The Graduate*
🔍 Graduated from the American Academy of Dramatic Arts. She was only six years older than Dustin Hoffman when she played Mrs. Robinson. Preparing for her role as Anne Sullivan in *The Miracle Worker* she blindfolded herself and learned sign language. Was married for 40 years to Mel Brooks. Fifteenth actor to win the Triple Crown of acting.
Major Awards: Oscar, Tony, Emmy, NBR, Cannes, GG, BAFTA, WOF

Bancroft, George

1928/29-(BA) *Thunderbolt*
    Winner: Warner Baxter, *In Old Arizona*
▪ Born 9/30/1882 in Philadelphia, PA. Died 10/2/56 of natural causes.
🖋 Curly, the driver in *Stagecoach*
🔍 He started out as a blackface performer in minstrel shows. Graduated from the Naval Academy in Annapolis, and served as an officer in the Navy. With his stardom established, his ego knew no bounds. He once refused a director's order to fall down when shot. He shouted, "One bullet can't kill Bancroft!"

Bannen, Ian

1965-(BSA) *The Flight of the Phoenix*
    Winner: Martin Balsam, *A Thousand Clowns*
▦ Born on 6/29/28 in Airdrie, Scotland.
    Died 11/3/99 in a car accident.
〃 The cantankerous cricket-loving Grandfather
in *Hope and Glory*
🔍 Served in the British Army and attended Ratcliffe
College. Awarded Life Achievement Award by the
British Academy of Film. Almost gave up acting to
become a monk in a cloistered monastery. When
director John Schlesinger wanted to cast him in
Sunday, Bloody Sunday he refused the role because
it required him to kiss a male actor. Peter Finch
took the role and was nominated for an Oscar.
Major Awards: London's Critic

Bardem, Javier

2000-(BA) *Before Night Falls*
    Winner: Russell Crowe, *Gladiator*
▦ Born 3/1/69 in Las Palmas, Spain.
〃 Cuban writer Reinaldo Arenas in above movie.
🔍 He is a hypochondriac and doesn't know how to
drive a car. Wanted to be a painter. Played rugby for
the Spanish National Team, toured the country with
a theatrical group. He was a construction worker
and male stripper. First Spaniard to be nominated
for an Oscar.
Major Awards: Goya, NBR, NSFC, ISA, VFF

Barrault, Marie-Christine

1976-(BA) *Cousin, Cousine*
    Winner: Faye Dunaway, *Network*
▦ Born 3/21/44 in Paris, France
〃 Marthe in above movie.
🔍 Her breakout movie *Cousin, Cousine* shattered
the foreign box office record set by an *A Man and
a Woman*. Married to French film director Roger
Vadim until his death. She trained at the Paris
Conservatoire. Was a staple on French television
in the '70s and '80s. She was a member of the jury
on the Venice Film Festival in 1981.

Barraza, Adrianna

2006-(BSA) *Babel*
    Winner: Jennifer Hudson, *Dreamgirls*
▦ Born on 3/5/56 in Toluca, Mexico.
〃 Amelia in nominated role.
🔍 She was a star on Mexican television in the 1990s.
She has directed on Telemundo and has been a dia-
lect coach and drama teacher. She has also served
as Vice President in Neutral Accent and Acting
Development for Telemundo. She had to gain 35
pounds for her role in *Babel*. She has suffered two
heart attacks, and nearly had heat stroke in the
desert while filming *Babel*.
Major Awards: SFFCC

Barrymore, Ethel

★ 1944-(BSA) *None but the Lonely Heart*
1946-(BSA) *The Spiral Staircase*
    Winner: Anne Baxter, *The Razor's Edge*
1947-(BSA) *The Paradine Case*
    Winner: Celeste Holm, *Gentleman's Agreement*
1949-(BSA) *Pinky*
    Winner: Mercedes McCambridge, *All the
King's Men*
▦ Born *Edith Blythe* on 8/15/1879 in Philadelphia, PA. Died 6/18/59 of a heart condition.
〃 Matriarch of politics in *The Farmer's Daughter*
🔍 She was educated in a convent and had dreams
of becoming a concert pianist. She was a big fan of
baseball, had a huge library, and is also known to have
a morbid sense of humor. When she was a young
woman, Winston Churchill once proposed to her,
however she turned him down. She and brother
Lionel were the first brother-sister Oscar winners.
Major Awards: Oscar, WOF

Barrymore, Lionel

1928/29-(BD) *Madame X*
★ 1930/31-(BA) *A Free Soul*
▦ Born *Lionel Blythe* on 4/28/1878 in Philadelphia, PA. Died 11/15/54 of a heart attack.

✒ Henry Potter in *It's a Wonderful Life*, (#6 on AFI's Villain List), Disko Troop in *Captains Courageous*

✎ Lived in Paris studying to be an artist. Wrote a novel and was a painter and etcher. Composed music that was played by the Philadelphia Symphony Orchestra. He was also a director, producer, and screenwriter. He also invented the boom microphone. From 1938 to the end of his acting days he was confined to a wheelchair due to arthritis and hip surgery.

Major Awards: Oscar, WOF (2)

Barthelmess, Richard

1927/28-(BA) *The Noose*
1927/28-(BA) *The Patent Leather Kid*
    Winner: Emil Jannings, *The Last Command*,
    The Way of all Flesh
▦ Born 5/9/1895 in New York, NY.
    Died 8/17/63 of throat cancer.
✒ Murderer Nickie Elkins in *The Noose*
✎ In the movie *Way Down East*, he made a very real ice-floe-to-ice-flow leap to save Lillian Gish, a dangerous and life-threatening stunt even by today's standards. One of the original founders of the Academy of Motion Picture Arts and Science. Joined Navy Reserve in WW II at the age of 47.
Major Awards: WOF

Baryshinikov, Mikhail

1977-(BSA) *The Turning Point*
    Winner: Jason Robards, *Julia*
▦ Born 1/27/48 in Riga, Latvia.
✒ World Class ballet dancer
✎ Defected to the U.S. from Communist Russia in 1974. Despite the rigors of staying in shape to dance, he was a smoker and serious drinker. Started his ballet lessons at a late age of 15. He was very athletic—swimming and playing rugby and soccer. Had a love child with actress Jessica Lange. Has his own perfume line called *Misha*.
Major Awards: Emmy (3), DDA

Basinger, Kim

★ 1997-(BSA) *L.A. Confidential*
▦ Born 12/8/53 in Athens, GA
✒ Lynn Bracken in *L.A. Confidential*
✎ She studied ballet at age three. She was a cheerleader. Once was the Breck Shampoo girl. First Oscar winner to appear nude in *Playboy*. Has agoraphobia and once wouldn't come out of her house for six months. Bought the town of Braselton, GA for $20 million. Later was sued for breach of contract and had to declare bankruptcy, leaving the town in a lurch. Once married to actor Alec Baldwin. She's a vegetarian. Once romantically linked to rock star Prince.
Major Awards: Oscar, SAG, GG, NBR, WOF

James Baskette

★ 1947-Honorary Oscar, *Song of the South*
    Winner, Ronald Coleman, *A Double Life*
▦ Born 2/16/04 in Indianapolis, IN.
    Died 9/9/48 of a heart ailment.
✒ Uncle Remus in *Song of the South*
✎ First black actor to win an Oscar. First live actor to be hired by Disney. This special award was perceived as an attempt to promote race relations without nominating him for BA—it backfired, the black community was incensed at his portrayal as a happy carefree slave. The NAACP denounced *Song of the South* as a racist movie and to this day Disney will not release the movie in the U.S.

Basserman, Albert

1940-(BSA) *Foreign Correspondent*
    Winner: Walter Brennan, *The Westerner*
▦ Born 9/7/1867 in Mannheim, Germany.
    Died 5/15/52 of a heart attack.
✒ Mr. Van Meer in *Foreign Correspondent*
✎ Once studied chemistry before gravitating to the stage. Made his first German movie in 1913. Fled Germany into Switzerland to escape the Nazi regime in 1933. Made his American acting debut at age 72. He did not speak English, and had to

phonically learn his lines for his Oscar nominated movie. It was years later when moviegoers finally learned he couldn't speak English.

Bassett, Angela

1993-(BA) *What's Love Got To Do With It*
    Winner: Holly Hunter, *The Piano*
▪ Born 8/16/58 in New York, NY
🖋 Tina Turner in above movie.
🔍 Her aunt raised her until she was five. Made her acting debut at age 15. She was the first black student in her high school to make the National Honor Society. She received an academic scholarship to Yale University where she earned a B.A. and Master's. Worked as a photo researcher for *US News & World Report*.
Major Awards: GG, Saturn, WFCA

Bates, Sir Alan

1968, (BA) *The Fixer*
    Winner: Cliff Robertson, *Charly*
▪ Born 2/19/34 in Allestree, Derbyshire England. Died 12/27/2003 of pancreatic cancer.
🖋 Nude shot in *Women In Love*
🔍 Started acting at age 11. Graduated from RADA. Served in the Royal Air Force in 1951. He became the darling of college coeds across the country when he shed his clothes for a full frontal nudity pose—the first Hollywood actor to do so. He was made CBE in 1995, knighted by the Queen in 2003.
Major Awards: Tony, BAFTA, SAG

Bates, Kathy

★ 1990-(BA) *Misery*
1998-(BSA) *Primary Colors*
    Winner: Judi Dench, *Shakespeare in Love*
2002-(BSA) *About Schmidt*
    Winner: Catherine Zeta-Jones, *Chicago*
▪ Born 6/28/48 in Memphis, TN

🖋 Annie Wilkes in *Misery* (#17 on AFI's Villain List)
🔍 Graduated from Southern Methodist University. Once worked in the New York Museum of Modern Art as a cashier in their gift shop. Since her first success on Broadway, she has owned and operated a very lucrative Talking Books audiocassette company. Lived with her future husband Tony Campisi for 12 years before they got married. They were divorced six years later.
Major Awards: Obie, GG, SAG, NBR

Baxter, Anne

★ 1946-(BSA) *The Razor's Edge*
1950-(BA) *All About Eve*
    Winner: Judi Holliday, *Born Yesterday*
▪ Born 5/7/23 in Michigan City, IN.
    Died 12/12/85 of a brain aneurysm.
🖋 Eve Harrington in *All About Eve* (#23 on AFI's Villain List)
🔍 She was the granddaughter of famed architect Frank Lloyd Wright. She retired to a huge sheep farm in Australia. After four years, disillusioned and very unhappy, she fled the farm and wrote a critically acclaimed novel *Intermission: A True Story*. Famed costume designer Edith Head was godmother to her daughter.
Major Awards: GG, WOF

Baxter, Warner

★ 1928/29-(BA) *In Old Arizona*
▪ Born 3/29/1891 in Columbus, OH.
    Died 5/7/51 of pneumonia.
🖋 The Cisco Kid in above movie.
🔍 He replaced Raoul Walsh as the Cisco Kid when Walsh lost his eye in an auto accident. Had a nervous breakdown. He also suffered from a severe arthritic condition so bad that he had a lobotomy to ease the pain. Unfortunately pneumonia set in after the operation thus eventually leading to his death.
Major Awards: WOF

Beatty, Ned

1976-(BSA) *Network*
Winner: Jason Robards, *All the President's Men*
▪ Born 7/6/37 in Louisville, KY
✍ Bobby Trippe, the salesman raped by the evil woodsman in *Deliverance*.
🔔 Started acting debut at age ten singing in the church choir. At one time wanted to enter the clergy for ordained religious service. Often called the busiest actor in Hollywood. Nominated for the Laurence Olivier Award, two Emmys, and a Golden Globe. He has eight children. Enjoys plucking away at his bass guitar and playing golf.

Beatty, Warren

1967-(BA) *Bonnie and Clyde*
Winner: Rod Steiger, *In the Heat of the Night*
1967-(Best Picture/Producer) *Bonnie and Clyde*
1975-(Best Writer) *Shampoo*
1978-(BA) *Heaven Can Wait*
Winner: Jon Voight, *Coming Home*
1978-(Best Director) *Heaven Can Wait*
1978-(Best Picture/Producer) *Heaven Can Wait*
1978-(Best Writer) *Heaven Can Wait*
1981-(BA) *Reds*
Winner: Henry Fonda, *On Golden Pond*
★ (Best Director) *Reds*
1981-(Best Picture/Producer) *Reds*
1981-(Best Writer) *Reds*
1991-(BA) *Bugsy*
Winner: Anthony Hopkins, *The Silence of the Lambs*
1998-(Best Writer) *Bullworth*
▪ Born *Warren Beaty* 3/30/37 in Louisville, KY
✍ Legendary lady-killer. Clyde Barrow, *Bonnie and Clyde* (#32 on AFI's Villain List.)
🔔 He made his acting debut as a child in amateur productions directed by his acting coach mother. He was class president and captain of the football team in high school. Turned down ten football scholarships. Dropped out of Northwestern to seek an acting career. Worked in a jazz bar playing the piano. He

is the younger brother of actress Shirley MacLaine. Married to actress Annette Bening, and they have four children. He is allergic to oysters. He has a photographic memory. He has been romantically linked to Julie Christie, Leslie Caron, Diane Keaton, Madonna, Natalie Wood, Joan Collins . . .
Major Awards: GG, NSFC, NBR, Irving Thalberg, BAFTA, DDA, DGA, VFF, WGA

Beery, Wallace

1929/30-(BA) *The Big House*
Winner: George Arliss, *Disraeli*
★ 1929/30-(BA) *The Champ*
▪ Born 4/1/1885 in Kansas, MO.
Died 4/15/49 of a heart attack.
✍ Long John Silver in *Treasure Island*
🔔 Once was an elephant boy in Ringling Bros. Circus. Quit after a leopard clawed him. For 35 years he held the world record for catching the largest black sea bass at 515 pounds. Once married to actress Gloria Swanson. He got violent when he drank and would often slap her around. In real life he was uncouth and totally devoid of the qualities he portrayed on the screen. Co-star Jackie Cooper said after the cameras stopped rolling he treated him like an unkept dog.
Major Awards: Oscar, WOF

Begley, Ed

★ 1962-(BSA) *Sweet Bird of Youth*
▪ Born 3/25/01 in Hartford, CT.
Died 4/28/70 of a heart attack.
✍ Boss Finlay in above movie.
🔔 Son of dirt poor Irish immigrants, he ran away from home at age ten and joined the circus. When of age enlisted in the U.S. Navy. After service he became a professional radio actor starring on *Richard Diamond, Private Detective*. Got his first big break starring in the movie *Boomerang*. Father of Ed Begley, Jr.
Major Awards: Oscar, Tony.

Bel Geddes, Barbara

1948-(BSA) *I Remember Mama*
  Winner: Claire Trevor, *Key Largo*
- Born 10/31/22 in New York, NY. Died 8/8/05 of lung cancer.
- Miss Ellie Ewing in TV soap *Dallas*
- At age 16 was expelled from swanky Putney Finishing School for being a "disruptive influence." She made her acting debut at age 18. Had a mastectomy in 1978. After years of smoking, quit in 1984 after a heart attack. Wrote two children's books *I Like To Be Me* and *So Do I*.

Major Awards: Emmy

Bellamy, Ralph

1937-(BSA) *The Awful Truth*
  Winner: Joseph Schildkraut, *The Life of Emile Zola*
1986-Honorary Oscar
- Born 6/17/04 in Chicago, IL. Died 11/29/91 of lung disease.
- FDR in *Sunrise at Campobello*
- For ten years he worked in 15 different traveling companies as an actor, director, producer, set designer, and prop man eventually starting his own company. One of the founders of the Screen Actors Guild. Among his peers, one of the most respected actors.

Major Awards: Tony, SAG Life Achievement, WOF

Bendix, William

1942-(BSA) *Wake Island*
  Winner: Van Heflin, *Johnny Eager*
- Born 1/4/06 in New York, NY. Died 12/14/64 of pneumonia.
- Chester Riley in TV series *The Life of Riley*
- Played in minor league baseball. He was a batboy for the New York Yankees and Giants. He used to fetch hot dogs for Babe Ruth, whom he later portrayed in the maligned *Babe Ruth Story*. His grocery store went under during the Depression and that's how he got into acting. He was a descendant of composer Felix Mendelssohn.

Major Awards: WOF

Benigni, Roberto

★ 1998-(BA) *Life Is Beautiful*
1998-(Best Director) *Life Is Beautiful*
1998-(Best Writing) *Life Is Beautiful*
- Born 10/27/52 in Tuscany, Italy
- After his win he said, "I am so full of joy. Every organ in my body is moving in a very bad way."
- His father was a prisoner in the Bergen-Belsen Nazi concentration camp. With his three nominations for actor, director, and producer he joined the ranks of Warren Beatty, Orson Welles, and Woody Allen as the Academy's only triple nominees in these categories.

Major Awards: Oscar, SAG, BAFTA, Cannes, César, DDA, NBR

Bening, Annette

1990-(BSA) *The Grifters*
  Winner: Whoopi Goldberg, *Ghost*
1999-(BA) *American Beauty*
  Winner: Hilary Swank, *Boys Don't Cry*
2004-(BA) *Being Julia*
  Winner: Hilary Swank, *Million Dollar Baby*
- Born 5/5/58 in Topeka, KS
- Convincing Warren Beatty that marriage is a good thing.
- Once was a cook on a charter boat to pay for her college expenses. Graduated from San Francisco State University majoring in theater. Listed as one of 12 promising new actors in *Screen World*. Publicly rebuked Hillary Clinton as a political opportunist in her bid for a senate seat in New York.

Major Awards: NSFC, SAG, NBR, BAFTA, BW, GG, WOF

Berenger, Tom

1986-(BSA) *Platoon*
  Winner: Michael Caine, *Hannah and Her Sisters*
▒ Born 5/31/50 in Chicago, IL
⬙ Sergeant Barnes in *Platoon*
⚲ A University of Missouri grad majoring in journalism. Tried out for acting on a bet in college. Studied at the Herbert Berghof Studio in New York. Once owned a restaurant and was a steelworker. Big break came when a landed he role on TV soap *One Life To Live*. Made his movie debut as Diane Keaton's pickup in *Looking for Mr. Goodbar*.
Major Awards: GG, BW

Bergen, Candice

1979-(BSA) *Starting Over*
  Winner: Meryl Streep, *Kramer vs. Kramer*
▒ Born 5/9/46 in Beverly Hills, CA
⬙ Murphy Brown in TV sitcom.
⚲ Daughter of world famous ventriloquist Edgar Bergman—reportedly wooden doll Charlie McCarthy's room was bigger than hers. Attended the University of Pennsylvania but flunked out. She is a vegetarian, and is fluent in French. She is an accomplished model, playwright, writer, and photographer.
Major Awards: Emmy, GG, BW

Bergman, Ingrid

1943-(BA) *For Whom the Bell Tolls*
  Winner: Jennifer Jones, *The Song of Bernadette*
★ 1944-(BA) *Gaslight*
1945-(BA) *The Bells of St. Mary's*
  Winner: Joan Crawford, *Mildred Pierce*
1948-(BA) *Joan of Arc*
  Winner: Jane Wyman, *Johnny Belinda*
★ 1956-(BA) *Anastasia*
★ 1974-(BSA) *Murder on the Orient Express*
1978-(BA) *Autumn Sonata*
  Winner: Jane Fonda, *Coming Home*
▒ Born 8/29/15 in Stockholm, Sweden. Died 8/29/82 of breast cancer.

⬙ Ilsa, Humphrey Bogart's girl in *Casablanca*
⚲ Her parents died when she was very young and she lived with her uncle. Her affair with director Rossalini, leaving her husband of 13 years, was a spectacular scandal—Hollywood boycotted her for seven years, eventually forgiving her for her transgressions. She is the third winner of the Triple Crown of acting. She was cremated and her ashes were spread to sea in Sweden. Only Oscar winner to die on her birthday. She was fluent in English, Swedish, French, German, and Italian.
Major Awards: Oscar, Emmy, Tony, GG, LAFC, NBR, NYFC, BAFTA, DDA, NSFA, César, WOF

Bergner, Elizabeth

1935-(BA) *Escape Me Never*
  Winner: Bette Davis, *Dangerous*
▒ Born *Elizabeth Ettel* on 8/22/1897 in Drohobycz, Poland. Died 5/12/86 of natural causes.
⬙ Gemma Jones in nominated movie
⚲ She was a favorite of famed director Max Reinhardt. Seeing the handwriting on the wall, she and her husband Dr. Paul Cziner fled the Nazi regime in 1933. Film critics of her day called her "the ablest actress in America." The city of Berlin named a city park after her.
Major Awards: German Film Award

Berlin, Jeannie

1972-(BSA) *The Heartbreak Kid*
  Winner: Eileen Heckart, *Butterflies Are Free*
▒ Born 11/1/49 in Los Angeles, CA
⬙ Lila Kolodny in nominated movie
⚲ She is the only daughter of actress, director, and screenwriter Elaine May. Made her acting debut at age 14 in *Alice's Restaurant*. Graduated from the University of New York. She is not only an actor but also a teacher, director, playwright, and screenwriter; she wrote the black comedy *In the Spirit*.
Major Awards: NYFC, NSFC

Halle Berry with Billy Bob Thornton in *Monster's Ball*.

Berry, Halle

★ 2001-(BA) *Monster's Ball*
■ Born 8/14/66 in Cleveland, OH.
〰 Storm in the movie *X-Men*.
𝄺 She won the Miss Teen America Pageant. Was runner-up in the 1986 Miss USA pageant. She was class president in high school, editor of the school paper, prom queen, and member of the National Honor Society. Once married to baseball's David Justice. She was involved in a hit-and-run accident in 2000 and was fined and given community service hours. Lost eighty percent of her hearing due to an abusive relationship. Currently the highest paid black actress in Hollywood.
Major Awards: Oscar, NBR, Emmy, SAG, GG, WFCA

Bickford, Charles

1943-(BSA) *The Song of Bernadette*
    Winner: Charles Coburn, *The More the Merrier*
1947-(BSA) *The Farmer's Daughter*
    Winner: Edmund Gwenn, *Miracle on 34th Street*
1948-(BSA) *Johnny Belinda*
    Winner: Walter Huston, *The Treasure of the Sierra Madre*
■ Born 1/1/1881 in Cambridge, MA. Died 11/9/67 of a blood infection.
〰 Pop Warner in *Jim Thorpe—All American*
𝄺 At the age of nine he was tried for attempted murder when he shot a motorman because he ran over his dog. Graduated from MIT. Bickford was once the sparring partner for James J. Corbett. In his first film, tired of being bullied by director Cecil B. DeMille, he hauled off and punched him out.
Major Awards: NBR, WOF

Bikel, Theodore

1958-(BSA) *The Defiant Ones*
    Winner: Burl Ives, *The Big Country*
■ Born 5/2/24 in Vienna, Austria
〰 Sheriff Mann Muller in the above movie.
𝄺 Bikel was an established folk singer and guitar player. He is fluent in six languages and plays and sings songs in 20 different dialects. He has mastered the guitar, mandolin, balalaika, and harmonica. He's a tireless political activist for NY's Greenwich Village Democratic Party.
Major Awards: WOF

Binoche, Juliette

★ 1996-(BSA) *The English Patient*
2000-(BA) *Chocolat*
    Winner: Julia Roberts, *Erin Brockovich*
■ Born 5/9/64 in Paris, France.
〰 Canadian nurse in *The English Patient*
𝄺 Her mother was an actress and her father a sculptor. Grew up in a Catholic boarding school. Once worked as a cashier. Plays the violin and is an avid painter. Her works have been exhibited in Paris art galleries. She is the highest paid actress in French history. Nominated eight times for a César.

Major Awards: Oscar, César, NBR, BAFTA, BIFF, VFF

Black, Karen

1970-(BSA) *Five Easy Pieces*
   Winner: Helen Hayes, *Airport*
▪ Born *Karen Ziegler* on 7/1/42 in Park Ridge, IL
✎ Rayette Dipesto in above movie.
🔑 Graduated from high school at age 14. Made her acting debut at age 14. Entered Northwestern University at age 15. Studied ballet as a young child until age 17. She is an avid Scientologist and chain-smoker. Her breakout movie was *Easy Rider*.
Major Awards: NBR, NYFC, GG

Blair, Betsy

1955-(BSA) *Marty*
   Winner: Jo Van Fleet, *East of Eden*
▪ Born *Betsy Boger* on 12/11/23 in Cliffside Park, NJ
✎ Shy schoolteacher Clara in *Marty*
🔑 She was a child model. Once married to Gene Kelly. She began auditioning for dance roles on Broadway and nightclubs as a teenager. She was blacklisted by Hollywood when she was erroneously accused of being a Communist. After splitting from Gene Kelly she was married for 40 years to director Karel Reisz until his death in 2002. Lives in England.
Major Awards: BAFTA

Blair, Linda

1973-(BSA) *The Exorcist*
   Winner: Tatum O'Neal, *Paper Moon*
▪ Born 1/22/59 in Westport, CT
✎ Regan MacNeil (#9 on AFI's Villain List)
🔑 Early pressures of success sidetracked her into a life of sex, drugs, and booze. After several bouts with the law and a rehab stint she eventually straightened herself out. She's an inveterate animal lover and accomplished horsewoman. She is a vegetarian and has received many animal rights awards.
Major Awards: Golden Globe

Blakley, Ronee

1975-(BSA) *Nashville*
   Winner: Lee Grant, *Shampoo*
▪ Born 8/24/45 in Caldwell, ID
✎ Barbara Jean in above movie.
🔑 Educated at Stanford University. She is an accomplished country western singer and songwriter who composed her own music for her role in *Nashville*. She produced, wrote, scored, directed and starred in the play *I Played It for You*. Sang background vocals on Bob Dylan's "Hurricane."
Major Awards: NBR

Blanchett, Cate

1998-(BA) *Elizabeth*
   Winner: Gwyneth Paltrow, *Shakespeare in Love*
★ 2004-(BSA) *The Aviator*
2006-(BSA) *Babel*
   Winner: Jennifer Hudson, *Dreamgirls*
▪ Born 5/14/69 in Melbourne, Australia.
✎ Elfin deity in *Lord of the Rings*
🔑 Attended Methodist Ladies College where she was the Drama Captain. Graduated from Australia's National Institute of Dramatic Art. First person to win the Critics Circle Theater Award for best newcomer and lead actress awards in the same year. She has the nervous habit of biting her nails and is an inveterate list maker.
Major Awards: Oscar, SAG, GG, NBR, BAFTA, KCFCC

Blethyn, Brenda

1996-(BA) *Secrets and Lies*
   Winner: Frances McDormand, *Fargo*

1998-(BSA) *Little Voices*
  Winner, Judi Dench, *Shakespeare in Love*
■ Born *Brenda Anne Bottle* on 2/20/46 in
  Ramsgate Kent, England
✒ Comedy work on British TV's *Outside Edge*
🔍 She is the youngest of eight siblings. Once worked
as a stenographer and bookkeeper. She was awarded
Officer of the British Empire. Ran in the 2002 London Marathon. She is polydactyl—she was born with
an extra finger.
Major Awards: Cannes, LAFC, GG, BAFTA,
BSFC

Blondell, Joan

1951-(BSA) *The Blue Veil*
  Winner: Kim Hunter, *A Streetcar Named
  Desire*
■ Born 8/30/06 in New York, NY. Died 1979.
✒ Ladyfingers in *The Cincinnati Kid*
🔍 Attended the Professional Child's School in New
York. She was one of the original *Katzenjammer Kids*,
touring the U.S., Europe and Australia. Made six
movies with James Cagney, more than any other
actress. He once said that she was the only woman
he ever loved—other than his wife. She penned the
best-selling novel *Centerdoor Fancy*.
Major Awards: NBR, WOF

Blyth, Anne

1945-(BSA) *Mildred Pierce*
  Winner: Anne Revere, *National Velvet*
■ Born 8/16/28 in Mt. Kisco, NY
✒ Spoiled daughter Veda Pierce in above movie
🔍 Started performing at age five and made her
Broadway debut at age 13. Broke her back in an
accident in 1945. She is devoutly Catholic. Marrying
in 1953 she obtained a rare benediction from Pope
Pius Xll. Her husband and she were awarded the
rank of Lady and Knight of the Holy Sepulchre by
Cardinal Cooke in 1971.
Major Awards: WOF

Bogart, Humphrey

1943-(BA) *Casablanca*
  Winner: Paul Lukas, *Watch on the Rhine*
★ 1951-(BA) *The African Queen*
1954-(BA) *The Caine Mutiny*
  Winner: Marlon Brando, *On the Waterfront*
■ Born 11/23/1899 in New York, NY.
  Died 1/14/57 of throat cancer.
✒ Rick Blaine in *Casablanca*, (#4 on AFI's Hero
  List). Allnut in *African Queen* , Fred C. Dobbs
  in *The Treasure of Sierra Madre*, Philip
  Marlowe in *The Big Sleep* (#32 on the AFI's
  Hero List)
🔍 He was expelled from Yale Medical School and
joined the Navy. During WW I transporting a manacled POW he was smashed in the mouth, accounting
for his scarred lip. He dropped the prisoner with one
shot from his .45. He was an expert chess player. He
had a photographic memory and would recite long
passages from Shakespeare on a regular basis. He
smoked five packs of Chesterfields a day and was a
world-class drinker. As they closed his coffin, a small
gold whistle was placed inside by his wife, Lauren
Bacall. "You know how to whistle. You put your lips
together and blow." A true Hollywood icon.
Major Awards: NBR, WOF

Bondi, Beulah

1936-(BSA) *The Gorgeous Hussy*
  Winner: Gale Sondergaard, *Anthony Adverse*
1938-(BSA) *of Human Hearts*
  Winner: Faye Bainter, *Jezebel*
■ Born *Beulah Bondi* on 5/3/1892 in Chicago,
  IL. Died 1/11/81 broken ribs and following
  heart complications.
✒ George Bailey's mother in *It's a Wonderful Life*
🔍 In her very first role at age seven she played Little
Lord Fauntleroy, her one and only role as a boy.
She remained a bachelorette her whole life and was
reportedly quite content. She broke her ribs when
at age 92 when she tripped over her beloved cat.
Major Awards: Emmy, WOF

Bonham Carter, Helena

1997-(BA) *The Wings of the Dove*
   Winner: Helen Hunt, *As Good As It Gets*
▣ Born 5/26/66 in London, England
✎ Kate Croy in above movie.
✑ She entered a national writing contest when she was 13. She won the contest and used the money to put her name in the actor's directory. Stayed at her parent's home until age 30, caring for her paralyzed father. Speaks French fluently. Great granddaughter to British Prime Minister H.H. Asquith (1908–16). As of this writing she is expecting her second child with director Tim Burton.
Major Awards: NBR, LAFC, BSFC, KCFCC

Booth, Shirley

★ 1952-(BA) *Come Back, Little Sheba*
▣ Born *Thelma Boothford* on 8/30/07 in New York, NY. Died 10/16/92 of natural causes.
✎ Title role in TV series *Hazel*
✑ Dropped out of grade school at age 13, against her parents' wishes, to pursue acting. Made stage debut at age 18 and had appeared in over 600 plays before hitting it big. Producer Hal Wallis liked Booth so much in the Broadway production of *Come Back, Little Sheba* he bought the rights to the play and insisted she reprise her role on the big screen. Won the Triple Crown of acting. One of only eight actors to win both an Oscar and Tony for playing the same role.
Major Awards: Oscar, Emmy, Tony, NBR, GG, Cannes, WOF

Borgnine, Ernest

★ 1955-(BA) *Marty*
▣ Born *Ermes Effron Borgnine* on 1/24/17 in Hamden, CT.
✎ Kind, shy butcher in *Marty*, Skipper Quinton McHale in TV comedy series *McHale's Navy*
✑ Once was a factory worker and enjoyed boxing.

He is fluent in Italian. He is a 33rd degree Mason. He almost made the Navy his career. He served ten years and was discharged at the rank of Gunner's Mate First Class after WW II. In 2004 he was made honorary U.S. Navy Chief Petty Officer.
Major Awards: Oscar, NBR, NYFC, GG, Cannes, BAFTA, WOF

Boyer, Charles

1937-(BA) *Conquest*
   Winner: Spencer Tracy, *Captains Courageous*
1938-(BA) *Algiers*
   Winner: Spencer Tracy, *Boys Town*
1942-Honorary Oscar
1944-(BA) *Gaslight*
   Winner: Bing Crosby, *Going My Way*
1961-(BA) *Fanny*
   Winner: Maximillian Schell, *Judgment at Nuremberg*
▣ Born 8/28/1899 in Figeac, France. Died 8/26/78 suicide.
✎ Pepe Le Moko in *Algiers*
✑ As WW II was raging, he started the French Research Foundation in Hollywood, collecting clippings and information on occupied France and working to change the image of the stereotypical French. His only son committed suicide. After his wife died of cancer, and despondent over these two tragedies, he took his own life two days later.
Major Awards: NYFC, Cannes

Bracco, Loraine

1990, (BSA) *Goodfellas*
   Winner: Whoopi Goldberg, *Ghost*
▣ Born 10/2/57 in Brooklyn, NY
✎ Dr. Jennifer Melfi the psychiatrist on HBO series *The Sopranos*
✑ She was once globally recognized as a high fashion model for the Wilhelmina agency. Worked as a disc jockey for Radio Luxembourg. She made her film debut in Paris. Surrealist painter Salvador Dali

once asked her to pose nude, she turned him down flat. Spokeswoman for Pfizer's anti-depressant drug *Zoloft*.
Major Awards: LAFC, SAG

Brady, Alice

1936-(BSA) *My Man Godfrey*
    Winner: Gale Sondergaard, *Anthony Adverse*
★ 1937-(BSA) *In Old Chicago*
▧ Born 11/2/1892 in New York, NY.
    Died 10/28/39 of cancer.
🏵 Mother O'Leary whose cow started the fire.
🔍 She couldn't attend the Oscar ceremony due to her illness—an unknown man came on to the stage and accepted the award. He and the Oscar disappeared never to be seen again. Shortly after completing the movie *Young Mr. Lincoln* she was tragically cut down at the age of 47 by cancer.
Major Awards: Oscar, WOF

Branagh, Kenneth

1989-(BA) *Henry V*
    Winner: Daniel Day Lewis, *My Left Foot*
1989-(BD) *Henry V*
1996-(BW) *Hamlet*
▧ Born 12/10/60 in Belfast, Northern Ireland
🏵 Henry V in nominated role
🔍 Graduated from RADA. Received honorary Doctorate from Queens University. Came from a poverty-stricken home. Co-founded England's Renaissance Theater Company. At 23, youngest actor in the history of the Royal Shakespeare Company to play the lead in *Henry V.*
Major Awards: Emmy, BAFTA, NBR, NYFC, VFF

Brandauer, Klaus Maria

1985-(BSA) *Out of Africa*
    Winner: Don Ameche, *Cocoon*
▧ Born Klaus George Steng on 6/22/44 in Aussee, Austria.

🏵 Baron Bror Blixen-Finecke in nominated role
🔍 He was a music and drama student at Stuttgarter Hochschule. Originally didn't like working in the movies. Played the same character—a man who sells his soul to the devil—in Szabo's trilogy of *Mephisto*, *Colonel Redl*, and *Hanussen*. Received an Honorary Doctorate from the University of Tel Aviv.
Major Awards: NBR, GG, KCFCC, DDA, NYFC

Brando, Marlon

1951-(BA) *A Streetcar Named Desire*
    Winner: Humphrey Bogart, *The African Queen*
1952-(BA) *Viva Zapata*
    Winner: Gary Cooper-*High Noon*
1953-(BA) *Julius Caesar*
    Winner: William Holden, *Stalag 17*
★ 1954-(BA) *On the Waterfront*
1957-(BA) *Sayonara*
    Winner: Alex Guinness, *The Bridge on the River Kwai*
★ 1972-(BA) *The Godfather*
1973-(BA) *Last Tango In Paris*
    Winner: Jack Lemmon, *Save the Tiger*
1989-(BSA) *A Dry White Season*
    Winner: Denzel Washington, *Glory*
▧ Born 4/13/24 in Omaha, NE.
    Died 7/1/2004 of pulmonary fibrosis
🏵 His two films with director Elia Kazan, *A Streetcar Named Desire*, and *On the Waterfront*, motorcycle rebel Johnny Strabler in the *The Wild One*, Don Vito Corleone in *The Godfather*, Colonel Kurtz in *Apocalypse Now*.
🔍 His mother Dorothy was an acting coach. One of her pupils was Henry Fonda. One of Marlon's closest friends was comedian Wally Cox. Tried to enlist in the Army during WW II but was rejected because of an old football knee injury. Drafted during the Korean War but rejected again because of mental problems—at the time he was under psychoanalysis. His son Christian killed his sister Cheyenne's boyfriend and did time for manslaughter. At the trial, Brando gave an hour-long uninterrupted pre-sentencing testimony entirely in French. Despon-

dent, his daughter committed suicide. He was a legendary trencherman, going on eating binges that almost defied comprehension. Once broke a paparazzo's jaw. After his death, *The Godfather* script, which he annotated, sold for a record $312,800. Sired 11 children by four wives and his maid.

Major Awards: Oscar, Emmy, Cannes, NYFC, NBR, GG, NSFC, GGWFF, BAFTA, KCFCC, BW, WOF

Brennan, Walter

★ 1936-(BSA) *Come And Get It*
★ 1938-(BSA) *Kentucky*
★ 1940-(BSA) *The Westener*
1941, (BSA) *Sergeant York*
   Winner: Donald Crisp, *How Green Was My Valley*
▥ Born 10/3/35 in Las Angeles, CA.
   Died 9/21/74 of emphysema.
🖉 Grandpa Amos McCoy in the TV series *The Real McCoy's*
🖋 Graduated from Cambridge as an engineer. At various times worked as a lumberjack, ditch digger, rancher, reporter, real estate agent, and bank clerk. Enlisted in the Army and was promoted to colonel. During WW I a poison gas attack affected his vocal cords and changed his voice forever. He was a stuntman and ended up losing all of his teeth in an accident. First and only actor to win three Best Supporting Actor Oscars. He recorded two hit records, *Dutchman's Gold* and *Old Rivers*.

Major Awards: Oscar, WOF

Brennen, Eileen

1980-(BSA) *Private Benjamin*
   Winner: Mary Steenburgen, *Melvin and Howard*
▥ Born 10/3/35 in Las Angeles, CA
🖉 Captain Doreen Lewis in nominated role.
🖋 Graduated from Georgetown University. She was a favorite of director Peter Bogdanovich. Sang and performed in NY night clubs with Charles

Nelson Reilly, and was a semi-regular on TV show *Laugh-In*. Was seriously injured when she was hit by a car, resulting in a long rehabilitation and being confined to a wheelchair.

Major Awards: Emmy, GG, Obie.

Breslin, Abigail

2006-(BSA) *Little Miss Sunshine*
   Winner: Jennifer Hudson, *Dreamgirls*
▥ Born 4/14/96 in New York, NY
🖉 Olive in nominated role
🖋 She has been in front of the screen since age three—doing commercials. Her brother is actor Spencer Breslin who starred in *Santa Claus 3*. As young as she is, at age ten she is already considered a total professional. She is double jointed.

Major Awards: Broadcast Film Critics Award

Bridges, Jeff

1971-(BSA) *The Last Picture Show*
   Winner: Ben Johnson, *The Last Picture Show*
1974-(BSA) *Thunderbolt and Lightfoot*
   Winner: Robert DeNiro, *The Godfather, Part II*
1984-(BA) *Starman*
   Winner: F. Murray Abraham, *Amadeus*
2000-(BSA) *The Contender*
   Winner: Benicio Del Torro, *Traffic*
▥ Born 12/4/49 in Las Angeles, CA
🖉 The Dude in *The Big Lebowski*
🖋 He fulfilled his military obligation in the Coast Guard during the Vietnam conflict. Made screen debut at age four months playing the infant of Jane Greer in *The Company She Keeps*. He plays the guitar, paints, composes, and is a practioneer of Transcendental Meditation. Was treated for marijuana dependency as a teenager. Recorded his own album *Be Here Now* in 2002. David Crosby was one of his collaborators. He is the son of Lloyd Bridges, and his brother is Beau Bridges. Pauline Kael once wrote that he "may be the most natural and least self-conscious screen actor that has ever lived."

Major Awards: NBR, Saturn, ISA, WOF

Broadbent, Jim

★ 2001-(BSA) *Iris*

▪ Born 5/24/49 in Lincolnshire, England.

⚘ John Bayley, devoted husband to noted British psychologist Dame Iris Murdock in nominated role.

⚘ He made his acting debut at age four in the stage production *The Doll's House*. Once was stage manager at the Open Air Theater in Regents Park. He got expelled from Leighton Park high school for drinking right before finals. Graduated from the London Academy of Music and Dramatic Arts after attending a Quaker boarding school.

Major Awards: Oscar, LAFC, GG, NBR, BAFTA, VFF

Brody, Adrien

★ 2002-(BA) *The Pianist*

▪ Born 4/14/73 in New York, NY.

⚘ Polish pianist Wladyslaw Szpilman

⚘ Attended Queens College. His father is a retired history teacher and his mother a photo-journalist. Did magic for children's show under the name The Amazing Adrien for $50.00 per hour. Favorite trick was breaking pencils in half with a dollar bill. He lost 30 pounds for his award-winning role from his already gaunt weight of 160 pounds. Only actor to win a Best Actor Oscar when competing against four previous winners. Youngest Best Actor Oscar winner at age 29 yrs, 11 months. He has also appeared in Diet Coke commercials and a Tori Amos music video.

Major Awards: Oscar, NSFC, César, BSFC

Brooks, Albert

1987-(BSA) *Broadcast News*
   Winner: Sean Connery, *The Untouchables*

▪ Born Albert Einstein on 7/22/47 in Los Angeles, CA.

⚘ Aaron Altman in nominated role.

⚘ Son of comedian Harry Einstein, sidekick to Eddie Cantor. Educated at Carnegie Institute of Technology. Called the West Coast Woody Allen. Richard Dreyfuss was his classmate at Beverly Hills High School. Started out as a stand up comedian. Is a musician and once worked as a sportswriter. One of the most versatile entertainers in the business.

Major Awards: NSFC, BSFC, NYFC

Browne, Leslie

1977-(BSA) *The Turning Point*
   Winner: Vanessa Redgrave, *Julia*

▪ Born 6/29/57 in New York, NY.

⚘ Emilia Rodgers in nominated role.

⚘ Her parents were both dancers with the American Ballet Theater. Nominated in her first film. Has worked with veteran choreographer Herbert Ross on many projects. She still performs but mainly teaches up-and-coming ballet hopefuls to fulfill their dreams. Nominated for an Oscar in her first film. She has only made made five films.

Brynner, Yul

★ 1956-(BA) *The King and I*

▪ Born *Taidje Khan* on 7/12/15 Sakhalin Island, "east of Siberia and north of Japan." Died 10/10/85 of lung cancer.

⚘ Chris the mercenary gunman dressed in black in *The Magnificent Seven*

⚘ Performing as a highflying trapeze artist, he had a near fatal fall, which permanently grounded him. He was fluent in several languages. Worked for the U.S. Office of War Information in WW II. He was hardcore all the way—once, when he was severely cut aboard his boat he took fishing line and a hook and sewed up his own wound. Played the guitar and Russian three-string balalaika. He was a first rate photographer. Smoked five packs of cigarettes a day. He liked to shroud his past in mystery. It is reported in some sources that he was born in Vladnostok, Russia.

Major Awards: Oscar, Tony, NBR, WOF

Bujold, Genevieve

1969-(BA) *Anne of the Thousand Days*
   Winner: Maggie Smith, *The Prime of Miss
   Jean Brodie*
▨ Born 7/1/42 in Montreal, Quebec
✎ Anne Boleyn in nominated role.
✎ She spent 12 years in Montreal's strict Hochelaga
convent. She was caught reading an unapproved novel
and was promptly given her exit papers. Graduated
from Quebec's Conservatory of Drama. She worked
as an usherette while attending drama school.
Major Awards: LAFC, GG

Buono, Victor

1962-(BSA) *What Ever Happened to Baby Jane?*
   Winner: Ed Begley, *Sweet Bird of Youth*
▨ Born 2/3/38 in San Diego, CA.
   Died 1/1/82 of a heart attack.
✎ Edwin Flagg in nominated role.
✎ Originally wanted to enroll in medical school.
Graduated from Villanova University. Got his big
break when he played poet Bongo Benny on TV's
77 Sunset Strip. Highly regarded as a gourmet chef
and poet. In 1971 recorded his own poetry on an
album called *Heavy.* He also published a book of
poems called *It Could Be Verse.*
Major Awards: Golden Globe

Burke, Billie

1938-(BSA) *Merrily We Live*
   Winner: Faye Bainter, *Jezebel*
▨ Born *Mary William Ethelbert Appleton* on
   8/6/1885 in Washington, DC. Died 5/14/70.
✎ Good witch Glenda in the *Wizard of Oz*
✎ Once married to legendary showman Florenz
Ziegfield. Her father was a singing clown whose name
she adopted. A sensation on Broadway. Some of her
backstage admirers were Enrico Caruso, W. Somerset
Maugham, and Mark Twain.
Major Awards: WOF

Burns, Catherine

1969-(BSA) *Last Summer*
   Winner: Goldie Hawn, *Cactus Flower*
▨ Born 9/25/45 in New York, NY
✎ Rhoda in nominated role.
✎ Graduated from the American Academy of the
Arts. She made only one other film *Red Sky at Morn-
ing.* She starred in the daytime TV soap *One Day at
a Time.* Nominated in her very first film. Made her
last screen appearance in the TV series *The Word.*
She is now retired from acting and is concentrating
on a writing career.
Major Awards: KCFCC

Burns, George

★ 1975-(BSA) *The Sunshine Boys*
▨ Born *Nathan Birnbaum* on 1/20/1896 in
   New York, NY. Died 3/9/96 of natural causes.
✎ Teaming with wife Gracie Allen on TV
   comedy series *Burns and Allen.*
✎ Originally broke into showbiz as a singer in the
Pee Wee Quartet. Only mildly successful until he
met Gracie Allen and became her straight man.
At age 80 years, 2 months, he was the oldest actor
to receive an Oscar (Best Supporting Actor), until
Jessica Tandy won. Jack Benny was his best friend
and also the best man at his and Gracie's wedding.
Smoked ten cigars a day right up until the day he
died. Discovered Ann-Margret.
Major Awards: Oscar, Saturn, SAG, VFF, WOF

Burstyn, Ellen

1971-(BSA) *The Last Picture Show*
   Winner: Cloris Leachman, *The Last Picture
   Show*
1973-(BA) *The Exorcist*
   Winner: Glenda Jackson, *A Touch of Class*
★ 1974-(BA) *Alice Doesn't Live Here Anymore*
1978-(BA) *Same Time Next Year*
   Winner: Jane Fonda, *Coming Home*

1980-(BA) *Resurrection*
    Winner: Sissy Spacek-*Coal Miner's Daughter*
2000-(BA) *Requiem for a Dream*
    Winner: Julia Roberts, *Erin Brockovitch*
▪ Born *Edna Gillooly* on 12/7/32 in Detroit, MI
▯ Mrs. MacNiel, Regan's mother in *The Exorcist*
▯ In her earlier years she had somewhat of an identity crisis—she used as her name at various times Edna Rae, Keri Flynn, Erica Jean and Ellen MacRae. She once worked as a showgirl on *The Jackie Gleason* Show and a nightclub dancer in Montreal. She is a vegetarian, stays away from alcohol, doesn't drink coffee, and practices yoga. She was the first female to be president of the Actor's Equity.
Major Awards: Oscar, Tony, NYFC, NSFC, GG, ISA, BSFC, KCFCC, NBR, BAFTA

Burton, Richard

1952-(BSA) *My Cousin Rachel*
    Winner: Anthony Quinn, *Viva Zapata!*
1953-(BA) *The Robe*
    Winner: William Holden, *Stalag 17*
1964-(BA) *Becket*
    Winner: Rex Harrison, *My Fair Lady*
1965-(BA) *The Spy Who Came in from the Cold*
    Winner: Lee Marvin, *Cat Ballou*
1966-(BA) *Who's Afraid of Virginia Woolf?*
    Winner: Paul Scofield, *A Man for All Seasons*
1969-(BA) *Anne of the Thousand Days*
    Winner: John Wayne, *True Grit*
1977-(BA) *Equus*
    Winner: Richard Dreyfuss, *The Goodbye Girl*
▪ Born *Richard Walter Jenkins Jr.* on 11/10/25 in Pontrhyfenigais South Wales. Died 8/5/84 of a cerebral hemorrhage.
▯ Stormy marriages to Elizabeth Taylor, Shakespearian roles.
▯ He was 12 of a family of 13. He took his surname from teacher Phillip Burton, who taught him English and helped get him a scholarship to Oxford University. Was a Royal Air Force cadet during WW II. He taught poetry at Oxford. Appointed CBE in 1970. He was best man at Laurence Oliver and Joan Plowright's wedding. He was a heavy smoker and world-class drinker. Doctors discovered in 1981 that his spinal column was coated in crystallized alcohol. Suffered from acute insomnia. Got into a Shakespearian sonnet recital contest with Robert F. Kennedy. They were neck-and-neck until Burton recited a sonnet backwards, which broke the tie and he won. He and Peter O'Toole are the only seven-time nominees never to be Oscar'd.
Major Awards: Tony, GG, BAFTA, DDA

Busey, Gary

1978-(BA) *The Buddy Holly Story*
    Winner: Jon Voight, *Coming Home*
▪ Born 6/29/44 in Goose Creek, TX
▯ Buddy Holly in nominated role.
▯ Graduated from Pittsburg College in Kansas. He once was a bull rider. Played the drums and guitar for Leon Russell, Kris Kristofferson, and Willie Nelson under the name Teddy Jack Eddy. Played his own guitar in *The Buddy Holly Story*. In 1966 he was almost killed in an auto accident. Another brush with death came in 1988—his near-fatal motorcycle accident resulted in tougher helmet laws in California.
Major Awards: NSFC, BAFTA, LAFC

Buttons, Red

★ 1957-(BSA) *Sayonara*
▪ Born *Aaron Chwatt* 2/5/19 in Bronx, NY. Died 7/13/06 of vascular disease.
▯ Dean Martin's celebrity roasts "Never Got a Dinner" routine, Sergeant Joe Kelley in Oscar'd role.
▯ At age 12 he won a local amateur entertainment contest. He was a singing bellhop at a Bronx tavern. His uniform had a shiny buttons and his red hair garnered his sobriquet. Joined the Marines during WW II. Honed his standup skills in the Catskills. Starred in his own TV variety show from 1952–55. There he created all kinds of characters among them the Kupke Kid, Sad Sack, and Keeglefarvin. He also recorded a novelty song in the '50s, *Strange Things*

Are Happening which hit No. 15 on the Billboard charts.

Major Awards: GG, WOF

Byington, Spring

1938-(BSA) *You Can't Take It with You*
    Winner: Faye Bainter, *Jezebel*
◾ Born 10/17/1893 in Colorado Springs, CO. Died 9/7/71 of cancer.
🍴 Penny Sycamore in nominated role.
🔦 Her father, a college professor, died when she was five. Her mother was a doctor. Made her acting debut on the Denver stage at age 14. Married in 1912 and moved to Buenos Aires, Argentina. Divorced in 1917 and moved to New York to pursue acting career. She spent considerable time reading sci-fi and had an avid interest in the occult. Her longtime companion was Marjorie Main.

Major Awards: WOF

Caan, James

1972-(BSA) *The Godfather*
    Winner: Joel Grey, *Cabaret*
◾ Born 3/26/39 in Bronx, NY
🍴 Sonny Corleone in nominated role
🔦 In high school he was captain of both the basketball and baseball teams. Also was class president. Attended Michigan State and played football. Graduated from Hofstra University. Was a professional rodeo rider for nine years and still maintains a stable of horses. Has a black belt in karate.

Major Awards: WOF

Caesar, Adolph

1984-(BSA) *A Soldier's Story*
    Winner: Haing S. Ngor, *The Killing Fields*
◾ Born 12/3/33 in Harlem, NY. Died 3/6/86 of a massive heart attack.
🍴 Master Sergeant Vernon Waters in nominated role

🔦 Joined the Navy as a teenager. Studied drama at NYU. Afterward joined the Negro Ensemble Company. Voice for the United Negro College Fund commercial, "A mind is a terrible thing to waste." Died of a sudden heart attack while filming *Tough Guys*, and was replaced by Eli Wallach.

Major Awards: Obie, LAFC

Cage, Nicholas

★ 1996-(BA) *Leaving Las Vegas*
2002-(BA) *Adaptation*
    Winner: Adrian Brody, *The Pianist*
◾ Born *Nicholas Coppola* on 1/7/64 in Long Beach, CA
🍴 Prolific drunk in *Leaving Las Vegas*, dual role in *Adaptation*, as an action hero in numerous films
🔦 His uncle is Francis Ford Coppola and his aunt is Talia Shire. A method actor to the extreme: in preparing for roles he has had two wisdom teeth pulled without Novocain, slashed his arm with a knife, and eaten a live cockroach. Suffers from vertigo and has an extensive comic book collection. Got Johnny Depp his first acting job. Married Lisa Presley and divorced her three months later.

Major Awards: Oscar, NBR, NYFC, NSFC, LAFC, GG, WOF

Cagney, James

1938-(BA) *Angels with Dirty Faces*
    Winner: Spencer Tracy, *Boys Town*
★ 1942-(BA) *Yankee Doodle Dandy*
1955-(BA) *Love Me Or Leave Me*
    Winner: Ernest Borgnine, *Marty*
◾ Born 7/17/04 in New York, NY. Died 3/30/86 of diabetes and a heart attack.
🍴 George M. Cohan in *Yankee Doodle Dandy*, Tom Powers in *Public Enemy* (#42 on AFI's Villain List). Smashing grapefruit in Mae Clarke's face. Cody Jarrett in *White Heat*, (#26 on AFI's Villain List)—"Top of the world, Ma!"
🔦 He once was a waiter, dancer, and pool racker. His first professional job was as a female impersonator.

James Cagney in *Yankee Doodle Dandy*.

He was a chorus girl in Keith's 81st Street Theater. In his role as George M. Cohan with Bob Hope as Edie Foy in *The 7 Little Foys*, he accepted no salary. Eddie Foy had befriended him in his struggling years and this was his way of repaying him. Talked war hero Audie Murphy into acting. His best friends were Pat O'Brien and Frank McHugh. He had a black belt in judo. President Reagan delivered the eulogy at his funeral. Possibly the most imitated actor in Hollywood history. Incidentally, he never said "You dirty rat" in any of his movies.
Major Awards: Oscar, NBR, NYFC, AFI's and SAG Life Achievement Awards, Presidential Medal of Freedom, WOF

Caine, Sir Michael

1966-(BA) *Alfie*
   Winner: Paul Scofield, *A Man for All Seasons*
1972-(BA) *Sleuth*
   Winner: Marlon Brando, *The Godfather*
1983-(BA) *Educating Rita*
   Winner: Robert Duvall, *Tender Mercies*
★ 1986-(BSA) *Hannah and Her Sisters*
★ 1999-(BSA) *The Cider House Rules*
2002-(BA) *The Quiet American*
   Winner: Adrian Brody, *The Pianist*
■ Born *Maurice Micklewhite* on 9/14/33 in London, England
⚜ Title role in *Alfie*
🍴 Early in his career he changed his last name to Caine, after the movie *The Caine Mutiny*. The British working class actor never has learned to drive a car. He speaks Yiddish and is excellent at telling Jewish dialect jokes. Awarded a CBE in 1993 and knighted by the Queen in 2000. In the '60s he was drinking two bottles of vodka and smoking four packs of cigarettes a day. Owns six restaurants and his own production company.
Major Awards: Oscar, GG, NSFC, SAG, BAFTA, KCFCC, NBR, WOF

Calhern, Louis

1950-(BA) *The Magnificent Yankee*
   Winner: Jose Ferrer, *Cyrano de Bergerac*
■ Born *Henry Vogt* on 2/16/1895 in New York, NY. Died 5/12/56 of a heart attack.
⚜ Crooked lawyer Alonzo D. Lon Emmerich in *Asphalt Jungle*
🍴 He was discovered by a traveling acting troupe while playing high school football. Served in the Army as an officer during WW I. He was married four times. Played mostly elderly distinguished gentlemen throughout his career. While filming *Teahouse of the August Moon*, he succumbed to a fatal heart attack.
Major Awards: VFF

Cannon, Dyan

1969-(BSA) *Bob & Carol & Ted & Alice*
   Winner: Goldie Hawn, *Cactus Flower*
1976-(Best Short Film) *Number One*
1978-(BSA) *Heaven Can Wait*
   Winner: Maggie Smith, *California Suite*
▣ Born *Samille Diane Friesten* on 1/4/39 in Tacoma, WA
✎ Married to legendary actor Cary Grant and mother of his only child Jennifer.
✎ Attended University of Washington. She was discovered by a talent scout while having lunch at a sidewalk café. Sponsored by AFI, she produced, directed, wrote, and co-edited a film short, *Number One*. Once held the title of Miss West Seattle. Her last name was changed to Cannon by producer Jerry Wald because of her explosive nature.
Major Awards: NYFC, GG, WOF

Cantor, Eddie

1956-Honorary Oscar
▣ Born *Edward Israel Itskowitz* on 1/31/1892in New York, NY. Died 10/10/64 of a heart attack.
✎ The moniker *Ole Banjo Eyes* and his signature song "Ida, sweet as apple cida"
✎ He wrote the song "Merrily We Roll Along." Inducted into the Radio Hall of Fame in 2000. The National Foundation of Infantile Paralysis got their campaign slogan from Eddie Cantor, "March of Dimes." After the slogan caught fire the foundation at the White House was deluged with over two and half million dimes. For dinner he always ate milk and corn flakes.
Major Awards: SAG Life Achievement, WOF

Carey, Harry

1939-(BSA) *Mr. Smith Goes to Washington*
   Winner: Thomas Mitchell, *Stagecoach*
▣ Born *Harry DeWitt Carey II* on 1/16/1878 in Bronx, NY. Died 5/21/47 of a coronary thrombosis and cancer.

✎ Cowboy roles in silent films
✎ Educated at Hamilton Military Academy and turned down an appointment to West Point. He was a practicing lawyer before breaking into movies at age 40. Got director John Ford his first job. Later in his career they had a falling out and they never talked again. A top star, he was making $1250 a week in 1919, that's over $15,000 in 2005 dollars. John Wayne paid tribute to Harry Carey in *The Searchers* by adopting some of Carey's mannerisms and gestures—the parting shot where John holds his elbow as he is walking out the doorway was a Careyism.
Major Awards: WOF

Carlin, Lynn

1968-(BSA) *Faces*
   Winner: Ruth Gordon, *Rosemary's Baby*
▣ Born *Lynn Kramer* 1/31/38 in Los Angeles, CA
✎ Maria Forst in nominated role.
✎ Made her stage debut at the Laguna Playhouse starring in *The Women*. Spotted by director/actor John Cassavetes. She was a secretary to director Robert Altman. John Cassavetes cast her in his avant-garde movie *Faces* shortly after director Robert Altman fired her.

Carney, Art

★ 1974-(BA) *Harry and Tonto*
▣ Born 11/4/18 in Mt. Vernon, NY. Died11/9/03 of natural causes.
✎ Ed Norton on Jackie Gleason's *The Honeymooners* TV series.
✎ Serving in WW II, he was wounded by shrapnel on Omaha Beach. This accounted for his slight limp. Never took any acting lessons, and taught himself to play the piano. Jackie Gleason said that Art was 90 percent responsible for the success of the *Honeymooners*.
Major Awards: Oscar, GG, Emmy, CA, NSFC, VFF, WOF

Caron, Leslie

1953-(BA) *Lili*
   Winner: Audrey Hepburn, *Roman Holiday*
1963-(BA) *The L-Shaped Room*
   Winner: Patricia Neal, *Hud*
▪ Born 7/1/31 in Boulogne-Billancourt Paris, France.
✇ Young ingénue in title role *Gigi*
✎ Her father was a chemist and her mother a dancer. Started as a ballerina at age ten. Once was married to meat packing heir George Hormel. Big break came when Gene Kelly chose her to play the lead in *An American in Paris*. Once romantically linked to actor Warren Beatty.
Major Awards: GG, BFAA, WFCA

Carroll, Diahann

1974-(BA) *Claudine*
   Winner: Ellen Burstyn, *Alice Doesn't Live Here Anymore*
▪ Born *Carol Diahann Johnson* on 7/17/35 in Bronx, NY.
✇ Title role in TV series *Julia*
✎ At age ten received the prestigious Metropolitan Opera Scholarship. She was a fashion model for *Ebony* magazine. She was a classmate of actor Billy Dee Williams. She is a breast cancer survivor. Was engaged to talk show host David Frost and Sidney Poitier, although not at the same time.
Major Awards: Tony, GG, WFCA, WOF

Carroll, Nancy

1929/30-(BA) *The Devil's Holiday*
   Winner: Norma Shearer, *The Divorcée*
▪ Born *Ann Veronica La Hife* on 11/19/04 in New York, NY. Died 8/6/65 of an aneurysm.
✇ Hallie Hobart in nominated role.
✎ Made her film debut at the tender age of 14. Popular in the mid-thirties. It was reported in the newspapers of the day that she received more fan mail than any other star. Paramount paid $500,000

for the script of her movie *Abie's Irish Rose*, the highest to that date. She was an avid painter and her works were exhibited in many art houses.
Major Awards: WOF

Cass, Peggy

1958-(BSA) *Auntie Mame*
   Winner: Wendy Hiller, *Separate Tables*
▪ Born *Mary Margaret Cass* 5/21/24 in Boston, MA. Died 3/8/99 of heart failure.
✇ TV game show panelist in the '70s
✎ She possessed a rare photographic memory and encyclopedic mind. She joined a USO troupe and toured Australia for seven months. She was a secretary, phone operator, and model before making it to the movies.
Major Awards: Tony

Cassavetes, John

1967-(BSA) *The Dirty Dozen*
   Winner: George Kennedy, *Cool Hand Luke*
1968-(BW) *Faces*
1974-(BD) *A Woman Under the Influence*
▪ Born 12/9/29 in New York, NY. Died 2/3/89 of cirrhosis of the liver.
✇ Victor Franko in nominated role.
✎ Produced his first independent film *Shadows* with his earnings from TV series *Johnny Staccato*, in which he starred as a piano-playing private eye. He was one of the few people in Hollywood who was a producer, director, screenwriter, and playwright. Appeared on a 2003 37-cent commemorative stamp. Close friends to Peter Falk and Ben Gazzara.
Major Awards: LAFC, NSFC, BIFF, VFF

Cassel, Seymour

1968-(BSA) *Faces*
   Winner: Jack Albertson, *The Subject Was Roses*
▪ Born 1/22/32 in Detroit, MI
✇ Chet, the aging beach bum, in *Faces*

🖋 Studied acting at the Actors Studio. Often collaborated with John Cassavetes and served as his associate producer. Known for his positive attitude and once said, if he likes a role, he would do the movie for the price of a plane ticket. Among his circle of close friends were Ben Gazzara, Gena Rowlands, Lynn Carlin, and Peter Falk.
Major Awards: NYFC, NSFC, Sundance

Castellano, Richard

1970-(BSA) *Lovers and Other Strangers*
   Winner: John Mills, *Ryan's Daughter*
▪ Born 9/4/33 in the Bronx, NY. Died 12/10/88 of a heart attack.
🖌 Clemenza in *The Godfather*.
🖋 Before joining the Yiddish Theater and making inroads into the movie business, he was the general manager of a construction company. Amazingly, he was the highest paid actor in *The Godfather*. When *Godfather II* was planned he was written out because of his ill-advised steep salary demands.

Castle-Hughes, Keisha

2002-(BA) *Whale Rider*
   Winner: Charlize Theron, *Monster*
▪ Born 3/24/90 in Donneybrook, Western Australia, Australia
🖌 Pai in nominated role.
🖋 She won the lead over hundreds of other competing hopefuls. At age 13 she was the youngest actress ever nominated for a Best Actress Oscar. Her father is Australian and her mother Maori. They were together nine years but never married. On the *Jay Leno Show* she revealed that she didn't know how to swim when she was cast in *Whale Rider*.
Major Awards: CFC

Chakiris, George

★ 1961-(BSA) *West Side Story*
▪ Born 9/16/33 in Norwood, OH.

🖌 Bernardo in nominated role.
🖋 He's the son of Greek immigrants. Made his acting debut at age 12. Worked as a clerk in a Los Angeles department store while attending singing and dancing classes. He was once a choirboy who initially wanted to become a professional singer. His interest in dancing took precedence.
Major Awards: Oscar, GG

Chandler, Jeff

1950-(BSA) *Broken Arrow*
   Winner: George Sanders, *All About Eve*
▪ Born *Ira Grossel* on 12/15/18 in Brooklyn, NY. Died 6/17/61 prematurely from blood poisoning after routine spinal surgery to repair a slipped disc.
🖌 Cochise in nominated role.
🖋 He was an officer in the Army during WW II, rising from infantryman to first lieutenant. He had his own publishing company. He played Cochise in three different movies. He played the violin and sang and recorded some hit songs for Liberty Records. Often rebelled against the studio, and was suspended numerous times. It was determined that malpractice occurred in his operation and early death, and his family was awarded a large sum.
Major Awards: WOF

Channing, Carol

1967-(BSA) *Throughly Modern Millie*
   Winner: Estelle Parsons, *Bonnie and Clyde*
▪ Born on 1/31/21 in Seattle, WA
🖌 Trademark song "Diamonds Are a Girl's Best Friend" in Broadway's *Gentlemen Prefer Blonds*.
🖋 Her father was a well-known Christian Science co-editor and lecturer. Graduated from Bennington College in Vermont. Her former high school, Lowell, named its school theater after her. Known for her stage performances, she once danced for the San Francisco Ballet. She is allergic to bleach—her splashy blond hair is actually a wig.
Major Awards: Tony, GG, WOF

Channing, Stockard

1993-(BA) *Six Degrees of Separation*
  Winner: Holly Hunter, *The Piano*
■ Born *Susan Stockard* on 2/13/44 in New York, NY.
✎ Rizzo in *Grease*
✐ Coming from well-to-do parents, she was sent to exclusive preparatory schools, and then graduated Harvard specifically from female-only Radcliff College cum laude, majoring in history and literature. She was 34 years old when she played the teenage part of Rizzo, the gang leader of the Pink Ladies in *Grease*.
Major Awards: Tony, Obie, SAG, Emmy, NBR, PC

Chaplin, Sir Charlie

1927/28-(BA) *The Circus*
  Winner: Emil Jannings, *The Last Command*
1927/28-(BD) *The Circus*
1927/28-Honorary Oscar
1940-(BA) *The Great Dictator*
  Winner: James Stewart, *The Philadelphia Story*
1940-(BP) *The Great Dictator*
1940-(BW) *The Great Dictator*
1947-(BW) *Monsier Verdoux*
1971-Honorary Oscar
★ 1972-(Best Musical Score) *Limelight*
■ Born 4/16/1889 in London, England.
  Died12/25/77 of natural causes
✎ The Little Tramp (#38 on AFI's Hero List)
✐ In 1918 he was making an incredible $125,000 a picture. Roomed with Stan Laurel in 1912 in a boarding house when they came to America. First actor to be on the cover of *Time* magazine. He was once indicted for violating the Mann Act, a law enacted to prevent the transportation of women across state lines for immoral purposes. He was found innocent. He was an accomplished musician and wrote musical scores for his silent movies. In France, on a lark, he entered a Charlie Chaplin look-a-like contest and came in third. Knighted by the Queen in 1975. He was awarded an Oscar for his musical score in *Limelight* 20 years after the film was made,

because it was never shown in a Los Angeles theater until then. A true original. His trademark bowler and cane sold at auction in 1987 for $150,000.
Major Awards: Oscar, NBR, NYFC, DG, BAFTA, VFF,WOF

Chatterton, Ruth

1928/29-(BA) *Madam X*
  Winner: Mary Pickford, *Coquette*
1929/30-(BA) *Sarah and Son*
  Winner: Norma Shearer, *The Divorcée*
■ Born 12/24/1893 in New York, NY.
  Died 11/24/61 of a brain hemorrhage.
✎ Jacqueline in *Madam X*
✐ Made her career move at age 14 as a chorus girl. One of the first real liberated ladies of Hollywood. She wrote a play and several novels, was a licensed pilot, and flew her own plane cross-crossing the country. She was fluent in French and translated French plays for the American stage.
Major Awards: WOF

Cheadle, Don

2004-(BA) *Hotel Rwanda*
■ Born 11/29/64 in Kansas City, MO
✎ Paul Rusesabagina in nominated role.
✐ His parents are a child psychologist and teacher. Had art and theater scholarship offers from four colleges. He's an accomplished jazz musician—he can play the sax, trumpet, and drums. He founded a company of artists, called the Elemental Prose, who are dedicated to passing down oral history through words and music. Recently beat poker pro Phil Ivey in a heads up Celebrity/Pro Hold'em poker tournament.
Major Awards: GG, LAFC, NSFC, SAG

Chekov, Michael

1945-(BSA) *Spellbound*
  Winner: James Dunn, *A Tree Grows in Brooklyn*

Born 8/29/1891 in Leningrad, Russia. Died 9/30/55 of a heart attack.

🍴 Dr. Alex Brulow in nominated role

🔍 He was the nephew of famed Russian playwright Anton Chekov. He started his own drama school in England, working closely with Stanislavski and Reinhardt. He taught acting in his own school. Among his prized students were Yul Bryner, Gary Cooper, Ingrid Bergman, Jack Palance, Gregory Peck, and Marilyn Monroe.

Cher

1983-(BSA) *Silkwood*
　Winner: Linda Hunt, *The Year of Living Dangerously*

★ 1987, (BA) *Moonstruck*

Born *Cherilyn Sarkisian La Piere* on 5/20/46 in El Centra, CA

🍴 Singing with long-time partner and husband Sonny Bono.

🔍 Her grade school friends called her "Pinky." She had an unstable childhood—her mother was married eight times, and her father abandoned the family when she was one. She's a non-smoker, non-drinker, and incessant dieter. She is dyslexic, has a fear of flying, and has had rhinoplasty. Oldest female recording artist with a No. 1 hit, "Believe." Has appeared on the cover of *People* 13 times. Reportedly worth over $600 million.

Major Awards: Oscar, GG, Cannes, Emmy, Grammy, DDA, KCFCC, WOF

Chevalier, Maurice

1929/30-(BA) *The Big Pond*
1929/30-(BA) *The Love Parade*
　Winner: George Arliss, *Disraeli*
1958-Honorary Oscar

Born 9/12/1888 in Paris, France. Died 1/1/72 of cardiac arrest following kidney surgery.

🍴 Signature song "Thank Heaven for Little Girls."

🔍 He was an acrobat as a youth but after a severe accident he turned his energies to acting. In his younger years he was the sparring partner for boxing champion Georges Carpentier. He fought and was wounded in WW I, and spent two years in the Altegrabow POW camp. After his release he was decorated with France's highest honor the *Croix de Guere*.

Major Awards: Oscar, C.B. DeMille, Tony, GG, WOF

Christie, Julie

★ 1965-(BA) *Darling*
1971-(BA) *McCabe & Mrs. Miller*
　Winner: Jane Fonda, *Klute*
1997-(BA) *Afterglow*
　Winner: Helen Hunt, *As Good as It Gets*

Born 4/14/41 in Chuka Assam, India.

🍴 Lara in *Doctor Zhivago*

🔍 She grew up on a tea plantation in India. She is fluent in French and Italian. Long-time girlfriend of Warren Beatty. He dedicated his movie *Reds* to her. She was only paid $7500 for her Oscar winning role. She is an avid campaigner for social and political causes, including animal rights and nuclear disarmament. Workaholic by nature and into transcendental meditation.

Major Awards: Oscar, NBR, NYFC, CA

Church, Thomas Hayden

2004-(BSA) *Sideways*
　Winner: Morgan Freeman, *Million Dollar Baby*

Born 6/17/61 in El Paso, TX.

🍴 Flint Marko in *Spider-Man 3*.

🔍 Started his career as a deejay at the local radio station KGFM in Harlingen, TX, doing voiceovers. He not only acts but is also a director, writer, and producer. He was semi-retired and working on his ranch when director Alexander Payne asked him to star in *Sideways*. Recently played a convincing grizzled cowboy in TV mini-series *Broken Trail* with Robert Duvall.

Major Awards: NBR, NSFC, SAG, ISA, KCFCC

Cilento, Diane

1963-(BSA) *Tom Jones*
  Winner: Margaret Rutherford, *The V.I.P.s*
■ Born 10/5/33 in Brisbane, Australia.
✎ Molly Seagrim in nominated role.
🔍 Her father was an attorney, who was knighted, and her mother was a doctor. With her acting career behind her she wrote her first novel in 1969. She has written several novels. Once was married to Sean Connery. She owns an open-air theater in a rainforest in Mossman, Queensland, way out in the sticks in Australia.

Clark, Candy

1973-(BSA) *American Graffiti*
  Winner: Tatum O'Neal, *Paper Moon*
■ Born June Clark on 6/20/47 in Norman, OK
✎ Debbie in nominated role
🔍 Once was a high-paid fashion model and Jeff Bridges's steady. She has played in a handful of films since her film debut in John Huston's *Fat City*. Once married to evangelist turned actor Marjoe Gortner, and auditioned for the role of Princess Leia in *Star Wars*.
Major Awards: Saturn

Elizabeth Taylor and Montgomery Clift
in *A Place in the Sun.*

Clarkson, Patricia

2003-(BSA) *Pieces of April*
  Winner: Renée Zellweger, *Cold Mountain*
■ Born 12/29/59 in New Orleans, LA
✎ Joy Burns in nominated role
🔍 Her mother was a long-time councilman representing the French Quarter. Studied Dramatic Arts at Yale. Graduated from Fordam University's College at the Lincoln Center. She has appeared in over 30 stage productions. Ingrid Bergman was her favorite actress.
Major Awards: Emmy, NBR, NSFC, NYFC, KCFCC, BSFC, Sundance

Clayburgh, Jill

1978-(BA) *An Unmarried Woman*
  Winner: Jane Fonda, *Coming Home*
1979-(BA) *Starting Over*
  Winner: Sally Field, *Norma Rae*
■ Born 4/30/44 in New York, NY.
✎ Marilyn Homberg in *Starting Over*
🔍 Attended posh Brearley Finishing School. She was educated at Sarah Lawrence College majoring, in philosophy and drama. Her interests include cooking and exercising and psychotherapy. Companion to Al Pacino from 1970 to 1975. She is a reformed smoker.
Major Awards: Cannes, Obie

Clift, Montgomery

1948-(BA) *The Search*
  Winner: Laurence Olivier, *Hamlet*
1951-(BA) *A Place in the Sun*
  Winner: Humphrey Bogart, *The African Queen*
1953-(BA) *From Here to Eternity*
  Winner: William Holden, *Stalag 17*
1961-(BSA) *Judgement at Nuremburg*
  Winner: George Chakiris, *West Side Story*
■ Born 10/17/20 in Omaha, NE. Died 7/23/66 of coronary occlusion.
✎ Matt Garth in *Red River*

He had a twin sister. He was fluent in French, Italian, and German. His father was violent, abusive and a bigot. He was involved in a near fatal accident, which facially disfigured him. Considered aloof, a loner, and non-conformist. Became dependant on painkillers and booze, which led to his early death of a heart attack at age 45. It is reported that Liz Taylor proposed to him. He declined the offer. He was good friends with Dean Martin, and helped him in his transition from singer to actor. Suffered from bouts of dysentery and colitis up until his death.
Major Awards: WOF

Clooney, George

★ 2005-(BSA) *Syriana*
2005-(BD) *Good Night, And Good Luck*
2005-(Best Original Screenplay) *Good Night, And Good Luck*

▪ Born 5/6/61 in Lexington, KY
🖉 Dr. Douglas Ross on TV's *ER*, perpetually charming leading man
He is the son of long-time newscaster Nick Clooney, and nephew to singer Rosemary Clooney. Attended Kentucky University. Tried out for the Cincinnati Reds baseball team. He is on medication for bleeding ulcers. Earned 20 million dollars for *Ocean's 11*. Clooney got into a slugfest with *The Three Kings* director David Russell over how the director was treating the extras.
Major Awards: GG, NBR, Saturn, SAG, VFF, KCFCC

Close, Glenn

1982-(BSA) *The World According To Garp*
  Winner: Jessica Lange, *Tootsie*
1983-(BSA) *The Big Chill*
  Winner: Jack Nicholson, *Terms of Endearment*
1984-(BSA) *The Natural*
  Winner: Peggy Ashcroft, *A Passage to India*
1987-(BA) *Fatal Attraction*
  Winner: Cher, *Moonstruck*
1988-(BA) *Dangerous Liaisons*
  Winner: Jodie Foster, *The Accused*

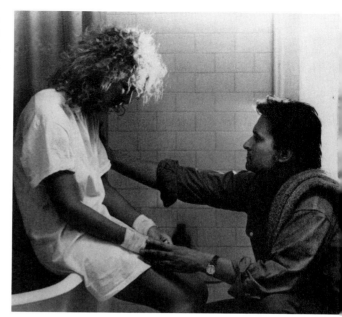

Glenn Close and Michael Douglas in *Fatal Attraction*.

▪ Born 3/19/47 in Greenwich, CN.
🖉 Alex Forrest in *Fatal Attraction* (#7 on AFI's Villain List)
Her father ran a health clinic in the Belgian Congo for 16 years. She lived alternately in Africa and in boarding school in Switzerland. Educated at William & Mary, majoring in anthropology. Once was a member of the folk singing group Up With People, which toured the United States and Europe. She collects costumes from her movies. Distant relative to Princess Diana and second cousin to Brooke Shields.
Major Awards: Obie, Tony, OCC, LAFC, Emmy, SAG, NBR, WFCA

Cobb, Lee J.

1954-(BSA) *On the Waterfront*
  Winner: Edmond O'Brian, *The Barefoot Contessa*
1958-(BSA) *The Brothers Karamazov*
  Winner: Burl Ives, *The Big Country*

Lee J. Cobb and Marlon Brando in *On the Waterfront*.

■ Born *Leo Jacoby* 12/9/11 in New York, NY.
   Died 2/11/76 of a heart attack.
✎ Willie Loman in *Death of a Salesman*
♀ A child prodigy—without any lessons he was a virtuoso talent on the violin and harmonica. His plans for a career in music were dashed when he broke his wrist. Ran away from home at the age of 16 and traveled to Hollywood to get into acting. He was a pilot in WW II for the Civil Air Patrol. Majored in Accounting at CCNY. Played Judge Garth on long-running TV western series *The Virginian*. When he was almost destitute, Frank Sinatra rescued him financially even though they had never met. Although nominated for many awards, never won one. He was supposed to be the original Colombo, but had to turn down the role because of previous commitments.

Coburn, Charles

1941-(BSA) *The Devil and Miss Jones*
   Winner: Donald Crisp, *How Green Was My Valley*
★ 1943-(BSA) *The More the Merrier*
1946-(BSA) *The Green Years*
   Winner: Harold Russell, *The Best Years of Our Lives*

■ Born 6/19/1877 in Savannah, GA.
   Died 8/30/61 of a heart attack.
✎ Mr. Merrick in *The Devil and Miss Jones*
♀ The epitome of a Southern gentleman, he ran his own theater troupe for years. Made Broadway debut in 1901. Performed at the White House for President Taft in 1910. Did not enter the movies and Hollywood until he was 58. Made his final film at age 84. When asked about his monocle he would say, "No point having two window panes when one will do."
Major Awards: NBR, WOF

Coburn, James

★ 1998-(BSA) *Affliction*
■ Born 8/31/28 in Laurel, NE.
   Died 11/18/2002 of a heart attack.
✎ *Our Man Flint*
♀ Cured himself of debilitating rheumatoid arthritis by practicing holistic medicine. One of the first celebrities to do TV commercials. Mr. Coburn was also a producer and screenwriter. He played the flute and was into fasting and meditating. Grandson of Charles Coburn. He was a pallbearer at Bruce Lee's funeral.
Major Awards: Oscar, GW, WOF

Coco, James

1981-(BSA) *Only When I Laugh*
   Winner: John Gielgud, *Arthur*
■ Born 3/21/29 in New York, NY.
   Died 2/25/87 of a heart attack
✎ Broadway success in *The Last of the Red Hot Lovers*
♀ Worked as a waiter, dishwasher, night clerk, and toy salesman before making it on Broadway. Wrote best-selling cookbook, *Cooking with Coco*. Battling weight problems his whole life he gained and lost and regained hundreds of pounds. Nominated for a Tony for his role in Broadway's *The Last of the Red Hot Lovers*.
Major Awards: Obie, Emmy

Colbert, Claudette

★ 1934-(BA) *It Happened One Night*
1935-(BA) *Private Worlds*
    Winner: Bette Davis—*Dangerous*
1944-(BA) *Since You Went Away*
    Winner: Ingrid Bergman, *Gaslight*
▪ Born *Claudette Lily Chauchoin* on 9/13/07 in Paris, France. Died 7/30/96 of a stroke
✎ Ellie Andrews in Oscar'd role
✑ She was once an aspiring artist. She always insisted that only one side of her face be photographed, which called for redesigning whole sets to appease her phobia about her "bad side." She was the highest paid actress in Hollywood in 1938. Lived on a 200-year-old plantation in Barbados where she entertained dignitaries such as President Reagan and Frank Sinatra. One of her favorite sayings was, "When you are born stupid it is for a very long time."
Major Awards: Oscar, GG, and WOF

Collette, Toni

1999-(BSA) *The Sixth Sense*
    Winner: Angelina Jolie, *Girl, Interrupted*
▪ Born *Antonia Collette* 11/1/72 in Sydney, New South Wales, Australia.
✎ Lynn Sloan—the mom in *The Sixth Sense*
✑ Won Australian Oscar for *Muriel's Wedding*. Gained 40 pounds in seven weeks for the above role. After losing the weight, she gained 25 pounds back for her role in *In Her Shoes*.
MMajor Awards: Australian Oscar, BSFC

Collinge, Patricia

1941-(BSA) *The Little Foxes*
    Winner: Mary Astor, *The Great Lie*
▪ Born 9/20/1892 in Dublin, Ireland. Died 1974.
✎ Aunt Birdie Hubbard in nominated role.
✑ First appeared on stage at the age of ten. She made her Broadway debut at age 14. Made her film debut in 1941 in *The Little Foxes*. She was a very talented

writer. She wrote many novels, which became best sellers, as well as short stories and even a play.
Major Awards: NBR

Collins, Pauline

1989-(BA) *Shirley Valentine*
    Winner: Jessica Tandy, *Driving Miss Daisy*
▪ Born 9/3/40 in Exmouth, Devon, England
✎ Starring as Sarah Moffat in TV series *Upstairs, Down Stairs*
✑ Before making her inroads on the stage and eventually movies, she was educated in a Catholic convent. Turned down a permanent role on the popular 1963 series *Dr. Who*. She was awarded the Officer of the British Empire (OBE) by the Queen in 2001.
Major Awards: Obie, Tony, BAFTA

Colman, Ronald

1929/30-(BA) *Bulldog Drummond*
1929/30-(BA) *Condemned*
    Winner: George Arliss, *Disraeli*
1942-(BA) *Random Harvest*
    Winner: James Cagney, *Yankee Doodle Dandy*
★ 1947-(BA) *A Double Life*
▪ Born 2/9/1891 in Richard Surrey, England. Died 5/19/58 of a lung infection.
✎ Anthony John in Oscar'd role.
✑ He intended to enter Cambridge, but his father died and he was orphaned at age 16. He joined the Scottish Reginals at the outbreak of WW I. He was seriously wounded in France in the Battle of Ypres and was invalided out. Came to New York with $37 in his pocket. Made his screen debut in 1923 with Lillian Gish.
Major Awards: Oscar, GG, WOF

Compson, Betty

1928/29-(BA) *The Barker*
    Winner: Mary Pickford, *Coquette*

■ Born Elenor Luicine Compson on 3/18/1897 in Beaver, UT. Died 4/18/74 of a heart attack.

✒ Carrie in nominated role.

✎ Started out in vaudeville at the age of 15. Billed as the "Vagabond Violinist." Once had her own movie production company and was a shrewd business woman who compiled a substantial fortune. In retirement she ran her business Ashtrays Unlimited until 1974, just at the start of the anti-smoking movement.

Connery, Sir Sean

★ 1987-(BSA) *The Untouchables*

■ Born 8/25/30 in Edinburgh, Scotland

✒ James Bond (#3 on AFI's Hero List)

✎ Quit school at age 15 and joined the British navy, mustered out because of ulcers. Once was a body builder and entered the Mr. Universe contest, finishing in the top ten. He has also worked as a milkman, coffin polisher, and nude model. In his youth he liked to live dangerously—he was romancing Lana Turner off screen and her mobster husband Johnny Stompanato nearly had him killed. Knighted by the Queen in 2000.

Major Awards: Oscar, GG, NBR, BAFTA, AFI's Life Achievement, WOF

Connelly, Jennifer

★ 2001-(BSA) *A Beautiful Mind*

■ Born 12/12/70 in New York, NY

✒ Alicia Nash in Oscar'd role.

✎ Attended Yale and Stanford Universities. At the tender age of ten she was already doing modeling ads in magazines and television spots. She is fanatical when it comes to exercising, with yoga being one of her favorite activities. Enjoys camping, biking, hiking, and gymnastics. Also into quantum physics and philosophy.

Major Awards: Oscar, AFI, GG, BAFTA, KCFCC

Conti, Tom

1983-(BA) *Reuben, Reuben*
    Winner: Robert Duvall, *Tender Mercies*

■ Born 11/22/41 in Paisley, Scotland

✒ Gowan McGland in nominated role.

✎ He was born of Italian and Irish parents. He is a classical pianist trained at the Royal Scottish Academy of Music. He is a gifted and talented comedic actor and has been married to actress Kara Wilson since 1967. Despite all of his fine performances, major stardom has eluded him.

Major Awards: Tony, OCC

Cooper, Chris

★ 2002-(BSA) *Adaptation*

■ Born 7/9/51 in Kansas City, MO

✒ Trainer Tom Smith in *Seabiscuit*

✎ Studied ballet at Stephan College—and majored in architecture at University of Missouri. Once worked as a construction foreman and helped build the Kansas City Royals stadium. His young son Jesse died of cerebral palsy in 2005.

Major Awards: Oscar, LAFC, NBR, GG, KCFCC, BW

Cooper, Gary

1936-(BA) *Mr. Deeds Goes to Town*
    Winner: Paul Muni, *The Story of Louis Pasteur*

★ 1941-(BA) *Sergeant York*

1942-(BA) *The Pride of the Yankees*
    Winner: James Cagney, *Yankee Doodle Dandy*

1943-(BA) *For Whom the Bell Tolls*
    Winner: Paul Lucas, *Watch on the Rhine*

★ 1952-(BA) *High Noon*

1960-Honorary Oscar

■ Born *Frank James Cooper* on 5/7/01 in Helena, MT. Died 5/13/61 of lung cancer.

✒ Sergeant York (#35 on AFI's Hero List), Will Kane, (#5 on AFI's Hero List), Lou Gehrig (#25 on AFI's Hero List).

🖋 Once was a guide at Yellowstone National Park and a political cartoonist. Changed his name to Gary at the request of his agent Nan Collins—she read where a fellow by the name of Frank James had just killed his wife. Fearing the public would be confused he used the name of the city she was from Gary, IN. He was an avid hunter, fisherman, gardener, swimmer, and horseback rider. He played the harmonica and guitar. Offscreen he was quite the Lothario, having affairs with numerous leading ladies.

Major Awards: Oscar (2), NYFC, GG, NBR, WOF

Cooper, Dame Gladys

1942-(BSA) *Now, Voyager*
  Winner: Teresa Wright, *Mrs. Miniver*
1943-(BSA) *The Song of Bernadette*
  Winner: Katina Paxinou, *For Whom the Bell Tolls*
1964-(BSA) *My Fair Lady*
  Winner: Lila Kedrova, *Zorba the Greek*
▦ Born 12/18/1888 in Lewisham, England. Died 11/17/71 of pneumonia.
🖋 Sister Vauzous in *The Song of Bernadette*.
🖋 She was posing as a model at age six. Made Dame Commander of the British Empire by the Queen in 1967. She was the British Army's pinup girl in WW I. Bette Davis once said that she was one of the few actresses she felt privileged to play a scene with.

Major Awards: WOF

Cooper, Jackie

1930/31-(BA) *Skippy*
  Winner: Lionel Barrymore, *A Free Soul*
▦ Born John Cooperman on 9/15/21 in Los Angeles, CA.
🖋 Perry White in the *Superman* movies
🖋 A child star, he was a member of the *Little Rascals*. Before he was 18 he was Joan Crawford's paramour. Had his own TV series *Hennessey* and *The People's Choice*. Became a powerful director and producer. He served in the Navy and held the rank of captain.

He is the youngest performer to be nominated for Best Actor, at age nine.

Major Awards: Emmy, WOF

Corby, Ellen

1948-(BSA) *I Remember Mama*
  Winner: Clair Trevor, *Key Largo*
▦ Born *Ellen Hansen* on 6/3/13 in Racine, WI. Died 4/14/99 of natural causes.
🖋 Grandma Walton on TV series *The Waltons*
🖋 She was a script girl in Hollywood for 12 years. She wrote a couple of Hopalong Cassidy episodes and the dialogue for *Murder My Sweet*. Suffered a near fatal stroke in 1976 but gamely bounced back to win a Emmy the next year. Received a Golden Boot award for all of her bit parts in westerns.

Major Awards: Emmy (3), GG

Cortese, Valentina

1974-(BSA) *Day for Night*
  Winner: Ingrid Bergman, *Murder on the Orient Express*
▦ Born 1/1/24 in Milan, Italy
🖋 Severine in nominated role.
🖋 Ingrid Bergman, in her acceptance speech, apologized to Valentina stating it was she that really deserved the Oscar.

Major Awards: NYFC, NSFC

Costner, Kevin

1990-(BA) *Dances with Wolves*
  Winner: Jeremy Irons, *Reversal of Fortune*
★ 1990-(Best Picture/Producer) *Dances with Wolves*
★ 1990-(Best Director) *Dances with Wolves*
▦ Born 1/15/55 in Lynwood, CA
🖋 Elliot Ness in *The Untouchables*, washed up flop *Waterworld*.
🖋 As a youth he sang in the choir in his Baptist church. He wrote poetry and took writing lessons.

Graduated from Cal State Fullerton. His was a star of the *The Big Chill*, however his part was left on the cutting room floor. At age 18 built a canoe and went down the same rivers that Lewis and Clark navigated. When he completed *Dances with Wolves*, the Sioux Indian tribe bequeathed him a tract of land on which he built a golf course.

Major Awards: Oscar, GG, NBR, BAFTA, BIFF, DGA, GG, NBR, PC, BW, WOF

Courtenay, Sir Tom

1965-(BSA) *Doctor Zhivago*
    Winner: Martin Balsam, *A Thousand Clowns*
1983-(BA) *The Dresser*
    Winner: Robert Duvall, *Tender Mercies*
▧ Born 2/25/37 in Hull Humberside, England
⚘ Pasha Antipov in *Doctor Zhivago*
⚲ Graduated from RADA. Awarded knighthood in 2001 by Queen Elizabeth. He now works mainly in stage and theatrical productions. He recently reprised his acclaimed performance in *The Dresser*.

Major Awards: GG, BAFTA, NBR, VFF

Coward, Sir Noel

1943-(BP) *In Which We Serve*
1943-(Best Original Screenplay) *In Which We Serve*
1943-Honorary Oscar
▧ Born 12/16/1899 in Teddington, England. Died 3/26/73 of a heart attack
⚘ *In Which We Serve*
⚲ Mr. Coward could truly be classified as a Renaissance man. His mother named him Noel because he was born close to Christmas. He was a playwright, screenwriter, director, producer, composer, actor, novelist, short story writer, and songwriter. He was knighted in 1970. During WW II he worked undercover for the British Intelligence. He achieved all of this without a grammar school education. He wrote 140 plays and over 100 songs.

Major Awards: Tony, NYFC

Crain, Jeanne

1949-(BA) *Pinky*
    Winner: Olivia de Havilland, *The Heiress*
▧ Born 5/25/25 in Barstow, CA
⚘ Patricia Johnson in nominated role. Died 12/14/2003 of a heart attack.
⚲ Won the Miss Long Beach beauty contest at age 16. Discovered by Orson Welles. Found domestic tranquility at age 18, and still continued her career despite having seven children. She was married for 57 years to Paul Brooks, once a double for Errol Flynn.

Crawford, Broderick

★ 1949-(BA) *All the King's Men*
▧ Born 12/9/11 in Philadelphia, PA. Died 4/26/86 of a series of strokes.
⚘ Dan Mathews in TV cop series *Highway Patrol*
⚲ Graduated from Harvard. Working in his youth as a stevedore and merchant seaman he was involved in many fights. He broke his nose six times. He was in the Army during WW II and fought in the Battle of the Bulge. Married three times and had a lifelong struggle with the bottle. Once engaged to Lucille Ball. His mother Helen named him after her maiden name.

Major Awards: Oscar, NYFC, GG, WOF (2)

Crawford, Joan

★ 1945-(BA) *Mildred Pierce*
1947-(BA) *Possessed*
    Winner: Loretta Young, *The Farmer's Daughter*
1952-(BA) *Sudden Fear*
    Winner: Shirley Booth, *Come Back, Little Sheba*
▧ Born *Lucille LeSuer* 3/23/08 in San Antonio, TX. Died 5/10/77 of pancreatic cancer.
⚘ Fay Dunaway's brutal portrayal of her in *Mommy Dearest*.
⚲ She attended Stephens College. She was a dancer and once an elevator girl. She would wash her hands

Ann Blyth, Zachary Scott, and
Joan Crawford in *Mildred Pierce*.

every ten minutes, and after guests left she would
wipe down the whole house. Her big break came
when she won a Charleston contest. She married
Pepsi-Cola tycoon Alfred Steele, who served on
the Board of Directors. She wrote two volumes
of her memoirs. She was an excessive smoker and
drinker and near the end she was consuming a quart
of vodka a day.
Major Awards: Oscar, NBR, CB DeMille, GG,
WOF

Crisp, Donald

★ 1941-(BSA) *How Green Was My Valley*
Born 7/27/1880 in Aberfeldy, Scotland.
Died 5/26/74 of a stroke.
Father Morgan in nominated role.
Graduated from Oxford University. He fought in
the Boer War and was wounded. He was a very astute
real estate investor amassing a huge fortune. Served
on the Board of Directors for the Bank of America.
Starred in over 174 films from 1908 until 1963.
Major Awards: Oscar, NBR, WOF

Cromwell, James

1995-(BSA) *Babe*
Winner: Kevin Spacey, *The Usual Suspects*
Born 1/27/40 in Las Angeles, CA
Arthur Hoggett in nominated role
Graduated from Middlebury College and Carnegie Institute of Technology. Once was a member of
the Black Panthers. Arrested for trespassing during
an animal rights protest at a Wendy's restaurant,
and was fined $1000. At 6'7" he is the tallest actor
ever to be nominated.
Major Awards: Bronze Wrangler

Cronyn, Hume

1944-(BSA) *The Seventh Cross*
Winner: Barry Fitzgerald, *Going My Way*
Born 7/18/11 in Ontario, Canada.
Died 6/15/2003 of prostate cancer.
Paul Roeder in nominated role.
Graduated from Ridley College. Married to
actress Jessica Tandy since 1942. Initially studied
to be a lawyer, like his dad. He was selected to the
Canadian boxing team in 1932. He had a glass eye,
having lost the real one to cancer.
Major Awards: Emmy, Tony, Obie, Humanitis,
WGA

Crosby, Bing

★ 1944-(BA) *Going My Way*
1945-(BA) *The Bells of St. Mary's*
Winner: Ray Milland, *The Lost Weekend*
1954-(BA) *The Country Girl*
Winner: Marlon Brando, *On the Waterfront*
Born *Harry Lillis Crosby* on 5/2/01 in Tacoma,
WA. Died 10/14/77 of a heart attack.
Singer and crooner par excellence.
Father O'Malley in *Going My Way*
It is reported that he drank so much in his youth
that his voice changed from a tenor to a baritone.
He was colorblind. An avid golfer his whole life,

Bing Crosby and Barry Fitzgerald in *Going My Way*.

he died on a course in Spain. Nicknamed after comic strip character Bingville Bugle. Despite being aloof, rude to fans, a philanderer, a womanizer, and cruel to his sons, he never suffered a tarnished public image. Up until his death he was the biggest recording artist of all time.

Major Awards: Oscar, Peabody, NBR, GG, C.B. DeMille, WOF

Crosse, Rupert

1969-(BSA) *The Reivers*
    Winner: Gig Young, *They Shoot Horses Don't They?*
▩ Born 1/1/27 in Jackson, MS. Died 3/5/73 of cancer.
𝄢 Ned McClaslin in nominated role.
🔍 At 6'5" he was one of Hollywood's tallest actors. Made his TV debut on *Bonanza*. Starred in the '70s TV comedy cop series *The Partners*. First black actor to earn a nomination for a supporting role. Career was cut short when he contracted cancer and died tragically at age 45. Jack Nicholson, his old buddy, wanted him to play Mulhall in *The Last Detail* but he was too sick.

Crouse, Lindsay

1984-(BSA) *Places in the Heart*
    Winner: Peggy Ashcroft, *A Passage to India*
▩ Born 5/12/48 in New York, NY
𝄢 Margaret Lomax in nominated role.
🔍 Graduated from Radcliffe in 1970 and was in the first class to receive Harvard diplomas. Listed as one of the most promising new actors of 1977. Once married to screenwriter, playwright, and director David Mamet. Her father Russell was an established novelist who authored *State of the Union* and *Life with Father*. She was named after her father's longtime writing partner, Howard Lindsay.

Crowe, Russell

1999-(BA) *The Insider*
    Winner: Kevin Spacey, *American Beauty*
★ 2000-(BA) *Gladiator*
2001-(BA) *A Beautiful Mind*
    Winner: Denzel Washington, *Training Day*
▩ Born 4/7/64 in Wellington, New Zealand
𝄢 Gen. Maximus Meridus (#50 on AFI's Hero List), throwing telephones at hotel employees

He is a high school dropout. Lives on 560-acre cattle farm in Sydney, Australia. Reportedly is ¹⁄₁₆ Maori. Was a target of an abduction threat and received FBI protection. Has his own band The Ordinary Fear of God in which he sings and writes his own songs. Once worked as a bingo caller. For his role in *The Insider* he gained 48 pounds.
Major Awards: Australian Oscar, LAFC, NSFC, NBR, BAFTA, SAG

Cruise, Tom

1989-(BA) *Born on the 4th of July*
    Winner: Daniel Day Lewis, *My Left Foot*
1996-(BA) *Jerry Maguire*
    Winner: Geoffrey Rush, *Shine*
1999-(BSA) *Magnolia*
    Winner: Michael Caine, *The Cider House Rules*
Born *Thomas Cruise Mapother IV* on 7/3/62 in Syracuse, NY.
Top Gun, Jerry Maguire in title role, generally freakish behavior
Son of nomadic parents, he attended 15 different schools by the time he was 14, when he enrolled in a Franciscan seminary. He dropped out after four years, deciding against becoming a priest and went to New York to pursue an acting career. A lifelong sufferer of dyslexia. He is a skydiver and scuba diver, as well as piloting his own plane. He is allergic to cats.
Major Awards: GG, NBR, BAFTA, Saturn, DDA, WOF

Cruz, Penelope

2006-(BA) *Volver*
    Winner: Helen Mirren, *The Queen*
Born *Penelope Cruz Sanchez* on 4/28/74 in Madrid, Spain.
Raimunda in nominated role.
She studied classical dance for nine years and ballet for three at Spain's National Conservatory. At age 15 she beat out 300 hopefuls to land a lucrative television contract. She is fluent in Spanish, Italian, English and French. She is a vegetarian, she has been linked romantically with Tom Cruise and Mathew McConaughey. She collects coat hangers.
Major Awards: Goya, NBR

Cummings, Quinn

1977-(BSA) *The Goodbye Girl*
    Winner: Vanessa Redgrave, *Julia*
Born 8/13/67 in Hollywood, CA
Lucy McFadden in nominated role.
She attended UCLA. Worked as a casting agent in the '80s. Her father invented the baby sling carrier *Hiphugger*. She was once a short story recruiter for a major book publisher. Listed as one of 100 greatest child actors. Started her own blog on the Internet in 2005.
Major Awards: Young Artist Award

Curtis, Tony

1958-(BA) *The Defiant Ones*
    Winner: David Niven, *Separate Tables*
Born *Bernard Schwartz* in Bronx, NY
Sidney Falco in *The Sweet Smell of Success*, gangster on the run playing with Marilyn Monroe in *Some Like It Hot*, father of actress Jamie Lee Curtis
His father was a tailor from Hungary and he still speaks the language fluently. Serving in the submarine corps during WW II in Guam he was seriously injured—he was knocked overboard and his legs were paralyzed for a month. Wildly promiscuous, and always open about having sex with both men and women. He has a fear of flying. He has authored two best selling novels, *Kid Andrew Cody* and *Julie Sparrow*, and is an accomplished and incredibly successful painter—his work has shown at New York's Metropolitan Museum of Art.
Major Awards: GGWFF, DDA, WOF

Cusack, Joan

1988-(BSA) *Working Girl*
    Winner: Geena Davis, *The Accidental Tourist*

1997-(BSA) *In and Out*
  Winner: Kim Basinger, *L.A. Confidential*
◼ Born 10/11/62 in Evanston, IL
⍰ Melanie Griffith girlfriend Cyn in *Working Girl*
⍰ Member of the improv comedy troupe The Ark at the University of Wisconsin, which in turn spurred her interest in acting. She was a regular on *Saturday Night Live* for one season but quit because of the quality of material for women. Sister to actor John Cusack.
Major Awards: CFC, NYFC

Dafoe, Willem

1986-(BSA) *Platoon*
  Winner: Michael Caine, *Hannah and Her Sisters*
2000-(BSA) *Shadow of the Vampire*
  Winner: Benicio Del Toro, *Traffic*
◼ Born 7/22/55 in Appleton, WI
⍰ Sergeant Elias in *Platoon*, Green Goblin in *Spider-Man*
⍰ Skilled in the trades—he held jobs as a carpenter and electrician. Toured Europe and U.S. with an experimental theater group. Did most of his own stunts in *Spider-Man*. Contracted yellow fever while filming *Platoon*. He is a vegetarian and is a regular yoga practioner.
Major Awards: LAFC, ISA

Dailey, Dan

1948-(BA) *When My Baby Smiles at Me*
  Winner: Laurence Olivier, *Hamlet*
◼ Born 12/14/14 in New York, NY
⍰ Major league pitcher Dizzy Dean in *The Pride of St. Louis*. Died 10/16/78 of pernicious anemia.
⍰ Worked as a grocery clerk, golf caddy, and shoe salesman, and he appeared in burlesque and minstrel shows. Served in WW II and came out a lieutenant. Mel Brooks wanted him to play the Waco Kid in *Blazing Saddles*. His only son committed suicide in 1975.
Major Awards: GG

Dall, John

1945-(BSA) *The Corn Is Green*
  Winner: James Dunn, *A Tree Grows in Brooklyn*
◼ Born *John Jenner Thompson* on 5/26/18 in New York, NY. Died 1/15/71 of a heart attack.
⍰ Welsh miner Morgan Evans in nominated role.
⍰ His career was cut short after he suffered a fatal heart attack at the age of 52. Made a memorable major picture as Brandon Shaw in Alfred Hitchcock's *Rope*.

Damon, Matt

1997-(BA) *Goodwill Hunting*
  Winner: Jack Nicholson, *As Good As It Gets*
★ 1997-(BW) *Goodwill Hunting*
◼ Born 10/8/70 in Cambridge, MA
⍰ Will Hunting in title role.
⍰ Attended Harvard, leaving two semesters short of a degree in English. Lost 40 pounds on his already thin frame to play a heroin addict in *Courage Under Fire*. This sudden weight loss injured his adrenal glands, which required months of medication. Plays the piano.
Major Awards: Oscar, NBR, GG, BIFF, Humanitis

Dandridge, Dorothy

1954-(BA) *Carmen Jones*
  Winner: Grace Kelly, *The Country Girl*
◼ Born 11/9/23 in Cleveland, OH. Died 9/8/65 from an overdose of barbiturates and alcohol.
⍰ Carmen Jones in title role.
⍰ Daughter of a minister. First black woman to appear on the cover of *Life* magazine. Although she was a great nightclub singer, she hated it. Suffered from stage fright and was diagnosed as manic depressive. Dated Peter Lawford and Otto Preminger. She was the first African American to be nominated for a Best Actress Oscar.
Major Awards: WOF

Darin, Bobby

1963-(BSA) *Captain Newman, Md.*
    Winner: Melvyn Douglas, *Hud*
▪ Born *Robert Cassotto* on 5/14/36 in New York, NY. Died 12/20/73 after undergoing two open-heart surgeries.
♫ Singing signature song "Mack the Knife"
♪ Started out in radio and recorded his own song "Splish, Splash" on *American Bandstand*. Suffered from a hereditary heart condition. Elected to the Rock 'n' Roll Hall of Fame in 1990. Fell in love with Connie Francis—they wanted to elope but her dad ran him off with a gun. Connie regretted not marrying him ever after. In the end he married actress Sandra Dee.
Major Awards: GG, Grammy, WOF

Darwell, Jane

★ 1940-(BSA) *The Grapes of Wrath*
▪ Born *Patti Woodward* 10/15/1879 in Palmyra, MO. Died 8/14/67 of a heart attack.
♫ Ma Joad in nominated role.
♪ She was a direct descendant of the seventh president of the United States, Andrew Jackson. Her father was president of the Louisville Southern railroad. She originally turned down the role of Birdwoman in *Mary Poppins*, however Walt Disney personally persuaded her to play the role.
Major Awards: NBR, WOF

Davidson, Jaye

1992-(BSA) *The Crying Game*
    Winner: Gene Hackman, *Unforgiven*
▪ Born Alfred Amey on 3/21/68 in Riverside, CA
♫ The hairdresser Dil in nominated role.
♪ His father is from Ghana and his mother from England. Dropped out of high school at age 16. He once was a hairdresser in real life, as well as a sales clerk for Walt Disney. Studied ballet as a child. First person to be nominated in a role in which he appeared in full frontal nudity.
Major Awards: NBR

Davis, Bette

★ 1935-(BA) *Dangerous*
★ 1938-(BA) *Jezebel*
1939-(BA) *Dark Victory*
    Winner: Vivien Leigh, *Gone with the Wind*
1940-(BA) *The Letter*
    Winner: Ginger Rogers, *Kitty Foyle*
1941-(BA) *The Little Foxes*
    Winner: Joan Fontaine, *Suspicion*
1942-(BA) *Now, Voyager*
    Winner: Greer Garson-*Mrs. Miniver*
1944-(BA) *Mr. Skeffington*
    Winner: Ingrid Bergman, *Gaslight*
1950-(BA) *All About Eve*
    Winner: Judy Holliday, *Born Yesterday*
1952-(BA) *The Star*
    Winner: Shirley Booth, *Come Back, Little Sheba*
1962-(BA) *Whatever Happened to Baby Jane?*
    Winner: Anne Bancroft, *The Miracle Worker*
▪ Born on 4/5/08 in Lowell, MA. Died 10/6/89 of breast cancer.
♫ Margo Channing in *All About Eve*, Regina Gunderson in *The Little Foxes*, and Baby Jane Hudson (#43 and #44 respectively on AFI's Villain List). Gutsy, perennial Hollywood icon.

Bette Davis and Henry Fonda in *Jezebel*.

🔎 Leading lady of Hollywood once took out an ad in the trade papers "Job Wanted" when work was scarce. She had osteomyelitis, which required an operation to remove half of her jaw. She was the only female president of the Academy of Motion Picture Arts and Sciences. She quit the same year she was elected. Director William Wyler was the love of her life, but he would not leave his wife. Suffered a series of strokes and had a mastectomy in 1983. She had a lifelong feud with sometime co-star Joan Crawford.

Major Awards: Oscar, Emmy, NBR, NYFC, Cannes, C.B. DeMille, César, GG, AFI's Lifetime Achievement, WFCA, WOF

Davis, Geena

★ 1988-(BSA) *The Accidental Tourist*
1991-(BA) *Thelma & Louise*
    Winner: Jodie Foster, *The Silence of the Lambs*
◾ Born *Virginia Davis* on 1/21/57 in
    Wareham, MA
🍴 Thelma (#24 on AFI's Hero List)
🔎 Graduated from Boston University. A part-time writer, she once wrote an episode for the television series *Buffalo Bill*. Working as a saleswoman in woman's department store, she posed as a human mannequin in their storefront window. She is a champion archer having placed on the Olympic Archery Team. She speaks Swedish, and is a Mensa member with an IQ of 140. She is a statuesque six feet tall.

Major Awards: Oscar, NBR, DDA, BSFC, GG, WFCA

Davis, Judy

1984-(BSA) *A Passage to India*
    Winner: Sally Field, *Places in the Heart*
1992-(BSA) *Husbands and Wives*
    Winner: Marisa Tomei, *My Cousin Vinny*
◾ Born 1956 in Perth, Western Australia
🍴 Adela Quested in *A Passage to India*
🔎 She studied to enter the religious life—though once there became disenchanted and dropped out of the convent. She then joined a rock band in Australia and became the lead singer. Hates being interviewed and plays the piano.

Major Awards: GG, Emmy, NSFC, NYFC, NBR, LAFC, BAFTA, ISA, SAG, Australian F.I.

Davison, Bruce

1990-(BSA) *Longtime Companion*
    Winner: Joe Pesci, *Goodfellas*
◾ Born 6/28/46 in Philadelphia, PA
🍴 Senator Kelly in *X-Men*
🔎 Graduated from Penn State University. Graduated from the prestigious NYU's School of the Arts. He has won Broadway's Dramalogue Award three times. Started out as a Shakespearian actor on the stage. Originally wanted to be a painter but quickly changed his mind after starring in his high school play.

Major Awards: NYFC, NSFC, GG, ISA, VFF

Day, Doris

1959-(BA) *Pillow Talk*
    Winner: Simone Signoret, *Ship of Fools*
◾ Born *Doris von Kappelhoff* on 4/3/22 in
    Cincinnati, OH
🍴 Singing Academy award winning song "Que Sera Sera" in Hitchcock's *The Man Who Knew Too Much*. Movies with co-star Rock Hudson.
🔎 She was studying to be a dancer when a near fatal auto accident turned her to acting. When her manager husband suddenly died, she found out she was destitute. Filed bankruptcy and sued her lawyer. She was awarded 22 million.

Major Awards: GGWFF, CB DeMille, WOF

Day-Lewis, Daniel

★ 1989-(BA) *My Left Foot*
1993-(BA) *In the Name of the Father*
    Winner: Tom Hanks, *Philadelphia*
2002-(BA) *Gangs of New York*
    Winner: Adrien Brody, *The Pianist*

■ Born 4/29/57 in London, England

✎ Hawkeye in *The Last of the Mohicans*

♦ Accidentally overdosed on migraine medicine at age 16 and suffered from hallucinations for two weeks. He was mistaken for a heroin addict and placed in a mental institution until he proved otherwise. He is an expert carpenter and woodworker and has learned how to be a cobbler. Has a son with actress Isabel Adjani.

Major Awards: Oscar, NYFC, NBR, NSFC, SAG, LAFC, BAFTA, BSFC, KCFCC

Dean, James

1955-(BA) *East of Eden*
   Winner: Ernest Borgnine, *Marty*
1956-(BA) *Giant*
   Winner: Yul Bryner, *The King and I*

■ Born 2/8/31 in Marion, IN. Died 9/30/55 in an auto accident.

✎ Rebel roles: Cal Trask and Jett Rink

♦ He was raised by his aunt and uncle on a farm in Fairmount, IN. In high school he won a statewide speech contest and was a champion pole vaulter. Before his fatal crash, he filmed a commercial for safe driving for the National Highway Committee. Two hours before his crash he was issued a speeding ticket. Marlon Brando was his idol.

Major Awards: GG, GGWFF, WOF

Richard Davalos, James Dean, and Julie Harris in *East of Eden*.

Olivia de Havilland and Montgomery Clift in *The Heiress*.

De Havilland, Olivia

1939-(BSA) *Gone with the Wind*
   Winner: Hattie McDaniel, *Gone with the Wind*
1941-(BA) *Hold Back the Dawn*
   Winner: Joan Fontaine, *Suspicion*
★ 1946-(BA) *To Each His Own*
1948-(BA) *The Snake Pit*
   Winner: Jane Wyman, *Johnny Belinda*
★ 1949-(BA) *The Heiress*

■ Born 7/1/16 in Tokyo, Japan

✎ Melanie in *Gone with the Wind*

♦ She was suspended six months by Warner Bros. because she complained about the roles she was getting. When they wouldn't release her from her contract she sued and won a landmark decision. Her sister Joan Fontaine and she were not close—a classic case of sibling rivalry was fatally exacerbated when Joan won the Oscar in 1941. From then on they were permanently estranged. She has lived in Paris since the early '50s and teaches Sunday school at her

local church. It was discovered that she was a distant cousin to frequent co-star Erroll Flynn.
Major Awards: Oscar, NBR, NYFC, GG, VFF, WOF

Del Toro, Benicio

★ 2000-(BSA) *Traffic*
2003-(BSA) *21 Grams*
    Winner: Tim Robbins, *Mystic River*
■ Born 2/19/67 in Santurce, Puerto Rico
🖋 Battle-worn cop Javier Rodriguez in *Traffic*
🔍 Moved to Philadelphia after his mother's death when he was 12. Co-captained his high school basketball team. Attended the University of California studying business. *Big Top Pee Wee* was his film debut. He is an artist and loves painting.
Major Awards: Oscar, NSFC, NYFC, SAG, GG, NBR, BAFTA, BIFF, ISA, KCFCC, VFF, Sundance

Demarest, William

1946-(BSA) *The Jolson Story*
    Winner: Harold Russell, *The Best Years of Our Lives*

Benicio Del Toro in *Traffic*.

■ Born 2/27/1892 in St. Paul, MN. Died 12/28/83 prostate cancer and pneumonia.
🖋 Uncle Charlie on television series *My Three Sons*
🔍 Started on the stage at age 13. Worked in vaudeville and was a circus barker. At one time entered the world of professional boxing. Was an ardent golfer hitting the links whenever he had any free time.
Major Awards: WOF

Dench, Dame Judi

1997-(BA) *Mrs. Brown*
    Winner: Helen Hunt, *As Good As It Gets*
★ 1998-(BSA) *Shakespeare in Love*
2000-(BSA) *Chocolat*
    Winner: Marcia Gay Harden, *Pollock*
2001-(BA) *Iris*
    Winner: Hallie Berry, *Monster's Ball*
2005-(BA) *Mrs. Henderson Presents*
    Winner: Reese Witherspoon, *Walk the Line*
2006-(BA) *Notes on a Scandal*
    Winner: Helen Mirren, *The Queen*
■ Born 12/9/34 in York, England
🖋 Queen Elizabeth I in Oscar'd role.
🔍 Her screen time in her award-winning role was only eight minutes, the second shortest in Oscar history. As a young woman she attended the Mount School and became a Quaker. Named Dame Commander of the British Empire by the Queen in 1960. Along with Audrey Hepburn won an Oscar and Tony the same year. Awarded Honorary Doctorate in Letters at Oxford and Trinity Universities. Nominated 17 times for a BAFTA and won eight.
Major Awards: Oscar, Tony, NSFC, GG, SAG, BAFTA, KCFCC

Deneuve, Catherine

1992-(BA) *Indocine*
    Winner: Emma Thompson, *Howard's End*
■ Born *Catherine Dorleac* on 10/22/43 in Paris, France
🖋 Elaine Devries in nominated role, crazed tenant in Roman Polanksi's *Repulsion*

⚲ She made her screen debut at age 13. She assumed her mother's maiden name. Despite having children with Roger Vadim and Marcello Mastroianni, she refused to marry either. She has never appeared in the theater because of stage fright. She speaks Italian, French, English, and German fluently.

Major Awards: César, BIFF, DDA, VFF, WFCA

De Niro, Robert

★ 1974-(BSA) *The Godfather Part II*
1976-(BA) *Taxi Driver*
   Winner: Peter Finch, *Network*
1978-(BA) *The Deer Hunter*
   Winner: Jon Voight, *Coming Home*
★ 1980-(BA) *Raging Bull*
1990-(BA) *Awakenings*
   Winner: Jeremy Irons, *Reversal of Fortune*
1991-(BA) *Cape Fear*
   Winner: Anthony Hopkins, *The Silence of the Lambs*
▦ Born 8/17/43 in New York, NY
⚗ Jake LaMotta. Travis Bickle, *Taxi Driver* (#30 on AFI's Villain List).
⚲ Grew up in New York's Little Italy where his childhood chum was director Martin Scorsese. Dropped out of high school to join a neighborhood gang. Co-owns the San Francisco eatery Rubicon with Francis Ford Coppola and Robin Williams.

Robert DeNiro in *Raging Bull*.

Returned French Legion of Honor award after being falsely accused of being involved in an international prostitution ring. Gained 60 pounds for his role in *Raging Bull*. His father came out of the closet and declared his homosexuality and then divorced his mother. Had prostate cancer surgery in 2003—it is now in remission. Accidentally broke Joe Pesci's rib when sparring while filming *Raging Bull*.

Major Awards: Oscar, NYFC, NSFC, LAFC, NBR, GG, AFI's Life Achievement, BSFC, VFF

Dennis, Sandy

★ 1966-(BSA) *Who's Afraid of Virginia Woolf?*
▦ Born 4/27/37 in Hastings, NE. Died 3/2/92 of ovarian cancer.
⚗ Honey in Oscar'd role
⚲ One of the few actresses to receive a Tony award in successive years: 1963 and 1964. Long-time companion of jazz saxophonist great Gary Mulligan but never married. Life cut prematurely short when she contracted cancer. She had a great fondness for cats.

Major Awards: Oscar, Tony

Depardieu, Gerard

1990-(BA) *Cyrano De Bergerac*
   Winner: Jeremy Irons, *Reversal of Fortune*
▦ Born 12/27/48 in Chateauroux, France.
⚗ Title in nominated role
⚲ As a youth he was a juvenile delinquent involved in petty theft and sexual battery. Eventually he was straightened out by a kindly social worker. He is a professional-level winemaker. Underwent quintuple heart bypass surgery following a heart attack in 2000. Announced his retirement from acting in 2005.

Major Awards: Cannes, GG, NSFC, César, VFF

Depp, Johnny

2003-(BA) *Pirates of the Caribbean: The Curse of the Black Pearl*
   Winner: Sean Penn, *Mystic River*

2004-(BA) *Finding Neverland*
　　Winner: Jamie Foxx, *Ray*
▪ Born 6/9/63 in Owensboro, KY
✅ Star of television series *21 Jump Street*, Jack Sparrow in *Pirates of the Caribbean*, uncanny knack for picking great roles.
🔦 He was a high school dropout at age 16. Nicholas Cage was his mentor who encouraged him to get into acting. He has a pathological fear of clowns. He is part Navajo Indian. Played the guitar for the band The Kids. He is fluent in French. Maintains homes in Paris and Los Angeles. Once engaged to Winona Ryder.
Major Awards: SAG, César, PC, WOF

Dern, Bruce

1978-(BSA) *Coming Home*
　　Winner: Christopher Walken, *The Deer Hunter*
▪ Born 6/4/36 in Chicago, IL
✅ Villain who killed John Wayne in *The Cowboys*
🔦 An avid runner—placed first in the Penn relays and for years ran 50 miles a week. His grandfather was Secretary of War in FDR's administration and Governor of Utah. His uncle was poet Archibald MacLeish. Once married to actress Diane Ladd and father to Laura Dern. He is the quintessential movie psychotic, beginning with parts as hippies and freaks in the '60s in Roger Corman's exploitation flicks.
Major Awards: NYFC, NSFC, BIFF

Dern, Laura

1991-(BA) *Rambling Rose*
　　Winner: Jodie Foster, *The Silence of the Lambs*
▪ Born 2/10/66 in Santa Monica, CA
✅ Heroine in *Jurassic Park*
🔦 Made screen debut at age seven. Laura's sister died when she accidentally drowned in the family pool. A nurse left her side momentarily to answer the phone. Her mother Diane Ladd was nominated for the same movie, an Oscar first.
Major Awards: LAFC, BSFC, GG, Sundance

Desica, Vittorio

★ 1947-Honorary Oscar, *Shoeshine*
★ 1949-Honorary Oscar, *The Bicycle Thief*
1957-(BSA) *A Farewell to Arms*
　　Winner: Red Buttons, *Sayonara*
★ 1964-(Best Foreign Film) *Yesterday, Today and Tomorrow*
★ 1971-(Best Foreign Film) *The Garden of the Finzi-Continis*
▪ Born 7/7/02 in Sora, Italy. Died 11/13/74 of natural causes.
✅ Great Italian director
🔦 Once worked as an office clerk and gave all of his earnings to his poor family. Because of Italian laws after living with future wife for 26 years was finally married after adopting French citizenship. He acted in over 150 films mainly to earn money to finance his projects. He was a compulsive gambler.
Major Awards: Oscar, NBR, Cannes, BIFF, DDA, KCFCC

Dewilde, Brandon

1953-(BSA) *Shane*
　　Winner: Frank Sinatra, *From Here to Eternity*
▪ Born 4/9/42 in Brooklyn, NY. Died 7/6/72 in an auto accident.
✅ Joey Starrett in nominated role—"Shane, come back Shane . . ."
🔦 Made Broadway debut at age seven in *The Member of the Wedding*, which he performed 492 times. First child to win the Donaldson Award. Starred in his own television series *Jamie* in 1953–54. Life was cut short when he was killed at age 29 in a horrific traffic accident. He left behind one son.
Major Awards: GG

DiCaprio, Leonardo

1993-(BSA) *What's Eating Gilbert Grape?*
　　Winner: Tommy Lee Jones, *The Fugitive*
2004-(BA) *The Aviator*
　　Winner: Jamie Foxx, *Ray*

2006, (BA) *Blood Diamond*
   Winner: Forest Whitaker, *The Last King of Scotland*
▨ Born 11/11/74 in Hollywood, CA
✎ Jack Dawson in *Titanic*
✎ Rejected at age ten by a talent agent because of a bad haircut. Successfully sued *Playgirl* magazine to block publication of unauthorized nude pictures. Suffered from an obsessive-compulsive disorder as a child and was kicked off of *The Romper Room Show* for disruptive behavior. Big supporter of environmental and conservation causes. Enjoys bungee jumping. He speaks German.
Major Awards: NBR, GG, LAFC, BIFF

Dietrich, Marlene

1930/31-(BA) *Morocco*
   Winner: Marie Dressler, *Min and Bill*
▨ Born *Marie Magdelene Dietrich von Losch* on 12/27/01 in Berlin, Germany. Died 5/6/92 of kidney failure.
✎ Legendary movie star
✎ In real life was recruited to be a Nazi spy and she refused. For her tireless work during WW II for the Allied Forces, she was awarded the U.S. Medal of Freedom, French Legion of Honor, and a Russian

Gary Cooper and Marlene Dietrich in *Morocco*.

Humanitarian Medal. She bragged about the fact that she slept with three of the Kennedy men, Joe Sr., Joe Jr., and John F. Had a torrid romance with General George Patton. She was terrified of germs and was an insomniac. She was adept at playing the violin and piano. Her best friend was Mae West. First German actress to be nominated.
Major Awards: Tony, WOF

Dillon, Matt

2005-(BSA) *Crash*
   Winner: George Clooney, *Syriana*
▨ Born 2/18/64 in New Rochelle, NY
✎ Officer Ryan in nominated role.
✎ He has five brothers and sisters. His uncles were the creators of the *Flash Gordon* and *Jungle Jim* comic strips. Publicly acknowledges Gene Hackman as his mentor and idol. He likes traveling and collecting baseball cards and vinyl LP records.
Major Awards: SAG, ISA

Dillon, Melinda

1977-(BSA) *Close Encounters of the Third Kind*
   Winner: Vanessa Redgrave, *Julia*
1981-(BSA) *Absence of Malice*
   Winner: Maureen Stapleton, *Reds*
▨ Born 10/13/39 in Hope, AZ
✎ Ralphies' mother in *The Christmas Story*
✎ The original Honey in her debut on Broadway in the play *Who's Afraid of Virginia Woolfe?* She got her start as an improvisational comedian. She is very selective in choosing her roles. She is a very private person and most personal information is unknown.
Major Awards: KCFCC

Dix, Richard

1930/31-(BA) *Cimarron*
   Winner: Lionel Barrymore, *A Free Soul*
▨ Born *Ernest Carlton Brimmer* on 7/18/84 in St. Paul, MN. Died 9/20/58 of a heart attack.

Paul Stewart and Kirk Douglas in *Champion*.

Yancey Cravet in nominated role.

He was very athletic in high school and captained the football and baseball teams. Attended the University of Minnesota. Once told by Charlie Chaplin that he would never make it in the business and becoming a star was out of the question. He was educated to be a surgeon.

Major Awards: WOF

Donat, Robert

1938-(BA) *The Citadel*
 Winner: Spencer Tracy, *Boys Town*
★ 1939-(BA) *Goodbye, Mr. Chips*
■ Born 3/18/05 in Withington Manchester, England. Died 6/9/58 of an asthma attack.
Arthur Chipping in winning role (#41 on AFI's Hero List)

As a child he took elocution lessons to overcome a stutter. He was a life-long sufferer of chronic and debilitating asthma attacks. He had severe self-doubts about his acting, although most of his peers revered his talent. He was picked to play the title role in *Captain Blood* but withdrew, opening the door for Errol Flynn.

Major Awards: Oscar, NBR, WOF

Donlevy, Brian

1939-(BSA) *Beau Geste*
 Winner: Thomas Mitchell, *Stagecoach*
■ Born 2/9/1899 in Portadown, Ireland. Died 4/15/72 of throat cancer.
Sergeant Markoff in nominated role.

As a teenager he joined General Pershing's expedition against Poncho Villa—as a bugler. In WW I he was a pilot in the famous Lafayette Escadrille. Attended the Naval Academy in Annapolis for two years. His hobbies were mining for gold and writing poetry. He also served as mayor of Malibu, CA. He was best man at William Holden's wedding. During the filming of *Beau Geste* he got so into the role that the cast was on the verge of killing him, until the director intervened.

Major Awards: WOF

Douglas, Kirk

1949-(BA) *Champion*
 Winner: Broderick Crawford, *All the King's Men*
1952-(BA) *The Bad and the Beautiful*
 Winner: Gary Cooper, *High Noon*
1956-(BA) *Lust for Life*
 Winner: Yul Brynner—*The King and I*
1995-Honorary Oscar
■ Born *Issur Danielovitch Demsky* on 12/9/16 in Amsterdam, NY
Spartacus in title role (#22 AFI's Hero List)

Kirk attended St. Lawrence University where he was a star wrestler. He was a lieutenant in the U.S. Navy and was injured in combat leading to an early discharge. For his solid efforts as a goodwill ambassador for the U.S., he was awarded the Medal of Freedom and the French Legion of Honor. He has published two novels and a best-selling autobiography *The Ragman's Son*. Speaks French and German fluently. Suffered a stroke in 1995 but gamely bounced back and at this writing is doing well.

Major Awards: GG, AFI and SAG Life Achievement Awards, César, C.B. DeMille, NBR, NYFC, WOF

Douglas, Melvyn

★ 1963-(BSA) *Hud*
1970-(BA) *I Never Sang for My Father*
 Winner: George C. Scott, *Patton*
★ 1979-(BSA) *Being There*
▪ Born *Melvyn Edouard Hesselberg* on 4/5/01 in Macon, GA. Died 8/4/81 of pneumonia and cardiac arrest.
✎ Homer Bannon, Paul Newman's principled father, in *Hud*
✎ His Russian father was a concert pianist. He dropped out of high school to pursue an acting career. One of the few Hollywood actors to have served in WW I and WW II. He enlisted at the age of 42 and completed the rigorous basic training and finished at the top. Won the Triple Crown of acting in 1967. His wife Helen was politically active for years, and was appointed Treasurer of the United States by John F. Kennedy.
Major Awards: Oscar, Emmy, Tony, NBR, GG, LAFC, NYFC, WOF

Douglas, Michael

★ 1975-(Best Picture/Producer) *One Flew Over the Cuckoo's Nest*
★ 1987-(BA) *Wall Street*
▪ Born 9/25/44 in New Brunswick, NJ.
✎ Gordon Gecko (#24 AFI's Villain List)
✎ Graduated from the University of California. As a struggling actor in New York he roomed with Danny DeVito. Worked as a gas jockey at a Mobil station and was awarded Mobil Man of the month. In 1998 he was named United Nations Messenger of Peace. Has undergone treatment for alcohol abuse. He, along with Laurence Olivier, are the only actors to win Oscars for Best Picture and Actor.
Major Awards: Oscar, GG, NBR, César, PC, LAFC, SAG, C.B. DeMille, KCFCC

Dourif, Brad

1975-(BSA) *One Flew Over the Cuckoo's Nest*
 Winner: George Burns, *The Sunshine Boys*

▪ Born 3/18/50 in Huntington Beach, WV.
✎ Grima Wormtongue in *The Lord of the Rings*
✎ Attended Marshall University. Originally wanted to be a professional artist. Taught a directing class at the University of Columbia for three years. Played music with the band The Deviants. Plays the Australian musical instrument, the didgeridoo. He was the voice of the killer doll Chucky.
Major Awards: GG, BAFTA

Downey, Robert Jr.

1992-(BA) *Chaplin*
 Winner: Al Pacino, *Scent of a Woman*
▪ Born 4/4/65 in New York, NY.
✎ Chaplin in title role, drug addiction problems
✎ He was a high school dropout. Plays the piano and sings opera. Has written and published 30 original songs. Studying for his Chaplin movie he learned to play tennis left handed. Has been in and out of rehab centers in his battle to overcome his drug and alcohol dependency. He even spent time in a prison rehab as a judge said it was necessary to save his life. Fired from the cast of *Ally McBeal* because of his drug problem.
Major Awards: GG, SAG, Saturn, BAFTA, VFF, Sundance

Dresser, Louise

1927/28-(BA) *A Ship Comes In*
 Winner: Janet Gaynor, *Seventh Heaven*
▪ Born *Louise Kerlin* on 10/5/1878 in Evansville, IN. Died 4/24/65 of an intestinal obstruction following surgery.
✎ Mamma Pleznick in nominated role.
✎ She took her name from famed songwriter Paul Dresser who wrote "My Gal Sal" and "On the Banks of the Wabash Far Away." She was Will Rogers's favorite co-star. After retiring in 1937, she devoted all her time and effort to Hollywood's Motion Picture Country House and Hospital.
Major Awards: WOF

Dressler, Marie

★ 1930/31-(BA) *Min and Bill*
1931/32-(BA) *Emma*
   Winner: Helen Hayes, *The Sin of Madelon Claudet*
▪ Born *Leila Marie Koerber* on 11/9/1869 in Co-burg Ontario, Canada. Died 7/28/34 of cancer.
🖋 Min in title role.
🔍 She ran away from home at age 14 and ended up being a chorus girl. Made her Broadway debut in 1892. She suffered from stage fright her whole career. One of America's most popular actresses. She was No. 1 at the box office for four years running.
Major Awards: WOF

Dreyfuss, Richard

★ 1977-(BA) *The Goodbye Girl*
1995-(BA) *Mr. Holland's Opus*
   Winner: Nicholas Cage, *Leaving Las Vegas*
▪ Born 10/29/47 in Brooklyn, NY.
🖋 Matt Hooper in *Jaws*
🔍 He donated $300,000 to Lupus research at UCLA. Was a conscientious objector during the Vietnam War, working two years at LA County Hospital. Before going into rehab, his daily intake was 2 grams of cocaine, 20 percodans, and 2 quarts of liquor. Youngest actor to win Oscar at age 30 until Adrian Brody won at age 29 in 2003. Hates rock music. Announced retirement from acting on the screen in 2004 to concentrate on the stage.
Major Awards: Oscar, LAFC, GG, DDA, BAFTA, KCFCC, WOF

Driscoll, Bobby

1949-Honorary Oscar, *The Window*
▪ Born 5/3/37 in Cedar Rapids, IA.
   Died 3/30/68 of hepatitis from drug abuse.
🖋 Jim Hawkins in *Treasure Island*
🔍 He was the first actor to be signed by Walt Disney Studios animation department. Unable to find work, he became a drug addict and was indigent up until his death. Died of a heart attack at age 30. He was buried in a pauper's grave. His body wasn't identified until a year later.
Major Awards: WOF

Driver, Minnie

1997-(BSA) *Good Will Hunting*
   Winner: Kim Basinger, *L.A. Confidential*
▪ Born *Amelia Driver* on 1/31/70 in Bridgetown, Barbados.
🖋 Skylar in nominated role.
🔍 She was a jazz singer in a London bistro and plays the guitar. Raised in the Caribbean until she was nine. She then attended finishing schools in Paris and Grenoble. Formed a production company with her sister called Two Drivers and received a recording contract in 2004. She has a tattoo on her right hip.
Major Awards: London Film Critics, Chicago Film Critics

Dukakis, Olympia

★ 1987-(BSA) *Moonstruck*
▪ Born 6/20/31 in Lowell, MA
🖋 Rose Castorini in Oscar'd role
🔍 Graduated from Boston University majoring in physical therapy. She taught acting at Yale and the University of New York. She is a relative to 1988 Democratic candidate for president Michael Dukakis. She is a strong advocate of women's rights and is an environmentalist. In 1989 her Oscar was stolen in a home burglary and has never been recovered.
Major Awards: Oscar, Obie, CA, NBR, LAFC, GG, BAFTA, KCFCCC

Duke, Patty

★ 1962-(BSA) *The Miracle Worker*
▪ Born *Anna Marie Duke* on 12/14/46 in Elmhurst, NY
🖋 A young Helen Keller in Oscar'd role

⚲ Professional actress at age seven. Before age 13 she had to her credit over 50 television appearances, 2 movies and 25 stage appearances. Starred as twins in television series *The Patty Duke Show*. Mother of actor Sean Astin. She is the youngest person, age 12, to have her name appear on a Broadway marquee. She has had a life-long struggle with manic depression. In 1965 she recorded a top selling gold record "Please Just Don't Stand There"
Major Awards: Oscar, Emmy, GG, BW, PC, WOF

Dunaway, Faye

1967-(BA) *Bonnie and Clyde*
   Winner: Katharine Hepburn, *Guess Who's Coming to Dinner*
1974-(BA) *Chinatown*
   Winner: Ellen Burstyn, *Alice Doesn't Live Here Anymore*
★ 1976-(BA) *Network*
▦ Born 1/14/41 in Bascom, FL
⫻ Bonnie Parker in title role (#32 on AFI's Villain List); Joan Crawford in *Mommie Dearest* (#41 on AFI's Villain List)
⚲ Daughter of career Army officer. Lived in dozens of towns in America and Europe. Graduated from the University of Florida and finished up at Boston University's School of Fine and Applied Arts. She turned down a Fullbright Scholarship to RADA. Once married to J. Geils Band lead singer Peter Wolf. She was more-or-less discovered by Warren Beatty, who cast her as his co-star in *Bonnie and Clyde*. Her portrayal of Joan Crawford changed the way we look at coat hangers.
Major Awards: Oscar, BAFTA, DDA, Emmy, KCFCC, WOF, GG

Duncan, Michael Clarke

1999-(BSA) *The Green Mile*
   Winner: Michael Caine, *The Cider House Rules*
▦ Born 12/10/57 in Chicago, IL.
⫻ John Coffey, the gifted healer in nominated role.

⚲ Played basketball at Kankakee Community College. Attended Alcorn State College but dropped out to help his ailing mother. Dug ditches for several years for the Chicago Gas Company. Once tried out for the Chicago Bears. Once was a bodyguard for Hollywood celebrities, Will Smith and Jamie Foxx. He gives five dollars to anyone who recognizes him on the street.
Major Awards: Saturn

Dunn, James

★ 1945-(BSA) *A Tree Grows in Brooklyn*
▦ Born 11/2/05 in New York, NY. Died 9/3/67 following stomach surgery.
⫻ Johnny Nolan in Oscar'd role.
⚲ His father was a stockbroker and wanted his son to get into the business. Gravitated to the stage instead and was a popular song and dance man in the '30s. Once was a used car salesman. After several setbacks, he gradually drifted into severe alcoholism. He died unemployed, destitute, and bankrupt. Featured on a U.S. postage stamp in the '70s.
Major Awards: Oscar, WOF

Dunn, Michael

1965-(BSA) *Ship of Fools*
   Winner: Martin Balsam, *A Thousand Clowns*
▦ Born *Gary Neil Miller* on 10/20/34 in Shattuck, OK. Died 8/29/73 of chrondrodystrophy, which is a defect in the formation of the long bone cartilages. This caused his stunted growth.
⫻ Dr. Miguelito Lovelass on television western series *The Wild, Wild West*
⚲ He was a concert pianist at the age of 15 but could not continue to play because of his disease. He graduated from the University of Florida. He was captain of the cheerleading team and editor of the college newspaper. Reportedly had an IQ of 178. At 3'6" he was the shortest person to be nominated for an Oscar. Famed artist Toulouse-Lautrec suffered the same disease.

Dunne, Irene

1930/31-(BA) *Cimmaron*
   Winner: Marie Dressler, *Min and Bill*
1936-(BA) *Theodora Goes Wild*
   Winner: Louise Rainer, *The Great Ziegfield*
1937-(BA) *The Awful Truth*
   Winner: Louise Rainer, *The Good Earth*
1939-(BA) *Love Affair*
   Winner: Vivian Leigh, *Gone with the Wind*
1948-(BA) *I Remember Moma*
   Winner: Jane Wyman, *Johnny Belinda*
▦ Born *Irene Marie Dunn* on 12/20/1898 in
   Louisville, KY. Died 9/4/90 of heart failure.
〰 Swedish mother Martha "Mama" Hanson in
   I Remember Mama
🔍 Graduated from the Chicago School of Music.
She was a music and art instructor at East Chicago
High School in Indiana. She was appointed by
President Eisenhower as a delegate to the United
Nations in 1957 and 1958. Unknowingly buying a
ticket to an event at Radio City Music Hall in 1934,
she found out it was the five millionth ticket sold.
One of the greats who truly should have received
an Honorary Oscar.
Major Awards: WOF

Dunnock, Mildred

1951-(BSA) *Death of a Salesman*
   Winner: Kim Hunter, *A Streetcar Named Desire*
1956-(BSA) *Baby Doll*
   Winner: Dorothy Malone, *Written on the Wind*
▦ Born 1/25/1906 in Baltimore, MD.
   Died 7/25/91 of natural causes.
〰 Linda Loman in *Death of a Salesman*
🔍 Graduated from John Hopkins University. Before
catching the acting bug, she was a teacher at Brearly
High School. She studied acting at Lee Strasberg's
Actors Studio. Married to her husband Keith Urmy
for 58 years.
Major Awards: WOF

Durbin, Deanna

★ 1938-Honorary Oscar
▦ Born *Edna Mae Durbin* on 12/4/21 in Winnepeg, Canada.
〰 Teen roles with Mickey Rooney and Judy
   Garland
🔍 Her hit movies in the '30s brought Universal
Studios out from the edge of bankruptcy. As the
highest paid actress in Hollywood and battling
weight problems, she suddenly dropped out of sight
and hasn't given an interview since 1949. Years later
she was tracked down living in France—married and
fabulously wealthy. She was Winston Churchill's
favorite actress.
Major Awards: WOF

Durning, Charles

1982-(BSA) *The Best Little Whorehouse in Texas*
   Winner: Louis Gossett Jr., *An Officer and a
   Gentleman*
1983-(BSA) *To Be or Not To Be*
   Winner: Jack Nicholson, *Terms of Endearment*
▦ Born 2/28/23 in Highland Falls, NY
〰 Lt. Snyder in *The Sting*
🔍 He survived Omaha Beach during the D-Day
Normandy invasion and was awarded the Silver and
Bronze Star, Combat Infantry Man's Badge, and three
Purple Hearts. He also was one of the few survivors of
the German machine-gunning of POWs in Malmedy,
Belgium, depicted in the movie *Battle of the Bulge*.
Started out in burlesque and graduated to Broadway.
Despite his beefy stature he was a ballroom dancer
for ten years. Starred on television series *Evening
Shade*. Nominated eight times for an Emmy—but
no victories to date.
Major Awards: GG, Obie, NBR, Tony

Duvall, Robert

1972-(BSA) *The Godfather*
   Winner: Joel Grey, *Cabaret*
1979-(BSA) *Apocalypse Now*
   Winner: Melvyn Douglas, *Being There*

1980-(BA) *The Great Santini*
   Winner: Robert DeNiro, *Raging Bull*
★ 1983-(BA) *Tender Mercies*
1997-(BA) *The Apostle*
   Winner: Jack Nicholson, *As Good As It Gets*
1998-(BSA) *A Civil Action*
   Winner: James Coburn-*Affliction*
▨ Born 1/5/31 in San Diego, CA
✍ Tom Hagen in *The Godfather*, Lt-Col Kilgore in *Apocalypse Now*, Boo Radley in *To Kill a Mockingbird*
✧ Son of a Navy Rear Admiral. He fought in the Korean War and won the National Defense Medal. Practices the tango every day. Wrote and performed his own songs in *Tender Mercies*. He is a direct descendant of Robert E. Lee and a distant relative to George Washington. He speaks Spanish fluently and Buenos Aires, Argentina, is his favorite city. The *Guinness Book of World Records* deemed him as the most versatile actor in the world. He is a lifelong Republican and was invited to George Bush's Presidential Inaugural Ball in 2001.
Major Awards: Oscar, Obie, GG, NYFC, LAFC, SAG, BAFTA, ISA, KCFCC, NBR, NSFC, VFF, BW, WOF

Eagels, Jeanne

1928/29-(BA) *The Letter*
   Winner: Mary Pickford, *Coquette*
▨ Born *Amelia Jean Eagles* 6/26/1894 in Kansas, MO. Died 10/3/29 of a heroin overdose.
✍ Leslie Crosbie in nominated role.
✧ Appeared on stage at age seven. Broke into the film industry early and enjoyed a meteoric rise to stardom. She was a full-blown alcoholic, at least in part due to sinusitis so bad that she developed ulcers on her eyes, which required surgery. She and Arthur Fiedler had an affair in the '20s, and until his death he proclaimed she was the great love of his life. First actress to be nominated for an award posthumously.

Eastwood, Clint

1992-(BA) *Unforgiven*
   Winner: Al Pacino, *Scent of a Woman*
★ 1992-(Best Picture/Producer) *Unforgiven*
★ 1992-(Best Director) *Unforgiven*
★ 2004-(Best Picture/Producer) *Million Dollar Baby*

Gene Hackman and Clint Eastwood in *Unforgiven*.

★ 2004-(Best Director) *Million Dollar Baby*
2004-(BA) *Million Dollar Baby*
  Winner: Jamie Foxx, *Ray*
▨ Born 5/31/30 in San Francisco, CA.
⬿ Man with No Name in Sergio Leone's Spaghetti westerns, Dirty Harry (#17 on AFI's Hero List); Merciless Will Munny in nominated role.
⚲ In route to the Korean War, his plane crashed, and he swam to shore. After that was made swimming instructor at Fort Ord. Ran for mayor of Carmel, CA—and won. He is a self-taught piano player and has written songs and scored movies. He also is an avid collector of western art. Part owner of famed Pebble Beach golf course. His favorite actor was James Cagney. Believe it or not, he is allergic to horses. At age 74 he is the oldest person to win a Best Director Oscar and shows no signs of slowing down.
Major Awards: Oscar, GG, NSFC, LAFC, GGWFF, AFI's and SAG Life Achievement, NBR, César, C.B. DeMille, Cannes, NYFC, BW, DG, Irving Thalberg, DDA, DGA, KCFCC, PC, VFF, BW, WOF

Eggar, Samantha

1965-(BA) *The Collector*
  Winner: Julie Christie, *Darling*
▨ Born *Victoria Eggar* on 3/5/39 in Hampton London England.
⬿ Miranda Grey in nominated role.
⚲ Her father was a Brigadier General in the British Army. She was trained and educated in Holy Cross Catholic Convent and Webber-Douglas Academy of Dramatic Arts. Starred in the short-lived TV series *Anna and the King*. Once married to actor Stuart Whitman. Starred in the short-lived TV series *Commander in Chief*.
Major Awards: Cannes, GG

Elliott, Denholm

1986-(BSA) *A Room with a View*
  Winner: Michael Caine, *Hannah and Her Sisters*

▨ Born 5/31/22 in London, England.
  Died 10/6/92 of complications of AIDS.
⬿ Indiana Jones's addled sidekick Dr. Marcus Brody in *Raiders of the Lost Ark*
⚲ He was in the RAF and his plane was shot down over Germany in 1942. He spent the next three years in a WW II POW camp. He was appointed by the Queen as a CBE in 1988. He was self-conscious of the fact he lost his thumb in a childhood accident. Nominated nine times for a BAFTA, won four times.
Major Awards: BAFTA, KCFCC

Emerson, Hope

1950-(BSA) *Caged*
  Winner: Josephine Hull, *Harvey*
▨ Born 10/27/1897 in Hawarden, IA.
  Died 4/25/60 of a liver ailment.
⬿ Evelyn Harper, the sadistic prison matron in nominated role
⚲ She was the tallest female thespian at 6'3" and 230 pounds to be nominated. She was the voice of Elsie the Cow on the Borden TV commercials. She was never married and never had any children. She was the bar owner mother in TV detective series *Peter Gunn*. She left *Peter Gunn* to take the role of a housekeeper named *Sarge* on the Dennis O'Keefe Show.

Erwin, Stuart

1936-(BSA) *Pigskin Parade*
  Winner: Walter Brennan, *Come and Get It*
▨ Born 2/14/02 in Squaw Valley, CA.
  Died 12/21/67 of a heart attack.
⬿ Starred in '50s TV series *Stu Erwin Show*
⚲ Graduated from the University of California at Berkeley. Mr. Erwin was popular in the '30s and was billed over Bing Crosby. Starred in his own TV series, the popular *Stu Erwin Show*, in the '50s. Due to prudent investments and steering clear of the stock market in the '20s, he died a very wealthy man.
Major Awards: WOF

Evans, Dame Edith

1963-(BSA) *Tom Jones*
   Winner: Margaret Rutherford, V.I.P.s
1964-(BSA) *The Chalk Garden*
   Winner: Lila Kedrova, *Zorba the Greek*
1967-(BA) *The Whisperers*
   Winner: Katharine Hepburn, *Guess Who's Coming to Dinner*
▨ Born 2/8/1888 in London, England. Died 10/14/76 of natural causes.
✇ Miss Western in *Tom Jones*
☌ In 1946 the Queen of England made Mrs. Evans Dame CBE. Wrote an autobiography. Oldest nominated person at the time, age 79, in last role. She was an ardent Christian Scientist. She made her first film at age 61. She is generally acknowledged as the greatest English stage actress of the twentieth century.
Major Awards: NBR, NYFC

Fairbanks Sr., Douglas

1939-Honorary Oscar
▨ Born *Douglas Elton Ulman* on 5/23/1883 in Denver, CO. Died 12/12/39 of a heart attack.
✇ He was the original swashbuckler, Thief of Bagdad in title role.
☌ His parents were divorced when he was five. He went to Harvard. He soon tired of school and traveled to Europe. He once was a clerk on Wall Street. Worked in a hardware store and was a cattle freighter. Fell in love and married Mary Pickford. Along with Charley Chaplin they formed United Artist in 1919. Performed almost all of his own stunts. He was featured on a commemorative 20-cent stamp in 1984.
Major Awards: Photoplay, WOF

Falk, Peter

1960-(BSA) *Murder Inc.*
   Winner: Peter Ustinov, *Spartacus*
1961-(BSA) *Pocketful of Miracles*
   Winner: George Chakiris, *West Side Story*
▨ Born 9/16/27 in New York, NY
✇ Detective Columbo in long-running TV series.
☌ Lost his eye to a childhood cancerous tumor at age three. Lettered in three sports in high school and was class president. He was in the Merchant Marines serving as a cook. Graduated with a MPA (Master of Public Administration) from Syracuse University and worked for the state of Connecticut as an efficiency expert. He is a Certified Public Accountant. Nominated for 12 Emmys and has won five. Wrote a book, released in 2006, *Just One More Thing*.
Major Awards: Emmy, Tony, GG

Farnsworth, Richard

1978-(BSA) *Comes A Horseman*
   Winner: Christopher Walken, *The Deer Hunter*
1999-(BA) *The Straight Story*
   Winner: Kevin Spacey, *American Beauty*
▨ Born 9/1/20 in Los Angeles, CA. Died 10/6/2000 of a self-inflicted gunshot after learning he had terminal cancer.
✇ Train robber Bill Miner in *The Grey Fox*
☌ He was a stunt man for 40 years before becoming an actor. Inducted into the Hall of Fame of Great Western Actors' Cowboy Museum. Doubled for Roy Rogers, Gary Cooper, and Steve McQueen. He is the oldest actor ever nominated in the Leading Actor category for an Oscar. Asked by Roger Ebert what he was most proud of in his movie career—it was that he never cussed. He abhorred bad language.
Major Awards: NBR, NYFC, NSFC, Gemini, ISA, WOF

Ferrer, Jose

1948-(BSA) *Joan of Arc*
   Winner: Walter Huston, *The Treasure of the Sierra Madre*
★ 1950-(BA) *Cyrano De Bergerac*
1952-(BA) *Moulin Rouge*
   Winner: Gary Cooper, *High Noon*
▨ Born *Jose Vincente Ferrer De Oteroy Cintron* on 1/8/1909 in Santurce, Puerto Rico. Died 1/26/92 of colon cancer.

José Ferrer in *Cyrano de Bergerac.*

✍ Title role *Cyrano de Bergerac*

🔍 Studied architecture at Princeton, but he dropped out to pursue an acting career. Received five Honorary degrees from various universities. He was George Clooney's uncle. First actor to receive the National Medal of the Arts. He was fluent in Spanish, English, and French. Only one of eight actors to win an Oscar and Tony for the same role, Cyrano de Bergerac.

Major Awards: Oscar, Tony, GG, WOF

Field, Sally

★ 1979-(BA) *Norma Rae*

★ 1984-(BA) *Places in the Heart*

■ Born 11/6/46 in Pasadena, CA

✍ Norma Rae (#15 on AFI's Hero List), *The Flying Nun* in TV series, *Sybil* in the made-for-TV movie.

🔍 Her stepfather was Jock Mahoney, who was a stuntman who once played Tarzan. She was a high school cheerleader. Dated Burt Reynolds for many years, turning down many proposals before they eventually broke up. Her favorite movie is *Smokey and the Bandit.* Her Oscar acceptance speech, "You like me, right now, you like me" is now legendary.

Major Awards: Oscar, Emmy, NBR, NSFC, NYFC, LAFC, GG, Cannes, KCFCC, PC, WFCA

Fiennes, Ralph

1993-(BSA) *Schindler's List*
   Winner: Tommy Lee Jones, *The Fugitive*
1996-(BA) *The English Patient*
   Winner: Geoffrey Rush, *Shine*

■ Born 12/22/62 in Suffolk, England.

✍ Evil concentration camp commander Amon Goeth (#15 on AFI's Villain List.)

🔍 Graduated from Chelsea College of Arts and Design and RADA. His cousin was a British explorer, his uncle a former priest and theology professor at Cambridge, and his great uncle a Benedictine monk. Gained 30 pounds for the role of the demonic Goeth in *Schindler's List.* Steven Spielberg saw him on TV playing Lawrence of Arabia and tapped him for the role.

Major Awards: Tony, NYFC, DD, NYFC, NSFC, BAFTA, BSFC

Finch, Peter

1971-(BA) *Sunday, Bloody Sunday*
   Winner: Gene Hackman, *The French Connection*

★ 1976-(BA) *Network*

■ Born *William Mitchell* on 9/28/16 in London, England. Died 1/14/77 of a massive heart attack.

✍ Howard Beale in Oscar'd role. Remember: "I'm mad as hell and I'm not going to take it anymore."

🔍 Only actor to receive an Oscar posthumously. He was a legendary hard drinker and womanizer. Suffered from stage fright and had a fear of flying. Despite being befriended by Laurence Olivier he had

an affair with Olivier's wife Vivien Leigh. Nominated seven times for the BAFTA and won five.
Major Awards: Oscar, NBR, NSFC, GG, BAFTA, BIFF

Finlay, Frank

1965-(BSA) *Othello*
  Winner: Martin Balsam, *A Thousand Clowns*
▨ Born 8/6/26 in Farnsworth Lancaster, England
✍ The scheming Iago in nominated role.
♀ Graduated from RADA. He made his stage debut at age 31. Played Inspector Lestrade in two Sherlock Holmes movies, *Murder by Decree* and *A Study in Terror*. He was awarded CBE by Queen Elizabeth in 1984. He formed his own theater company in 1970.
Major Awards: BAFTA

Finney, Albert

1963-(BA) *Tom Jones*
  Winner: Sidney Poitier, *Lilies of the Field*
1974-(BA) *Murder on the Orient Express*
  Winner: Art Carney, *Harry and Tonto*
1983-(BA) *The Dresser*
  Winner: Robert Duvall, *Tender Mercies*
1984-(BA) *Under The Volcano*
  Winner: F. Murray Abraham, *Amadeus*
2000-(BSA) *Erin Brockovich*
  Winner: Benicio Del Toro, *Traffic*
▨ Born 5/9/36 in Salford Manchester, England.
✍ Title role *Tom Jones*, Ed Masry, the law firm owner in *Erin Brockovich*
♀ Graduated from RADA. Declined the award of the Order of the British Empire in 1980. In 1977 recorded an album and wrote all the songs himself. Laurence Olivier hand picked him to head the British National Theater but again he declined. Nominated 12 times for a BAFTA, won twice. A truly gifted actor who has been overlooked time and again by the Academy, especially in 2000. He definitely marches to his own drum.
Major Awards: NBR, NYFC, Emmy, GG, LAFC, SAG, BAFTA, BIFF, VFF

Firth, Peter

1977-(BSA) *Equus*
  Winner: Jason Robards, *Julia*
▨ Born 10/27/53 in Bradford Yorkshire, England.
✍ Alan Strang in nominated role.
♀ Dropped out of school at the age of 16 to get into acting. Listed in *Screen World* as one of twelve promising actors in 1977. Initially got into acting because of his interest in girls. Early on he was a major star on an England children's TV series *The Double Deckers*.
Major Awards: BAFTA, GG, KCFCC

Fishburne, Lawrence

1993-(BA) *What's Love Got to Do with It*
  Winner: Tom Hanks, *Philadelphia*
▨ Born 7/30/61 in Augusta, GA
✍ Morpheus in *The Matrix*
♀ Studied acting at Lincoln Square Academy. He was a regular on TV soap *One Life to Live* for four years. Wrote directed and stared in his own play, *Riff Raff*. At age 14, his mother had a role in *Apocalypse Now*, and he ended up working on the epic for 18 months. Founded the Guggenheim Motorcycle Club—they arrange rides to art museums all over the world.
Major Awards: Tony, Emmy, BSFC

Fitzgerald, Barry

★ 1944-(BSA) *Going My Way*
1944-(BA) *Going My Way*
  Winner: Bing Crosby, *Going My Way*
▨ Born *William Joseph Shields* on 3/10/1888 in Dublin, Ireland. Died 1/14/61 of a heart attack.
✍ Father Fitzgibbon in Oscar'd role. Michelene in *The Quiet Man*
♀ Worked for the civil service until age 41 and then went into acting. Just months before the Oscar ceremony he beat, with the help of L.B. Mayer, a vehicular homicide charge after he hit and fatally

killed an elderly woman crossing the street. Only actor to be nominated for a Best Actor and Best Supporting Actor for the same role.

Major Awards: Oscar, NYFC, GG, WOF

Fitzgerald, Geraldine

1939-(BSA) *Wuthering Heights*
  Winner: Hattie McDaniel, *Gone with the Wind*
- Born 11/24/14 in Dublin, Ireland. Died 4/17/2005 of complications of Alzheimer's disease.
- Isabella Linton in nominated role.
- Her father was an attorney whose law firm represented author James Joyce and poet W.B. Yeats. Good friends with Bette Davis. Vivien Leigh was her one-time roommate. When she confronted studio execs about the roles she was getting she was blackballed and her career stalled for years.

Major Awards: Obie, WOF

Fletcher, Louise

★ 1975-(BA) *One Flew Over the Cukoo's Nest*
- Born 7//34 in Birmingham, AL
- Nurse Ratched (#5 on AFI's Villain List)
- Her father was an Episcopal minister. Like Lon Chaney Sr., both of her parents were deaf, and she had to learn sign language at a very early age. She worked as a doctor's receptionist during the day and studied acting at night. Had a little hiccup in 2000 when she rammed her car into a police squad car.

Major Awards: Oscar, GG, Saturn, BAFTA

Foch, Nina

1954-(BSA) *Executive Suite*
  Winner: Eva Marie Saint, *On the Waterfront*
- Born *Nina Consuelo Maud Fock* on 4/20/24 in Leiden, Holland, Netherlands.
- Erica Martin in nominated role.
- Her mother was a famous pin-up girl in WW I in Europe. Her father was a musician, conductor,

and composer for the Dutch Symphony Orchestra. Early in her career she was a concert pianist and a painter of note before enrolling in the American Academy of the Arts. She taught acting at USC and had her own drama school.

Major Awards: NBR, WOF

Fonda, Jane

1969-(BSA) *They Shoot Horses, Don't They?*
  Winner: Maggie Smith, *The Prime of Miss Jean Brodie*
★ 1971-(BA) *Klute*
1977-(BA) *Julia*
  Winner: Diane Keaton, *Annie Hall*
★ 1978-(BA) *Coming Home*
1979-(BA) *The China Syndrome*
  Winner: Sally Field, *Norma Rae*
1981-(BSA) *On Golden Pond*
  Winner: Maureen Stapleton, *Reds*
1986-(BA) *The Morning After*
  Winner: Marlee Matlin, *Children of a Lesser God*
- Born 12/21/37 in New York, NY
- Nicknamed Hanoi Jane for her anti-war views during the Vietnam conflict.
- She once was a model, and was on the cover of *Vogue*. She is a descendant of Samuel Adams, leader of the American Revolution. She has been married to a French film director, a peace activist, and a media mogul—Roger Vadim, Tom Hayden, and Ted Turner respectively. She was arrested for drug smuggling in 1970 but charges were dropped—it was actually vitamins she had in her possession. She speaks French fluently. Recently, once again, she has picked up the anti-war banner. She had a stormy relationship with her father Henry, however they mended the fences in his later years.

Major Awards: Oscar, Emmy, GG, NYFC, NSFC, LAFC, GGWWF, BAFTA, DDA, KCFCC, NBR, PC, WFCA

Fonda, Henry

1940-(BA) *The Grapes of Wrath*
  Winner: James Stewart, *The Philadelphia Story*

Shirley Mills, Jane Darwell, and Henry Fonda in *The Grapes of Wrath*.

Peter Fonda in *Easy Rider*.

1957-(BP) *12 Angry Men*
1980-Honorary Oscar
★ 1981-(BA) *On Golden Pond*
▓ Born 5/16/05 in Grand Island, NE.
Died 8/12/82 of cardiac arrest.
⬚ Tom Joad, *Grapes of Wrath* (#12 on AFI's Hero List), Juror No. 8, *12 Angry Men* (#28 on AFI's Hero List)
⸙ Served in WW II as a Lieutenant and was awarded a Bronze Star and Presidential Citation. His wife, mother of Jane and Peter, suffered a mental breakdown and committed suicide. A first-class painter, he saw his works displayed in art galleries and exhibitions worldwide. Also enjoyed needlepoint and gardening, bee keeping, model airplanes, and kites. On two occasions roomed with lifelong friend James Stewart. He and Jane and John and Haley Mills are the only two father/daughter Oscar winners. He was the oldest performer to win the Best Actor Oscar at age 76 years, 9 months. Won the Triple Crown of acting.
Major Awards: Oscar, Tony, DD, Grammy, NBR, CB DeMille, AFI's Life Achievement Award, BAFTA, DDA, GG, WOF

Fonda, Peter

1969-(BW) *Easy Rider*

1997-(BA) *Ulee's Gold*
Winner: Jack Nicholson, *As Good As It Gets*
▓ Born 2/23/40 in New York, NY
⬚ Captain America in *Easy Rider*
⸙ Graduated from the University of Omaha. When he heard of his mother's death, he shot himself damaging his liver and kidneys. A rebel in his youth, he was considered the guru of the drug movement in the '60s. Beatles wrote the song "She Said, She Said" with him in mind. Broke his back two times while riding his motorcycle. He was puffing on a blunt the whole time while filming *Easy Rider*, which made him a millionaire and no doubt skewed the government's statistics on the debilitating effects of marijuana.
Major Awards: NYFC, GG, ISA, WOF

Fontaine, Joan

1940-(BA) *Rebecca*
Winner: Ginger Rogers, *Kitty Foyle*
★ 1941-(BA) *Suspicion*
1943-(BA) *The Constant Nymph*
Winner: Jennifer Jones, *The Song of Bernadette*
▓ Born *Joan Beauvoir de Havilland* on 10/22/17 in Tokyo, Japan.
⬚ Lina McLaidlaw in Oscar'd role

Sister to Olivia de Havilland. She and Olivia have IQs approaching genius. They had a well-publicized falling out. She is the epitome of a Renaissance woman. She is a licensed pilot, champion balloonist, prize-winning fisherman, licensed interior decorator, cordon bleu cook, and expert golfer. Even scored a hole-in-one. Howard Hughes once proposed to her. She and her sister Olivia de Havilland are still estranged after all of these years. Sisters please listen, life is too short.

Major Awards: NBR, NFC, WOF

Fontanne, Lynn

1931/32-(BA) *The Guardsman*
   Winner: Helen Hayes, *The Sin of Madelon Claudet*
- Born 12/6/1892 in Woodford, England. Died 1993.
- Many stage roles
- She was married to actor Alfred Lunt. They were considered the first couple in Hollywood. They made almost all of their stage appearances together, never alone, however not their films. She and her husband were featured on the U.S. 33-cent stamp in 1999. She and her husband were the first husband and wife to be nominated in the same movie.

Major Awards: Emmy, Tony

Ford, Harrison

1985-(BA) *Witness*
   Winner: William Hurt, *Kiss of the Spider Woman*
- Born 7/13/42 in Chicago, IL
- Han Solo (#14 on AFI's Hero List), Indiana Jones (#2 on AFI's Hero List).
- Worked as a carpenter in his struggling years, working for many Hollywood stars. Owns a helicopter and three planes. Has used them to rescue a stranded mountain climber and a lost boy scout. His films have grossed over U.S. $5.65 billion worldwide. No other actor is even close. His Indiana Jones whip and fedora are on display at the Smithsonian

Institute. Holds the distinction of going through the most expensive divorce in Hollywood history with his wife of 21 years, Melissa Mathison.
Major Awards: GG, AFI's Lifetime Achievement, PC, KCFCC, Saturn, CB DeMille, WOF

Forrest, Fredrick

1979-(BSA) *The Rose*
   Winner: Melvyn Douglas, *Being There*
- Born 12/23/38 in Waxahachie, TX
- Blue Duck in *Lonesome Dove*
- In his early years suffered from stage fright so bad that he would bolt for the exit when he auditioned. Graduated from Texas Christian University. He was the first actor signed by Francis Ford Coppola for his newly formed Zoetrope Studios. Studied under famed acting teachers Lee Strasberg and Sanford Meisner.

Major Awards: NSFC

Forster, Robert

1997-(BSA) *Jackie Brown*
   Winner: Robin Williams, *Good Will Hunting*
- Born *Robert Foster* 7/13/41 in Rochester, NY.
- Max Cherry in nominated role
- Graduated from Rochester University majoring in psychology. Has been a door-to-door vacuum cleaner salesman, construction worker, and substitute teacher. He appeared nude in *Reflections in a Golden Eye* and *Medium Cool*. He added the R to his name to make it more noticeable. Starred in TV detective series *Banyon*. In between movies he was a motivational speaker and acting coach.

Major Awards: KCFCC

Foster, Jodie

1976-(BSA) *Taxi Driver*
   Winner: Beatrice Straight, *Network*
★ 1988-(BA) *The Accused*
★ 1991-(BA) *The Silence of the Lambs*

1994-(BA) *Nell*
Winner: Jessica Lange, *Blue Sky*
▥ Born *Alicia Christian Foster* on 11/19/62 in Los Angeles, CA
✍ Clarice Starling in *The Silence of the Lambs.*
♜ As a child, she was the bare-bottomed Coppertone girl. She was Valedictorian in high school and gave her graduation speech in French. She went on to Yale University where she graduated Cum Laude. Her hobbies are yoga, kickboxing, karate, aerobics, and collecting kitchenware. She is fluent in French and Italian.
Major Awards: Oscar, GG, NYFC, BAFTA, NBR, DDA, ISA, LAFC, KCFCC, NSFC, PC, SAG, WFCA

Foxx, Jamie

2004-(BSA) *Collateral*
Winner: Morgan Freeman, *MIllion Dollar Baby*
★ 2004-(BA) *Ray*
▥ Born *Eric Bishop* on 12/13/67 in Terrell, TX.
✍ Ray Charles in nominated role
♜ He was adopted by his grandparents and sang in the choir as a child. Took piano lessons at age three and studied classical music at Julliard. In high school worked as a shoe salesman and was quarterback on the football team. Started out as a standup comedian. Gave himself the last name Foxx after his favorite comedian Redd Foxx. Only one of five performers to have a No. 1 Billboard hit and to have won an Oscar—the others being Cher, Frank Sinatra, Bing Crosby, and Barbra Streisand.
Major Awards: GG, NBR, NSFC, SAG, BAFTA, BSFC

Franciosa, Anthony

1957-(BA) *A Hatful of Rain*
Winner: Alex Guinness, *The Bridge on the River Kwai*
▥ Born *Anthony Papaleo* 10/28/28 in New York, NY. Died 1/19/2006 of a stroke.
✍ Polo in nominated role.
♜ His father was a construction worker and his mother a seamstress. They divorced when he was one year old and he rarely saw his father the rest of his life. Starred in the TV series *Name of the Game* and was fired. Actors Robert Culp, Peter Falk, Robert Wagner, and Darren McGavin replaced him. Once married to Shelley Winters. He was an ardent civil rights activist. He was difficult to work with and once spent 10 days in jail for slugging a photographer.
Major Awards: GG, VFF

Jamie Foxx in *Ray.*

Freeman, Morgan

1987-(BSA) *Street Smart*
Winner: Sean Connery, *The Untouchables*
1989-(BA) *Driving Miss Daisy*
Winner: Daniel Day Lewis, *My Left Foot*
1994-(BA) *The Shawshank Redemption*
Winner: Tom Hanks, *Forrest Gump*
★ 2004-(BSA) *Million Dollar Baby*
▥ Born 6/1/37 in Memphis, TN
✍ Red in *The Shawshank Redemption*
♜ Studied ballet, tap dancing, and jazz. He was a mechanic in the U.S. Air Force but really wanted to be a fighter pilot. His first job in Hollywood was as a clerk typist. He has a pilot's license and can fly

Morgan Freeman in *Million Dollar Baby*.

Fricker, Brenda

★ 1989-(BSA) *My Left Foot*
▪ Born 2/17/45 in Dublin, Ireland.
〰 Mrs. Brown in Oscar'd role.
🔍 In her teen years she was in a car accident and was bedridden for months. Later she contracted tuberculosis and had to have a kidney removed. Starred in the popular BBC hospital drama *Casualty*. Started her career with the Royal Shakespeare Company. One of her memorable quotes: "When you're lying drunk at the airport you're Irish. When you win an Oscar, you're British."
Major Awards: Oscar, LAFC

Gable, Clark

★ 1934-(BA) *It Happened One Night*
1935-(BA) *Mutiny on the Bounty*
    Winner: Victor McLaglen, *The Informer*
1939-(BA) *Gone with the Wind*
    Winner: Robert Donat, *Goodbye, Mr. Chips*
▪ Born 2/1/02 in Cadiz, OH. Died 11/16/60 of a massive heart attack.
〰 Rhett Butler in *Gone with the Wind*.
    The King of Hollywood.
🔍 His mother died when he was seven. Grief-stricken after the death of his wife, Carole Lombard, he enlisted in WW II at the age of 42. He was an aerial

jets. Keeps a boat docked in the Caribbean. He was the Easy Reader for five years on PBS's children's series *The Electric Company*. Started his own production company Revelation Entertainment. Hates watching his own movies. Recently has taken up golf and is a self-professed addict.
Major Awards: Obie, NYFC, NSFC, LAFC, NBR, GG, BIFF, KCFCC, SAG, BW, WOF

Frey, Leonard

1971-(BSA) *Fiddler on the Roof*
    Winner: Ben Johnson, *The Last Picture Show*
▪ Born 9/4/38 in Brooklyn, NY. Died 8/24/88 of AIDS.
〰 Motel the Tailor in nominated role
🔍 Originally studied to be an artist. Got into acting while in college and ended up studying under Sanford Meisner. Following his screen success he continued to work on the stage and in TV throughout the '70s and '80s. Nominated for a Tony in 1975.

Clark Gable and Claudette Colbert in *It Happened One Night*.

gunner and pilot and flew five bombing missions. He came out a captain and won the Distinguished Flying Cross and Air Medal. An avid skeet shooter. Adolph Hitler offered a bounty of $5000 for Gable, dead or alive. He was dyslexic. He had cosmetic surgery on his ears and because of pyorrhea had almost all of his teeth extracted. He had a gun collection valued at the time of his death at one-half million dollars. He had a child out of wedlock with actress Loretta Young.

Major Awards: Oscar, WOF

Garbo, Greta

1929/30-(BA) *Anna Christie, Romance*
  Winner: Norma Shearer, *The Divorcée, Their Own Desire*
1937-(BA) *Camille*
  Winner: Louise Rainer, *The Good Earth*
1939-(BA) *Ninotchka*
  Winner: Vivian Leigh, *Gone with the Wind*
1954-Honorary Oscar
▧ Born *Greta Louisa Gustafsson* on 9/18/05 in Stockholm, Sweden. Died 4/15/90 of pneumonia.
▨ Anna Christie in title role.
♀ She was Adolf Hitler's favorite actress. Planned to be married to actor John Gilbert, but on the wedding day, she never showed up and left him standing at the

altar. She was highly disciplined and a perfectionist to the extreme. The *Guiness Book of World Records* voted her the most beautiful woman who ever lived. She suffered from chronic depression and only ate health foods, however she never gave up smoking, and she liked her toddies. It was rumored that she was bisexual. Ingrid Bergman once received a telegram from her. "I would like to see you when I am free, if you are willing?" She never married and died a multi-millionaire, alone to the end.

Major Awards: NYFC, NBR, WOF

Garcia, Andy

1990-(BSA) *The Godfather Part III*
  Winner: Joe Pesci, *Goodfellas*
▧ Born *Andres Garcia-Menendez* on 4/12/56 in Havanna, Cuba
▨ Vincent Mancini nominated role.
♀ Family fled Cuba during the Bay of Pigs. Produced and directed a documentary of famed Cuban musician Israel Lopez. He wrote songs and scored music for several movies. He was born with a twin attached to his shoulder. The twin was no bigger than a tennis ball and was removed minutes after birth. Collects hats and conga drums.

Major Awards: WOF

Gardenia, Vincent

1973-(BSA) *Bang the Drum Slowly*
  Winner: John Houseman, *The Paper Chase*
1987-(BSA) *Moonstruck*
  Winner: Sean Connery, *The Untouchables*
▧ Born *Vincent Scognamiglio* on 1/7/22 in Naples, Italy. Died 12/9/92 of a heart attack.
▨ Cosmo Castorini in *Moonstruck*
♀ After migrating to the United States he dropped out of school at age 14. He doctored his birth certificate and joined the Army. Served as a private for two years during WW II. The city of Brooklyn renamed 16th Avenue in his old neighborhood Vincent Gardenia Avenue in honor of his memory.

Major Awards: Emmy, Obie, Tony

Greta Garbo and Melvyn Douglas in *Ninotchka*.

Ava Gardner (left) with Grace Kelly
and Clark Gable in *Mogambo*.

John Garfield and Artie Dorrell
in *Body and Soul*.

Gardner, Ava

1953-(BA) *Mogambo*
   Winner: Audrey Hepburn, *Roman Holiday*
 Born *Ava Lavinia Gardner* on 12/24/22 in
   Smithfield, NC. Died 1/25/90 of bronchial
   pneumonia.
Stormy relationship with Frank Sinatra.
She was one of six children born to a dirt-poor
tenant farmer. Her brother-in-law secretly submitted
her photograph to an MGM casting office, and, as
they say, the rest is history. Was married to Mickey
Rooney, bandleader Artie Shaw, and the Chairman of
the Board, Frank Sinatra. It was Frank who paid all
of her medical expenses when she had a stroke in 1989,
which left her bedridden and semi-paralyzed.
Major Awards: WOF

Garfield, John

1938-(BSA) *Four Daughters*
   Winner: Walter Brennan, *Kentucky*
1947-(BA) *Body and Soul*
   Winner: Ronald Coleman, *A Double Life*
Born *Julius Garfinkle* 3/4/13 in New York,
   NY. Died 5/21/52 coronary thrombosis.

Charlie Davis in *Body and Soul*
Once a juvenile delinquent and gang member.
Attended school for troubled children. Won a state
debating contest sponsored by the *New York Times*.
He was wrongfully accused as a Communist by the
McCarthy led House Un-American Activities Com-
mittee. Although innocent, he was black-listed in
Hollywood. The strain led to a fatal heart attack at
age 39. Over 10,000 people attended his funeral.
Major Awards: WOF

Gargan, William

1940-(BSA) *They Knew What They Wanted*
   Winner: Walter Brennan, *The Westener*
Born 7/17/05 in Brooklyn, NY. Died 2/17/79
   of a heart attack.
Martin Kane on TV detective series.
He was a star on Broadway one year after he
graduated from high school. Picked up a few dollars selling bootleg booze during prohibition. His
partner was future restaurateur David Chasen, who
owned the popular Brown Derby in Hollywood.
He was stricken with cancer of the larynx. Taught
himself esophageal speech, and in turn taught his
method for the American Cancer Society.
Major Awards: SAG Life Achievement

Garland, Judy

1939-Honorary Oscar
   Juvenile Performance for *The Wizard of Oz*
1954-(BA) *A Star Is Born*
   Winner: Grace Kelly, *The Country Girl*
1961-(BSA) *Judgement at Nuremburg*
   Winner: Rita Moreno, *West Side Story*
▦ Born *Frances Gumm* on 6/10/22 in Grand
   Rapids, MN. Died 6/22/69 accidental over-
   dose of barbiturates.
✏ Dorothy Gale in *The Wizard of Oz*
♀ Studio execs alarmed at her weight gain put her
on diet pills. This led to a lifelong dependency.
Shirley Temple was originally slated to star in *The
Wizard of Oz*. The day Judy died there was a tornado
over Kansas. Her daughter is Liza Minnelli. Sang
"Somewhere Over the Rainbow" to JFK on the
phone on several occasions. Overcame her stage
fright with a little jolt of Irish whiskey. She had a
photographic memory and could remember long
songs or passages after a glance. She was a distant
relative to President Ulysses S. Grant. When she
passed away 22,000 people paid their respects, filing
pass her coffin over a 24-hour period.
Major Awards: GG, CBD, Grammy, Tony,
WOF

Jack Haley, Judy Garland, and
Ray Bolger in the *Wizard of Oz*.

Garner, James

1985-(BA) *Murphy's Romance*
   Winner: William Hurt, *Kiss of the Spider Woman*
▦ Born *James Scott Baumgarner* on 4/7/28 in
   Norman, OK.
✏ TV western series *Maverick* in title role. TV private eye James Rockford in *The Rockford Files*.
♀ A high school dropout, he joined the Marines
at age 16. He was wounded in the Korean War and
received a Purple Heart. He is quite a golfer with a
four handicap. He was constantly at odds with the
studio brass. When royalty issues arose he sued
and after a bitter court battle, he won. He is part
Cherokee Indian. He married his wife 14 days after
they met. He had four heart bypasses in 1988 and
both knees replaced in 2000.
Major Awards: Emmy, GG, BW, WOF

Garner, Peggy Ann

1945-Honorary Oscar
   Juvenile Performance, *A Tree Grows in Brooklyn*
▦ Born 2/3/31 in Canton, OH. Died 10/16/84
   of pancreatic cancer.
✏ Princess in *A Tree Grows in Brooklyn*
♀ Her divorced mother got her a modeling contract
at age four. She made several more movies and
was on some TV dramas. She moved to New York
to study at the Actors Studio and stayed with Ed
Sullivan whose daughter she was close friends with.
Unable to find work in Hollywood she became a
successful sales manager for a Pontiac dealership.
Major Awards: WOF

Garr, Teri

1982-(BSA) *Tootsie*
   Winner: Jessica Lange, *Tootsie*
▦ Born 12/11/49 in Lakewood, OH.
✏ Sandy Lester in nominated role.
♀ Graduated from California State. Daughter
of actor-comedian Ed Garr. She made her screen
debut in the offbeat movie *Head*, starring the Mon-
kees. She was a dancer in nine Elvis Presley movies.

She has been battling multiple sclerosis since 1983 but has been working the whole time. She suffered a severe brain aneurysm in 2006 and is currently recovering from this setback.

Major Awards: NBR

Garson, Greer

1939-(BA) *Goodbye, Mr. Chips*
   Winner: Vivian Leigh, *Gone with the Wind*
1941-(BA) *Blossoms in the Dust*
   Winner: Joan Fontaine, *Suspicion*
★ 1942-(BA) *Mrs. Miniver*
1943-(BA) *Madame Curie*
   Winner: Jennifer Jones, *The Song of Bernadette*
1944, (BA) *Mrs. Parkington*
   Winner: Ingrid Bergman, *Gaslight*
1945-(BA) *The Valley of Decision*
   Winner: Joan Crawford, *Mildred Pierce*
1960-(BA) *Sunrise at Campobello*
   Winner: Elizabeth Taylor, *Butterfield 8*
▪ Born 9/29/08 in County Down, Ireland. Died 4/6/96 of heart failure.
⫻ Mrs. Miniver in title role.
⚲ Graduated with honors from the University of London and also studied at the University of Grenoble. Originally wanted to be a teacher. Mar-

ried co-star Richard Ney, ten years her junior. The marriage lasted four years. Gave the longest Oscar acceptance speech on record (six minutes), which prompted the Academy to limit future acceptance speeches. Her Oscar was destroyed in a fire but was replaced by the Academy. Donated millions to the Santa Fe College Drama School. Along with Bette Davis, holds the record for consecutive nominations at five.

Major Awards: NBR, GG, WOF

Gaynor, Janet

★ 1927/28-(BA) *Seventh Heaven, Street Angel, Sunrise*
1937-(BA) *A Star Is Born*
   Winner: Luise Rainer, *The Good Earth*
▪ Born *Laura Gainor* 10/6/06 in Philadelphia, PA. Died 9/14/84 of pneumonia.
⫻ Vicki Lester in *A Star is Born*
⚲ She once sold shoes for $18 a week and was an usherette in a local movie house. Retired in 1939 to her husband's Brazilian cattle ranch. She was involved in a life-threatening auto accident with Mary Martin, whose agent was killed. Later in life she started to paint and exhibited her works at many galleries in New York.

Major Awards: WOF

Greer Garson (second from left) in *Mrs. Miniver.*

Gazzo, Michael V.

1974-(BSA) *The Godfather, Part II*
   Winner: Robert DeNiro, *The Godfather, Part II*
- Born 4/5/23 in Hillside, NJ. Died 2/14/95 of a stroke.
- Frankie Pentangeli in nominated role.
- He served in the Air Force during WW II. He was a noted playwright before appearing in movies. He wrote the much-acclaimed Broadway play *A Hatful of Rain*, a harrowing groundbreaking account of a war veteran in the throes of addiction, which was made into a movie in 1957. The play ran for over two years with 389 performances.

Genn, Leo

1951-(BSA) *Quo Vadis*
   Winner: Karl Malden, *A Streetcar Named Desire*
- Born 8/9/05 in London. England. Died 1/26/78 of a heart attack.
- Petronius in nominated role.
- Studied law at Cambridge and was a practicing barrister before appearing on Broadway and breaking into the movies. He was a Lt. Colonel in the Royal Artillery during WW II and was awarded the Croix de Guerre for gallantry. He was one of the prosecuting attorneys during the Belsen war crimes trial.

George, Chief Dan

1970-(BSA) *Little Big Man*
   Winner: John Mills, *Ryan's Daughter*
- Born Tes-Wah-No on 17/24/1899 in No. Vancouver, British Columbia, Canada. Died 9/23/81 of heart failure.
- Old Lodge Skins in nominated role
- Worked as a longshoreman, construction worker, and school bus driver. He was chief of his tribe the Squamish Indians. A Canadian Indian, he did not enter the movies until he was in his '70s. He was an ardent campaigner for environmental causes. He pushed Hollywood to cast real Indians in movies instead of extras with greasepaint. First Native American nominated.
Major Awards: NYFC, NSFC

George, Gladys

1936-(BA) *Valient Is the Word for Carrie*
   Winner: Luise Rainer, *The Great Ziegfeld*
- Born *Gladys Ann Clare* 9/13/04 in Patten, ME. Died 12/8/54 of a cerebral hemorrhage.
- Wisecracking Panama in *The Roaring '20s*
- Daughter of Shakespearian actor Sir Arthur Clare. Started her acting career at the age of three. Suffered severe facial burns in a fiery explosion at her home. After a long struggle, died of throat cancer. It was suspected that she died of an overdose of barbiturates, but it was never proven.

Giamatti, Paul

2005-(BSA) *Cinderella Man*
   Winner: George Clooney, *Syriana*
- Born 6/6/67 in New Haven, CT.
- Joe Gould in nominated role.
- Graduated from Yale, majoring in drama and English. His father, the late Bart Giamatti, was a professor of Renaissance Literature at Yale, went on to become its youngest president, and later was appointed the Commissioner of Baseball. He is a big Boston Red Sox backer.
Major Awards: NBR, NYFC, SAG

Giannini, Giancarlo

1976-(BA) *Seven Beauties*
   Winner: Peter Finch, *Network*
- Born 8/1/42 in Spezia, Italy.
- Pasqualino Settebellezze in nominated role.
- He was trained in the prestigious Rome Academy of Drama. He hooked up with famed director Lina Wertmuller. He became her favorite actor and appeared in many of her films. His melancholy eyes conveyed a wide range of emotions without even

saying a word. He was nominated seven times for the Italian Oscar (DDA) and won six times.
Major Awards: Cannes, DDA

Gibson, Mel

★ 1995-(Best Director) *Braveheart*
★ 1995-(Best Picture/Producer) *Braveheart*
▪ Born 1/3/56 in Peekskill, NY.
⚜ *Mad Max* in title role.
🔍 His father moved the family from New York to Sydney, Australia, so his sons wouldn't be drafted to serve in the Vietnam War. The night before he was to audition for the part of Mad Max, he got into a barroom brawl and came out of the fight all bruised up. He won the part. He produced the controversial and surprise box office blockbuster *The Passion*, putting in 40 million of his own money. The movie is the No. 11 all-time box office hit grossing $371 million. He was awarded Australia's highest honor, officer of the Australian Order, in 1997. Got himself in deep with a drunk driving bust and anti-Semitic remarks in 2006.
Major Awards: Oscar, GG, PC, NBR, Australian F.I.

Mel Gibson in *Braveheart*.

Gielgud, Sir John

1964-(BSA) *Becket*
  Winner: Peter Ustinov, *Topkapi*
★ 1981-(BSA) *Arthur*
▪ Born 4/14/04 in London, England. Died 5/21/2000 of natural causes.
⚜ The butler Hobson in Oscar'd role.
🔍 In Broadway circles his interpretation of Hamlet onstage is considered the greatest. Due to monetary constraints he took a lot of lesser roles on the screen in order to finance his stage work and independent projects. He was knighted by the Queen of England and has won the Superfecta of acting. He was a lifetime PETA contributor. His career spanned an incredible 76 years.
Major Awards: Oscar, GG, Grammy, Emmy, Tony, NYFC, LAFC, BAFTA, NSFC

Gilford, Jack

1973-(BSA) *Save the Tiger*
  Winner: John Houseman, *The Paper Chase*
▪ Born *Yankel Gellman* on 7/25/07 in New York, NY. Died 6/2/90 of stomach cancer.
⚜ Phil Greene in nominated role. Cracker Jack commercial.
🔍 Started his career in vaudeville as a comedian. Entertained for years at the Greenwich Village nightclub Café Society. Made his film debut in 1944 with dancer Ann Miller in an entertainment vehicle for the servicemen in WW II called *Hey, Rookie*. He and his wife were blacklisted by the government during the '50s communist witch-hunt, although they were entirely innocent.

Gish, Lillian

1946-(BSA) *Duel in the Sun*
  Winner: Anne Baxter, *The Razor's Edge*
1970-Honorary Oscar
▪ Born 10/14/1896 in Springfield, OH. Died 2/27/93 of heart failure.
⚜ The First Lady of the Silent Screen

Her father was an alcoholic and abandoned the family when she was six, the same age she started acting. Her childhood friend Gladys Smith was soon to become Mary Pickford and she introduced Pickford to famed director D.W. Griffith. In her first film, directed by Griffith, *An Unseen Enemy*, she appeared with her sister and mother. MGM dropped her in 1928 in favor of Greta Garbo. She never married. She wrote several autobiographies.

Major Awards: NBR, AFI's Life Achievement, WFCA, WOF

Gleason, Jackie

1961-(BSA) *The Hustler*
 Winner: George Chakiris, *West Side Story*
 Born *Herbert John Gleason* on 2/26/16 in Brooklyn, NY. Died 6/24/87 of liver cancer.
 Minnesota Fats in nominated role. Ralph Kramden on TV's *The Honeymooners*
 Orson Welles coined Jackie's nickname, "The Great One." Started in vaudeville, carnivals, and nightclubs. He had a vast library on the occult, and he reported that President Nixon had escorted him to a secret area where he claims he was shown alien bodies. The story was never disputed. He composed, arranged, and conducted recordings of mood music. He wrote the opening music to *The Honeymooners*, entitled "Melancholy Serenade." He made all of his own shots on the pool table in *The Hustler*. Despite being the reigning King of TV in the '50s he never won an Emmy—a great showbiz injustice.

Major Awards: Tony, NBR, Peabody, WOF

Gleason, James

1941-(BSA) *Here Comes Mr. Jordan*
 Winner: Donald Crisp, *How Green Was My Valley*
 Born 5/23/1886 in New York, NY.
 Died 4/12/59 of an asthma attack.
 Manager Max Corkle in nominated role.
 His parents were actors and he started on the stage almost right out of the cradle. Served in the Spanish-American War and WW I. Before he started acting he was a screenwriter, director, and dialogue specialist. He was also a noted playwright and wrote several musicals.

Major Awards: WOF

Jackie Gleason and Paul Newman square off in *The Hustler*.

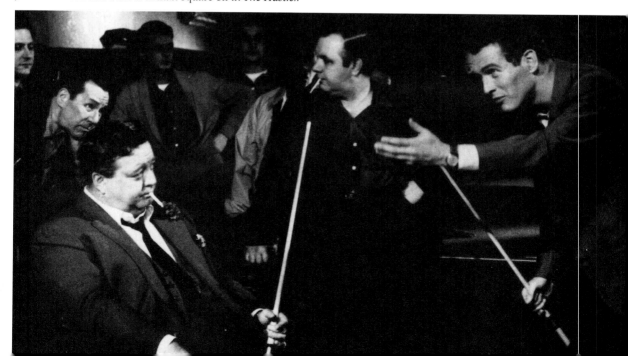

Goddard, Paulette

1943-(BSA) *So Proudly We Hail!*
  Winner: Katina Paxinou, *For Whom the Bell Tolls*
▦ Born *Marion Levy* on 6/3/11 in Great Neck Long Island, NY. Died 4/23/90 of heart failure.
✐ Lt. Jean O'Doul in nominated role.
✎ She was, at one time, married to Charlie Chaplin. She was one of the finalists for the role of Scarlett O'Hara in *Gone with the Wind*. She was also married to actor Burgess Meredith and novelist Erich Maria Remarque. Left 20 million to the University of New York. Although married four times she never had any children.
Major Awards: WOF

Goldberg, Whoopi

1985-(BA) *The Color Purple*
  Winner: Geraldine Page, *The Trip to Bountiful*
★ 1990-(BSA) *Ghost*
▦ Born 11/13/49 in New York, NY.
✐ Oda Mae Brown in *Ghost*
✎ Held a variety of odd jobs before making movies: bricklayer, hairdresser, bank teller, and mortician.

Whoopi Goldberg with Patrick Swayze in *Ghost*.

Shook a heroin habit in the '70s. Co-owned restaurant Eclipse with Joe Pesci and Steven Segal. Hates to fly, is dyslexic, collects Fiestaware china, and uses a customized bus to travel. Has won the Superfecta of acting. She received an Honorary degree from Wilson College.
Major Awards: Oscar, GG, OCC, Tony, NBR, DD, Grammy, Emmy, BAFTA, KCFCC, PC, WFCA, WOF

Gomez, Thomas

1947-(BSA) *Ride the Pink Horse*
  Winner: Edmund Gwenn, *Miracle on 34th Street*
▦ Born 4/10/05 in New York, NY. Died 6/18/71 in an auto accident.
✐ Curley Hoff the gangster in *Key Largo*
✎ After high school he answered an ad, which led to his acting career. Made his acting debut on the stage. Performed for many years with Broadway greats Alfred Lunt and Lynn Fontanne. He was a strong union man and served on the Board of Directors of the Actors Guild for over forty years. He was a restaurant connoisseur, dining at all of Hollywood's best. He weighed over 290 pounds but went on a crash diet and lost 140 pounds—he was 150 pounds at time of his death.

Gooding, Cuba

★ 1996-(BSA) *Jerry Maguire*
▦ Born 1/2/68 in Bronx, NY.
✐ Rod Tidwell in Oscar'd role.
✎ He attended four different high schools and was elected class president in three of them. Studied Japanese marital arts for three years. Worked as a construction worker and busboy. Father's band The Main Ingredient hit it big with "Everybody Plays the Fool." Father left the family after moving to Los Angeles and mother and the kids went on welfare. Now commands over one million a picture.
Major Awards: Oscar, SAG, WOF

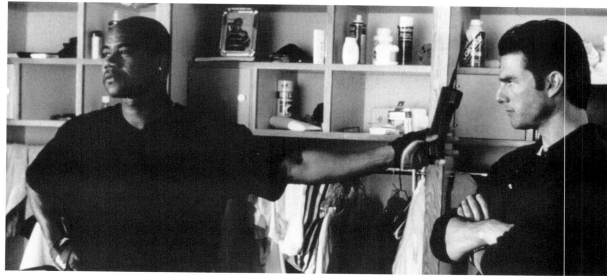

Cuba Gooding, Jr. with Tom Cruise in *Jerry Maguire*.

Gordon, Dexter

1986-(BA) *Round Midnight*
   Winner: Paul Newman, *The Color of Money*
▪ Born 2/27/23 in Los Angeles, CA.
   Died 4/25/90 of kidney failure.
▨ Dale Turner in nominated role
⚲ Not an actor by trade, rather one of the all-time great jazz musicians. He has played the saxophone for many big-name bands, including those of Louis Armstrong and Lionel Hampton, and released many classic records as a leader on the famous Blue Note label. Well respected among his peers and fans. Suffered from cancer of the larynx. Elected to the Jazz Hall of Fame in 1988. This was the only starring movie he ever appeared in. He served time in Chino penitentiary for heroin possession.
Major Awards: DDA, LAFC

Gordon, Ruth

1947-(BW) *A Double Life*
1950-(BW) *Adam's Rib*
1952-(BW) *Pat and Mike*
1965-(BSA) *Inside Daisy Clover*
   Winner: Shelley Winters, *A Patch of Blue*
★ 1968-(BSA) *Rosemary's Baby*
▪ Born 10/30/1896 in Wollaston, MA.
   Died 8/28/85 of a stroke.
▨ The witch Minnie Castevet in Oscar'd role.
⚲ Her father was a ship's captain. She went into acting against his objections. She had a brilliant Broadway career. She had an out-of-wedlock son with producer Jed Harris. She married talented playwright and screenwriter Garson Kanin and collaborated with him on many over the years. She was a member of the infamous Algonquin Round Table.
Major Awards: Oscar, Emmy, SWG, GG, WOF

Gosling, Ryan

2006-(BA) *Half Nelson*
   Winner: Forest Whitaker, *The Last King of Scotland*
▪ Born 11/12/80 in London, Ontario, Canada.

🖌 Dan Dunne in nominated role

🔍 He was home-schooled until high school because he was constantly bullied in the lower grades. Starred in the short-lived *New Mickey Mouse Club* beating out 17,000 hopefuls. His fellow Mousketeers were Britney Spears, Christina Aguilera, and Justin Timberlake. Lived with the Timberlake family for a short while. He is an accomplished jazz guitarist. Since the movie *Notebook*, he and his co-star Rachel McAdams have been companions.

Major Awards: NBR

Gossett, Louis Jr.

★ 1982-(BSA) *An Officer and a Gentleman*

▦ Born 5/27/36 in Brooklyn, NY.

🖌 Sergeant Emil Fowley in Oscar'd role

🔍 He was a star basketball player in college and went on to try out with the New York Knicks. Won prestigious Donaldson Award as best newcomer on Broadway. In addition to acting he occasionally sang in various nightclubs. Wrote the anti-war song "Handsome Johnny," which was performed by Richie Havens at Woodstock.

Major Awards: Oscar, Emmy, GG, WOF

Louis Gossett, Jr. in *An Officer and a Gentleman*.

Gould, Elliott

1969-(BSA) *Bob & Carol & Ted & Alice*
   Winner: Gig Young, *They Shoot Horses, Don't They?*

▦ Born *Elliott Goldstein* on 8/29/38 in Brooklyn, NY.

🖌 Trapper John in *M*A*S*H*

🔍 He performed on the Borscht Belt in the Catskills. Once was a ballet dancer in the chorus line on Broadway. Was married to actress Barbra Streisand. Constantly being called "Mr. Streisand" led him to receive psychiatric help and eventually a divorce. Has served as a regular guest host on the Fox News Network. He was a major box office star in 1970 and 1971.

Major Awards: Laurel

Grahame, Gloria

1947-(BSA) *Crossfire*
   Winner: Celeste Holm, *Gentleman's Agreement*

★ 1952-(BSA) *The Bad and the Beautiful*

▦ Born *Gloria Hallward* on 11/28/24 in Los Angeles, CA. Died 10/5/81 of cancer and peritonitis.

🖌 Rosemary Bartlow in Oscar'd role. Violet Bick in *It's a Wonderful Life*.

🔍 Started on the stage at age nine at the Pasadena Playhouse. She was a high school dropout. Always played the fallen wife or sexy, cheating woman. She was married four times. She raised eyebrows by marring her stepson from her second marriage. Died battling cancer. She has royalty in her blood—she is a direct descendant of King Edward III of England.

Major Awards: Oscar, WOF

Grant, Cary

1941-(BA) *Penny Seranade*
   Winner: Gary Cooper, *Sergeant York*
1944-(BA) *None but the Lonely Heart*
   Winner: Bing Crosby, *Going My Way*
1969-Honorary Oscar

Cary Grant and Eva Marie Saint in *North by Northwest*.

■ Born *Archibald Alexander Leach* on 1/18/1904 in Bristol, England. Died 11/29/86 of a stroke.

✎ C.K. Dexter Haven in *The Philadelphia Story*

✐ His father was a philanderer, and his mother suffered a nervous breakdown. Dropped out of school at age 14 and joined the circus as an acrobat and stilt walker. He was a workaholic and a notorious tightwad, even though he donated his salary in *The Philadelphia Story* and *Arsenic and Old Lace* to the British war effort. Once married to Woolworth heiress Barbara Hutton. Had a fear of knives and heights and was a lifelong insomniac. Sired his only child, a daughter, with actress Dyan Cannon. In a nasty subsequent divorce, she claimed he took LSD.

Major Awards: Jean Hersholt Humanitarian, WOF

Grant, Lee

1951-(BSA) *Detective Story*
Winner: Kim Hunter, *A Streetcar Named Desire*
1970-(BSA) *The Landlord*
Winner: Helen Hayes, *Airport*
★ 1975-(BSA) *Shampoo*
1976-(BSA) *Voyage of the Damned*
Winner: Beatrice Straight, *Network*

■ Born *Lyova Haskell Rosenthal* on 10/31/27 in New York, NY.

✎ Felicia Carr in Oscar'd role.

✐ Debuted on stage at age four and was a member of the American Ballet at age 11. She was blacklisted for 12 years during the McCarthy era. She enjoys painting and cooking. She is one of the few actresses to become an accomplished director. Turned down the role of Dorothy on *The Golden Girls*. In 1983 she was awarded the Congressional Arts and Caucus Award for Outstanding Achievement in Acting and filmmaking.

Major Awards: Oscar, Emmy, Obie, Cannes, WFCA

Granville, Bonita

1936-(BSA) *These Three*
Winner: Gale Sondergaard, *Anthony Adverse*
■ Born 2/2/23 in New York, NY. Died 10/11/88 of cancer.

✎ Mary Tilford in nominated role.

✐ Daughter of show people, she was on stage at age three. Played mischievous and naughty girls in most of her movies. Played plucky detective reporter Nancy Drew in the movie series. She married a

wealthy Texas oilman and became an executive of a huge business empire which included hotels and corporations, as well as controlling a number of TV series, including *Lassie* and *The Lone Ranger*.
Major Awards: WOF

Greene, Graham

1990-(BSA) *Dances with Wolves*
  Winner: Joe Pesci, *Goodfellas*
▪ Born 6/22/52 in Six Nations Reserve, Ontario, Canada.
 Kicking Bird in nominated role.
 Graduated from the Centre for Indigenous Theater Natives. He is a full-blooded Onieda Indian. Suffering from severe mental strain, he was hospitalized after a tense standoff with the police. No charges were filed since he agreed to undergo a psychiatric evaluation.
Major Awards: NBR, Gemini

Greenstreet, Sydney

1941-(BSA) *The Maltese Falcon*
  Winner: Donald Crisp, *How Green Was My Valley*
▪ Born 12/27/1879 in Sandwich, England. Died 1/18/54 of diabetes and Bright's Disease.
 Casper Gutman in nominated role.
 At age 18 moved to Sri Lanka in hopes to make a fortune as a tea planter but went bankrupt. After appearing on the British stage and Broadway for years he made his screen debut at age 62. Once managed a brewery out of boredom. Starred with Peter Lorre in ten movies. His career only lasted eight years, and he made only made 23 films. Heaviest actor to be nominated, tipping the scales at over 300 pounds.
Major Awards: NBR

Grey, Joel

★ 1972-(BSA) *Cabaret*
▪ Born *Joel Katz* on 4/11/32 in Cleveland, OH

 Master of Ceremonies in Oscar'd role.
 Son of comedian Mickey Katz of the Spike Jones Orchestra. The 5'4" actor made his stage debut at age nine and was a seasoned professional entertainer at age 15. Performed in the Catskills and later appeared on Broadway. His daughter is actress Jennifer Grey. Once hosted the *Muppet Show* and was the first mystery guest on the revived *What's My Line* in the '60s.
Major Awards: Oscar, Tony, OCC, NBR, NSFC, GG, BAFTA, KCFCC

Griffith, Corrine

1928/29-(BA) *The Divine Lady*
  Winner: Mary Pickford, *Coquette*
▪ Born *Corrine Griffin* on 11/24/1894 in Texarkana, TX. Died 7/13/79 of cardiac arrest.
 Emma Hart, Lady Hamilton in nominated role.
 Stared mainly in silent films making her debut in 1916. She was executive producer in eleven of her movies. She retired in 1932. She was a savvy businesswoman having invested in real estate. She was an accomplished writer having published more than a dozen plus books, among them the best seller *Papa's Delicate Condition*. At the time of her death her fortune was estimated to be worth over 150 million.
Major Awards: WOF

Griffith, Hugh

★ 1959-(BSA) *Ben-Hur*
1963-(BSA) *Tom Jones*
  Winner: Melvyn Douglas, *Hud*
▪ Born 5/30/12 in Marian Glas, Anglesby, North Wales. Died 5/14/80 of natural causes.
 Sheik Ilderim in *Ben-Hur*
 After graduating from high school he wanted to attend college but couldn't pass the English exam. Enlisted in the British Army and spent six years stationed in India. After his hitch in the service he was employed as a bank clerk. He made his stage debut at age 28. Had a 30-year career in the film industry.
Major Awards: Oscar, NBR

Griffith, Melanie

1988-(BA) *Working Girl*
   Winner: Jodie Foster, *The Accused*
▦ Born 8/9/57 in New York, NY.
🖋 Tess McGill in nominated role
𝒬 She is the daughter of Hitchcock protégé Tippi Hedren. She ran away from home at age 14 with actor Don Johnson who she eventually married and divorced. Addicted to alcohol and drugs she entered the Hazelton Clinic for rehab. Clawed in the face by a lion when filming *Roar*. She was blasted by a car when crossing the street and thrown over 12 feet into a curb. She has experienced pain from that event ever since.
Major Awards: GG, NSFC

Griffiths, Rachel

1998-(BSA) *Hillary and Jackie*
   Winner: Judi Dench, *Shakespeare in Love*
▦ Born 6/4/68 in Melbourne, Victoria, Australia.
🖋 Hilliary du Pre' in title role
𝒬 Her mother was an art consultant and her uncle a Jesuit priest. Attended a Catholic girl's school where she studied ballet. Her father left home with an 18-year-old when she was just 11. She hasn't seen him since. She and her husband donated all of their wedding gifts to the Sacred Heart Mission in Melbourne, Australia. She once protested the sins of gambling by running topless through Melbourne's Crown Casino.
Major Awards: GG, Australian Film Institute

Guinness, Sir Alec

1952-(BA) *The Lavender Hill Mob*
   Winner: Gary Cooper, *High Noon*
★ 1957-(BA) *The Bridge on the River Kwai*
1958-(BW) *The Horse's Mouth*
1977-(BSA) *Star Wars*
   Winner: Jason Robards, *Julia*
1979-Honorary Oscar
1988-(BSA) *Little Dorrit*
   Winner: Kevin Kline, *A Fish Called Wanda*
▦ Born *Alec Guinness de Cuffe* on 4/2/14 in Marylebone, England. Died 8/5/2000 of liver cancer.
🖋 Obi-Won Kenobi in *Star Wars*.
𝒬 Alec was born illegitimate and took the last name of his real father's best friend. He joined the Royal Navy and was commissioned an officer after a year during WW II. He was discovered by John Geilgud and started working in his acting troupe. In his youth he was a short distance sprinter and won many trophies. Knighted by the Queen in 1955. He was a heavy smoker all his life but quit shortly before his death. He often lamented that he didn't take enough chances as an actor. Although widely known as Obi-Won Kenobi he hated *Star Wars* and threw away all of his fan mail.
Major Awards: Oscar, Tony, NBR, NYFC, GG, LAFC, BAFTA, KCFCC, VFF, WOF

Gwenn, Edmond

★ 1947-(BSA) *Miracle On 34th Street*
1950-(BSA) *Mister 880*
   Winner: George Sanders, *All About Eve*
▦ Born 9/26/1875 in Glamorgan, Wales, England. Died 9/7/59 of pneumonia and a stroke.
🖋 Kris Kringle in Oscar'd role
𝒬 He was kicked out of the house at age 17 when he announced he wanted to become an actor. He was discovered and sponsored by famed playwright George Bernard Shaw. He was a captain in the Royal Army during WW I. He was 71 years old when he won his Oscar, the oldest winner ever at that time.
Major Awards: Oscar, GG, WOF

Gyllenhaal, Jake

2005-(BSA) *Brokeback Mountain*
   Winner: George Clooney, *Syriana*
▦ Born 12/19/80 in Los Angeles, CA.
🖋 Homer Hickum in *October Sky*
𝒬 Attended Columbia University but dropped out after two years to pursue an acting career. His Godmother is Jamie Lee Curtis, and Paul Newman taught him how to drive. Worked as a lifeguard,

busboy and chef. Favorite book is *To Kill a Mock-ingbird*. Has two dogs, named Atticus and Boo.
Major Awards: NBR

Hackett, Joan

1981-(BSA) *Only When I Laugh*
    Winner: Maureen Stapleton, *Reds*
▫ Born 5/1/42 in New York, NY. Died 10/8/83 of ovarian cancer.
✒ Toby Landau in nominated role.
✎ Started out as a highly paid fashion model in New York. Eventually she was taken under the wing of famed acting guru Lee Strasberg. She debuted on Broadway in 1961. She was a staunch believer in the paranormal and occult. She needed a lot of sleep, 10 to 12 hours at a stretch, and would put a sign on the door that would say "Go Away I'm Asleep."
Major Awards: GG, Obie

Hackman, Gene

1967-(BSA) *Bonnie and Clyde*
    Winner: George Kennedy, *Cool Hand Luke*
1970-(BSA) *I Never Sang for My Father*
    Winner: John Mills, *Ryan's Daughter*
★ 1971-(BA) *The French Connection*
1988-(BA) *Mississippi Burning*
    Winner: Dustin Hoffman, *Rain Man*
★ 1992-(BSA) *Unforgiven*
▫ Born 1/30/31 in San Bernardino, CA
✒ Popeye Doyle in *The French Connection* (#44 on AFI's Hero List), Buck Barrow in *Bonnie and Clyde*
✎ He quit school when he was 16. Had the steel bracelets slapped on him for stealing candy and pop. After that he enlisted in the Marines. Was honorably discharged and kicked around the country for ten years in all kinds of odd jobs before enrolling in acting class to realize his dreams. He and Dustin Hoffman were voted Most Unlikely to Succeed, and were roommates in New York as struggling actors. In *The French Connection* he did his own driving in the car chase scenes.

Major Awards: Oscar, NSFC, NBR, LAFC, NYFC, GG, Cannes, AFI, CB DeMille, BAFTA, BIFF, KCFCC, SAG, BW

Hagen, Jean

1952-(BSA) *Singin' in the Rain*
    Winner: Gloria Grahame, *The Bad and the Beautiful*
▫ Born *Jean Shirley Verhagen* 8/3/23 in Chicago, IL. Died 8/29/77 of throat cancer at age 54.
✒ Lina Lamont in nominated role.
✎ Graduating from Northwestern she moved to New York. There she worked in radio and as an usherette, which introduced her on Broadway. She played Danny Thomas's wife on the TV series *Make Room for Daddy* from 1953 to 1957. Debbie Reynolds lip-synced her song in *Singin' in the Rain*—it was Jean Hagen who was really singing it. She was nominated for two Emmys.
Major Awards: WOF

Haley, Jackie Earl

2006-(BSA) *Little Children*
    Winner: Alan Arkin, *Little Miss Sunshine*
▫ Born 7/14/61 in Northridge, CA.
✒ Ronnie J. McGorley in nominated role.
✎ His dad Haven was a radio actor. Jackie's first gig at age six was doing TV commercials. After his initial screen appearances, roles dried up and the phone stopped ringing. During this down time he was a limo driver, furniture refinisher, security cop, and pizza pusher. Then, as fate would have it, the phone rang once again. Director Steve Zaillian had remembered him.
Major Awards: NYFC

Hall, Grayson

1964-(BSA) *The Night of the Iguana*
    Winner: Lila Kedrova, *Zorba the Greek*
▫ Born *Shirley Grossman* on 9/18/23 in Philadelphia, PA. Died 8/7/85 of cancer.

🍴 Julia in *Dark Shadows*

🔍 Appeared on the TV soap opera *One Life to Live* where her husband and her son were writers. She landed the lead in TV cult series *Dark Shadows*. When dating Sam Hall he affectionately called her Grayson, after an army buddy. She adopted it as her professional name.

Hanks, Tom

1988-(BA) *Big*
   Winner: Dustin Hoffman, *Rain Man*
★ 1993-(BA) *Philadelphia*
★ 1994-(BA) *Forrest Gump*
1998-(BA) *Saving Private Ryan*
   Winner: Roberto Benigni, *Life is Beautiful*
2000-(BA) *Cast Away*
   Winner: Russell Crowe, *Gladiator*
▦ Born 7/9/56 in Concord, CT.
🍴 Forrest Gump, Sergeant Miller *Saving Private Ryan*. Andrew Becket *Philadelphia* (#49 on AFI's Hero List)
🔍 Lived with his divorced father, who was an itinerant cook, and changed elementary schools five times. Once worked as a bellhop. Dropped out of Cal State to pursue an acting career. Hates talking on the phone and is a recluse at times. His hobby is collecting old typewriters, and he is a huge *Star Trek* fan. He received the Navy's highest civilian award, The Distinguished Public Service Award, for his work in *Saving Private Ryan*. He gained and lost 50 pounds for his role in *Cast Away*. He is a distant cousin to Abraham Lincoln, whose mother was Nancy Hanks.
Major Awards: Oscar, AFI's Life Achievement, SATURN, BIFF, Emmy, KCFF, PC, WOFLAFC, NBR, GG, SAG, NYFC, WOF

Harden, Marcia Gay

★ 2000-(BSA) *Pollock*
2003-(BSA) *Mystic River*
   Winner: Renee Zellweger, *Cold Mountain*
▦ Born 8/14/59 in La Jolla, CA.

🍴 Lee Krasner in Oscar'd role.

🔍 Educated in Greece and Germany before returning to the states and graduating from the University of Texas. Her father was a military man and the family was constantly moving. A casting agent said she would never make it in show business because of her "flaring nostrils." She was intending to make it big in the circus and is adept on the trapeze and tightrope as well as juggling.
Major Awards: OSCAR, NYFC, BSFC, NBR, BW

Harding, Ann

1930/31-(BA) *Holiday*
   Winner: Marie Dressler, *Min and Bill*
▦ Born *Dorothy Walton Gatley* on 8/7/1901 in Ft. Sam Houston, TX. Died 9/1/81 of natural causes.
🍴 Linda Seaton in nominated role.
🔍 Daughter of career Army officer, she moved all over the country and Cuba. Dropped out of Bryn Mawr College and became an insurance clerk and a free-lance script reader. Retired from the screen in 1937 after marrying orchestra conductor Werner Janssen, but was coaxed out for a role in *The Man in the Gray Flannel Suit* in 1956.
Major Awards: WOF

Harper, Tess

1986-(BSA) *Crimes of The Heart*
   Winner: Diane Wiest, *Hannah and Her Sisters*
▦ Born 1952 in Mammoth Springs, AR.
🍴 Chick Boyle in nominated role
🔍 After graduating from the University of Texas she performed in children's plays and dinner theater. She debuted on TV and made several appearances before landing in the movies. She was nominated for a Golden Globe as Robert Duvall's holy and pious love in *Tender Mercies*. She worked very hard to shed her southern accent but kept getting roles as Southerners.

Harrelson, Woody

1996-(BA) *The People vs. Larry Flynt*
    Winner: Geoffrey Rush, *Shine*
▪ Born 7/23/61 in Midland, TX.
⚘ Bartender Woody Boyd in TV comedy *Cheers*
⚲ He was hyperactive as a child and placed in a school for troubled children. His father was convicted of murdering a federal judge and was sentenced to life in prison. Climbed the Golden Gate Bridge once to hang a banner calling for the protection of the redwood trees. Has been featured on the cover of *High Times* magazine. He has admitted to being a sex addict.
Major Awards: Emmy, BW

Harris, Barbara

1971-(BSA) *Who Is Harry Kellerman and Why Is He Saying All Those Terrible Things About Me?*
    Winner: Cloris Leachman, *The Last Picture Show*
▪ Born *Sandra Markowitz* on 7/5/35 in Evanston, IL.
⚘ Allison in nominated role.
⚲ Graduated from Chicago University. Her mother was a concert pianist and her father was an arborist and tree surgeon. She was a founding member of Chicago's famous Second City Players improvisation, that which included Alan Arkin and Elaine May.
Major Awards: Tony

Harris, Ed

1995-(BSA) *Apollo 13*
    Winner: Kevin Spacey, *The Usual Suspects*
1998-(BSA) *The Truman Show*
    Winner: James Coburn, *Affliction*
2000-(BA) *Pollock*
    Winner: Russell Crowe, *Gladiator*
2002-(BSA) *The Hours*
    Winner: Chris Cooper, *Adaptation*
▪ Born 11/28/50 in Tenafly, NJ.
⚘ Jackson Pollock, John Glenn in *The Right Stuff*

⚲ Graduated from the University of Columbia where he played football. By his own admission he claims acting helped him get over his innate shyness. Took acting lessons and played summer stock before enrolling at the California Institute of Arts. Married to actress Amy Madigan. Ed has also produced and directed several productions.
Major Awards: NBR, GG, DD, Obie, SAG, NSFC

Harris, Julie

1952-(BA) *The Member of the Wedding*
    Winner: Shirley Booth, *Come Back*, *Little Sheba*
▪ Born 12/2/25 in Grosse Point, MI
⚘ Frankie Adams in nominated role.
⚲ Her father was an investment banker who sent her to Yale Drama School and New York's Actors Studio. She made her Broadway debut and startled the audience by playing the part of a 12-year-old at the age of 27! She is the most honored actor in Tony history with ten nominations. She was also nominated 11 times for an Emmy—winning three times. Had brain surgery in 1999, the result of an accidental fall.
Major Awards: DD, OCC, Emmy, Tony (5)

Harris, Richard

1963-(BA) *This Sporting Life*
    Winner: Sidney Poitier, *Lilies of the Field*
1990-(BA) *The Field*
    Winner: Jeremy Irons, *Reversal of Fortune*
▪ Born 10/1/33 in Limerick, Ireland.
    Died 10/25/2002 of Hodgkin's disease.
⚘ Frank Machin and Bull McCabe in nominated roles.
⚲ Graduated from Sacred Heart Jesuit School. As a teenager he contracted tuberculosis and was incapacitated for two and half years. Recorded No. 1 hit song "MacArthur Park." His drinking binges and barroom brawls were legendary. He wrote poetry.
Major Awards: Cannes, GG, BW

Harris, Rosemary

1994-(BSA) *Tom and Viv*
  Winner: Dianne Wiest, *Bullets over Broadway*
▧ Born 9/19/30 in Ashby, Suffolk, England.
𝄞 May Parker in *Spider-Man*
⚲ Although born in England, she was raised in India. Has starred on the American stage for years. She initially wanted to be a nurse. Competed against her own daughter for Best Performance by a Leading Actress in the play *Waiting in the Wings*. Her daughter, Jennifer Ehle, took home the Tony.
Major Awards: Emmy, GG, NBR, Obie, Tony

Harrison, Sir Rex

1963-(BA) *Cleopatra*
  Winner: Sidney Poitier, *Lilies of the Field*
★ 1964-(BA) *My Fair Lady*
▧ Born *Reginald Carey Harrison* on 3/5/08 in Huyton, England. Died 6/2/90 of pancreatic cancer.
𝄞 Professor Henry Higgins in Oscar'd role.
⚲ Due to a case of measles as a child he lost most of his sight in his left eye. During WW II he was a flight lieutenant for the Royal Air Force. Hollywood columnist Hedda Hopper nicknamed him "Sexy Rexy." Early in his career he was told to get out of the business because he wasn't talented enough in an already crowded field.
Major Awards: Oscar, Tony, NBR, GG, NYFC, WOF

Hartman, Elizabeth

1965-(BA) *A Patch of Blue*
  Winner: Julie Christie, *Darling*
▧ Born 12/23/41 in Youngstown, OH. Died 6/10/87 of suicide.
𝄞 Selina D'Arcey in nominated role.
⚲ Graduated from Carnegie-Tech. Nominated in her first film. She became emotionally unstable with her lack of movie roles. Mentally fragile and distraught she underwent psychiatric treatment, but in the end, she took her own life by leaping from her fifth-story apartment.
Major Awards: GG

Harvey, Lawrence

1959-(BA) *Room at the Top*
  Winner: Charlton Heston, *Ben-Hur*
▧ Born *Laruska Mischa Skikne* on 10/1/28 in Yomishkis, Lithuania. Died 11/25/73 of stomach cancer.
𝄞 Joe Lampton in nominated role.
⚲ Joined South African Navy at age 14, but it was discovered that he was lying, and he was returned him to his parents. Four years later he enlisted in the army during WW II. Married briefly to Columbia movie mogul Harry Cohn's widowed wife Joan and fathered a child out of wedlock while married to her. First Lithuanian to be nominated.
Major Awards: BW

Hawke, Ethan

2001-(BSA) *Training Day*
  Winner: Jim Broadbent, *Iris*
2004-(BW) *Under the Sunset*
▧ Born 11/6/70 in Austin, TX.
𝄞 Todd Anderson *Dead Poets Society*
⚲ Dropped out of Carnegie Mellon for two months to film *Dead Poets Society*. Sang his own songs on the *Reality Bites* soundtrack. Wrote a novel, *The Hottest State*, which sold for $400,000. Co-founded the New York theater company Malaparte. He is a big *Star Wars* fan and once was married to actress Uma Thurman. Has publicly stated he never wanted to be an actor! Ethan, say it ain't so.

Hawn, Goldie

★ 1969-(BSA) *Cactus Flower*
1980-(BA) *Private Benjamin*
  Winner: Sissy Spacek, *Coal Miner's Daughter*
▧ Born *Goldie Stulendgehawn* on 11/21/45 in Takoma Park, MD.

🦋 Private Benjamin, dumb blonde on TV comedy series *Laugh In*

🔍 She took tap-dancing and ballet lessons when she was three. During the 1964 World's Fair she was a chorus line cancan dancer. Paid her college tuition by teaching dance lessons. Enjoys cooking, sewing, knitting, and collecting antiques. Has been a long-time companion to actor Kurt Russell since 1983. Her daughter is actress Kate Hudson.

Major Awards: Oscar, GG

Hawthorne, Sir Nigel

1994-(BA) *The Madness of King George*
   Winner: Tom Hanks, *Forrest Gump*

◼ Born 4/5/29 in Coventry, England. Died 12/26/2001 of a heart attack.

🦋 King George III in nominated role.

🔍 He was a staunch vegetarian. Queen Elizabeth II made him Commander of the British Empire in 1987 and he was knighted in 1999. He was considered for the role of Gandolf in *The Lord of the Rings*. Battled pancreatic cancer until it was thought to be in remission before he suffered a fatal heart attack.

Major Awards: BAFTA (6), LCC, Tony

Hayakawa, Sessue

1957-(BSA) *The Bridge on the River Kwai*
   Winner: Red Buttons, *Sayonara*

◼ Born 6/10/1889 in Chiba, Japan. Died 11/23/73 of cerebral thrombosis.

🦋 Colonel Saito in nominated role

🔍 He had to abandon a navy career because of a punctured eardrum. Overwrought, he tried to commit hara-kiri, stabbing himself 30 times but he miraculously lived. After doing several movies in Hollywood he moved to France, where during WW II and the Nazi occupation, he earned a living as an artist. He authored a novel and a play, and he worked as a screenwriter for a time.

Major Awards: NBR, WOF

Hayek, Salma

2002-(BA) *Frida*
   Winner: Nichole Kidman, *The Hours*

◼ Born 9/2/66 in Coatzacoalcos, Vera Cruz, Mexico.

🦋 Frida Kahlo in title role.

🔍 Her father was a Lebanese oil executive and her mother a Mexican opera singer. Achieved stardom on Mexican TV, and the family moved to Los Angeles. She graduated from high school in only two years. She was expelled from boarding school for setting all the alarm clocks back three hours. Co-wrote the script for her film *Frida*. She is fluent in English, Spanish, Arabic, and Portuguese. She is a big dog lover. Produces TV hit *Ugly Betty*.

Major Awards: Emmy

Hayes, Helen

★ 1931/32-(BA) *The Sin of Madelon Claudet*
★ 1970-(BSA) *Airport*

◼ Born *Helen Hayes Brown* on 10/10/1900 in Washington, DC. Died 3/17/93 of congestive heart failure.

🦋 First Lady of American Theater

🔍 Made her stage debut at age five. Married playwright and screenwriter Charles MacArthur in 1928. Unhappy, she left Hollywood for Broadway. Won a Tony Award in the first year they were presented. Prompted by the sudden death of her daughter she wrote several memoirs. Actor James MacArthur is her son. First actress to portray a prostitute on the screen. Won the Superfecta of acting.

Major Awards: Oscar, Tony, Grammy, Emmy, VR, OCC, WOF

Hayward, Susan

1947-(BA) *Smash Up—The Story of a Woman*
   Winner: Loretta Young, *The Farmer's Daughter*
1949-(BA) *My Foolish Heart*
   Winner: Olivia de Havilland, *The Heiress*
1952-(BA) *With a Song in My Heart*
   Winner: Shirley Booth, *Come Back, Little Sheba*

Susan Hayward in *I Want to Live!*

1955-(BA) *I'll Cry Tomorrow*
  Winner: Anna Magnani, *The Rose Tattoo*
★ 1958-(BA) *I Want To Live!*
▪ Born *Edythe Marrener* 6/30/18 in Brooklyn, NY. Died 3/14/75 of a cancerous brain tumor.
✎ Barbara Graham in Oscar'd role.
🔍 She was once a stenographer, dress designer, and photographer's model. She was one of the many who auditioned for the part of Scarlett O'Hara. In a bitter courtroom custody battle over her twin sons, she attempted suicide. Her footprints are the only ones set in gold dust at Grauman's Chinese Theatre. The film *The Conqueror* in which she starred was filmed at a former nuclear testing site in Utah. All of her co-stars died from cancer.
Major Awards: Oscar, GGWFF, Cannes, NYFC, WOF

Heckart, Eileen

1956-(BSA) *The Bad Seed*
  Winner: Dorothy Malone, *Written on the Wind*
★ 1972-(BSA) *Butterflies Are Free*
▪ Born 3/29/19 in Columbus, OH.
  Died 12/31/01 of cancer.
✎ Mrs. Baker in Oscar'd role.

🔍 Graduated from Ohio State, majoring in Drama. Her mother was married five times. Her marriage lasted 53 years. Her hoarse voice came from a childhood bout of Whooping Cough. She was collecting unemployment when she learned she had won the Oscar. She has won the Triple Crown of acting.
Major Awards: Oscar, GG, DD, Emmy, NBR, Tony, WOF

Heflin, Van

★ 1942-(BSA) *Johnny Eager*
▪ Born *Emmett Evan Heflin, Jr.* on 12/13/10 in Walters, OK. Died 7/23/71 of a heart attack while swimming.
✎ Brave rancher Joe Starett in *Shane*
🔍 When his acting debut bombed he took to the sea. He was a sailor and merchant seaman for three years before returning to Hollywood. He also was a combat cameraman during WW II. In accordance with his will he was cremated and his ashes were cast into the Pacific Ocean. Turned down the role of Elliott Ness on TV's *The Untouchables*.
Major Awards: Oscar, WOF

Hemingway, Mariel

1979-(BSA) *Manhattan*
  Winner: Meryl Streep, *Kramer vs. Kramer*
▪ Born 11/22/61 in Ketchum, Idaho
✎ Tracy in nominated role.
🔍 Granddaughter of famed writer Ernest Hemingway. A savvy businesswoman, she was executive producer of one of her pictures and she's also the owner of a popular New York eating establishment called *Sam's Place*, named after a Cuban fishing village that was a favorite of her father and grandfather.
Major Awards: Broadcast Film Critics

Henry, Justin

1979-(BSA) *Kramer vs. Kramer*
  Winner: Melvyn Douglas, *Being There*
▪ Born 5/25/71 in Rye, NY

⚉ Billy Kramer in nominated role.

↳ At age seven he was discovered by his next-door neighbor who happened to be a casting director. Later on he got his degree at Skidmore College. His acting stints have been sporadic at best. Youngest performer to be nominated for a Best Supporting Actor Oscar at age eight. As of this writing he is the director of sales and strategies for Flavorpill.

Major Awards: DDA

Hepburn, Audrey

★ 1953-(BA) *Roman Holiday*
1954-(BA) *Sabrina*
    Winner: Grace Kelly, *The Country Girl*
1959-(BA) *The Nun's Story*
    Winner: Simone Signoret, *Room at the Top*
1961-(BA) *Breakfast At Tiffany's*
    Winner: Sophia Loren, *Two Women*
1967-(BA) *Wait Until Dark*
    Winner: Katharine Hepburn, *Guess Who's Coming to Dinner*

Audrey Hepburn and Cary Grant in *Roman Holiday.*

■ Born *Audrey Kathleen Ruston* on 5/4/29 in Brussels, Belgium. Died 1/20/93 of colon cancer.

⚉ Princess Anne in Oscar'd role

↳ Her father was a banker and her mother a Dutch baroness. One of her uncles and a cousin were killed in a Nazi concentration camp. She was fluent in English, Spanish, French, Dutch, Italian, and Flemish. Broke her back horseback riding while filming *The Unforgiven* (1960). Everybody remembers Marilyn Monroe singing "Happy Birthday Mr. President" to JFK. What is forgotten is that at his final birthday in 1963 it was Hepburn who sang "Happy Birthday." One of the few actors to win the Superfecta of acting.

Major Awards: Oscar, Tony, NYFC, GG, CB DeMille, SAGLA, Jean Hersholt Humanitarian, Emmy, GGWFF, BAFTA, WFCA, WOF

Hepburn, Katharine

★ 1932/33-(BA) *Morning Glory*
1935-(BA) *Alice Adams*
    Winner: Bette Davis, *Dangerous*
1940-(BA) *The Philadelphia Story*
    Winner: Ginger Rogers, *Kitty Foyle*
1942-(BA) *Woman of the Year*
    Winner: Greer Garson, *Mrs. Miniver*
1951-(BA) *The African Queen*
    Winner: Vivien Leigh, *A Streetcar Named Desire*
1955-(BA) *Summertime*
    Winner: Anna Magnani, *The Rose Tattoo*
1956-(BA) *The Rain Maker*
    Winner: Ingrid Bergman, *Anastasia*
1959-(BA) *Suddenly Last Summer*
    Winner: Simone Signoret, *Room at the Top*
1962-(BA) *Long Day's Journey into Night*
    Winner: Anne Bancroft, *The Miracle Worker*
★ 1967-(BA) *Guess Who's Coming to Dinner*
★ 1968-(BA) *The Lion in Winter*
★ 1981-(BA) *On Golden Pond*
■ Born 11/8/09 in Hartford, CT. Died 6/29/03 of natural causes.
⚉ Eleanor of Aquitaine in *The Lion in Winter;* Spencer Tracy's soul mate for 27 years
↳ Her father was a doctor and her mother a woman's activist. She won a Bronze Medal for figure

Spencer Tracy and Katharine Hepburn in *Guess Who's Coming to Dinner.*

skating at Madison Square Garden. She won the state of Connecticut Golf Championship. She was expelled from Bryn Mawr College for smoking a cigarette. She was readmitted and graduated with a degree in history and philosophy. Her grandfather, her uncle, and her brother all committed suicide. She was a descendent of King John of England. She made nine films with Spencer Tracy. A bronze bust of Spencer Tracy that she made went for $316,000 at her estate auction.
Major Awards: Oscar (4), Emmy, NYFC, Cannes, SAGLA, BATF, WOF

Hershey, Barbara

1996-(BSA) *The Portrait of a Lady*
  Winner: Juliette Binoche, *The English Patient*
■ Born *Barbara Herzstein* on 2/5/48 in Hollywood, CA.
Ⅶ Myrna Fleenor in *Hoosiers*
🔍 Her father was editor of *The Racing Form*. She was a member of the high school bands drill team and a pom-pom girl. During her hippie years she changed her last name to Seagull and named her son "Free." She since changed his name to Tom. First and only actor to win back-to-back awards at the Cannes Film Festival.
Major Awards: Emmy, GG, Cannes, NSFC, BW, LAFC

Heston, Charlton

★ 1959-(BA) *Ben-Hur*
■ Born *John Charlton Carter* on 10/4/24 in Evanston, IL
Ⅶ Moses, *The Ten Commandments* (#43 on AFI's Hero list)
🔍 Served three years in the Air Force during WW II as a radio operator on a B25. In his struggling years he was a nude model in NY working for a $1.25 an hour. He is a talented artist. His drawings have been exhibited in galleries in the U.S. and Europe. He was the president of the Screen Actors Guild from 1966 to 1971. Loves peanut butter. Longtime president of the National Rifle Association. Made a memorable cameo in Michael Moore's anti-gun flick *Bowling for Columbine*. Don't get Charlton riled—on the set of *Major Dundee* he threatened to knock out director Sam Peckinpah if he didn't quit riding him.
Major Awards: Oscar, GG, CB DeMille, Jean Hersholt Humanitarian, SAGLA, BW, WOF

Hickey, William

1985-(BSA) *Prizzi's Honor*
  Winner: Don Ameche, *Cocoon*
■ Born 9/19/28 in Brooklyn, NY. Died 6/29/97 of emphysema and bronchitis.
Ⅶ Don Corrado in nominated role.
🔍 Began career as a child actor in traveling variety shows. Was featured on TV in the early '50s. Found his niche as an acting teacher at the HB Studio in Greenwich Village. Some of his students were Steve McQueen, Sandy Dennis, George Segal, and Barbra Streisand.

Hiller, Dame Wendy

1938-(BA) *Pygmalion*
  Winner: Bette Davis, *Jezebel*
★ 1958-(BSA) *Separate Tables*
1966-(BSA) *A Man for All Seasons*
  Winner: Sandy Dennis, *Who's Afraid of Virginia Woolf?*

Born 8/15/12 in Bramshall, Cheshire, England. Died 5/14/03 of natural causes.

Eliza Doolittle in *Pygmalion*

Legendary playwright George Bernard Shaw, after seeing her on the stage, personally recommended her for the part in the movie. She was awarded an honorary degree from Manchester College. She received the Order of the British Empire in 1971 and was made Dame Commander by Queen Elizabeth in 1975.

Major Awards: Oscar, GG

Hirsch, Judd

1980-(BSA) *Ordinary People*
   Winner: Timothy Hutton, *Ordinary People*

Born 3/15/35 in New York, NY.

Alex Rieger in popular TV comedy series *Taxi*

Graduated from CCNY with a degree in physics and engineering. Started out on TV doing commercials for Lava soap, TWA, GTE, and Swiss Miss Hot Chocolate. Nominated six times for an Emmy and seven times for a Golden Globe. He holds the distinction of starring in two primetime TV series *Numbers* and *Studio 60 on Sunset Strip*.

Major Awards: Emmy, GG, Obie, Tony

Hoffman, Dustin

1967-(BA) *The Graduate*
   Winner: Rod Stieger, *In the Heat of the Night*
1969-(BA) *Midnight Cowboy*
   Winner: John Wayne, *True Grit*
1974, (BA) *Lenny*
   Winner: Art Carney, *Harry and Tonto*
★ 1979-(BA) *Kramer vs. Kramer*
1982-(BA) *Tootsie*
   Winner: Ben Kingsley, *Gandhi*
★ 1988-(BA) *Rain Man*
1997-(BA) *Wag the Dog*
   Winner: Jack Nicholson, *As Good as It Gets*

Born 8/8/37 in Los Angeles, CA.

Ben Braddock in *The Graduate*, Ratso Rizzo *Midnight Cowboy*

Tom Cruise and Dustin Hoffman in *Rain Man*.

Attended Santa Monica City College but couldn't cut it because of bad grades and dropped out. Initially wanted to be a concert pianist and doctor. As a struggling actor, bunked out with Gene Hackman and Robert Duvall, sleeping on the kitchen floor. His mother named him after silent screen star Dustin Farnum. Lost the tip of his finger while filming *Finding Neverland*. Believe it or not, he was 30 years old when he played Ben Braddock in *The Graduate*, only six years younger than Ann Bancroft. Has played characters of age 17 (*The Graduate*) to age 121 (*Little Big Man*), a *Guinness Book* world record. His hobby is collecting antique toys.

Major Awards: Oscar, Emmy, Obie, NSFC, NYFC, LAFC, GG, CBD, AFI's Life Achievement Award, WOF

Hoffman, Philip Seymour

★ 2005-(BA) *Capote*

Born 7/23/67 in Fairpark, NY

Truman Capote in title role.

He was an all-star wrestler in high school before a neck injury ended his mat dreams. Graduated from New York University's Tisch School of Arts. Taught directing classes at Columbia University. He is a prolific and dependable character actor, wildly respected by his peers, and has appeared in 14 movies in the last five years. Once worked as a lifeguard and waiter.

Major Awards: GG, LAFC, NBR, NSFC, BAFTA, KCFCC, BSFC, SAG

Holden, William

1950-(BA) *Sunset Boulevard*
    Winner: Jose Ferrer, *Cyrano de Bergerac*
★ 1953-(BA) *Stalag 17*
1976-(BA) *Network*
    Winner: Peter Finch, *Network*
▦ Born *William Franklin Beedle* on 4/17/18 in O'Fallon, IL. Died 11/16/81 in a serious fall.
▥ Sefton in Oscar'd role.
▢ As a fledgling actor, he was befriended by Barbara Stanwyck and they became lifelong friends. He was a distant relative to President Warren G. Harding. He owned a 1200-plus-acre ranch in Kenya, and he donated large sums of money to African wildlife preservation. He was best man at Ronald and Nancy Reagan's wedding. He was obsessive compulsive and would take up to four showers a day. Battled alcoholism his whole life and eventually died when, in a drunken state, he tripped on a rug, fell, gashed his head, and bled to death.

Major Awards: Oscar, Emmy, VFF, NBR, WOF

Holliday, Judy

★ 1950-(BA) Born Yesterday
▦ Born *Judith Tuvim* on 6/21/65 in New York, NY. Died 6/7/65 of breast cancer.
▥ Billy Dawn in Oscar'd role.
▢ Once worked as a switchboard operator and stage manager for Orson Welles's Mercury Theater. Often played dumb blondes but had a recorded IQ of 172. She was a known Marxist. In her greatest performance ever, essentially resurrecting her Billy Dawn role, she confronted McCarthy's HUAC committee so successfully that she didn't have to "name names" and wasn't blacklisted.

Major Awards: Oscar, Emmy, GG, Tony, WOF

Holloway, Stanley

1964-(BSA) *My Fair Lady*
    Winner: Peter Ustinov, *Topkapi*
▦ Born 10/1/1890 in London, England. Died 1/30/82 of natural causes.
▥ Alfred Doolittle in nominated role.
▢ His first job was a clerk in a fish market. Son of a law clerk whose family had showbiz connections. WW I cut short his solo singing career, and he served in the British Army in France. Starred on TV in the comedy *Our Man Higgins*.

Holm, Celeste

★ 1947-(BSA) *Gentleman's Agreement*
1949-(BSA) *Come to the Stable*
    Winner: Mercedes McCambridge, *All the King's Men*
1950-(BSA) *All About Eve*
    Winner: Josephine Hull, *Harvey*
▦ Born 4/29/1919 in New York, NY.
▥ Anne Detrie in Oscar'd role.
▢ Her father was a Norwegian insurance executive and her mother a portrait artist. She was educated in France, Holland, and the U.S. Performed as a child with legendary showman George M. Cohan. Knighted by King Olav of Norway. In 1957. She was a regular on the TV series *Nancy* and the *Delphi Bureau*. She is a spokesperson for UNICEF and received an honorary degree from Seton Hall University.

Major Awards: Oscar, GG, WOF

Holm, Ian Sir

1981-(BSA) *Chariots of Fire*
    Winner: John Gielgud, *Arthur*
▦ Born *Ian Holm Cuthbert* 9/12/31 in Goodmayes, England.

🎞 Homicidal android in *Alien*, Bilbo Baggins in *The Lord of the Rings*

🎭 Spent 13 years with the Royal Shakespeare Company. Suffered a severe case of stage fright in 1976 and abruptly left the stage. Even professionals aren't immune. Appointed Commander of the British Empire in 1990 and was knighted by the Queen in 1998. Overcame a bout of prostate cancer in 2001.

Major Awards: Tony, Cannes, NBR, BAFTA, BSFC, KCFCC, SAG

Homolka, Oscar

1948-(BSA) *I Remember Mama*
    Winner: Walter Huston, *The Treasure of the Sierra Madre*
▦ Born 8/12/1898 in Vienna, Austria.
    Died 1/27/78 of pneumonia at age 80.
🎞 Uncle Chris in nominated role.
🎭 The bushy eye-browed actor worked for Max Reinhardt and appeared in many German silent films until Hitler came into power. Left for England, then to the U.S. Became a U.S. citizen in 1943.

Major Awards: German Film Award

Hope, Bob

1940-Honorary Oscar
1944-Honorary Oscar
1952-Honorary Oscar
1965-Honorary Oscar
▦ Born *Leslie Townes Hope* on 5/29/03 in Eltham, England. Died 4/27/2003 of natural causes.
🎞 Tireless USO entertainer for the troops. Emceeing the Oscar awards. Rapid-fire quips and ad libs. Signature song "Thanks for the Memories."
🎭 Quit school at age 16 to become a boxer under the name Packy East. An avid golfer his whole life, it is noted he shot twelve holes-in-one during his lifetime. Wrote ten best-selling books. Emceed the Oscars 18 times. In 1998 was awarded Honorary British Knighthood. Once was part owner of the Cleveland Indians. Arguably the richest entertainer ever with a net worth over $700 million. His most cherished of his 2000 lifetime awards was the Honorary Veteran Award bestowed on him by Congress in 1997, the only one ever awarded. A true American icon and legend.

Major Awards: GG, Emmy, CB DeMille, SAG, Jean Hersholt Humanitarian, Civilian Congressional Medal of Honor, WOF

Hopkins, Sir Anthony

★ 1991-(BA) *The Silence of the Lambs*
1993-(BA) *The Remains of the Day*
    Winner: Tom Hanks, *Philadelphia*
1995-(BA) *Nixon*
    Winner: Nicholas Cage, *Leaving Las Vegas*
1997-(BSA) *Amistad*
    Winner: Robin Williams, *Good Will Hunting*
▦ Born 12/31/37 in Port Talbot, South Wales, England.
🎞 Hannibal Lector in Oscar'd role (#1 on AFI's Villain List)
🎭 Originally studied to be a concert pianist and is a virtuoso player. Served in the British Royal Navy. Volunteer teaches at Ruskin School of acting. Is related to poet William Butler Yeats. Almost bought the farm while filming *The Edge* when he fell into a river and had to be treated for hypothermia. Overcame alcoholism. Awarded Commander of the British Empire in 1987 and was knighted in 1993.

Major Awards: Oscar, Emmy, NBR, NYFC, LAFC, WOF

Hopkins, Miriam

1935-(BA) *Becky Sharp*
    Winner: Bette Davis, *Dangerous*
▦ Born on 10/18/1902 in Bainbridge, GA.
    Died 10/9/72 of a heart attack.
🎞 Becky Sharp in title role.
🎭 Studied to a ballerina until she broke her ankle. A very temperamental and self-centered actress, she was once rebuked on set by an otherwise gentlemanly Edward G. Robinson, and she had a running feud with Bette Davis. Auditioned for the role of Scarlet O'Hara in *Gone with the Wind*. She adopted

a boy in 1932 as a single parent, which was unheard of at the time.
Major Awards: WOF

Hopper, Dennis

1969-(BW) *Easy Rider*
1986-(BSA) *Hoosiers*
  Winner: Michael Caine, *Hannah and Her Sisters*
▦ Born 5/17/36 in Dodge City, KS
⚡ Shooter in nominated role, Frank Booth in *Blue Velvet* (#36 on AFI's Villain List)
⚚ He was raised on a farm by his grandparents. Tired of the Hollywood establishment he and Peter Fonda raised $400,000 and made *Easy Rider*. It became a box office smash grossing 16 million. Dropped out of Hollywood and spent years battling drug dependency. Is one of the foremost collectors of art in the world. He is an accomplished photographer, having his work exhibited in galleries in the U.S., Europe, and Japan.
Major Awards: LAFC, NSFC, GG

Hoskins, Bob

1986-(BA) *Mona Lisa*
  Winner: Paul Newman, *The Color of Money*
▦ Born 10/26/42 in Bury St. Edmunds, Suffolk, England.
⚡ The chauffer George in nominated role.
⚚ Dropped out of school at the age of 15. He once worked in the circus as a fire-eater. Got into the show business in a fateful way: He was sitting in a pub where a small play was to be staged, and they needed an extra. He has never taken professional acting lessons.
Major Awards: Cannes, NBR, NYFC, NSFC, GG, BAFTA, BSFC, NBR, KCFCC

Hounsou, Djimon

2003-(BSA) *In America*
  Winner: Tim Robbins, *Mystic River*

2006-(BSA) *Blood Diamond*
  Winner: Alan Arkin, *Little Miss Sunshine*
▦ Born 4/24/64 in Cotenou, Benin, Africa.
⚡ Juba in *The Gladiator*
⚚ Migrated to Paris when he was 13. Unable to find work, he lived under bridges and foraged for food in trashcans and dumpsters. He was rescued from poverty and became a fashion model, appearing in music videos. Signed a contract with clothing designer Thierry Mugler. He is only the fourth African to be nominated for an Oscar. Learned how to speak English by watching television.
Major Awards: ISA

Houseman, John

1953-(BP) *Julius Caesar*
★ 1973-(BSA) *The Paper Chase*
▦ Born *Jacques Haussmann* on 9/22/1902 in Bucharest, Romania. Died 10/31/88 of spinal cancer.
⚡ Professor Kingsfield in Oscar'd role.
⚚ He was an actor, producer, scriptwriter, playwright, and director and co-founded the Mercury Theater with Orson Welles. He developed the story of *Citizen Kane*. Quit as VP of Selznick Productions when WW II broke out. Was chief of radio operations for the OWI. Over the years the films that he produced were nominated for twenty Oscars and won seven.
Major Awards: Oscar, NBR, GG, WOF

Howard, Leslie

1932/33-(BA) *Berkeley Square*
  Winner: Charles Laughton, *The Private Life of Henry the VIII*
1938-(BA) *Pygmalion*
  Winner: Spencer Tracy, *Boys Town*
▦ Born *Leslie Stainer* on 4/3/1893 in London, England. Died 6/2/43 in a plane crash.
⚡ Ashley Wilkes in *Gone with the Wind*.
⚚ Suffered from shell shock in WW I and received a medical discharge. He befriended Humphrey Bogart when he insisted he reprise his role of Duke

Mantee on film in *The Petrified Forest*. He lost his life on a secret decoy mission during WW II when his plane was shot down at sea by German fighters. They thought Winston Churchill was aboard.
Major Awards: WOF, VFF

Howard, Terrence

2005-(BA) *Hustle & Flow*
    Winner: Philip Seymour Hoffman, *Capote*
▪ Born 3/11/69 in Chicago, IL
🖋 DJ in nominated role.
🔍 Graduated from Pratt Institute majoring in chemical engineering. Discovered on the streets of New York by a casting director. Taught himself how to play the piano and guitar. During a flight from Toronto to Cleveland he got into a row with a stewardess and upon landing was tossed in the can for a night. His father spent five years in jail when he defended himself against an assailant with a knife.
Major Awards: LAFC, NBR, SAG

Howard, Trevor

1960-(BA) *Sons and Lovers*
    Winner: Burt Lancaster, *Elmer Gantry*
▪ Born 9/29/16 in Cliftonville, England.
    Died 1/7/88 of influenza and bronchitis.
🖋 Walter Moral in nominated role.
🔍 He was trained at the Royal Academy of Dramatic Arts. While fighting in WW II with the Royal Artillery he was wounded in battle and was honorably discharged. He had a clause written into all of his movie contracts that he would not be working when Britain's International cricket team was playing. One of Britain's most polished actors, he never forgot his lines.
Major Awards: Emmy, BAFTA

Hudson, Jennifer

★ 2006-(BSA) *Dreamgirls*
▪ Born 9/12/81 in Chicago, IL

🖋 Effie White in nominated role.
🔍 Started her singing career at age seven singing gospel songs in her church choir. Her prowess landed her a job on the Disney cruise lines. She opted to jump ship, literally, when her contract came up for renewal. She landed a spot on *American Idol* and didn't win. Those people really know how to judge talent. However it was a launching pad for her singing and acting career. She beat out over 780 hopefuls for the *Dreamgirls* role.
Major Awards: NBR, NYFC,

Hudson, Kate

2000-(BSA) *Almost Famous*
    Winner: Marcia Gay Harden, *Pollock*
▪ Born 4/19/79 in Los Angeles, CA
🖋 Penny Lane in nominated role.
🔍 Daughter of Goldie Hawn and Bill Hudson. Her adoptive father, Kurt Russell, and her mom raised her. She is estranged from her father. She enjoys playing the guitar, writes her own music, and is into arts and crafts. Her brother nicknamed her "Hammerhead." Started the production company Cosmic Entertainment with her mother and Kurt Russell. Speaks French and is a yoga practitioner. Was married to Chris Robinson of the Black Crowes.
Major Awards: GG, Grammy, LAFC, KCFCC

Hudson, Rock

1956-(BA) *Giant*
    Winner: Yul Brynner, *The King and I*
▪ Born *Roy Harold Scherer Jr.* on 11/17/25 in
    Winnetka, IL. Died 10/2/85 of AIDS.
🖋 Charming leading man and first Hollywood star to admit his homosexuality and go public with the details of his battle with AIDS.
🔍 During WW II he was an airplane mechanic. Worked as a movie usher, mail carrier, telephone lineman, and truck driver. His high school classmates were Ann-Margret and Charlton Heston. Starred in TV series *McMillan and Wife*. One line in his first movie *Fighter Squadron* took 38 takes. His long-time

companion, Marc Christian, successfully sued his estate after his death.
Major Awards: GG, GGWFF, WOF

Huffman, Felicity

2005-(BSA) *Transamerica*
   Winner: Rachel Weisz, *The Constant Gardner*
- Born 12/9/62 in Bedford, NY
- Lynette Scavo on TV's *Desperate Housewives*
- She has six sisters and she is the youngest. Graduated from New York University's Tisch School of the Arts. Attended RADA. Met future husband William Macy while attending his school the Atlantic Theater Company. Her idol is Tina Turner, and she got to sing backup for Turner on the *Oprah Winfrey Show*. Her nickname is Flicka.
Major Awards: Emmy, GG, NBR, SAG

Hulce, Tom

1984-(BA) *Amadeus*
   Winner: F. Murray Abraham, *Amadeus*
- Born 12/6/53 in White Water, WI
- Mozart in nominated role.
- Attended North Carolina School of arts. Originally wanted to become a singer until his voice changed. Once worked as a ticket taker and usher. After his movie *Amadeus*, Mozart music sales shot up 30 percent. Directed eight-hour stage production of *The Cider House Rules*, which required two days to see the whole performance.
Major Awards: Emmy, DDA

Hull, Josephine

★ 1950-(BSA) *Harvey*
- Born *Josephine Sherwood* on 1/3/1886 in Newtonville, MA. Died 3/12/57 of a cerebral hemorrhage.
- Veta Louise Simmons in Oscar'd role.
- Graduated from Radcliffe and the New England Conservatory of Music. She was a star on Broadway for 50 years. Actor Henry Hull was her brother-in-law. Despite her thespian prowess she only appeared in five movies. Made her TV debut in 1949 on *The Ford Theater Hour*.
Major Awards: GG, WOF

Hunnicut, Arthur

1952-(BSA) *The Big Sky*
   Winner: Anthony Quinn, *Viva Zapata!*
- Born 2/17/11 in Gravelly, AR. Died 9/26/70 of mouth cancer.
- Uncle Zeb in nominated role.
- Attended Arkansas State College in hopes of becoming a teacher but had to drop out due to the lack of funds. He picked up a stage job at a theater in Massachusetts. Eventually made his way to Broadway and starred in the production of *Tobacco Road*. It was then Hollywood took notice. He was the original grizzled western old-timer.

Hunt, Helen

★ 1997-(BA) *As Good as It Gets*
- Born 6/15/63 in Los Angeles, CA.
- Jamie Buchman in TV comedy *Mad About You*
- She got her first staring role at age nine on the TV movie *Pioneer Woman*. Dropped out of UCLA after one month. Hates signing autographs, only signs with an "H." Nominated seven times for an Emmy and has won four times. She is only the second actor to win a Golden Globe, Emmy, and Oscar in the same year (Liza Minnelli was the first). She likes to vacation in Hawaii. She was making $1 million per episode in the last year of production of the television series *Mad About You.*
Major Awards: Oscar, GG, Emmy (4), SAG, PC

Hunt, Linda

★ 1983-(BSA) *The Year of Living Dangerously*
- Born 4/2/45 in Morristown, NJ
- Billy Kwan in Oscar'd role.

She is only 4'9" tall and weighs a little over 80 pounds. She studied directing at the prestigious Goodman Theater School in Chicago. First performer to win an Oscar portraying someone of the opposite sex. She was the narrator of the Oscar-nominated documentary *Amazon*. She is a charter member of the Interlochen Arts Academy.
Major Awards: Oscar, NYFC, LAFC, NBR, Obie

Hunter, Holly

1987-(BA) *Broadcast News*
    Winner: Cher, *Moonstruck*
1993-(BSA) *The Firm*
    Winner: Anna Paquin, *The Piano*
★ 1993-(BA) *The Piano*
2003-(BSA) *Thirteen*
    Winner: Renèe Zellweger, *Cold Mountain*
◾ Born 3/20/58 in Conyers, GA.
Ada McGrath in Oscar'd role.
The youngest of seven children. She was raised on a huge cattle and hay farm in Georgia where she drove a tractor. Started acting at age nine. Graduated from Carnegie Mellon. A very accomplished pianist, she played all of her own music in *The Piano*. Frances McDormand was her roommate in New York. Her uncle was the first commander of the USAF Thunderbirds, and her cousin is pro baseball player Tim Salmon.
Major Awards: Oscar, CA, Emmy, NBR, NSFC, NYFC, LAFC, Cannes, GG, Australian Film Institute, BAFTA, BIFF, BSFC, Sundance, WOF

Hunter, Kim

★ 1951-(BSA) *A Streetcar Named Desire*
◾ Born *Janet Cole* on 11/12/22 in Detroit, MI. Died 9/11/2002 of a heart attack.
Stella Kowalski in Oscar'd role.
Her name appeared in a communist pamphlet, and she was blacklisted in the '50s. She recovered her career when the pamphlet was discredited. Her testimony to the New York Supreme Court cleared many other actors who were erroneously accused. Wrote an autobiographical cookbook called *Loose in the Kitchen*.
Major Awards: Oscar, GG, WOF

Hurt, John

1978-(BSA) *Midnight Express*
    Winner: Christopher Walken, *The Deer Hunter*
1980-(BA) *The Elephant Man*
    Winner: Robert DeNiro, *Raging Bull*
◾ Born 1/22/40 in Shirebrook, Derbyshire, England.
Kane, officer on the *Nostromo* in *Alien*— the monster jumps out of his chest.
He is the son of a clergyman. Attended RADA. Studied to be a painter at the Grimsby Art School. His longtime companion and fiancée Marie Pierrot tragically died in a riding accident. He was awarded Commander of the British Empire by the Queen in 2004. Received Honorary Doctorate degree from Hull University in Yorkshire.
Major Awards: GG, BAFTA, Obie, WOF

Hurt, William

★ 1985-(BA) *Kiss of the Spider Woman*
1986-(BA) *Children of a Lesser God*
    Winner: Paul Newman, *The Color of Money*
1987-(BA) *Broadcast News*
    Winner: Michael Douglas, *Wall Street*
2005-(BSA) *A History of Violence*
    Winner: George Clooney, *Syriana*
◾ Born 3/20/50 in Washington DC.
Luis Molina in Oscar'd role.
His father worked in the State Department. He has lived in the South Pacific, Europe, England, and Africa. He is the stepson to *Time-Life* empire heir Henry Luce III. Studied theology for three years. Flies his own plane and speaks French fluently. He was awarded an Honorary Doctorate from Tufts University. Once dated co-star Marlee Matlin.
Major Awards: Cannes, NBR, LAFC, BAFTA, Obie, NYFC

Hussey, Ruth

1940-(BSA) *The Philadelphia Story*
  Winner: Jane Darwell, *The Grapes of Wrath*
▪ Born *Ruth Carol O'Rourke* on 10/30/14 in Providence, RI. Died 4/19/2005 of a botched appendectomy.
🖋 Cynical photographer Elizabeth Imbrei.
🔍 Graduated from University of Michigan. Worked as a fashion commentator and model. Was queen of the MGM "B movie unit" in the '30s and '40s. Married radio magnate Robert Longenecker and went into semi-retirement. She was a distant relative of one of the original purchasers of Nantucket Island.
Major Awards: WOF

Huston, Angelica

★ 1985-(BSA) *Prizzi's Honor*
1989-(BSA) *Enemies, A Love Story*
  Winner: Brenda Fricker, *My Left Foot*
1990-(BA) *The Grifters*
  Winner: Kathy Bates, *Misery*
▪ Born 7/8/51 in Santa Monica, CA.
🖋 Maerose Prizzi in Oscar'd role
🔍 She is the third generation of Hustons to win an Oscar. Once modeled for *Vogue* magazine. She has dual citizenship in the U.S. and Ireland. Suffered from dyslexia as a child. Her mother, ballerina Ricki Soma, died in an auto accident when she was 18. Gave Jack Nicholson the boot after a 17-year relationship after discovering he had a love child with a 26-year-old waitress.
Major Awards: Oscar, NBR, NSFC, LAFC, NYFC

Huston, John

1940-(BW) *Dr. Ehrlich's Magic Bullet*
1941-(BW) *Sergeant York*
1941-(BW) *The Maltese Falcon*
★ 1948-(BEST DIRECTOR) *The Treasure of the Sierra Madre*

★ 1948-(Best Writer) *The Treasure of the Sierra Madre*
1950-(BD) *The Asphalt Jungle*
1950-(BW) *The Asphalt Jungle*
1951-(BD) *The African Queen*
1951-(BW) *The African Queen*
1952-(BD) *Moulin Rouge*
1952-(BP) *Moulin Rouge*
1957-(BW) *Heaven Knows, Mr. Allison*
1963-(BSA) *The Cardinal*
  Winner: Melvyn Douglas, *Hud*
1975-(BW) *The Man Who Would Be King*
1985-(BD) *Prizzi's Honor*
▪ Born 8/5/1906 in Nevada, MO. Died 8/28/87 of emphysema.
🖋 Noah Cross in *Chinatown* (#16 on AFI's Villain List)
🔍 Won Amateur lightweight boxing championship in California. Was an officer in the Mexican Cavalry. At a party in Hollywood he took exception to a catty remark directed at his date by Errol Flynn. It is reported that both men needed medical attention after the brawl. He didn't fare so well with John Wayne, when directing him in the *Barbarian and the Geisha*. He pressed the wrong buttons with the Duke and was knocked out cold. He is the only person to have directed both a parent and a sibling to Academy Award wins. He was the oldest nominee for director at age 79 years, 7 months, and he was a true Hollywood eccentric.
Major Awards: Oscar, GG, LAFC, NBR, NSFC, NYFC, WGA, SWG, Cannes, AFI's Life Achievement, BSFC, ISA, KCFCC, VFF, DGA, WOF

Huston, Walter

1936-(BA) *Dodsworth*
  Winner: Paul Muni, *The Life of Louis Pasteur*
1941-(BA) *The Devil and Daniel Webster*
  Winner: Gary Cooper, *Sergeant York*
1942-(BSA) *Yankee Doodle Dandy*
  Winner: Van Heflin, *Johnny Eager*
★ 1948-(BSA) *The Treasure of the Sierra Madre*
▪ Born *Walter Houghston* 4/6/1884 in Toronto, Ontario, Canada. Died 4/7/50 of an aneurysm.

🎗 Howard, the wise miner in Oscar'd role.

🔍 He was a lifelong sufferer of stage fright. As a young man he had an engineering job, which, in his attempts to fix the town reservoir, nearly caused widespread flooding. In 1938 he was the first actor to introduce a song in a movie that would become a No. 1 hit, "September Song." Father of John Huston.

Major Awards: Oscar, NBR, NYFC, GG, WOF

Hutton, Timothy

★ 1980-(BSA) *Ordinary People*

▪ Born 8/16/60 in Malibu, CA

🎗 Conrad Jarrett in Oscar'd role.

🔍 Son of actor Jim Hutton. At the time was the youngest actor to win a BSA Oscar. Once directed a rock video for the band The Cars. His wife Aurore is the niece of former French President Valery Giscard d'Estaing. He is the youngest Best Supporting Actor winner at age 20 years, 7 months. In 2004 he was elected president of the exclusive Players Club in New York City.

Major Awards: Oscar, LAFC, KCFCC, GG

Hyer, Martha

1958-(BSA) *Some Came Running*
    Winner: Wendy Hiller, *Separate Tables*

▪ Born 8/10/24 in Fort Worth, TX.

🎗 Gwen French in nominated role.

🔍 Graduated from Northwestern University where her classmates were Charlton Heston and Patricia Neal. Auditioned for Janet Leigh's role in Hitchcock's *Psycho*. Universal Studios labeled her the answer to MGM's Grace Kelly. She was married to legendary Hollywood producer Hal B. Wallis until his death.

Major Awards: BW

Ireland, John

1949-(BSA) *All the King's Men*
    Winner: Dean Jagger, *12 O'clock High*

▪ Born 1/30/14 in Vancouver, Canada.
    Died 3/21/92 of leukemia.

🎗 Jack Burden in nominated role.

🔍 Began his show biz career as a professional swimmer in a water carnival. He was the first actor from Vancouver to be nominated for an Oscar. Wed to actress Joanne Dru. Brother-in-law to *Hollywood Squares* emcee Peter Marshall. John was quite a Romeo off the screen and his "physical endowment" was common knowledge among Hollywood starlets.

Major Awards: WOF

Irons, Jeremy

★ 1990-(BA) *Reversal of Fortune*

▪ Born 9/19/48 in Crowes, Isle of Wight, England.

🎗 Claus Von Bulow in Oscar'd role.

🔍 Originally wanted to be a veterinarian. Started out as a busker, a person who sings and plays a guitar to pull in people, outside of movie theaters. He was also a stage manager, housecleaner, and gardener. He is a man of many talents. Along with the guitar he plays the clarinet and fiddle, excels in rugby, and is an excellent horseman and skier. He is winner of the rare Triple Crown of acting.

Major Awards: Oscar, Tony, Emmy, NSFC, LAFC, NYFC, GG, César

Irving, Amy

1983-(BSA) *Yentl*
    Winner: Linda Hunt, *The Year of Living Dangerously*

▪ Born 9/10/53 in Palo Alto, CA.

🎗 Hadass in nominated role.

🔍 Her late father Jules Irving founded the Actors Workshop in San Francisco. She made her first stage appearance at the age of ten and her Broadway debut at age 17. Once married to director Steven Spielberg. It is reported she received a cool 100 million when their split was official. In 1990 had a child out of wedlock with Brazilian director Bruno Barreto.

Major Awards: Obie, SAG

Ives, Burl

★ 1958-(BSA) *The Big Counrty*

▨ Born *Burle Icle Ivanhoe* in Hunt City Township, IL. Died 4/15/95 of cancer of the mouth.

✐ Big Daddy in *Cat on a Hot Tin Roof a*nd singing the yuletide favorite song, "A Holly Jolly Christmas"

✎ Played fullback for a semi-professional football team. Traveled the country as a busker, singing ballads and playing the banjo. Recorded over 50 albums on Columbia and Decca records. He did many free benefits for the Boy Scouts, Indians, and children's medicine. Poet Carl Sandburg called him "the mightiest ballad singer in this century." He was a 33rd degree Mason.

Major Awards: Oscar, Grammy, GG

Jackson, Glenda

★ 1970-(BA) *Women in Love*

1971-(BA) *Sunday, Bloody Sunday*
    Winner: Jane Fonda, *Klute*

★ 1973-(BA) *A Touch of Class*

1975-(BA) *Hedda*
    Winner: Louise Fletcher, *One Flew Over the Cuckoo's Nest*

▨ Born 5/9/36 in Birkenhead, Cheshire, England

✐ Elizabeth I in the BBC TV production.

✎ Dropped out of school at the age of 16 to join an amateur theater group. Is afraid to fly. Appointed Commander of the British Empire in 1978. She is the first and only member of the British Parliament to win an Oscar. She resigned from her civic duties to run for mayor of London. Nominated for a Tony four times.

Major Awards: Oscar, Emmy, NBR, NSFC, NYFC, GG, BAFTA, DDA

Jackson, Samuel L.

1994-(BSA) *Pulp Fiction*
    Winner: Martin Landau, *Ed Wood*

▨ Born 12/21/48 in Washington DC.

✐ Jules the hit man in nominated role.

✎ To overcome a severe childhood stuttering problem he got into acting at the suggestion of his speech therapist. Graduated from Moorhead University despite being expelled for a radical sit in protest. He is an accomplished French horn and trumpet player. He was a stand-in for Bill Cosby on the *Bill Cosby Show* for three years. He was an admitted drug user and spent time in rehab to kick his habit. He is an avid golfer with a scratch handicap. He was an usher at Martin Luther King's funeral.

Major Awards: Cannes, NYFC, BAFTA, BIFF, ISA, KCFCC, WOF

Jaeckel, Richard

1971-(BSA) *Sometimes a Great Notion*
    Winner: Ben Johnson, *The Last Picture Show*

▨ Born 10/10/26 in Long Beach, NY.
    Died 6/14/97 of cancer.

✐ Sergeant Clyde Bowren in *The Dirty Dozen*.

✎ Louella Parsons, Hollywood gossip columnist, got him his first job as a mailman at 20th Century Fox Studio. Served in the Navy during WW II. Paul Newman wanted Jaeckel for his nominated role so much that he battled with the Hollywood brass until they relented. His son Barry was a former PGA golfer. Had to file for bankruptcy in his later life—he lost his home and retired to the Hollywood Retirement Center.

Major Award: Golden Boot

Jaffe, Sam

1950-(BSA) *The Asphalt Jungle*
    Winner: George Sanders, *All About Eve*

▨ Born *Shalom Jaffe* 3/8/1891 in New York, NY.
    Died 3/24/84 of cancer.

✐ Doc Riedenschneider in nominated role.
    Grand Lama in *Lost Horizon*, Dr. Zorba in TV's *Ben Casey*

✎ His mother was a Russian actress and his father an Irish jeweler. He was a teacher and dean of math at the Bronx Cultural Institute before he started a stage and movie career. Founded the Equity Library Theater for young actors in New York. He was

victimized by the Communist witch-hunt of the '50s and was blacklisted for years.
Major Awards: Venice Film Festival

Jagger, Dean

★ 1949-(BSA) *12 O'clock High*
▨ Born *Dean Jeffries* on 11/7/1903 in Lima, OH. Died 2/5/91 of heart disease.
✍ Major Harvey Stovall in Oscar'd role.
✎ Dropped out of high school twice and then ended up graduating from Wabash College in Indiana. After graduation he was a teacher for a short time. Appeared in vaudeville and touring groups before debuting on Broadway. Played high school principal Albert Vance in TV series *Mr. Novak*.
Major Awards: Oscar, Venice Film Festival, WOF

Jandl, Ivan

★ 1948-Honorary Oscar, *The Search*
▨ Born 1/24/37 in Prague, Czechoslovakia. Died 1987. He was worked to death in a Communist gulag.
✍ Karl Malik in honored role.
✎ Director Fred Zinnemann plucked Ivan out of a camp for displaced children for the role of an Auschwitz survivor. He spoke no English and learned his lines by rote. He gave so much hope to the people of Czechoslovakia that the Russians pulled him out of school and placed him in a labor camp working in a rock quarry. He was condemned to work there until he died at the age of 49.

Jannings, Emil

★ 1927/28-(BA) *The Last Command*, *The Way of all Flesh*
▨ Born *Theodor Janenz* on 7/23/1884 in Roschach, Switzerland. Died 1/3/50 of cancer.
✍ Grand Duke Sergius Alexander in Oscar'd role.
✎ He ran away from home at the age of 16 to be a sailor. He discovered acting when he returned and

went on to be an important stage actor of his era. Being a known supporter of the Nazi ideology he was used by Joseph Goebbels for propaganda purposes. After WW II he was blacklisted and died a lonely and bitter man. First actor to win an Oscar.
Major Awards: WOF

Jarman, Claude

★ 1946-Honorary Oscar, *The Yearling*
▨ Born 9/27/34 in Nashville, TN.
✍ Jody Baxter in honored role.
✎ MGM had a nationwide search, and he was selected for the coveted role. He graduated from Vanderbilt University and served in the Navy for three years. His career stalled and he became an executive for Amway and eventually was director of Cultural Affairs for the city of San Francisco. His last screen appearance was on the TV mini-series *Centennial*.

Jean-Baptiste, Marianne

1996-(BSA) *Secrets and Lies*
  Winner: Juliette Binoche, *The English Patient*
▨ Born 4/26/67 in London, England.
✍ Hortense Cumberbatch in nominated role.
✎ First black British actress to be nominated for an Oscar. Amazingly she was also the first black actress not to receive the NAACP Image Award for being nominated. She was trained at RADA and has performed at the Royal National Theater. She is singer, songwriter, and composer recording a hit album in England. Composed the music score for the film *Career Girls*.

Johns, Glynis

1960-(BA) *The Sundowners*
  Winner: Shirley Jones, *Elmer Gantry*
▨ Born 10/5/23 in Pretoria, South Africa
✍ Mrs. Firth in nominated role.
✎ She made her screen debut on the London stage when she was 12 years old. Her mother was a concert

pianist and the family toured all over Europe. Once starred in the ABC TV series *Batman* as villainess Lady Penelope Peasoup. Stephen Sondheim wrote "Send in the Clowns" especially for her in his show *A Little Night Music*.

Major Awards: Tony

Johnson, Ben

★ 1971-(BSA) *The Last Picture Show*

▓ Born 6/13/18 in Pawhuska, OK. Died 4/8/96 of a heart attack.

✍ Sam the Lion in Oscar'd role.

✇ Started out as a horse wrangler and stuntman and doubled for John Wayne, Gary Cooper, and James Stewart. In 1953 won the World Calf Roping championship as did his father years earlier. His award was stolen in 1976 and was returned ten years later by the guilt-ridden thief. He was inducted into the Rodeo Hall of Fame in 1982. He was part Osage Indian.

Major Awards: NBR, NYFC, GG, BW, BAFTA, WOF

Johnson, Dame Celia

1946-(BA) *Brief Encounter*
   Winner: Olivia de Havilland, *To Each His Own*

▓ Born 12/18//1908 in Elleuker Gate, Richmond, Surrey, England. Died 4/26/82 of a stroke.

✍ Laura Jesson in nominated role.

✇ She was trained at RADA. She was knighted Dame Commander of the British Empire. Her husband of 36 years was travel writer Peter Fleming. He was the older brother to Ian Fleming, author of the James Bond novels.

Major Awards: NBR, BAFTA, NYFC, NBR

Jolie, Angelina

★ 1999-(BSA) *Girl, Interrupted*

▓ Born *Angelina Jolie Voight* on 6/4/75 in Los Angeles, CA.

✍ Lara Croft *Tomb Raider*

✇ Daughter to actor Jon Voight. Godmother is actress Jacqueline Bisset and godfather is Maxmilian Schell. She has a morbid infatuation about death—had aspirations to be a funeral director, has a death tattoo in Japanese, gave ex-husband Billy Bob Thornton twin grave plots as a anniversary present, and had their wills signed in blood! She was made a citizen of Cambodia by the King for her environmental efforts. She and current partner Brad Pitt are raising several children.

Major Awards: Oscar, NBR, GG, SAG, PC

Jones, Carolyn

1957-(BSA) *The Bachelor Party*
   Winner: Miyoshi Umeki, *Sayonara*

▓ Born *Carolyn Sue Baker* on 4/28/29 in Amarillo, TX. Died 8/3/83 of colon cancer.

✍ Morticia in TV series *The Addams Family*

✇ Her father abandoned the family when she was five years old. Her grandfather paid her tuition to the Pasadena Playhouse. Not satisfied with her nose, she underwent a painful rhinoplasty operation before auditioning for her first movie role. Once married to movie mogul, Aaron Spelling. She was part Indian (Cherokee).

Major Awards: GG

Jones, James Earl

1970-(BA) *The Great White Hope*
   Winner: George C. Scott, *Patton*

▓ Born 1/17/31 in Arkabutla, MS.

✍ Jack Jefferson in nominated role. Voice of Darth Vader in the *Star Wars* trilogy

✇ Son of a prizefighter, Robert Earl Jones, a.k.a. Battling Stoval. Suffered from a severe stuttering problem as a child and had to communicate through notes. Studied to become a doctor before switching to drama and graduating from the University of Michigan. He was a member of the Pershing Rifles in the ROTC program whose members were Gen. Colin Powell and G. Gordon Liddy. He became an officer in the Army. He is part Indian.

Major Awards: Tony, Emmy, CA, DDA, OCC, GG, NBR, KCFCC

Jones, Jennifer

★ 1943-(BA) *The Song of Bernadette*
1944-(BSA) *Since You Went Away*
    Winner: Ethel Barrymore, *None but the Lonely Heart*
1945-(BA) *Love Letters*
    Winner: Joan Crawford, *Mildred Pierce*
1946-(BA) *Duel in the Sun*
    Winner: Olivia de Havilland, *To Each His Own*
1955-(BA) *Love Is a Many Splendored Thing*
    Winner: Anna Magnani, *The Rose Tattoo*
▧ Born *Phyllis Isley* on 3/2/19 in Tulsa, OK.
⟋ Bernadette Soubirous in Oscar'd role.
⚲ Once married to actor Robert Walker. Discovered by legendary movie producer David O. Selznick. Directing her career, he immediately changed her name. They eventually married in 1949 and were together until his death 16 years later. After his death she lost interest in acting and married philanthropist Norton Simon. In 1967 she failed in an attempted suicide. Her daughter Mary tried the same thing in 1976 but tragically succeeded.
Major Awards: Oscar, GG, DDA, WOF

Jones, Shirley

★ 1960-(BSA) *Elmer Gantry*
▧ Born 3/31/34 in Smithton, PA.
⟋ Lulu Bains in Oscar'd role and mother on TV series *The Partridge Family*
⚲ Took singing lessons at age six and began formal training at age twelve. Her mother named her after Shirley Temple. Won Miss Pittsburgh Pageant in 1952. Got the lead on Broadway in *South Pacific* at age 18. Originally wanted to be a veterinarian. Stepmother to teen singing idol David Cassidy. As of this writing she has been married to comedian Marty Ingals for 32 years. Received an Honorary Doctorate from Park Point College.
Major Awards: Oscar, NBR, WOF

Jones, Tommy Lee

1991-(BSA) *JFK*
    Winner: Jack Palance, *City Slickers*
★ 1993-(BSA) *The Fugitive*
▧ Born 9/15/46 in San Saba, TX.
⟋ Sam Gerard in Oscar'd role.
⚲ Graduated from Harvard cum laude. Played guard on the football team. His college roommate was Al Gore. He is a champion polo player. Owns a 3000-acre ranch in San Antonio. His ex-wife is sports writer Ring Lardner's granddaughter. He is first cousin to country singer Boxcar Willie. Speaks Spanish fluently.
Major Awards: Oscar, Emmy, LAFC, GG, Cannes, KCFCC, BW, WOF

Jurado, Katy

1954-(BSA) *Broken Lance*
    Winner: Eva Marie Saint, *On the Waterfront*
▧ Born *Maria Christina Jurado de Garcia* on 1/16/24 in Guadalajara, Jalisco Mexico. Died 7/5/2002 of a heart attack.
⟋ Helen Ramirez in *High Noon*
⚲ Worked as a radio reporter, bullfight critic, and movie columnist. Discovered by John Wayne at a bullfight. Once married to actor Ernest Borgnine who described her as beautiful but a tiger. First Mexican actress to be nominated for an Oscar. In the movie *Stay Away* she gained 22 pounds in 22 days to land the part of Annie Lightgood.
Major Awards: GG, WOF

Kahn, Madeline

1973-(BSA) *Paper Moon*
    Winner: Tatum O'Neal, *Paper Moon*
1974-(BSA) *Blazing Saddles*
    Winner: Ingrid Bergman, *Murder on the Orient Express*
▧ Born *Madeline Gail Wolfson* on 9/29/42 in Chelsea, MA. Died 12/3/99 of ovarian cancer.
⟋ The floozy Trixie Delight in *Paper Moon*

She attended Hofstra University and majored in speech therapy. She was going to get her Doctorate but acting sidetracked her. She originally studied to be an opera singer. Starred in the TV series *Oh Madeline*. Battled ovarian cancer for over a year before succumbing to the disease—a real trooper to the end.

Major Awards: Tony, KCFCC

Kaminska, Ida

1966-(BA) *The Shop on Main Street*
  Winner: Elizabeth Taylor, *Butterfield 8*
Born 9/18/1899 in Odessa, Ukraine. Died 5/21/80 of heart disease.
Rozalie Lautmannova in nominated role.
Started her acting career at age five. Performed in the Yiddish theater in Poland prior to WW II. After the war she founded the Jewish State Theater in Warsaw where she often directed. Migrated to the United States and eventually moved to Israel.

Major Awards: Cannes

Kane, Carol

1975-(BA) *Hester Street*
  Winner: Louise Fletcher, *One Flew over the Cuckoo's Nest*
Born 6/18/52 in Cleveland, OH.
Simka, Andy Kauffman's wife, in TV comedy *Taxi*
At age 12 she was sent to a psychotherapist and remained a patient for 15 years. Started acting career at age 14. Early on she sometimes went by the stage name Lisa LeBlanc. Debuted in 1962 on the TV Western series *The Virginian*. Noted for her versatility, she has played a wide variety of offbeat and bizarre characters: immigrants, witches, peasants, and she has done voice-overs in animated movies.

Major Awards: Emmy

Kaye, Danny

1954-Honorary Oscar
Born *David Daniel Kominski* on 1/18/1913 in Brooklyn, NY. Died 3/3/87 of hepatitis due to contaminated blood during heart bypass surgery.
The Court Jester. The "pellet with the poison's in the vessel with the pestle" routine
Dropped out of school at the age of 13 and worked as a busboy in the Catskills. He once was a soda jerk and insurance salesman. Besides being a singer, dancer, and actor, he was a licensed airplane pilot, gourmet cook, and symphony conductor and was once a part owner of the Seattle Mariners. Goodwill ambassador for UNICEF. Bob Hope was his favorite comedian.

Major Awards: Jean Hersholt, Emmy, GG, SAGLA, Tony, WOF

Keaton, Buster

1959-Honorary Oscar
Born *John Francis Keaton, Jr.* on 10/4/1895 in Piqua, KS. Died 2/1/66 of lung cancer.
Moniker "Old Stone Face"
His godfather was the great magician Harry Houdini. It was he who gave him the nickname Buster. He never had a stunt double. Stated he learned everything about show biz from Fatty Arbuckle. He was honored by being placed on a commemorative 29-cent stamp. Voted by *Entertainment Weekly* as the 7th Greatest Director of all time.

Major Awards: WOF

Keaton, Diane

★ 1977-(BA) *Annie Hall*
1981-(BA) *Reds*
  Winner: Katharine Hepburn, *On Golden Pond*
1996-(BA) *Marvin's Room*
  Winner: Frances McDormand, *Fargo*
2003-(BA) *Something's Gotta Give*
  Winner: Charlize Theron, *Monster*

■ Born Diane Hall on 1/5/46 in Los Angeles, CA

✎ Annie Hall in Oscar'd role.

🔍 She was in the original cast of *Hair* and was the only member of the production who refused to remove her clothes. She once sang for the band the Roadrunners. She goes for psychoanalysis on a weekly basis. Was romantically involved with Warren Beatty and Woody Allen. While dating Woody Allen he wrote *Annie Hall* specifically for her. She has never been married.

Major Awards: Oscar, NYFC, NSFC, GG, NBR, BAFTA, DDA, KCFCC, WFCA

Kedrova, Lila

★ 1964-(BSA) *Zorba the Greek*

■ Born 10/9/18 in Petrograd, Russia.
Died 2/16/2000 of congestive heart failure.

✎ Madame Hortense in Oscar'd role.

🔍 She and her family fled Russia during the Stalin regime. Maintained homes in Toronto and Paris. Spoke Russian, French, English, and Italian fluently. Suffered from Alzheimer's and eventually died of congestive heart failure.

Major Awards: Oscar, Tony, GG

Keener, Catherine

1999-(BSA) *Being John Malkovich*
Winner: Angelina Jolie, *Girl, Interrupted*
2005-(BSA) *Capote*
Winner: Rachel Weisz, *The Constant Gardner*

■ Born 3/26/60 in Miami, FL.

✎ Maxie Lund in nominated role.

🔍 Graduated from Wheaton College majoring in History and English. She was bumped from a photography class in college and took an acting class, which led to Hollywood. Dubbed the queen of independent cinema in the '90s. She was an intern for the Hughes-Moss casting agency.

Major Awards: NYFC, BSFC, KCFCC, LAFC

Keitel, Harvey

1991-(BSA) *Bugsy*
Winner: Jack Palance, *City Slickers*

■ Born 5/13/39 in New York, NY.

✎ Mickey Cohan in nominated role.

🔍 Overcame a childhood stuttering problem. He was a borderline juvenile delinquent and truant. After dropping out of high school and at age 16 he joined the Marines and was sent to Lebanon. Struggling as an actor he worked as a court stenographer and sold woman's shoes. Once worked as a production assistant to Martin Scorsese. Listed in 1998 as one of *Entertainment Weekly*'s 25 Best Actors.

Major Awards: NSFC, Australian Film Institute, BIFF, ISA

Kellaway, Cecil

1948-(BSA) *The Luck of the Irish*
Winner: Walter Huston, *The Treasure of the Sierra Madre*
1967-(BSA) *Guess Who's Coming to Dinner*
Winner: George Kennedy, *Cool Hand Luke*

■ Born 8/22/1893 in Cape Town, South Africa.
Died 2/28/73 of arteriosclerosis.

✎ Horace the leprechaun in nominated role.

🔍 Moved to Australia at age 18 and began his successful stage and screen career. Cousin to actor Edmund Gwenn. He also wrote and directed several productions. His son, Dr. Peter Kellaway pioneered the use of electroencephalograms (EEGs) in diagnosing neurological disorders and testified at Jack Ruby's murder trial of Lee Harvey Oswald. He was the first actor from South Africa to be nominated.

Kellerman, Sally

1970-(BSA) *M*A*S*H*
Winner: Helen Hayes, *Airport*

■ Born 6/2/37 in Long Beach, CA

✎ Major "Hot Lips" Houlihan in nominated role

🔍 She almost turned down the role that made her famous. Director Robert Altman calmed her down

when she objected to the role. He stated that her unbridled rage is just what he wanted for the Major "Hot Lips" Houlihan part. Often makes nightclub singing appearances. Once was a TV and radio narrator.
Major Awards: NBR

Kelly, Gene

1945-(BA) *Anchors Aweigh*
Winner: Ray Milland, *The Lost Weekend*
1951-Honorary Oscar
Born Eugene Curran Kelly on 8/23/1912 in Pittsburgh, PA. Died 2/2/96 of a stroke.
Dancer and choreographer extraordinaire
Graduated from the University of Pittsburg with a degree in Economics. Enlisted in the Navy and was stationed stateside. Taught gymnastics at the YMCA. Childhood ambition was to be shortstop for the Pittsburg Pirates. Scar on cheek was the result of a bicycle accident as a child. His father was the road manager for Al Jolson. Awarded the National Medal of Freedom in 1994. He was known to be a perfectionist and was quite a taskmaster when teaching dancing.
Major Awards: CBD, NBR, SAGLA, BIFF, Emmy, César, AFI's Life Achievement, WOF

Kelly, Grace

1953-(BSA) *Mogambo*
Winner: Donna Reed, *From Here to Eternity*
★ 1954-(BA) *Country Girl*
Born 11/12/29 in Philadelphia, PA. Died 9/14/82 in an auto accident.
Princess Grace of Monaco.
Her mother was a cover girl and her father and brother were Olympic gold medalist oarsmen on America's rowing team. Her uncle George was a Pulitzer Prize–winning playwright. Met Prince Rainier of Monaco while filming *To Catch a Thief* and they were married shortly after. Before that he miffed the Kelly family when he demanded a dowry of two million dollars—and he got it! She was the first actress to appear on a stamp, in her case Monaco celebrating her marriage to the Prince. A commemorative U.S. stamp was issued in 1993 in her honor.
Major Awards: Oscar, GG, GGWFF, NYFC, NBR,WOF

Kelly, Nancy

1956-(BA) *The Bad Seed*
Winner: Ingrid Bergman, *Anastasia*
Born 3/25/21 in Lowell, MA. Died 1/21/1995 of diabetes.
Christine Penmark in *The Bad Seed*
Began as a baby model and child actor and later gravitated to radio for a short period. She made over 50 silent films during the '20s. In 1929 she was deemed the most photographed child in America. Once was married to actor Edmond O'Brien. He brother was Jack Kelly who was Bart Maverick on the TV western series.
Major Awards: Tony, WOF

Kennedy, Arthur

1949-(BSA) *Champion*
Winner: Dean Jagger, *12 O'Clock High*
1951-(BSA) *Bright Victory*
Winner: Humphrey Bogart, *The African Queen*
1955-(BSA) *Trial*
Winner: Jack Lemon, *Mister Roberts*
1957-(BSA) *Peyton Place*
Winner: Red Buttons, *Sayonara*
1958-(BSA) *Some Came Running*
Winner: Burl Ives, *The Big Country*
Born 12/17/1914 in Worcester, MA. Died 1/5/1990 of a brain tumor.
Biff in Arthur Miller's play *Death of a Salesman*
He began as a protégé of acting great James Cagney. Graduated from Carnegie-Mellon. Enlisted in the Army during WW II. Abruptly quit the business in the mid '80s and retired to a small town in the east. Although nominated five times, the Academy never honored him for his achievements.
Major Awards: GG, NYFC, Tony, WOF

Kennedy, George

★ 1967-(BSA) *Cool Hand Luke*
■ Born 2/18/1925 in New York, NY
✐ Dragline in Oscar'd role.
✎ Made his stage debut at age two. Enlisted in the Army during WW II and saw combat. Served for 16 years and later was an armed forces radio and TV officer. He served under General George Patton. He was a technical advisor for the TV series *Sgt. Bilko*. Starred in over 200 TV and film productions. Only actor to appear in all four *Airport* movies.
Major Awards: Oscar, WOF

Kerr, Deborah

1949-(BA) *Edward My Son*
    Winner: Olivia de Havilland, *The Heiress*
1953-(BA) *From Here to Eternity*
    Winner: Audrey Hepburn, *Roman Holiday*
1956-(BA) *The King and I*
    Winner: Ingrid Bergman, *Anastasia*
1957-(BA) *Heaven Knows, Mister Allison*
    Winner: Joanne Woodward, *The Three Faces of Eve*
1958-(BA) *Separate Tables*
    Winner: Susan Hayward, *I Want to Live*
1960-(BA) *The Sundowners*
    Winner: Elizabeth Taylor, *Butterfield 8*
1993-Honorary Oscar
■ Born *Deborah Jane Kerr-Trimmer* on 9/30/21 in Helensburgh, Scotland.
✐ Karen Holmes in *From Here to Eternity*
✎ Originally trained as a ballet dancer. Based on her performance in *Major Barbara*, MGM brought her to Hollywood to play opposite Clark Gable in *The Hucksters*. Her singing was dubbed by Marni Nixon in *The King and I*. She was awarded Commander of the British Empire in 1997. Only actress to be nominated six times for an Oscar and not win. She suffers from Parkinson's Disease.
Major Awards: NYFC, GG, GGWFF, BAFTA, WOF

Kidman, Nicole

2001-(BA) *Moulin Rouge*
    Winner: Halle Berry, *Monster's Ball*
★ 2002-(BA) *The Hours*
■ Born 6/20/67 in Honolulu, HI.
✐ Virginia Woolf in *The Hours*
✎ She dropped out of high school to pursue acting. First Australian actress to win an Oscar. She's a devoted member of the Church of Scientology. Won libel damages from the *London Daily*, the *Star*, and *Express on Sunday*. Australia's tenth-richest woman. *Entertainment Weekly*'s Entertainer of the Year in 2001. Once married to actor Tom Cruise.
Major Awards: Oscar, GG, NYFC, NBR, Saturn, Australian Film Institute, BAFTA, BIFF, BSFC, KCFCC, WOF

Kikuchi, Rinko

2006-(BSA) *Babel*
    Winner: Jennifer Hudson, *Dreamgirls*
■ Born 1/6/81 in Kanagana, Japan.
✐ Chieko in nominated role
✎ She is an expert motorcycle and horseback rider. She is also quite proficient at the Japanese arts of *Kenjutsu*, sword fighting; *Kyudo*, archery; and *Nihonbuyo*, dancing. She also knows sign language. She began her acting and modeling career at the age of 15, and she does commercials for Fujitsu.
Major Awards: NBR

Kingsly, Sir Ben

★ 1982-(BA) *Gandhi*
1991-(BSA) *Bugsy*
    Winner: Jack Palance, *City Slickers*
2001-(BSA) *Sexy Beast*
    Winner: James Broadbent, *Iris*
2003-(BA) *The House of Sand and Fog*
    Winner: Sean Penn, *Mystic River*
■ Born *Krishna Bhanji* on 12/31/43 in Snaiton, Yorkshire, England.

🍴 Title role as Mohandas K. Gandhi (#21 on AFI's Hero List)

🔍 His mother was a fashion model born in England and his father was a Kenyan born physician whose family was from India. His relatives' home state was Gujarat, India, the same state where Gandhi was born. Adopted stage name from his grandfather, called the "Clove King," who traded spices in Zanzibar. Writes music and plays guitar. The Beatles once told him to get into music or he'd never be happy. Knighted by Queen Elizabeth in 2001.

Major Awards: Oscar, SAG, NBR, NYFC, LAFC, GG, BAFTA, KCFCC, BSFC

Kinnear, Greg

1997-(BSA) *As Good As It Gets*
    Winner: Robin Williams, *Good Will Hunting*
🍴 Born 6/17/63 in Logansport, IN.
🍴 Simon Bishop in nominated role.
🔍 His father was a career diplomat for the U.S. State Department. Lived in Beirut, Lebanon until civil war broke out. Family moved to Greece where learned to speak the language fluently. Graduated from the University of Arizona with a degree in journalism and was hired by Empire Entertainment in Los Angeles as a Marketing Assistant.

Major Awards: NBR

Kirkland, Sally

1987-(BA) *Anna*
    Winner: Cher, *Moonstruck*
🍴 Born 10/31/44 in New York, NY.
🍴 Title role in *Anna*
🔍 Appeared on the cover of *Vogue* magazine as a teenager. First actress to appear nude in a Broadway play (*Sweet Eros*). Had a drug problem in 1964 and attempted suicide. She is an ordained minister of the Church of the Movement of Spiritual Inner Awareness and teaches yoga and meditation. Has received humanitarian awards from the Blue Cross and the Crippled Childrens' Society.

Major Awards: LAFC, GG, ISA

Kline, Kevin

★ 1988-(BSA) *A Fish Called Wanda*
🍴 Born 10/24/47 in St. Louis, MO
🍴 President Bill Mitchell in *Dave*
🔍 Graduated from the University of Indiana and the prestigious Juilliard. Turned down the role of Batman. Toured the U.S. with John Houseman's Acting Company. Known for his humility. Married to actress Phoebe Cates.

Major Awards: Oscar, Tony, Obie, WOF

Knight, Shirley

1960-(BSA) *The Dark at the Top of the Steps*
    Winner: Shirley Jones, *Elmer Gantry*
1962-(BSA) *Sweet Bird of Youth*
    Winner: Patty Duke, *The Miracle Worker*
🍴 Born 7/5/37 in Groessel, KS.
🍴 Heavenly Finley in *Sweet Bird of Youth*
🔍 Trained at the Pasadena Playhouse. Her classmates were Jack Nicholson and Dean Stockwell. Disenchanted with Hollywood, she left for roles on Broadway. Eventually she moved to England, staring in the British theater and marrying playwright John Hopkins. Nominated seven times for an Emmy—winning twice.

Major Awards: Emmy, Tony, GG

Knightley, Keira

2005-(BA) *Pride and Prejudice*
    Winner: Reese Witherspoon, *Walk the Line*
🍴 Born 3/26/85 in Teddington, Middlesex, England.
🍴 Elizabeth Bennet in nominated role.
🔍 She made her film debut at age nine. Diagnosed as a borderline dyslexic. Never took any formal acting lessons. She did a nude scene at the age of 16 in the movie *The Hole*. Enjoys painting. Considers herself a tomboy and doesn't like parties. Third youngest actress to be nominated for Best Actor Oscar.

Major Awards: London Critics Circle

Knox, Alexander

1944-(BA) *Wilson*
　　Winner: Bing Crosby, *Going My Way*
▧ Born 1/16/1907 in Strathroy, Ontario,
　　Canada. Died 4/25/1995 of bone cancer.
▨ President Woodrow Wilson in title role.
✎ Graduated from the University of Western Ontario. After a successful career on the British stage
came to Hollywood in 1941. Landed the role of the
ship bookkeeper to Wolf Larson (E.G. Robinson)
in *The Sea Wolf*. In addition to his thespian talents
he was a screenwriter, playwright, mystery writer,
and novelist.
Major Awards: GG

Kohner, Susan

1959-(BSA) *Imitation of Life*
　　Winner: Shelly Winters, *The Diary of Anne
　　Frank*
▧ Born 11/11/36 in Los Angeles, CA.
▨ Sara Jane in nominated role.
✎ Her mother, Lupita Tovar, was a star in the Mexican cinema. Portrayed a light-skinned black girl in
nominated role, a casting choice that would never
happen in today's racially sensitive society. She serves
on the Board of Directors for the Julliard School
of Music and hosts a weekly radio program for the
blind. Retired from films in 1964.
Major Awards: GG

Korjus, Miliza

1938-(BSA) *The Great Waltz*
　　Winner: Faye Bainter, *Jezebel*
▧ Born 8/18/1900 in Warsaw, Poland.
　　Died 4/25/80 of bone cancer.
▨ Carla Donner in nominated role.
✎ She was trained as an opera singer at the Kiev
Conservatory. Two weeks before starting production
on her second movie she was in an auto accident
which almost cost her life. The doctors were within
an inch of having to amputate her leg. It was the last
and only American picture she ever made.

Kruschen, Jack

1960, (BSA) *The Apartment*
　　Winner: Peter Ustinov, *Spartacus*
▧ Born 3/20/22 in Winnepeg, Manitoba,
　　Canada. Died 4/2/2002 of natural causes.
▨ Jake Birnbaum in *McLintock*
✎ Starred in the first episode of the TV detective
series *Dragnet* in 1951. Very prolific and versatile
character actor who always was employed. Appeared
in 88 movies and over 100 television productions
either as the bully, staunch friend, ally, or dependable sidekick.

Ladd, Diane

1974-(BSA) *Alice Doesn't Live Here Anymore*
　　Winner: Ingrid Bergman, *Murder on the
　　Orient Express*
1990-(BSA) *Wild at Heart*
　　Winner: Whoopi Goldberg, *Ghost*
1991-(BSA) *Rambling Rose*
　　Winner: Mercedes Ruehl, *The Fisher King*
▧ Born *Rose Diane Ladner* on 11/29/39 in
　　Mewridian, MO.
▨ Marietta Pace in *Wild at Heart*
✎ Once was a model in New York and a dancer
at the Copacabana nightclub. Her ex-husband is
actor Bruce Dern, and she is the mother of actress
Laura Dern. First cousin to playwright Tennessee
Williams.
Major Awards: GG, BAFTA, ISA

LaGallienne, Eva

1980-(BSA) *Resurrection*
　　Winner: Mary Steenburgen, *Melvin and
　　Howard*
▧ Born 1/11/1899 in London, England, UK.
　　Died 6/3/91 of a heart attack.
▨ Grandma Pearl in nominated role.
✎ Her father was a poet, and their family friend
was Sarah Bernhardt. Founder of the Civic Reper-
tory Theater. Won a Pulitzer Prize for the play
Alison's House. Awarded National Medal of the Arts

by President Reagan in 1986. In her 60 years in the theater she was a director, producer, manager, and stage coach.

Major Awards: Tony, NBR, Emmy, Pulitzer Prize

LaGarde, Jocelyn

1966-(BSA) *Hawaii*
Winner: Sandy Dennis, *Who's Afraid of Virginia Woolf?*
▪ Born 1924 in Tahiti. Died 9/12/79 of unknown causes.
Queen Malama in nominated role.
She was a real life Tahitian princess with no previous acting experience. She was six feet tall. She only spoke French and had to learn her lines by rote, that is pronouncing every line phonetically. She is the only actress to ever be nominated in her first and only film, and, weighing in at over 400 pounds, the heaviest.

Major Awards: GG

Lahti, Christine

1984-(BSA) *Swing Shift*
Winner: Peggy Ashcroft, *A Passage to India*
★ 1995-(Best Short Film) *Lieberman In Love*
▪ Born 4/4/50 in Birmingham, MI.
Hazel Zanussi in nominated role.
Majored in drama at the University of Michigan and toured Europe with a group of pantomimes. Upon her arrival in New York she worked as a waitress and a mime in Central Park. Very multi-talented actress who has starred on stage, TV, movies, and even Oscar'd for her work on a short film. She has never posed nude in any of her movies.

Major Awards: GG, CA, Obie, Emmy, NYFC, LAFC

Lancaster, Burt

1953-(BA) *From Here to Eternity*
Winner: William Holden, *Stalag 17*
★ 1960-(BA) *Elmer Gantry*

Burt Lancaster in *Elmer Gantry*.

1962-(BA) *Bird Man of Alcatraz*
Winner: Gregory Peck, *To Kill a Mockingbird*
1981-(BA) *Atlantic City*
Winner: Henry Fonda, *On Golden Pond*
▪ Born 11/2/1913 in New York, NY.
Died 10/2/94 of a heart attack.
Many roles including Jim Thorpe, Wyatt Earp, Elmer Gantry (#35 on AFI's Villains List), J.J. Hunsecker in *Sweet Smell of Success*
Received an athletic scholarship to NYU. Joined the circus and formed an acrobatic team with childhood friend Nick Cravat. Once was a fireman, refrigerator repairman, floorwalker, and salesman. Never took an acting lesson. During WW II he was in Special Services in North Africa and Italy. Turned down the lead role in *Ben-Hur* because he was a self-professed atheist. He was a notorious philanderer, which eventually led to his wife Nancy leaving him. Almost died from a routine gall bladder operation in 1980. Life-long friend with Kirk Douglas.

Major Awards: Oscar, GG, SAGLA, NYFC, NBR, LAFC, BAFTA, BIFF, BSFC, DDA, NSFC, VFF, WOF

Lancaster, Elsa

1949-(BSA) *Come to the Stable*
  Winner: Mercedes McCambridge, *All the King's Men*
1957-(BSA) *Witness for the Prosecution*
  Winner: Miyoshi Umeki, *Sayonara*
▦ Born *Elizabeth Sullivan* on 10/28/1902 in Lewisham, England. Died 12/26/86 of bronchial pneumonia.
✐ Miss Plimsol in *Witness for the Prosecution*
♈ Danced with Isadore Duncan's troupe in Paris as a child. Her husband's homosexuality evidently wasn't a problem as she remained married to actor Charles Laughton for 33 years. Starred in the title role in the *Bride of Frankenstein*. Appeared in over 100 movie and television productions. Posed nude for an artist in her struggling years. She wrote two autobiographies.
Major Awards: GG

Landau, Martin

1988-(BSA) *Tucker: The Man and His Dream*
  Winner: Kevin Kline, *A Fish Called Wanda*
1989-(BSA) *Crimes and Misdemeanors*
  Winner: Denzel Washington, *Glory*
★ 1994-(BSA) *Ed Wood*
▦ Born 6/20/31 in Brooklyn, NY.
✐ Rollin Hand in TV hit series *Mission Impossible*
♈ Once worked as a cartoonist for the *New York Daily News*. Originally was Gene Roddenberry's first choice to play Mr. Spock in *Star Trek*. Of the 2000 hopefuls who auditioned for Lee Strasberg's acting school—only he and Steve McQueen were accepted. Married to *Mission Impossible* co-star Barbara Bain for 36 years, until their divorce in 1993.
Major Awards: GG, CA, NYFC, NSFC, LAFC, SAG, Saturn, BSFC, KCFCC, WOF

Lane, Diane

2002-(BA) *Unfaithful*
  Winner: Nicole Kidman, *The Hours*
▦ Born 1/22/65 in New York, NY.

✐ Connie Sumner in nominated role.
♈ Her grandmother was a Pentecostal minister and her mother was a former *Playboy* Bunny and centerfold. In 1979, at the age of 14, she was featured on the cover of *Time* magazine. Her eye is permanently dilated as a result of a tennis accident when a ball hit her. She was a multi-millionaire by age 18.
Major Awards: NYFC, NSFC

Lange, Hope

1957-(BSA) *Peyton Place*
  Winner: Miyoshi Umecki, *Sayonara*
▦ Born 11/28/31 in Redding Ridge, CT. Died 12/19/2003 of an ischemic colitis infection.
✐ Mrs. Muir in TV's *The Ghost and Mrs. Muir*
♈ Made her Broadway debut in Sid Kingsley's Pulitzer Prize–winning play *The Patriots* at age 12. Her father arranged music for Florenz Ziegfield. Once married to actor Don Murray. She had surgery to remove a brain tumor in 1991. After donating a major portion of her money to the US Relief Fund she lived like a pauper using shipping crates for coffee tables.
Major Awards: Emmy

Lange, Jessica

1982-(BA) *Frances*
  Winner: Meryl Streep, *Sofie's Choice*
★ 1982-(BSA) *Tootsie*
1984-(BA) *Country*
  Winner: Sally Field, *Places in the Heart*
1985-(BA) *Sweet Dreams*
  Winner: Geraldine Page, *The Trip to Bountiful*
1989-(BA) *Music Box*
  Winner: Jessica Tandy, *Driving Miss Daisy*
★ 1994-(BA) *Blue Sky*
▦ Born 4/20/49 in Cloquet, MN.
✐ Julie Nichols in *Tootsie*
♈ Majored in Art at the University of Minnesota. Studied mime and dancing in Paris. Worked for Wilhemeina Modeling agency in New York. Once was a waitress at the Lion's Head Restaurant in Greenwich Village. Had a child out of wedlock

with Mikhail Baryshnikov. Has been in a relationship with playwright Sam Shepard since 1982, and they have three children and live in Minnesota and New York.
Major Awards: Oscar, GG, NYFC, NSFC, LAFC

Lansbury, Angela

1944-(BSA) *Gaslight*
  Winner: Ethel Barrymore, *None but the Lonely Heart*
1945-(BSA) *The Picture of Dorian Gray*
  Winner: Ann Revere, *National Velvet*
1962-(BSA) *The Manchurian Candidate*
  Winner: Patty Duke, *The Miracle Worker*
▦ Born 10/16/25 in London, England
▥ Jessica Fletcher in TV series *Murder She Wrote.* Mrs. Iselin in *The Manchurian Candidate* (#21 on AFI's Villain List)
◌ She was only three years older than Lawrence Harvey when she played his mother in *The Manchurian Candidate*. Awarded Commander of the British Empire by Queen Elizabeth. Nominated 15 times for an Emmy and an incredible 12 consecutive years and has never won! However she is four for four with the Tony award.
Major Awards: GG, Tony, NBR, SAGLA, WOF

Laughton, Charles

★ 1932/33-(BA) *The Private Life of Henry VIII*
1935-(BA) *Mutiny on the Bounty*
  Winner: Victor McLaglen, *The Informer*
1957-(BA) *Witness for the Prosecution*
  Winner: Alec Guinness, *The Bridge on the River Kwai*
▦ Born 7/1/1899 in Scarsborough, England. Died 12/15/62 of cancer.
▥ Captain Bligh in *Mutiny on the Bounty* (#19 on AFI's Villain List)
◌ He was gassed during WW I which affected him for the rest of his life. He was not only an actor but also a writer, producer, and director. Only directed one movie *Night of the Hunter*. Married to actress

Charles Laughton (left) in *Witness for the Prosecution.*

Elsa Lanchester for 33 years even though he was a self-professed homosexual. He discovered actress Maureen O'Hara.
Major Awards: Oscar, Grammy, NYFC, NBR, WOF

Laurel, Stan

★ 1960-Honorary Oscar
▦ Born *Arthur Stanley Jefferson* in Ulverston, Cumbria England on 6/16/1890.
  Died 2/23/65 of a heart attack.
▥ Comedic partner with Oliver Hardy
◌ Onetime roommate and understudy to the great Charlie Chaplin. Was featured on a 29-cent U.S. commemorative postage stamp in 1991. He was married eight times, three times to the same woman. Suffered a nervous breakdown on the death of partner Oliver Hardy and never fully recovered. He was Peter Sellers's favorite actor. Dick Van Dyke delivered the eulogy at Stan's funeral.
Major Awards: SAG, WOF

Laurie, Piper

1961, (BA) *The Hustler*
  Winner: Sophia Loren, *Two Women*
1976, (BSA) *Carrie*
  Winner: Beatrice Straight, *Network*
1986, (BSA) *Children of a Lesser God*
  Winner: Dianne Wiest, *Hannah and Her Sisters*
▨ Born *Rosetta Jacobs* on 1/22/32 in Detroit, MI.
✎ Sarah Packard in *The Hustler*
✎ Her father was a Polish immigrant. Moved to Los Angeles when she was six. In 1950 Universal signed her to a $2000-a-week contract when she was only 17! Fed up with crummy roles she moved to New York and starred on Broadway. She then retired to upstate New York and settled into the domestic life cooking, baking, and raising her daughter.
Major Awards: Emmy, GG

Law, Jude

1999-(BSA) *The Talented Mr. Ripley*
  Winner: Michael Caine, *The Cider House Rules*
2003-(BA) *Cold Mountain*
  Winner: Sean Penn, *Mystic River*
▨ Born *David Jude Law* on 12/29/72 in Lewisham, London, England.
✎ Inman in *Cold Mountain*
✎ Started acting at age 12. Dropped out of school at age 17. His former roommate was actor Ewan McGregor. He is a vegetarian. His parents choose his middle name Jude after the Beatles' hit song "Hey Jude." Has a tattoo on his arm that says "Sexy Sadie," the name of his wife. Taught himself to play the sax for his nominated role.
Major Awards: BAFTA, NBR

Leachman, Cloris

★ 1971-(BSA) *The Last Picture Show*
▨ Born 4/30/26 in Des Moines, IA
✎ Ruth Popper in Oscar'd role.
✎ Attended Northwestern University on an Edgar Bergen scholarship and was Miss Chicago in 1946.

Former mother-in-law to actress Sharon Stone. Son overdosed on ulcer medication. Only actress to win five Emmys in five different categories. Nominated 21 times for an Emmy.
Major Awards: Oscar, Emmy (5), GG, BAFTA, WOF, NBR, KCFCC

Ledger, Heath

2005-(BA) *Brokeback Mountain*
  Winner: Philip Seymour Hoffman, *Capote*
▨ Born 4/4/79 in Perth, Australia
✎ Ennis Del Mar in nominated role.
✎ Attended a private boy's grammar school. Left school at age 17 and drove cross-country to Sidney. He only had 69 cents in his pocket. Played soccer for the semi-pro Kalamunda team. Almost played professional hockey, but choose acting. Once dated Naomi Watts. Has a daughter with his current girlfriend, Michelle Williams, whom he met on the set of *Brokeback Mountain*.
Major Awards: NYFC

Lee, Peggy

1955-(BSA) *Pete Kelly's Blues*
  Winner: Jo Van Fleet, *East of Eden*
▨ Born *Norma Deloris Engstrom* on 5/26/20 in Jamestown, ND. Died 1/21/2002 of a heart attack.
✎ Nightclub singer par excellence
✎ Worked as a milkmaid on her parent's farm. Sang at PTA meetings for 50 cents a gig. She was also a songwriter, lyricist, and arranger. Sued Walt Disney for royalties from her work on *The Lady and the Tramp* and won. The courts awarded her 2.3 million. She was married four times. She was inducted into the Jazz Hall of Fame in 1992.
Major Awards: Grammy, WOF

Leeds, Andrea

1937-(BSA) *Stage Door*
  Winner: Alice Brady, *In Old Chicago*

■ Born *Antoinette Lees* 8/18/1914 in Butte, MT. Died 5/21/84 of cancer.

✔ Kay Hamilton in nominated role.

🔍 Only appeared in the movies for four years, and then she married millionaire Robert Howard and retired. Auditioned for the role of Melanie Hamilton in *Gone with the Wind*. Owned and operated a jewelry store in Palm Springs until her death from cancer at age 70.

Leigh, Janet

1960-(BSA) *Psycho*
    Winner: Shirley Jones, *Elmer Gantry*
■ Born *Jeanette Helen Morrison* on 7/6/27 in Merced, CA. Died 10/3/04 of vaculitis.

✔ Marion Crane in nominated role.

🔍 Eloped at the age of 14 but her marriage was annulled. Graduated from high school at age 15. Majored in music at the College of the Pacific. Discovered by Norma Shearer. Married to actor Tony Curtis for 11 years. Awarded an Honorary Doctorate of Fine Arts from Pacific University. Mother to actress Jamie Lee Curtis, and they appeared together in the movie *The Fog*.

Major Awards: GG, WOF

Leigh, Vivien

★ 1939-(BA) *Gone with the Wind*
★ 1951-(BA) *A Streetcar Named Desire*
■ Born *Vivian Mary Hartley* on 11/5/1913 in Darjeeling, India. Died 7/7/67 of chronic tuberculosis.

✔ Scarlett O'Hara in *Gone with the Wind*

🔍 Was educated in a convent in England. Her childhood friend was Maureen O' Sullivan. Once a chain smoker, smoking four packs a day while filming *Gone with the Wind*. She only got paid $15,000 for her role as Scarlet O'Hara. Godmother to actress Juliette Mills. Married to actor Laurence Olivier for 20 years. Once had an affair with Peter Finch, who was discovered by Laurence, but he forgave her and took her back, however his relationship with Peter cooled off considerably. Suffered from manic depression and tuberculosis. She was an avid cat lover. Her Oscar for *Gone with the Wind* sold at auction for $510,000, a record amount.

Major Awards: Oscar, NYFC, Tony, BAFTA, VFF, WOF

Leighton, Margaret

1971-(BSA) *The Go-Between*
    Winner: Cloris Leachman, *The Last Picture Show*
■ Born 2/26/22 in Barnt Green, England. Died 1/13/76 of multiple sclerosis

✔ Mrs. Maudsley in nominated role.

🔍 Made her stage debut at age 16. Her mentor directors were Ralph Richardson and Laurence Olivier. She was married to publisher Max Reinhardt and actors Michael Wilding and Laurence Harvey. She was quite a trooper—after she was diagnosed with multiple sclerosis in 1971 she kept acting right up until the end.

Major Awards: BAFTA, KCFCC, Tony, Emmy

Lemmon, Jack

★ 1953-(BSA) *Mister Roberts*
1959-(BA) *Some Like It Hot*
    Winner: Charlton Heston, *Ben-Hur*
1960-(BA) *The Apartment*
    Winner: Burt Lancaster, *Elmer Gantry*
1962-(BA) *The Days of Wine and Roses*
    Winner: Gregory Peck, *To Kill a Mockingbird*
★ 1973-(BA) *Save the Tiger*
1979-(BA) *The China Syndrom*
    Winner: Dustin Hoffman, *Kramer vs. Kramer*
1980-(BA) *Tribute*
    Winner: Robert DeNiro, *Raging Bull*
1982-(BA) *Missing*
    Winner: Ben Kingsley, *Gandhi*
■ Born *John Uhler Lemmon III* on 2/8/25 in Boston, MA. Died 6/27/01 of cancer.

✔ Ensign Pulver in *Mister Roberts*

🔍 He was born in a hospital elevator. In his earlier years was a singing waiter in New York. A self-taught piano virtuoso, he recorded several albums and wrote

Jack Lemmon in *Mister Roberts*.

the theme music for the movie *Tribute*. He was an officer in the Navy during WW II and graduated from Harvard with a degree in War Service Science. Was a reformed alcoholic, and faultlessly polite. Nominated for 20 Golden Globe awards winning five times. Made ten movies with his lifelong buddy Walter Matthau, and died almost exactly a year after Walter passed away.
Major Awards: Oscar, GG, Cannes, CB DeMille, Emmy NBR, BAFTA, SAGLA, AFI's Life Achievement , DDA, BIFF, VFF, WOF

Lenya, Lotte

1961-(BSA) *The Roman Spring of Mrs. Stone*
 Winner: Rita Moreno, *West Side Story*
 Born *Karoline Blamauer* on 10/18/00 in Hitzing, Austria. Died 11/27/81 of cancer.
 Rosa Klebb in *From Russia with Love*
 She was a tightrope walker at age eight. Trained in classical ballet and opera in Zurich, Switzerland. Bobby Darin mentions her name in his rendition of "Mack the Knife," a song her husband, Kurt Weill, wrote for her.
Major Awards: Tony

Lerner, Michael

1991-(BSA) *Barton Fink*
 Winner: Jack Palance, *City Slickers*
 Born 6/22/41 in Brooklyn, NY.
 Jack Lipnick in nominated role.
 Attended Brooklyn College and graduated from Berkeley. Also attended the London Academy of Music and Dramatic Arts. Once worked in a Manhattan deli. He is a long-time professor at San Francisco State College. Has starred in over 90 movies and has made numerous TV appearances.
Major Awards: LAFC

Lewis, Juliette

1991-(BSA) *Cape Fear*
 Winner: Mercedes Ruehl, *The Fisher King*
 Born 6/21/73 in Los Angeles, CA.
 Danielle Bowden in nominated role.
 Made her acting debut at age 12. Dropped out of high school when she was a freshman. Legally emancipated from her acting father Geoffrey Lewis at age 14. Drove without a driver's license until she was 21. She was almost named Snowlake. Her sister's name is Lightfield. Tours and records with her rock band Juliette and the Licks.

Linney, Laura

2000-(BA) *You Can Count On Me*
 Winner: Julia Roberts, *Erin Brockovich*
2004-(BSA) *Kinsey*
 Winner: Cate Blanchett, *The Aviator*
 Born 2/5/64 in New York, NY.
 Samantha Prescott in nominated role.
 Graduated from Brown University and Julliard. Her mother is a nurse and her father an off-Broadway playwright. Suffers from stage fright and has a morbid fear of flying. Only made $10 thousand for her Oscar-nominated role. Put on 20 pounds for her role in Kinsey by stuffing herself with donuts.
Major Awards: Emmy, NYFC, BSFC, NBR, NSFC

Lithgow, John

1982-(BSA) *The World According to Garp*
    Winner: Louis Gossett Jr., *An Officer and a Gentleman*
1983-(BSA) *Terms of Endearment*
    Winner: Jack Nicholson, *Terms of Endearment*
▓ Born 10/19/45 in Rochester, NY
⧄ Professor Dick Solomon in TV series *Third Rock from the Sun*
⚲ His mother was an actress and his father a producer and director. Graduated from Harvard in Literature/History Magna Cum Laude. Was named a Fulbright Scholar. Married to an economics professor at UCLA.
Major Awards: Emmy, GG, Tony, DDA, NYFC, LAFC, SAG, WOF

Lloyd, Harold

1952-Honorary Oscar
▓ Born 4/20/1893 in Burchard, NE. Died 3/8/71 of prostate cancer.
⧄ Lonesome Luke two-reelers
⚲ Once worked as a pool hall proprietor. Lost his right thumb and index finger when a prop bomb accidentally detonated in his hand. He wore white gloves thereafter. Did all of his own stunt work using no safety nets. Had his trademark glasses insured for 25 thousand dollars. His hobbies were painting and photography —he was a pioneer in stereoscopic photography.
Major Awards: WOF

Locke, Sandra

1968-(BSA) *The Heart Is a Lonely Hunter*
    Winner: Ruth Gordon, *Rosemary's Baby*
▓ Born 5/28/47 in Shelbyville, TN.
⧄ One time girlfriend of Clint Eastwood.
⚲ Graduated from Middle Tennessee State University. She battled breast cancer and won. Brought a palimony suit against Clint Eastwood and was awarded a sizeable amount. Directed several movies.

She has settled down with longtime doctor friend who is the director of surgery at Cedars Sinai Hospital.

Lockhart, Gene

1938-(BSA) *Algiers*
    Winner: Walter Brennan, *Kentucky*
▓ Born 7/18/1891 in London, Ontario, Canada. Died 3/31/57 of coronary thrombosis.
⧄ Bob Cratchit in *A Christmas Carol* (1938)
⚲ Danced and sang with his father, a Scottish tenor, and toured England. He was a writer, director, songwriter, lyricist, lecturer and instructor at the Juilliard School of Music. Wrote the million-selling song "The World is Waiting for the Sunrise" in 1949. Father of actress June Lockhart. Starred in over 125 films during his career.
Major Award: WOF

Loggia, Robert

1985-(BSA) *The Jagged Edge*
    Winner: Don Ameche, *Cocoon*
▓ Born 1/3/30 in New York, NY.
⧄ Sam Ransom in nominated role.
⚲ Raised in Manhattan's Little Italy. Served in the Army as a news reporter in Panama. Graduated from the University of Missouri-Columbia with a degree in journalism. Studied with Stella Adler at the famed Actors Studio. Has appeared in over 100 movies and 100 TV productions. Nominated for two Emmys.
Major Awards: Saturn

Lombard, Carole

1936-(BA) *My Man Godfrey*
    Winner: Luise Rainer, *The Great Ziegfield*
▓ Born *Jane Alice Peters* on 10/6/1908 in Ft. Wayne, IN. Died 1/19/42 in a plane crash.
⧄ Irene Bullock in nominated role.
⚲ Made her movie debut at age 12. Her mother named her Carole after consulting a numerologist. Shortly after marrying Clark Gable, she died

tragically in a plane crash following a WW II war bond drive. Her mother had a premonition and pleaded to no avail for her not to fly that day. She was awarded the Medal of Freedom, as the first female casualty of war posthumously by FDR. Clark affectionately called her Ma and she called him Pa.
Major Awards: WOF

Loren, Sofia

★ 1961-(BA) *Two Women*
1964-(BA) *Marriage, Italian Style*
   Winner: Julie Andrews, *Mary Poppins*
1990-Honorary Oscar
▪ Born *Sofia Scicolone* on 9/20/34 in Rome, Italy
⚲ Cesira in Oscar'd role.
⚲ She was an illegitimate child who grew up in the slums of Naples during WW II. She has a shrapnel wound on her head as a result of the war. Her sister Maria married Benito Mussolini's son, Romano. Spent 18 days in prison for tax evasion in Italy. Cary Grant once proposed to her, but she turned him down. First actress to receive an Oscar for a foreign language film,
Major Awards: NYFC, Cannes, GGWFF, CBD, GG, NBR, BIFF, César, DDA, VFF, Grammy, WOF

Lorring, Joan

1945-(BSA) *The Corn Is Green*
   Winner: Anne Revere, *National Velvet*
▪ Born *Mary Magdalena Ellis* on 4/17/26 in Hong Kong, China.
⚲ Bessie Watty in nominated role.
⚲ At the outbreak of WW II, she and her family fled to America in 1939 when she was 13. She was very versatile as she worked in stage, TV, and radio in her latter years. In 1975 she was a regular on the TV soap, *Ryan's Hope*. She has a lifelong passion for baking, especially exotic breads, and has written articles for *Vogue* magazine.

Love, Bessie

1928/29-(BA) *Broadway Melody*
   Winner: Mary Pickford, *Coquette*
▪ Born *Juanita Horton* on 9/10/1898 in Midland, TX. Died 4/26/86 of natural causes.
⚲ Hank Mahoney in nominated role.
⚲ Discovered by D.W. Griffith while still in high school. He also gave her, her stage name. First person to perform the Charleston on screen. Career ended in 1931 and she moved to England. Worked for the Red Cross in WW II. Wrote the play *The Homecoming* in 1958.
Major Awards: WOF

Loy, Myrna

1990-Honorary Oscar
▪ Born *Myrna Williams* on 8/2/1905 in Raidersburg, MT. Died 12/14/93 following a routine surgery.
⚲ Nora Charles in *The Thin Man* series.
⚲ Made stage debut at age 12. Did her first screen text with Rudolf Valentino. In 1936 she was voted "Queen of the Movies," Clark Gable being the King. She served as film advisor to UNESCO for five years. Sculpting and dancing were her lifelong hobbies. She was on Hitler's "hit list" during WW II, but conversely was one of FDR's favorite actresses.
Major Awards: LAFC Life Achievement, NBR Life Achievement, WOF

Lukas, Paul

★ 1943-(BA) *Watch On The Rhine*
▪ Born *Pal Lukac* on 5/26/1894 in Budapest, Hungary. Died 8/15/71 of heart failure
⚲ Kurt Muller in Oscar'd role.
⚲ He was a pilot in the Hungarian Air Corps prior to WW I. He made his acting debut in 1916 on the Budapest stage. Achieved matinee-idol status in Hungary in the '20s. Brought to Hollywood by producer Adolph Zucor. Became a U.S. citizen in 1933. Made over 100 movies during his acting career.
Major Awards: Oscar, GG, NYFC, WOF

Lunt, Alfred

1931/32-(BA) *The Guardsman*
   Winner: Wallace Beery, *The Champ*
■ Born 8/12/1892 in Milwaukee, WI.
   Died 8/3/77 of bladder cancer.
✎ He and his wife Lynn Fontanne will be forever remembered as the First Royalty of Broadway.
🔍 Made his acting debut in Boston in 1912. He and his wife Lynn Fontanne were the premiere acting team in the history of the American Theater. They were the first married couple to be nominated for Oscars in the same movie. They were married for 35 years, and the couple appeared on a 33-cent U.S. postage stamp in 1999.
Major Awards: Emmy, Tony

MacGraw, Ali

1970-(BA) *Love Story*
   Winner: Glenda Jackson, *Women in Love*
■ Born *Elizabeth Alice MacGraw* on 4/1/38 in Pound Ridge, NY.
✎ Jenny Cavilleri in nominated role. Forever associated with the line, "Love means never having to say you're sorry."
🔍 Made her stage debut at age six. After graduating from Wellesley she was an editorial assistant at *Harper's Bazaar*. *People* magazine chose her as one of the 50 Most Beautiful people in the world in 1991. She left Paramount production chief Robert Evans to marry actor Steve McQueen. Spokesman for PETA.
Major Awards: GGWFF, GG, DDA

MacLaine, Shirley

1958-(BA) *Some Came Running*
   Winner: Susan Hayward, *I Want to Live!*
1960-(BA) *The Apartment*
   Winner: Elizabeth Taylor, *Butterfield 8*
1963-(BA) *Irma Ladouce*
   Winner: Patricia Neal, *Hud*
1976-(Best Documentary) *The Other Half of the Sky: A China Memoir*

Jack Nicholson and Shirley MacLaine in *Terms of Endearment*.

1977-(BA) *The Turning Point*
   Winner: Diane Keaton, *Annie Hall*
★ 1983-(BA) *Terms of Endearment*
■ Born *Shirley MacLean Beatty* on 4/24/34 in Richmond, VA.
✎ Aurora Greenway in Oscar'd role; Rat Pack moll.
🔍 Started ballet lessons at age two. Mother named her after Shirley Temple. She was understudy to lead dancer, Carol Haney in Broadway's production of *The Pajama Game*. As luck would have it Carol broke her leg. The first night Shirley filled in, producer Hal Wallis was in the audience and signed her to a five-year movie contract. Campaigned for Bobby Kennedy. Sister to actor Warren Beatty. Has written several books on reincarnation.
Major Awards: GG, NBR, NYFC, LAFC, Emmy, BAFTA, BIFF, DDA, CBD, VFF, WOF

MacMahon, Aline

1944-(BSA) *Dragonseed*
   Winner: Ethel Barrymore, *None but the Lonely Heart*
■ Born 5/3//1899 in McKeesport, PA.
   Died 10/12/91 of pneumonia.
✎ Mrs. Ling Tan in nominated role.
🔍 Educated at Erasmus and graduated from Barnard College. Toast of Broadway in 1926 for her performance in Eugene O'Neill's *Beyond the Horizon*. Her career spanned 40 years with roles on television as well as movies. Married for 47 years to Clarence Stein, chief planner of the 1915 World's Fair in San Diego.

Macy, William H.

1996-(BSA) *Fargo*
    Winner: Cuba Gooding Jr., *Jerry Maguire*
- Born 3/13/50 in Miami, FL.
- Car salesman Jerry Lundegaard in nominated role.
- Attended Bethany and Goddard colleges and studied under David Mamet. Founding member of the St. Nicholas Theater in Chicago and the Atlantic Theater in New York. National spokesman for the United Cerebral Palsy. Initially wanted to be a veterinarian. Spokesman for United Cerebral Palsy. He also plays a mean ukulele. Married to actress Felicity Hoffman.
Major Awards: NBR, Emmy, SAG, BSFC, ISA

Madigan, Amy

1985-(BSA) *Twice in a Lifetime*
    Winner: Anjelica Huston, *Prizzi's Honor*
- Born 9/11/51 in Chicago, IL.
- Sunny MacKenzie in nominated role. Annie Kinsella in *Field of Dreams*.
- Her father was lawyer/radio commentator John Madigan. She toured with her band Jelly singing and playing the piano. Appeared in *Playboy* Magazine but not in the conventional way—she was smeared with jelly to promote her musical band Jelly. Married to actor Ed Harris for over 20 years.
Major Awards: GG

Madsen, Virginia

2004-(BSA) *Sideways*
    Winner: Cate Blanchett, *The Aviator*
- Born 9/11/63 in Chicago, IL
- Maya in nominated role
- Her father is a fireman, her mother is Emmy-winning writer and producer Elaine Madsen, and her brother is actor Michael Madsen. Former daughter-in-law of director John Huston. Her left eye is brown and her right eye is green. If bitten by a bee she would go into anaphylactic shock.

Major Awards: LAFC, NSFC, NYFC, SAG, BSFC, ISA

Magnani, Anna

★ 1955-(BA) *The Rose Tatoo*
1957-(BA) *Wild Is the Wind*
    Winner: Joanne Woodward, *The Three Faces of Eve*
- Born 3/7/1908 in Rome, Latium, Italy. Died 9/26/73 of pancreatic cancer
- Serna Delle Rose in Oscar'd role.
- She was born out of wedlock and raised by her grandmother. Initially made her living singing earthy ballads in low-class nightclubs. She was buried in the family mausoleum of long-time friend director Roberto Rossellini.
Major Awards: BAFTA, GG, NBR, NYFC, BIFF, VFF, WOF

Main, Marjorie

1947-(BSA) *The Egg & I*
    Winner: Celeste Holm, *Gentleman's Agreement*
- Born *Mary Tomlinson* on 2/24/1890 in Acton, IN. Died 4/10/75 of lung cancer.
- Ma Kettle in nominated role and popular series with Percy Kilbride as Pa Kettle.
- Daughter of a minister. Attended Franklin College in Indiana. Appeared with W.C. Fields on Broadway in 1916. Starred in over 100 films. She had a propensity to wear white gloves and surgical masks because of her morbid fear of germs. Her companion for years was actress Spring Byington.

Mako

1966-(BSA) *The Sand Pebbles*
    Winner: Walter Matthau, *The Fortune Cookie*
- Born *Mako Inamatsu* on 12/10/33 in Kobe, Japan. Died 7/21/06 of esophageal cancer.
- The coolie Po-Han in nominated role.
- At the onset of WW II, lived with grandparents in Japan while his parents were in the U.S. working for

the Office of War Information. Gave up a career as an architect for acting. Founder of the Asian Theater. Enlisted in the army and served in the Korean War. Became a naturalized citizen in 1956.
Major Awards: WOF

Malden, Karl

★ 1951-(BSA) *A Streetcar Named Desire*
1954-(BSA) *On the Waterfront*
  Winner: Edmond O'Brien, *The Barefoot Contessa*
▩ Born *Malden Sekulovich* on 3/22/1914 in Gary, IN.
🌿 Harold "Mitch" Mitchel in Oscar'd role. Lt. Mike Stone in TV series *The Streets of San Francisco*.
🔍 Worked the steel mills as a young man in Gary. Earned a basketball scholarship to Arkansas State Teachers College. Served in service during WW II. Broke Marlon Brando's nose in a sparring match on the set of *A Streetcar Named Desire*. Served as the President of the Academy of Motion Pictures Arts and Sciences. Pitchman for American Express for 21 years. Married to the same woman for 67 years.
Major Awards: Oscar, Emmy, SAG Life Achievement, WOF

Malkovich, John

1984-(BSA) *Places in the Heart*
  Winner: Haing S. Ngor, *The Killing Fields*
1993-(BSA) *In the Line of Fire*
  Winner: Tommy Lee Jones, *The Fugitive*
▩ Born 12/9/53 in Christopher, IL.
🌿 Vicomte De Valmont in *Dangerous Liaisons*, and the title role in offbeat *Being John Malkevich*.
🔍 Played the tuba in his high school band, and also donned the cleats on the football field. Educated at Illinois State. Co-founded the Steppenwolf Theatre in Chicago in 1976. Maintains a home and owns a disco in Portugal. He was presented an official diploma from Illinois State, even though he didn't graduate.
Major Awards: Emmy, Obie, DDA, OCC, NBR, NSFC

Malone, Dorothy

★ 1956-(BSA) *Written on the Wind*
▩ Born *Dorothy Eloise Maloney* on 1/30/25 in Chicago, IL.
🌿 Marylee Hadley in Oscar'd role.
🔍 Beauty contest winner who attended Southern Methodist where she was spotted by a Hollywood talent scout. Starred in the TV series *Peyton Place*. Her brother was fatally struck by lightning while playing golf on a Dallas course. She dedicated her Oscar to him. She won the Golden Apple for Most Cooperative Actor in 1965, however after she was written off *Peyton Place*, she took the studio to the mat and won a sizeable settlement.
Major Awards: Oscar, WOF

Mantell, Joe

1955-(BSA) *Marty*
  Winner: Jack Lemmon, *Mister Roberts*
▩ Born 12/21/20 in New York, NY.
🌿 Angie in nominated role
🔍 Nominated for an Oscar in only his fourth movie. (Remember the catchphrase, "So whaddaya wanna do tonight, Marty?") Has made over 50 appearances on television. From 1952 to 1982 he mainly worked on TV. The last movie he appeared in was *The Two Jakes*.

March, Frederic

1930/31-(BA) *The Royal Family of Broadway*
  Winner: Lionel Barrymore, *A Free Soul*
★ 1931/32-(BA) *Dr. Jekyll and Mr. Hyde*
1937-(BA) *A Star Is Born*
  Winner: Spencer Tracy, *Captains Courageous*
★ 1946-(BA) *The Best Years of Our Lives*
1951-(BA) *Death of a Salesman*
  Winner: Humphrey Bogart, *The African Queen*
▩ Born *Ernest Frederick McIntyre Bickel* on 8/31/1897 in Racine, WI. Died 4/14/75 of cancer.
🌿 As Dr. Jekyll and Mr. Hyde in Oscar'd role.

He was an artillery Lieutenant in WW I. After graduating from the University of Wisconsin went into the banking business. Worked as a part-time newspaper magazine model. Took his stage name March from his mother's maiden name Marcher. Only actor to win an Oscar for playing a monster. He was Marlon Brando's favorite actor. Gave a dramatic reading of "The Gettysburg Address" before a joint session of Congress.
Major Awards: Oscar, Tony, GG, WOF

Marchand, Colette

1952-(BSA) *Moulin Rouge*
    Winner: Gloria Grahame, *The Bad and the Beautiful*
  Born 4/29/25 in Paris, France.
  Marie Charlet in nominated role.
  Nominated for an Oscar in her film debut. Trained as a ballerina. Played a streetwalker who became Toulose-Lautrec's mistress. Honored as Hollywood's Best Newcomer in 1954. Only made four movies, then faded from the public's eye and is now a watercolor painter residing in France.
Major Awards: GG

Marley, John

1970-(BSA) *Love Story*
    Winner: John Mills, *Ryan's Daughter*
  Born 10/17/1907 in New York, NY.
  Died 5/22/84 following open-heart surgery.
  Jack Woltz as the director in *The Godfather*
  He was a high school dropout. Fought in WW II in the Army Signal Corps. Joined the theater to avoid being swept into the gang life. He was the recipient of the famous horse head in *The Godfather*—they used a real horse head, but the blood was fake.
Major Awards: Venice Film Festival

Marvin, Lee

★ 1965-(BA) *Cat Ballou*

Born 2/19/24 in New York, NY. Died 8/29/87 of a heart attack.
Kid Shelleen/Tim Strawn in Oscar'd role, Major John Reisman in *The Dirty Dozen*
He was kicked out of dozens of schools for unruly behavior. In WW II, as a Marine, he was wounded in the Battle of Saipan and received a Purple Heart and disability pay from the government for life. Elected to the Cowboy Hall of Fame. Received a Gold Record for the song "Wandering Star." His brother was a two-star general in the Army. Distant relative to Robert E. Lee and a direct descendant of Thomas Jefferson. He turned down the role of George S. Patton but recommended George C. Scott.
Major Awards: Oscar, NBR, GG, WOF

Marx, Groucho

★ 1973-*Honorary Oscar*
Born *Julius Henry Marx* on 10/2/1890 in New York, NY. Died 8/19/77 of pneumonia.
A string of films with his brothers Chico, Harpo, and Zeppo, and his "straight man," Margaret Dumont. Host of '50s TV quiz show *You Bet Your Life*. His bushy eyebrows, grease-paint mustache, horned glasses, and duck walk are recognizable anywhere in the world.
Suffered from insomnia and would call friends up in the middle of the night and insult them. Invited to the New York Stock Exchange he stopped trading cold for 15 minutes while he told jokes, sang, and entertained the group. Close friend to rocker Alice Cooper and *Exorcist* author William Peter Blatty. Never a good golfer, once shot a hole in one at Brae Burn Country Club.
Major Awards: Emmy, WOF

Mason, James

1954-(BA) *A Star Is Born*
    Winner: Marlon Brando, *On the Waterfront*
1966-(BSA) *Georgy Girl*
    Winner: Walter Matthau, *The Fortune Cookie*
1982-(BSA) *The Verdict*

Winner: Louis Gossett Jr., *An Officer and a Gentleman*

▨ Born 5/15/09 in Huddlesfield, England. Died 7/27/84 of a heart attack.

✍ Field Marshal Erwin Rommel in *The Desert Fox* and *The Desert Rats*. Capt. Nemo in *20,000 Leagues Under the Sea*

♦ Graduated from Cambridge University with a degree in architecture. A conscientious objector and pacifist, refused military service during WW II which caused a family rift for years. Bought Buster Keaton's Hollywood mansion. Discovered a secret room, which contained Keaton's lost films.

Major Awards: GG, NBR, WOF

Mason, Marsha

1973-(BA) *Cinderella Liberty*
   Winner: Glenda Jackson, *A Touch of Class*
1977-(BA) *The Goodbye Girl*
   Winner: Diane Keaton, *Annie Hall*
1979-(BA) *Chapter Two*
   Winner: Sally Field, *Norma Rae*
1981-(BA) *Only When I Laugh*
   Winner: Katharine Hepburn, *On Golden Pond*

▨ Born 4/3/42 in St. Louis, MO.

✍ Paula McFadden in *The Goodbye Girl*

♦ Graduated from Webster College. Married and divorced from writer and playwright Neil Simon. Has her own herbal medicine business (she grows her own herbs) called Resting in the River. Turned down the role of Norma Rae, which won Sally Field an Oscar.

Major Awards: GG

Massey, Daniel

1968-(BSA) *Star*
   Winner: Jack Albertson, *The Subject Was Roses*

▨ Born 10/10/33 in London, England. Died 3/25/98 of Hodgkin's Disease.

✍ Playing his real life godfather Noel Coward in nominated role.

♦ His father was actor Raymond Massey. Made his movie debut at age nine. His parents divorced when he was young, and he only saw his father sporadically the rest of his life. Won the Laurence Olivier Theater Award in 1982.

Major Awards: GG

Massey, Raymond

1940-(BA) *Abe Lincoln in Illinois*
   Winner: James Stewart, *The Philadelphia Story*

▨ Born 8/30/1896 in Toronto, Ontario Canada. Died 7/29/83 of pneumonia.

✍ Abe Lincoln in nominated role.

♦ Graduated from Balliol College. Enlisted with the Canadian Field Artillery during WW I. As a major he was wounded in France. He also served as a major in WW II and again was wounded and invalided out. Had a fear of flying and hated travel by sea. He was a good golfer and an avid fisherman. He was heir to the Massey-Ferguson Tractor Company.

Major Awards: WOF

Mastrontonio, Mary Elizabeth

1986-(BSA) *The Color of Money*
   Winner: Dianne Wiest, *Hannah and Her Sisters*

▨ Born 11/17/58 in Lombard, IL

✍ Carmen in nominated role.

♦ She originally trained as an opera singer at the University of Illinois. Voted a promising new actor in 1986. Has the distinction of having the longest name of anyone who has ever been nominated for an Oscar. Has been on an extended sabbatical to raise a family while living in London, England.

Major Awards: Gracie Allen Award

Mastroianni, Marcello

1962-(BA) *Divorce—Italian Style*
   Winner: Gregory Peck, *To Kill a Mockingbird*
1977-(BA) *A Special Day*
   Winner: Richard Dreyfuss, *The Goodbye Girl*
1987-(BA) *Dark Eyes*
   Winner: Michael Douglas, *Wall Street*

■ Born *Marcello Mastrojanni* in Fontana Liri, Italy. Died 12/19/96 of pancreatic cancer.

⚜ Fernando in Divorce-Italian Style

⚲ In WW II he was captured by the Nazis and was sent to a German Labor Camp. He made a daring escape and hid in an attic of friends in Venice until end of war. An international star he worked with famed directors Federico Fellini, Luchino Visconti and Michelangelo Antonioni. Fathered a child with French actress Catherine Deneuve.

Major Awards: GG, Cannes, NBR, César, BAFTA , DDA, VFF

Matlin, Marlee

★ 1986-(BA) *Children of a Lesser God*

■ Born 8/24/65 in Morton Grove, IL.

⚜ Sarah Norman in Oscar'd role.

⚲ Afflicted with *Roseola Infantum* when a child which resulted in her lifelong deafness. Took criminal law courses in college and eventually married a police officer. Instrumental in helping pass a bill which required all TV sets 13 inches or larger to have closed captioning. Travels the world as a front person on behalf of the hearing impaired. Once dated Oscar winner William Hurt.

Major Awards: Oscar, GG

Matthau, Walter

★ 1966-(BSA) *The Fortune Cookie*

1971-(BA) *Kotch*
    Winner: Gene Hackman, *The French Connection*

1975-(BA) *The Sunshine Boys*
    Winner: Jack Nicholson, *One Flew over the Cuckoo's Nest*

■ Born *Walter Matthow* 10/1/20 in New York, NY. Died 7/1/2000 of a heart attack.

⚜ Oscar Madison in *The Odd Couple*

⚲ Served in the Army Air Corps as a radio cryptographer during WW II and returned home a sergeant with six battle stars. His father, Melos Matuschanskayasky was an Orthodox priest in Rus-

sia. Once was a boxing instructor, forester and gym teacher. An incorrigible gambler, it is estimated that his losses were over five million in his lifetime.

Major Awards: Oscar, GG, Tony, BAFTA, KCFCC, DDA, WOF

McCambridge, Mercedes

★ 1949-(BSA) *All the King's Men*

1956-(BSA) *Giant*
    Winner: Dorothy Malone, *Written on the Wind*

■ Born 3/17/18 in Joliet, IL. Died 3/17/04 of natural causes.

⚜ Sadie Burke in Oscar'd role.

⚲ Orson Welles, her co-star, called her "the world's greatest living radio actress." Suffered from alcoholism for years and finally beat her addiction. She was the uncredited voice of the demon in *The Exorcist*. She appealed to the SAG. All new prints have her name in the credits. Her only son John tragically killed himself, his wife, and children in 1987.

Major Awards: Oscar, GG, WOF

McCarthy, Kevin

1951-(BSA) *Death of a Salesman*
    Winner: Karl Malden, *A Streetcar Named Desire*

■ Born 2/15/14 in Seattle, WA.

⚜ Dr. Miles Bennell in *The Invasion of the Body Snatchers*

⚲ Majored in journalism at the University of Minnesota. Close personal friend of actor Montgomery Clift. Has starred in over 100 movies and has made over 125 TV appearances. Starred in the TV series *Flamingo Road*. His cousin was presidential candidate and Senator Eugene McCarthy.

Major Awards: GG

McCormack, Patty

1956-(BSA) *The Bad Seed*
    Winner: Dorothy Malone, *Written on the Wind*

■ Born *Patty Russo* on 8/21/45 in Brooklyn, NY.

🍴 Rhoda Penmark in nominated role

🔍 Started modeling career at age four. Never fully shed her image as the pig-tailed homicidal demon Rhoda in *The Bad Seed*, much akin to Linda Blair's role as Regan in *The Exorcist*. She appeared in a few more films and starred in her own TV sitcom in the '50s—*Peck's Bad Girl*. Voted the nation's most promising young actor in 1957.

Major Awards: WOF

McDaniel, Hattie

★ 1939-(BSA) *Gone with the Wind*

▪ Born 6/10/1895 in Wichita, KS.
Died 10/26/52 of breast cancer.

🍴 Mammy in Oscar'd role.

🔍 Her father was a Baptist preacher. She was the first black woman to sing on the radio and the first to win an Academy Award. Decided not to attend *Gone with the Wind* premiere in Atlanta because of the virulent racism that still stained the city. Her Oscar was willed to Howard University. However during the race riots in the '60s it was lost forever. Featured on a U.S. 39-cent commorative stamp in 2006.

Major Awards: Oscar, WOF

Vivien Leigh and Hattie McDaniel in *Gone with the Wind*.

McDonnell, Mary

1990-(BSA) *Dances with Wolves*
Winner: Whoopi Goldberg, *Ghost*
1992-(BA) *Passion Fish*
Winner: Emma Thompson, *Howard's End*

▪ Born 4/28/52 in Wilkes-Barre, PA.

🍴 Stands With Fist in nominated role.

🔍 Graduated from Fredonia State in New York. To keep herself busy, when she isn't on the stage, she teaches acting with her husband. She has the distinction of being the only actor to play both a First Lady (*Independence Day*) and the President (*Battlestar Galactica*).

McDormand, Frances

1988-(BSA) *Mississippi Burning*
Winner: Geena Davis, *The Accidental Tourist*
★ 1996-(BA) *Fargo*
2000-(BSA) *Almost Famous*
Winner: Marcia Gay Harden, *Pollock*
2005-(BSA) *North Country*
Winner: Rachel Weisz, *The Constant Gardner*

▪ Born 6/23/57 in Chicago, IL.

🍴 Marge Gunderson in Oscar'd role (#33 on AFI's Hero List)

🔍 She was the adopted daughter of a Disciples of Christ preacher. Graduated from Bethany College and Yale Drama School. Close friends to actress Holly Hunter. Married to movie director Joel Coen. They adopted a baby boy (Pedro) from Paraguay in 1994. One of only six women to be nominated for a movie that was directed by their spouse—and the only one to win the Oscar.

Major Awards: Oscar, NBR, SAG, LAFC, GG

McGovern, Elizabeth

1981-(BSA) *Ragtime*
Winner: Maureen Stapleton, *Reds*

▪ Born 7/18/61 in Evanston, IL.

🍴 Evelyn Nesbit in nominated role.

🖐 Dropped out of college to accept role in *Ordinary People*. Once engaged to actor Sean Penn.

McGuire, Dorothy

1947-(BA) *Gentleman's Agreement*
  Winner: Loretta Young, *The Farmer's Daughter*
▪ Born 6/14/18 in Omaha, NE. Died 6/14/2001 of cardiac arrest.
🖐 Kathey Lacey in nominated role.
🖐 Made her acting debut at age 13 opposite Henry Fonda. Married 36 years to noted *Life* magazine photographer John Swope. Always reclusive, turned down many ovations to pose for pictures, negated all efforts to publicize her life, and refused to wear makeup in many of her roles.
Major Awards: NBR, WOF

McKellen, Sir Ian

1998-(BA) *Gods and Monsters*
  Winner: Roberto Benigni, *Life is Beautiful*
2001-(BSA) *The Lord of the Rings: The Fellowship of the Ring*
  Winner: James Broadbent, *Iris*
▪ Born 5/25/39 in Burnley, Lancashire, England
🖐 Gandolf, the Sorcerer, in nominated role.
🖐 Graduated from Cambridge University with aspirations to be a journalist. In 1988 on the BBC radio he announced his homosexuality. He has been in a relationship for the past eight years. He was named Commander of the British Empire in 1979 and was knighted in 1990. He is a vegetarian.
Major Awards: CA, GG, Tony, DDA, OCC, NBR, LAFC, SAG, BIFF, ISA, KCFCC, Saturn.

McLaglen, Victor

★ 1935-(BA) *The Informer*
1952-(BSA) *The Quiet Man*
  Winner: Anthony Quinn, *Viva Zapata!*
▪ Born 12/10/1886 in Tunbridge Wells, Kent England. Died 11/7/59 of a heart attack.

John Wayne and Victor McLaglen in *The Quiet Man*.

🖐 Squire "Red" Will Danaher in *The Quiet Man*
🖐 Son of a Protestant Bishop. Enlisted to fight in the Boer War, but was shown the door when it was discovered he was only 14. He was a captain of the Irish Fusiliers during WW I. Also served as provost marshal of Bagdad, Iraq. Turned boxer, he battled famed Jack Johnson to a six-round draw and also boxed future champion Jess Willard. Worked in the circus, was a farmer, and mined gold in Australia. First Oscar winner to be nominated for a Best Supporting Oscar.
Major Awards: Oscar, WOF

McNamara, Maggie

1953-(BA) *The Moon Is Blue*
  Winner: Audrey Hepburn, *Roman Holiday*
▪ Born 6/18/28 in New York, NY. Died 2/18/78 of a drug overdose. A suicide note was left.
🖐 Patti O'Neill in nominated role.
🖐 She was a fashion model in her teens. She was twice featured on the cover of *Life* magazine. Her film career stalled out, and she eked out a living as

a typist. She had a history of mental illness. Her starring movie was condemned by The Catholic Legion of Decency.

McQueen, Steve

1966-(BA) *The Sand Pebbles*
    Winner: Paul Scofield, *A Man for All Seasons*
▪ Born 3/24/30 in Beech Grove, IN.
    Died 11/7/80 of lung cancer.
✏ Lt. Frank Bullitt in *Bullitt*
✎ He was abandoned as a baby and dropped out of school at age 14. He enlisted in the Marines and was thrown in the brig for 41 days for going AWOL. Had a gazillion jobs, from bartender to oil wildcatter. Beat out 2000 hopefuls for Lee Strasberg's Actors Studio. Did his own motorcycle driving in *The Great Escape*. Taught *Jeet Kune Do*, the fighting form developed by Bruce Lee. Racecar enthusiast, finishing second at Sebring in 1970. Flew his own plane. Was almost totally deaf due to a deep-sea diving accident. Threatened to punch out Howard Hughes if he kept harassing mutual friend Mamie Van Doren.
Major Awards: GGWFF, GG, WOF

McTeer, Janet

1999-(BA) *Tumbleweeds*
    Winner: Hilary Swank, *Boys Don't Cry*
▪ Born 5/8/61 in Newcastle, England, UK.
✏ Mary Jo Walker in nominated role.
✎ Graduated from RADA. She is very statuesque at 6'1." She grew so fast that her knees needed to be bandaged to ease her growing pains. While filming in North Africa she contracted a virus, which permanently ruined the vision in her right eye.
Major Awards: Tony, NBR, GG, Sundance

Medford, Kay

1968-(BSA) *Funny Girl*
    Winner: Ruth Gordon-*Rosemary's Baby*

▪ Born *Maggie O'Regin* on 9/14/14 in New York, NY. Died 4/10/80 of cancer.
✏ Rose Brice in nominated role.
✎ Her Irish parents died unexpectedly when she was a teenager. After her parents' deaths she fell back on humor as a comforting mechanism. Supported herself as a waitress in a nightclub where she developed her comedic stage routine. Won NY Drama Critics Award for her role in *Bye, Bye Birdie*. Was a regular on the *Dean Martin Comedy Hour*.

Menjou, Adolf

1930/31-(BA) *The Front Page*
    Winner: Lionel Barrymore, *A Free Soul*
▪ Born 2/18/1890 in Pittsburgh, PA.
    Died 10/29/63 of chronic hepatitis.
✏ The Menjou mustache. Always sophisticated, suave, debonair, and sartorially dressed.
✎ Attended Culver Military Academy. Graduated from Cornell University with a degree in engineering. Served as a captain of the Ambulance Corps in WW I. Voted Hollywood's Best Dressed Actor for nine straight years. Co-founder of the Motion Picture Alliance for the Preservation of American Ideals. Willingly cooperated with the HUAC in the '40s which torpedoed many fellow actors' careers.
Major Awards: WOF

Merchant, Vivien

1966-(BSA) *Alfie*
    Winner: Sandy Dennis, *Who's Afraid of Virginia Woolf?*
▪ Born *Ada Thomson* on 7/22/29 in Manchester, England. Died 10/3/82 of cirrhosis of the liver due to acute alcoholism.
✏ Lily in nominated role.
✎ First appeared on stage at age 14. Formerly married to playwright Harold Pinter. Essentially died of a broken heart. She fell into acute alcoholism following her divorce from Harold Pinter. Nominated for a Tony for *The Homecoming* in 1967.
Major Awards: NBR

Mercouri, Melina

1960-(BA) *Never on Sunday*
Winner: Elizabeth Taylor, *Butterfield 8*
▪ Born 10/18/23 in Athens, Greece.
Died 3/16/94 of lung cancer.
🖋 Ilya in nominated role. Known as "The Last Greek Goddess."
🔑 Her father was Minister of the State and Deputy Mayor of Athens. Politics were in her blood and she was a thorn in the side of the then-ruling junta. She was declared an enemy of the state, her citizenship was revoked, and she was forced into exile. She returned triumphantly, ran for a seat in the Parliament, and won. She was the first woman to hold a cabinet post in the Greek government, as Minister of Culture.
Major Awards: Cannes, OCC

Meredith, Burgess

1975-(BSA) *The Day of the Locust*
Winner: George Burns, *The Sunshine Boys*
1976-(BSA) *Rocky*
Winner: Jason Robards, *All the President's Men*
▪ Born 11/16/1907 in Cleveland, OH. Died 9/9/97 of cancer and Alzheimer's disease.
🖋 Role of the Penguin on TV's *Batman* series, and Mickey the trainer in *Rocky*.
🔑 Started out as a newspaper reporter, and seaman and was a captain in the Air Force during WW II. He was blacklisted by the House Un-American Activities Committee in the '50s. Besides acting he also wrote and directed. He was a staunch environmentalist. Once married to actress Paulette Goddard.
Major Awards: Emmy, NBR, WOF

Merkel, Una

1961-(BSA) *Summer and Smoke*
Winner: Rita Moreno, *West Side Story*
▪ Born 12/10/1903 in Covington, KY. Died 1/2/86 of natural causes.
🖋 Lily Belle Callahan in *Destry Rides Again*. Remember the knock-down drag-out fight between her and Marlene Dietrich . . . ?
🔑 Started out on the stage and later filled in as Lillian Gish's double. Starred in over 100 films of which 60 were made in the '30s. Her mother committed suicide in 1946 by turning on the gas stove. Una, in the next room, almost died. She was signed on as the original Blondie but the deal fell through in the last minute.
Major Awards: Tony, WOF

Midler, Bette

1979-(BA) *The Rose*
Winner: Sally Field, *Norma Rae*
1991-(BA) *For the Boys*
Winner: Jodie Foster, *The Silence of the Lambs*
▪ Born 12/1/45 in Paterson, NJ
🖋 "The Divine Miss M," Mary Rose Foster in nominated role, a fictional pseudo-bio of Janis Joplin.
🔑 Worked in a Dole pineapple factory. Graduated from the University of Hawaii. At age 21 headed for New York to kick-start her singing career. Barry Manilow was her pianist. Dedicated her first album to her sister Judy who died in an auto accident. Ranked #51 in VH 1's Greatest Women of Rock. Sang to Johnny Carson on his Farewell Show. Wrote best selling baby's book *The Saga of Baby Devine*.
Major Awards: Emmy, Grammy, Tony, GG, NBR, WFCA, PCA, WOF

Miles, Sarah

1970-(BA) *Ryan's Daughter*
Winner: Glenda Jackson, *Women in Love*
▪ Born 12/31/41 in Ingatestone, England.
🖋 Rosy Ryan in nominated role.
🔑 Enrolled in London's RADA at age 15. Married to Oscar-winning screenwriter Robert Bolt twice. Her career was hurt when she was enmeshed in a scandal when her manager committed suicide in her motel room. Is rather reclusive, a loner but an incessant talker, and she suffers from dyslexia.
Major Awards: NY International Film and Video

Miles, Sylvia

1969-(BSA) *Midnight Cowboy*
   Winner: Goldie Hawn, *Cactus Flower*
1975-(BSA) *Farewell, My Lovely*
   Winner: Lee Grant, *Shampoo*
▦ Born 9/9/32 in New York, NY.
✇ Cass in *Midnight Cowboy*
✎ She was married at the age of 16. She was almost cast in the role of Sally Rogers in *The Dick Van Dyke Show*. Peeved by a review, she dumped a plate of food on critic John Simon's head in a busy restaurant. Nominated for an Oscar for the shortest performance ever. Famous on the New York scene, she will reportedly attend "the opening of an envelope."

Milford, Penelope

1978-(BSA) *Coming Home*
   Winner: Maggie Smith, *California Suite*
▦ Born 3/1948 in St. Louis, MO.
✇ Viola Munson in nominated role.
✎ She made her acting bones in the Chicago and New York theaters. She was quite close to her younger brother Kim Milford, an actor, singer, and songwriter who died at age 37 following open-heart surgery. She had a five-year relationship with actor Richard Gere. Graduated from the high school of the stars New Treir in Winnetka, IL. Other alumni of that school were Charton Heston and Rock Hudson.

Milland, Ray

★ 1945-(BA) *The Lost Weekend*
▦ Born *Reginald Truscott-Jones* on 1/3/1905 in Neath, Glamorganshire, Wales, UK. Died 3/10/86 of lung cancer.
✇ Don Birnam in Oscar'd role.
✎ Served as a member of the King's Household Cavalry in Buckingham Palace. Rode as a jockey in the Grand National Steeplechase. He was an expert horseman. Had a tattoo of a skull and snake on his right arm. Only actor to not give an acceptance speech after being awarded the Oscar. He just nodded and walked off the stage.

Major Awards: Oscar, NBR, NYFC, GG, Cannes, WOF

Miller, Jason

1973-(BSA) *The Exorcist*
   Winner: John Houseman, *The Paper Chase*
▦ Born 4/22/39 in Long Island, NY. Died 5/13/2001 of a massive heart attack.
✇ Father Karras in nominated role.
✎ Very versatile and talented. He was an actor, writer, director, poet, producer, and playwright. Graduated from Scranton. He wrote *That Championship Season*, which garnered him the Pulitzer Prize in Literature. Married to Jackie Gleason's daughter Linda, and their son is actor Jason Patric.
Major Awards: Pulitzer Prize, Tony, NYDC

Mills, Haley

1960-Honorary Oscar
▦ Born 4/18/46 in London, England.
✇ Pollyanna
✎ Daughter of actor John Mills. Signed a five-year contract with Walt Disney. Jolted Hollywood when she shed her wholesome image and appeared nude in the *The Family Way*. Married the director, Roy Boulting, who was 33 years older than she. She had two godfathers, Sir Laurence Olivier and Sir Noel Coward. She and her father John were the first father/daughter Oscar winners. Her sister is actress Juliet Mills.
Major Awards: GG, BAFTA

Mills, Sir John

★ 1970-(BSA) *Ryan's Daughter*
▦ Born *Lewis Ernest Mills* on 2/22/1908 in Felixstone, Suffolk, England.
✇ Father Robinson in *The Swiss Family Robinson*
✎ Started as a song and dance boy in the London Revue. Served in the army during WW II. Father of actresses Haley and Juliet Mills. Appointed Commander of the British Empire in 1960 and knighted

by the Queen in 1976. Close friend Richard Attenborough gave the eulogy at his funeral.
Major Awards: Oscar, GG, NBR, KCFCC, VFF

Mineo, Sal

1955-(BSA) *Rebel Without a Cause*
  Winner: Jack Lemon, *Mister Roberts*
1960-(BSA) *Exodus*
  Winner: Peter Ustinov, *Spartacus*
▦ Born 1/10/39 in The Bronx, NY.
  Died 2/12/76, a homicide victim.
⫸ Plato Crawford in *Rebel Without a Cause*.
⚲ His father was a casket maker. A regular juvenile
delinquent, he was booted out a school at age eight
and arrested at age ten for robbery. Judge gave him a
choice, reform school or acting school. As a singer he
had two Top-40 hit songs in the '50 s. Walking home,
he was assaulted and stabbed to death by a drifter,
who would do a life sentence for the crime.
Major Awards: GG

Minnelli, Liza

1969-(BA) *The Sterile Cuckoo*
  Winner: Maggie Smith, *The Prime of Miss
  Jean Brodie*
★ 1972-(BA) *Cabaret*
▦ Born 3/12/46 in Los Angeles, CA.
⫸ Sally Bowles in Oscar'd role; many Broadway
  roles, troubled marriages, and well-publicized
  struggles with substance abuse; her version of
  "New York! New York!"
⚲ Daughter of Legendary Judy Garland and direc-
tor Vincent Minnelli. Made her film debut at age
two. She attended over 20 schools in California and
Europe. Liza has had her hip replaced twice and has
undergone three knee operations. She and Judy
were the first mother/daughter to be nominated for
Oscars. She is one of the few to win the Superfecta
of acting.
Major Awards: Oscar, Tony, Grammy, Emmy,
BAFTA, WOF

Mirren, Dame Helen

1994-(BSA) *The Madness of King George*
  Winner: Dianne Weist, *Bullets over
  Broadway*
2001-(BSA) *Gosford Park*
  Winner: Jennifer Connelly, *A Beautiful Mind*
★ 2006-(BA) *The Queen*
▦ Born *LLynea Lydia Mironoff* on 7/26/45 in
  Chiswick, London, England.
⫸ Mrs. Wilson in *Gosford Park*, title role in
  The Queen.
⚲ Her father was of Russian nobility. He was stranded
in England when the Russian Revolution broke out.
Married to director Taylor Hackford. She reportedly
refused an appointment as Commander of the British
Empire 1996. In an evident change of heart accepted
the Queen's offer and was made Dame of the British
Empire in 2003.
Major Awards: Emmy, Cannes, GG, NSFC,
NBR, NYFC, SAG, BAFTA, VFF

Mitchell, Thomas

1937-(BSA) *The Hurricane*
  Winner: Joseph Schildkraut, *The Life of
  Emile Zola*
★ 1939-(BSA) *Stagecoach*
▦ Born 7/11/1892 in Elizabeth, NJ.
  Died 12/17/62 of cancer.
⫸ Uncle Billy in *It's a Wonderful Life*
⚲ Started as a reporter for the local paper. Later
wrote several plays, which were adapted into movies.
His nephew, James Mitchell, was a former Secre-
tary of State under Dwight Eisenhower. One of
Hollywood's great character actors. First actor to
achieve the Triple Crown of acting.
Major Awards: Oscar, Tony, Emmy, WOF

Mitchum, Robert

1945-(BSA) *The Story of G.I. Joe*
  Winner: James Dunn, *A Tree Grows in Brooklyn*
▦ Born 8/6/17 in Bridgeport, CT. Died 7/1/97
  of lung cancer emphysema.

Robert Mitchum (left) in *The Story of G.I. Joe.*

🖋 Max Cady in *Cape Fear* (#28 on AFI's Villain List), Rev. Harry Powell in *Night of the Hunter* (#29 on AFI's Villain List)

🔍 Ran away from home at age 14. Sentenced to a chain gang in Georgia for vagrancy and escaped. Worked as a bouncer, boxer (27 professional fights), astrology writer, freighter wiper, and factory worker. Private in the army during WW II, and was awarded the Victory Medal. Got his start as an extra in Hopalong Cassidy films. Convicted of smoking marijuana in 1948. Had to dry out in an alcohol rehab facility in 1984. Played the sax and wrote poetry. Turned down the role of Patton and recommended George C. Scott. Recorded an album of Calypso songs, *Calypso is Like So.*

Major Awards: GG, NBR, LAFC, WOF

Montenegro, Fernanda

1998-(BA) *Central Station*
    Winner: Gwyneth Paltrow, *Shakespeare in Love*
▪ Born *Arlette Pinhero Esteves de Silva* on 10/16/29 in Rio de Janeiro, Brazil.
🖋 Dora in nominated role.
🔍 First broke into radio and began appearing in soap operas. Made her film debut when she was 19. Known as the Grand Dame of Brazilian television. First actress from Brazil to be nominated for an Academy Award. Turned down the appointment by Brazil's president to be the nation's Minister of Culture.
Major Awards: NBR, LAFC

Montgomery, Robert

1937-(BA) *Night Must Fall*
    Winner: Spencer Tracy, *Captains Courageous*
1941-(BA) *Here Comes Mr. Jordon*
    Winner: Gary Cooper, *Sergeant York*
▪ Born 5/21/1904 in Beacon, NY.
    Died 9/27/81 of cancer.
🖋 Mr. Jordan in nominated role
🔍 Worked as a railroad mechanic. He was a Lt. Commander of a PT Boat in the Pacific during WW II. He won the Bronze Star and was decorated a Knight in the French Legion of Honor. On the board of directors of Macy's, Milwaukee Phone Co., and Lincoln Center for the Performing Arts. Served as president of the Screen Actors Guild for years. Daughter was Elizabeth Montgomery star of TV series *Bewitched.*
Major Awards: Tony, Emmy, WOF

Moody, Ron

1968-(BA) *Oliver*
    Winner: Cliff Robertson, *Charly*
▪ Born *Ronald Moodnick* on 1/8/24 in London, England
🖋 Fagin in nominated role
🔍 Didn't get into acting until age 29. He was educated at the London School of Economics and ended up an economist and sociologist before his foray into acting. He was a staunch advocate for decreasing violence in movies. He was offered the part of Dr. Who on the BBC, but turned it down.
Major Awards: GG

Moore, Dudley

1981-(BA) *Arthur*
    Winner: Henry Fonda, *On Golden Pond*
▪ Born 4/19/35 in London, England.
    Died 3/27/2002 of pneumonia due to complications of supranuclear palsy.
🖋 Arthur in nominated role.
🔍 He was born with a clubfoot and was only 5'2" tall. Graduated from Oxford with a degree in music.

He was a concert pianist, composer, writer, actor and comedian. Once married to actress Tuesday Weld. He was arrested and charged with domestic violence in 1984. He was made Commander of the British Empire (CBE) in 2001.
Major Awards: GG, Tony, WOF

Moore, Grace

1934-(BA) *One Night of Love*
  Winner: Claudette Colbert, *It Happened One Night*
▥ Born 12/5/1898 in Slabtown, TN. Died 1/26/47 in a plane crash in Sweden following a concert.
⍗ As the Tennessee Nightingale
⚲ Wanted to be a missionary. Sang soprano at the Metropolitan Opera House. She was decorated as a Knight of the Legion of Honor in France in 1939. Elvis Presley named his mansion *Graceland* in her honor. Once refused to appear on stage with the Mills Brothers because of their color. Loews cancelled her contract.
Major Awards: WOF

Moore, Juanita

1959-(BSA) *Imitation of Life*
  Winner: Shelly Winters, *The Diary of Anne Frank*
▥ Born 10/19/22 in Los Angeles, CA.
⍗ Annie Johnson in nominated role.
⚲ One of the first black actresses to be given a substantial role in a movie. She benefited from the change in the social climate of the '50s. She went on to appear in over 40 movies and 20 television roles. She was nominated for a Golden Globe and came in second for the Laurel Award.

Moore, Julianne

1997-(BSA) *Boogie Nights*
  Winner: Kim Basinger, *L.A. Confidential*

1999-(BA) *The End of the Affair*
  Winner: Hilary Swank, *Boys Don't Cry*
2002-(BA) *Far From Heaven*
  Winner: Nichole Kidman, *The Hours*
2002-(BSA) *The Hours*
  Winner: Catherine Zeta-Jones, *Chicago*
▥ Born *Julie Ann Smith* on 12/3/60 in Fayetteville, NC.
⍗ Amber Waves in *Boogie Nights*
⚲ She was an Army brat. Her father was a military judge. Graduated from high school in Frankfort, Germany. Worked as a waitress. Graduated from Boston College with a degree in the Arts. Started out her career on the TV soap opera *As the World Turns*. She is pro-choice and a member of Planned Parenthood.
Major Awards: LAFC, NSFC, NBR, Emmy, GG, NYFC, BIFF, BSFC, ISA, KCFCC, VFF

Moore, Mary Tyler

1980-(BA) *Ordinary People*
  Winner: Sissy Spacek, *Coal Miner's Daughter*
▥ Born 12/29/36 in Brooklyn, NY.
⍗ Laura Petrie on TV comedy series *The Dick Van Dyke Show* and star of her own long-running sitcom
⚲ Started out as a dancer. First appeared on TV in a Hotpoint commercial 1955. She is a vegetarian and a strong animal rights activist. Has been a diabetic for 30 years. Spent a brief time at the Betty Ford Clinic. Her only son Richie accidentally shot and killed himself. Her sister died of a drug overdose and her brother attempted suicide but later died of cancer.
Major Awards: Emmy (6), GG, Tony, WOF

Moore, Terry

1952-(BSA) *Come Back, Little Sheba*
  Winner: Gloria Grahame, *The Bad and the Beautiful*
▥ Born *Helen Koford* on 1/7/29 in Los Angeles, CA.
⍗ Jill Young in the ape classic *Mighty Joe Young*

She worked as a child model before breaking into the movies at age eight. Once dated former Secretary of State Henry Kissinger. She was secretly married to billionaire Howard Hughes. When he died she sued his estate and received an undisclosed settlement after a lengthy court battle. Married six times.
Major Awards: WOF

Moorehead, Agnes

1942-(BSA) *The Magnificent Ambersons*
    Winner: Teresa Wright, *Mrs. Miniver*
1944-(BSA) *Mrs. Parkington*
    Winner: Ethel Barrymore, *None but the Lonely Heart*
1948-(BSA) *Johnny Belinda*
    Winner: Claire Trevor, *Key Largo*
1964-(BSA) *Hush . . . Hush, Sweet Charlotte*
    Winner: Lila Kedrova, *Zorba the Greek*
▩ Born 12/6/1906 in Clinton, MA.
    Died 4/30/74 of lung cancer.
✠ Endora the Witch on the TV series *Bewitched*
✎ Made her professional debut at age 11 as a ballerina. Graduated from Bradley University with a PhD in literature. Her father also had his PhD. She was the first woman to host the Academy Awards. The film *The Conqueror* was filmed near a nuclear test site, and she along with 91 cast members including John Wayne, Susan Hayward, and Dick Powell all died of cancer-related illnesses.
Major Awards: NBR, NYFC, GG, Emmy, WOF

Moreno, Catalina Sandino

2004-(BA) *Maria Full of Grace*
    Winner: Hilary Swank, *Million Dollar Baby*
▩ Born 1981 in Bogotá, Columbia
✠ Maria Alvarez in nominated role.
✎ She was attending acting class when she was plucked out to play the lead in nominated role. Moved to New York City in 2003. She is the first person from her country to be nominated for an Academy Award. She is also the first person to be nominated in an all-Spanish-speaking movie.
Major Awards: BIFF, ISA, LAFC

Rita Moreno in *West Side Story*.

Moreno, Rita

★ 1961-(BSA) *West Side Story*
▩ Born *Rosita Dolores Alverio* on 12/11/31 in Humacao, Puerto Rico.
✠ Anita in Oscar'd role.
✎ Immigrated to Hollywood at age 14 and worked as a dancer. Made her television debut on *Father Knows Best* in 1954. National spokesman for the Osteoporosis Foundation. First actor to garner an Oscar, Emmy, Grammy, and Tony. She is listed in the *Guinness Book of World Records*. Ninth person to win the Triple Crown and the Superfecta of acting. Married to an internist and cardiologist.
Major Awards: Oscar, Tony, Emmy, Grammy, Presidential Medal of Freedom, WOF

Morgan, Frank

1934-(BA) *The Affairs of Cellini*
    Winner: Clark Gable, *It Happened One Night*

127

1942-(BSA) *Tortilla Flat*
  Winner: Van Heflin, *Johnny Eager*

▨ Born *Frances Wupperman* on 6/1/1890 in New York, NY. Died 9/18/49 of natural causes.

▨ Five roles in *The Wizard of Oz*—the wizard, the gateman, the wizard's guard, Professor Marvel, and the horse-of-a-different-color's cart driver

⚲ His father was a wealthy manufacturer of cocktail bitters. He sang soprano in his local church. He was one of 11 children. In his youth he was a bronco buster and sold toothbrushes. Owned a yacht, *The Dolphin*, and won many races throughout the Pacific. Member of the "Irish Mafia" with James Cagney, Pat O'Brien, Spencer Tracy, and Frank McHugh, even though he wasn't Irish.
Major Awards: WOF

Moriarty, Cathy

1980-(BSA) *Raging Bull*
  Winner: Mary Steenburgen, *Melvin and Howard*

▨ Born 11/29/60 in The Bronx, NY.

▨ Vicki La Motta in nominated role.

⚲ She was involved in a horrific auto accident, which required back surgery and extensive therapy. A heavy smoker until she found out she was pregnant with twins and quit cold turkey. Co-owns Mulberry St. Pizza with Raquel Welch's husband, Richard Palmer.
Major Awards: Cable Ace

Morita, Noriyuki (Pat)

1984-(BSA) *The Karate Kid*
  Winner: Haing S. Ngor, *The Killing Fields*

▨ Born 6/28/32 in Isleton, CA.

▨ Malt shop owner Arnold on TV sitcom *Happy Days*

⚲ He had spinal tuberculosis as a child and doctors said he'd never walk. He was discovered by comedian Redd Foxx. He debuted as a standup comic calling himself "The Hip Nip." Owned a Japanese restaurant on Sunset Blvd. in Hollywood. At Pat's funeral, his young co-star in *The Karate Kid*, Ralph Macchio, offered a brief eulogy: "Forever My Sensei."
Major Awards: WOF

Morley, Robert

1938-(BSA) *Marie Antonette*
  Winner: Walter Brennan, *Kentucky*

▨ Born 5/25/1908 in Semley, Wiltshire, England. Died 6/3/92 of a stroke.

▨ Witty and rotund talk show guest on TV in the '50s.

⚲ Graduated from Wellington and intended to be an international diplomat. He wrote several plays when he wasn't acting. Appointed Commander of the British Empire in 1957. When asked to be a speaker at his alma mater he said the only reason he would return is to burn the place down.
Major Awards: LAFC, NSFC

Morris, Chester

1928/29-(BA) *Alibi*
  Winner: Warner Baxter, *In Old Arizona*

▨ Born 2/16/1901 in New York, NY. Died 9/11/70 of a drug overdose.

▨ Boston Blackie on the radio and film.

⚲ Made his acting debut in silents at age nine. Billed himself as the "youngest leading man in the country." Made 13 movies as super sleuth Boston Blackie. Claimed he heard the deathbed confession of director Roland West, who claimed it was he who murdered actress Thelma Todd. The crime is still unsolved. Died in a motel room of an overdose of barbiturates.

Morton, Samantha

1999-(BSA) *Sweet and Lowdown*
  Winner: Angelina Jolie, *Girl, Interrupted*
2003-(BA) *In America*
  Winner: Charlize Theron, *Monster*

▨ Born 5/13/77 in Nottinghamshire, England

▨ Agatha, the Precog, in *Minority Report*

Hit the TV circuit when she was 13, the same year she dropped out of school. Later on she attended West Bridgeford Comprehensive School. Acting is in her genes—her father is a schooled actor himself. She has eight brothers and sisters. Turned down the title role in *Iris*. She is currently engaged to Harry Holm, whose dad is English actor Ian Holm.

Major Awards: London Film Critics, Boston Film Critics

Mueller-Stahl, Armin

1996-(BSA) *Shine*
  Winner: Cuba Gooding, Jr., *Jerry Maguire*
  Born 12/17/30 in Tilsit, East Prussia, Germany
  Grandpa Sam Krischinsky in *Avalon*
  As a teen he was considered somewhat a musical prodigy and was a concert violinist. He got into acting and became famous for his stunning stage performances. He got in trouble with the Communist party because of his active stance against musical suppression by the government and was blacklisted, eventually escaping to West Germany.

Major Awards: German Film Award, BIFF

Muni, Paul

1928/29-(BA) *The Valiant*
  Winner: Warner Baxter, *In Old Arizona*
1932/33-(BA) *I Am a Fugitive from a Chain Gang*
  Winner: Charles Laughton, *The Private Life of Henry Vlll*
★ 1936-(BA) *The Story of Louis Pasteur*
1937-(BA) *The Life of Emile Zola*
  Winner: Spencer Tracy, *Captains Courageous*
1959-(BA) *The Last Angry Man*
  Winner: Charlton Heston, *Ben-Hur*
  Born *Muni Weiserfreund* on 9/22/1895 in Lemberg, Australia. Died 8/25/67 of a severe heart ailment.
  Louis Pasteur in Oscar'd role
  First appeared on stage at age seven. Family migrated to the U.S. in 1902. Suffered from a rheumatic heart his whole life. Only actor ever to be nominated

for an Oscar in his first and last film performances. Went blind toward the end of his life. He was the first person to win an Oscar for portraying a real person, Louis Pasteur. Due to his failing health in later years, he used a radio transmitter to help him remember his lines.

Major Awards: NYFC, TONY, WOF

Murphy, Eddie

2006-(BSA) *Dreamgirls*
  Winner: Alan Arkin, *Little Miss Sunshine*
  Born 4/3/61 in Brooklyn, NY.
  Saturday Night Live TV show, Reggie Hammond in *48 Hours*, the *Eddie Murphy Raw* concert film
  His dad was a policeman and died when Eddie was five. Started writing and performing his own skits at age 15. He was voted most popular in high school. He was doing standup routines at Manhattan's Comic Strip at age 19. Dated Halle Berry and Whitney Houston. He was the first actor to get a million dollars for a first movie, *48 Hours*. Paid for his comedy idol Redd Foxx's funeral. Co-owns the restaurant Georgia in Los Angeles, with Denzel Washington.

Major Awards: Grammy, GG, NSFC, PC, Saturn, WOF

Murray, Bill

2003-(BA) *Lost in Translation*
  Winner: Sean Penn, *Mystic River*
  Born 9/21/50 in Wilmette, IL.
  Paul Venkman in *Ghostbusters*, *Saturday Night Live*.
  He has eight brothers and sisters. Paid for his college tuition (Loyola University) by being a caddie. Once was a pre-med student at St. Regis but dropped out after a marijuana possession incident. He is a diehard Cubs fan and named his son Homer Banks after Cubs great Ernie Banks. His sister is a Dominican nun. He has no lawyer or agent and handles all of his own business affairs.

Major Awards: LAFC, NYFC, NSFC, GG, Emmy

Murray, Don

1956-(BSA) *Bus Stop*
　Winner: Anthony Quinn, *Lust for Life*
▪ Born 7/31/29 in Hollywood, CA
▨ Father Charles Dismas Clark in *The Hoodlum Priest*
🔍 His mother was a Ziegfield Girl. He was a conscientious objector during the Korean War. Because of his principles he turned down many roles that didn't agree with his social and political beliefs. Once married to actress Hope Lange.
Major Awards: WOF

Naish, J. Carrol

1943-(BSA) *Sahara*
　Winner: Charles Coburn, *The More the Merrier*
1945-(BSA) *A Medal for Benny*
　Winner: James Dunn, *A Tree Grows in Brooklyn*
▪ Born 1/21/1897 in New York, NY.
　Died 1/24/73 of emphysema.
▨ Giuseppe in *Sahara*
🔍 He joined the navy when he was 16 and was in the Signal Corps in WW II. After the war he traveled all over the world. Appeared in over 191 films. Although of Irish descent, never played an Irishman on film.
Major Awards: GG, WOF

Natwick, Mildred

1967-(BSA) *Barefoot in the Park*
　Winner: Estelle Parsons, *Bonnie and Clyde*
▪ Born 6/19/1905 in Baltimore, MD.
　Died 10/25/94 of cancer.
▨ Mrs. Ethel Banks in nominated role.
🔍 Graduated from Bryn Mawr College. Favorite of director John Ford. Starred on TV series *The Snoop Sisters* costarring with Helen Hayes. She was a devout follower of Christian Science. She was nominated for two Tonys.
Major Awards: Emmy

Neal, Patricia

★ 1963-(BA) *Hud*
1968-(BA) *The Subject Was Roses*
　Winner: Katharine Hepburn, *The Lion in Winter*
▪ Born 1/20/26 in Packard, KY.
▨ Alma Brown in Oscar'd role.
🔍 She took speech and drama courses at Northwestern University. Her classmates were Charlton Heston and Paul Lynde. She turned down the role of Mrs. Robinson in *The Graduate*. Suffered a nervous breakdown after a romantic entanglement with Gary Cooper, while he was married. Suffered a debilitating stroke which left her paralyzed and wheelchair bound. She made a miraculous recovery and regained her speech and movement.
Major Awards: GG, NBR, NYFC, BAFTA

Neeson, Liam

1993-(BA) *Schindler's List*
　Winner: Tom Hanks, *Philadelphia*
▪ Born 6/7/52 in Ballymena, Northern Ireland
▨ Oscar Schindler in nominated role (#13 on AFI's Hero List), Qui-Gon-Jinn in *Star Wars I*
🔍 He was an amateur boxer for eight years winning the Irish Youth Championship. He attended the Queens College in Belfast but college wasn't for him, and he flunked out. He was also a truck driver, fork lift operator, and architect. Was named Officer of the British Empire (OBE) by the Queen in 1999. Seriously hurt when he crashed his Harley after hitting a deer. Fly fishing is one of his hobbies.
Major Awards: LAFC, VFF

Nelligan, Kate

1991-(BSA) *The Prince of Tides*
　Winner: Mercedes Ruehl, *The Fisher King*
▪ Born 3/16/50 in London, Ontario, Canada.
▨ Eleni in movie of same name.
🔍 Attended the University of Toronto and Central School of Speech and Drama in London. She has

been nominated four times for a Tony award. Had her own TV series, *The Onedin Line*, in 1976.
Major Awards: NBR, BAFTA

Newman, Paul

1958-(BA) *Cat on a Hot Tin Roof*
   Winner: David Niven, *Separate Tables*
1961-(BA) *The Hustler*
   Winner: Maximillian Schell, *Judgment at Nuremberg*
1963-(BA) *Hud*
   Winner: Sidney Poitier, *Lilies of the Field*
1967-(BA) *Cool Hand Luke*
   Winner: Rod Steiger, *In the Heat of the Night*
1981-(BA) *Absence of Malice*
   Winner: Henry Fonda, *On Golden Pond*
1982-(BA) *The Verdict*
   Winner: Ben Kingsley, *Gandhi*
1985-Honorary Oscar
★ 1986-(BA) *The Color of Money*
1994-(BA) *Nobody's Fool*
   Winner: Tom Hanks, *Forrest Gump*
2002-(BSA) *Road to Perdition*
   Winner: Chris Cooper, *Adaptation*
▪ Born 1/26/25 in Shaker Heights, OH.
▨ Fast Eddie Felson in *The Hustler*; Luke Jackson (#30 on AFI's Hero List), in *Cool Hand Luke*,

Butch Cassidy in *Butch Cassidy and the Sundance Kid (#20 on AFI's Hero List)* Henry Gondorff in *The Sting*
⚲ Served in WW II as a radioman. Attended Yale Drama School. Has been married to actress Joanne Woodward for 47 years. His only son Scott died of a drug overdose. Donates all earnings ($100+ million) from his food line *Newman's Own* to children's cancer charity. He entered into the racing world and finished second at LeMans in 1979. Placated his passion for car racing by owning his own team with Carl Hass. Only one of four actors to be nominated over a five-decade period. Top Ten money-making star for 17 years. Liked to tip a few beers in his day and is credited with the saying "24 hours in a day, 24 beers in a case, coincidence, I don't think so."
Major Awards: Cannes, GGWFF, GG, NYFC, CBR, NBR, SAGLA, Jean Hersholt Humanitarian, BAFTA, NSFC, WOF, Emmy

Ngor, Haing S.

★ 1984-(BSA) *The Killing Fields*
▪ Born 3/22/40 in Samrong Young, Cambodia. Died 2/25/96: resisting an attempt to rob him, he was fatally shot by the Oriental Lazy Boyz gang. It was speculated they were contracted by the Khmer Rouge.

Paul Newman in *Cool Hand Luke*.

Hang S. Ngor in *Killing Fields*.

🖌 Dith Pran in Oscar'd role.

🕯 He was a gynecologist and surgeon and officer in the Cambodian Army. He was captured and tortured (cut off his finger) by the Khmer Rouge. After four years of imprisonment and the death of his wife and child he escaped to the U.S. First amateur since Harold Russell to win an Oscar. Only the third Asian to win the Award.

Major Awards: GG, BAFTA, BSFC

Nicholson, Jack

1969-(BSA) *Easy Rider*
  Winner: Gig Young, *They Shoot Horses, Don't They?*
1970-(BA) *Five Easy Pieces*
  Winner: George C. Scott, *Patton*
1973-(BA) *The Last Detail*
  Winner: Jack Lemmon, *Save the Tiger*

Jack Nicholson in *One Flew Over the Cuckoo's Nest*.

1974-(BA) *Chinatown*
  Winner: Art Carney, *Harry and Tonto*
★ 1975-(BA) *One Flew Over the Cuckoo's Nest*
1981-(BSA) *Reds*
  Winner: Sir John Gielgud, *Arthur*
★ 1983-(BSA) *Terms of Endearment*
1985-(BA) *Prizzi's Honor*
  Winner: William Hurt, *Kiss of the Spider Woman*
1987-(BA) *Ironweed*
  Winner: Michael Douglas, *Wall Street*
1992-(BSA) *A Few Good Men*
  Winner: Gene Hackman, *Unforgiven*
★ 1997-(BA) *As Good As It Gets*
2002-(BA) *About Schmidt*
  Winner: Adrien Brody, *The Pianist*
◼ Born 4/22/37 in Neptune, NJ.
🖌 R.P. McMurphy in *One Flew Over the Cuckoo's Nest*; Jack Torrance, *The Shining*, (#25 on AFI's Villain List)
🕯 He was born out of wedlock, and his father deserted him and his mother. He was raised to believe his grandmother was his mother and his real mother his sister. He was voted class clown in high school. Most nominated actor ever (12 times). Friends with Danny DeVito since childhood. Had a 17-year relationship with Angelica Huston. Big L.A. Lakers fan and never misses a home game. Only he and Laurence Olivier have been nominated in five consecutive decades.

Major Awards: NYFC, NSFC, NYFC, GG, Cannes, NBR, SAG, AFI's Life Achievement Award, BAFTA, CB DeMille, DDA, KCFCC, LAFC, WOF

Niven, David

★ 1958-(BA) *Separate Tables*
◼ Born 3/1/1910 in Kirriemuir, Scotland.
  Died 7/29/83 of Lou Gehrig's Disease
🖌 Phileas Fogg in *Around the World in 80 Days*
🕯 His father was a Captain in the British Army and was killed in Gallipoli. He was a Lieutenant in the Highland Infantry. Re-entered the service as a Lt. Colonel when WW II broke out. His valet was Pvt. Peter Ustinov. He was Ian Fleming's first choice to

play James Bond. Once roomed with Errol Flynn; they nicknamed their bachelor pad Cirrhosis by the Sea. Wrote two best-selling memoirs, *The Moon Is Blue* and *Bring on the Empty Horses*. His first wife Primmie died in a tragic fall playing hide-and-seek at Tyrone Powers's home when she opened a door to the basement and suffered a fatal concussion when she tumbled down the stairs.

Major Awards: GG, NYFC, WOF

Nolte, Nick

1991-(BA) *The Prince of Tides*
　Winner: Anthony Hopkins, *The Silence of the Lambs*
1998-(BA) *Affliction*
　Winner: Roberto Benigni, *Life Is Beautiful*
▪ Born 2/8/41 in Omaha, NE.
✍ Jack Cates in *48 Hours*
✎ He attended Arizona State on a football scholarship. He was arrested in 1962 for selling fake draft cards and was put on five years probation. Likes to live it up and has a couple of DUIs under his belt. Checked into a rehab hospital for alcohol counseling. Gained 50 pounds for his role in *Q&A*.
Major Awards: GG, LAFC, NSFC, NYFC, BSFC

Norton, Edward

1996-(BSA) *Primal Fear*
　Winner: Cuba Gooding Jr., *Jerry Maguire*
1998-(BA) *American History X*
　Winner: Roberto Benigni, *Life Is Beautiful*
▪ Born 8/18/69 in Columbia, MD.
✍ Aaron Stampler in *Primal Fear*
✎ His father is an attorney, and his mother died from brain cancer. Discovered by famed playwright Edward Albee. Graduated from Yale majoring in history. Auditioned for his role in *Primal Fear* beating out 2000 hopefuls. Once played guitar for the band Hole. Learned to speak Japanese when he worked in Osaka and is also fluent in Spanish.
Major Awards: NBR, LAFC, GG, Obie, BSFC, KCFCC

Oakie, Jack

1940-(BSA) *The Great Dictator*
　Winner: Walter Brennan, *The Westener*
▪ Born *Lewis DeLaney Offield* on 11/12/1903 in Sedalia, MO. Died 1/23/78 of an aortic aneurysm.
✍ Benzini Napaloni in nominated role.
✎ Had a brush with death in 1920 when terrorists blew up the Wall St. Treasury Building where he was working as a clerk. Always refused to wear makeup. He took his name from the state of Oklahoma where he grew up as a kid. Starred on Broadway in George M. Cohan's *Little Nellie Kelly*.
Major Awards: WOF

Oberon, Merle

1935-(BA) *Dark Angel*
　Winner: Bette Davis, *Dangerous*
▪ Born *Estelle Merle Thompson* on 2/19/11 in Kolkata, India. Died 11/23/79 of a massive stroke.
✍ Kitty Vane in nominated role.
✎ Her mother was born in Ceylon and her father in Ireland. Left India at age 17 for London. Due to her sensitive skin, she suffered cosmetic poisoning twice. She was involved in a near-fatal auto accident which left her facially scarred. Her director husband, Alexander Korda, convinced her to change her name from Queenny Thompson.
Major Awards: WOF

O'Brian, Edmund

★ 1954-(BSA) *The Barefoot Contessa*
1964-(BSA) *Seven Days in May*
　Winner: Peter Ustinov, *Topkapi*
▪ Born 5/8/1915 in The Bronx, NY. Died 5/8/85 of Alzheimer's disease.
✍ Newspaper editor Dutton Peabody in *The Man Who Shot Liberty Valance*
✎ His neighbor Harry Houdini taught him magic at age ten. Graduated from Columbia University majoring in drama. Once was member of Orson Welles's Mercury Theater. Attained rank of sergeant

during WW II. Always had his pet German shepard at his side. Starred in the '50s TV detective series, *Johnny Midnight*.
Major Awards: GG, Western Heritage, WOF

O'Brien, Margaret

1944-Honorary Oscar
▦ Born 1/15/37 in San Diego, CA.
🗡 Tootie Smith in *Meet Me in St. Louis*
🖊 Made her screen debut at age four. Her splendid movie career as a child actor only lasted ten years. Thereafter she made many TV appearances. Her Oscar was stolen shortly after the award ceremonies. It was returned 50 years later by a dealer who found it in an antique shop. Although a prodigy, she couldn't make the transition to adult roles and retired in 1951.
Major Awards: Oscar, WOF

O'Connell, Arthur

1955-(BSA) *Picnic*
    Winner: Jack Lemmon, *Mister Roberts*
1959-(BSA) *Anatomy of a Murder*
    Winner: Hugh Griffith, *Ben-Hur*
▦ Born 3/29/1908 in New York, NY.
    Died 5/18/81 of Alzheimer's disease.
🗡 Parnel McCarthy in *Anatomy of a Murder*
🖊 Originally wanted to become a priest. Worked the vaudeville circuit for years. Hooked up with Orson Welles's Mercury Theater players. Made his film debut unbilled in *Citizen Kane*.
Major Awards: Laurel Award

O'Herlihy, Dan

1954-(BA) *Adventures Of Robinson Crusoe*
    Winner: Marlon Brando, *On the Waterfront*
▦ Born 5/1/19 in Wexford, Ireland.
    Died 2/17/2005 of natural causes.
🗡 Robinson Crusoe in nominated role.
🖊 Graduated from the University of Ireland majoring in architecture. His son Lorcan also majored

in architecture. Gravitated to Irish radio and then the stage with the Abbey Players. Discovered by the great director Carol Reed who gave him a part in his movie *The Odd Man Out*.

O'Keefe, Michael

1980-(BSA) *The Great Santini*
    Winner: Timothy Hutton, *Ordinary People*
▦ Born 4/24/55 in Paulland, NJ.
🗡 Ben Meechum in nominated role.
🖊 Graduated from NYU and studied at the American Academy of Dramatic Arts. He is a Buddhist and an ordained Zen priest. Co-wrote the song "Longing in Their Hearts" with then wife Bonnie Raitt, which won a Grammy for her. Enjoys hiking in his spare time.

Okonedo, Sofia

2004-(BSA) *Hotel Rwanda*
    Winner: Cate Blanchett, *The Aviator*
▦ Born 1/1/69 in London, England
🗡 Tatianna Rusesabagina in nominated role.
🖊 Her father is Nigerian. She dropped out of high school at age 16, but went on to graduate from Cambridge. Answered an ad for a writer's workshop that eventually led into acting. Received a scholarship to the Royal Academy of Dramatic Arts.
Major Awards: Black Reel Award

Olin, Lena

1989-(BSA) *Enemies, A Love Story*
    Winner: Brenda Fricker, *My Left Foot*
▦ Born 3/22/56 in Stockholm, Sweden.
🗡 Masha in nominated role.
🖊 She made her film debut in famed director Ingmar Bergman's *Karleken*. She served on the jury of the Cannes Film Festival. Recorded a hit song that topped the charts in Sweden. She has been nominated for a BAFTA, Golden Globe, Screen Actors Guild, and an Emmy.
Major Awards: NYFC

Oliver, Edna May

1939-(BSA) *Drums Along the Mohawk*
  Winner: Hattie McDaniel, *Gone with the Wind*
▨ Born *Edna May Nutter* on 11/9/1883 in
  Malden, MA. Died 11/9/42 of intestinal
  complications.
✏ Widow McKlennar in nominated role.
🔍 She was a descendant of President John Quincy
Adams. Quit school at age 14. Toured the country
playing the piano with an all-female orchestra. She was
readily recognizable for her long facial features.
Major Awards: WOF

Olivier, Sir Laurence

1939-(BA) *Wuthering Heights*
  Winner: Robert Donat, *Goodbye, Mr. Chips*
1940-(BA) *Rebecca*
  Winner: James Stewart, *The Philadelphia Story*
1946-(BA) *Henry V*
  Winner: Frederick March, *The Best Years of
  Our Lives*
1946-(BP) *Henry V*
1946-Honorary Oscar
1948-(BA) *Hamlet*
1948-(Best Picture/Producer) *Hamlet*
1948-(BD) *Hamlet*
1956-(BA) *Richard III*
  Winner: Yul Brynner, *The King and I*
1960-(BA) *The Entertainer*
  Winner: Burt Lancaster, *Elmer Gantry*
1965-(BA) *Othello*
  Winner: Lee Marvin, *Cat Ballou*
1972-(BA) *Sleuth*
  Winner: Marlon Brando, *The Godfather*
1976-(BSA) *The Marathon Man*
  Winner: Jason Robards, *All the President's Men*
1978-(BA) *The Boys from Brazil*
  Winner: Jon Voight, *Coming Home*
1978-Honorary Oscar
▨ Born 5/22/1907 in Dorking, Surrey, England.
  Died 5/11/89 of a muscle disorder.
✏ Hamlet and all Shakespearean roles,
  Dr. Christian Szell in *The Marathon Man*
  (#34 on AFI's Villain List)

🔍 Son of a strict Anglican minister. Made stage debut at age 15. Joined the Fleet Air Arm of the Royal
Navy during WW II. Refused to talk to anyone who
wouldn't call him Larry. Thought of himself as a
failure according to his son Tarquin. Knighted by
the Queen in 1947. Married to Vivien Leigh for
20 years. Was slated to play Don Corleone in *The
Godfather* but got sick. He and Jack Nicholson were
the only actors to be nominated in five consecutive
decades. He and Roberto Benigni are the only actors to have directed themselves in Oscar-winning
performances.
Major Awards: Oscar, Emmy, BIFF, DDA, VFF,
NBR, NYFC, GG, BAFTA, CB Demille, WOF

Olmos, Edward James

1988-(BA) *Stand and Deliver*
  Winner: Dustin Hoffman, *Rain Man*
▨ Born 2/24/47 in East Los Angeles, CA.
✏ Lt. Martin Castillo in TV cop series *Miami Vice*
🔍 As a teenager he sang for various bands on Sunset
Strip. Always wanted to be a professional baseball
player. Once delivered furniture to make ends meet.
He is a spokesman and ambassador for UNICEF
and has received numerous awards. Spent 20 days
in the can for trespassing on the Island of Vieques,
Puerto Rico, which was a U.S. bomb test site. He
was protesting. Currently stars in TV sci-fi series
Battlestar Gallactica.
Major Awards: Emmy, GG, WOF

Olson, Nancy

1950-(BSA) *Sunset Boulevard*
  Winner: Josephine Hull, *Harvey*
▨ Born 7/14/28 in Milwaukee, WI.
✏ Betsy Carlisle in *The Absent Minded Professor*
🔍 Graduated from Wisconsin University. Once
married to famed songwriter Alan Jay Lerner. Did a
few Disney movies but essentially put her career on
hold and never recovered. In 1984 she starred in one
of the first prime-time soap operas, *Paper Dolls*.

O'Neal, Ryan

1970-(BA) *Love Story*
  Winner: George C. Scott, *Patton*
- Born 4/20/41 in Los Angeles, CA.
- Relationship with longtime live-in Farrah Fawcett
- Graduated from high school in Munich, Germany. Once was a lifeguard and stuntman. Boxed in the West Coast Golden Gloves. In 1970 won the Los Angeles Silver Handball Tournament. Thrown in jail for 51 days for assault and battery at a New Years party. Father of Tatum O'Neal. Battled leukemia, which is now in remission.
Major Awards: David di Donatello

O'Neal, Tatum

1973-(BSA) *Paper Moon*
- Born 11/5/63 in Los Angeles, CA
- Addie Loggins in Oscar'd role.
- Lived with her mother in a hippie commune until age eight when she ran away to live with her father, Ryan. She was a young Fagin, leading a gang of bicycle thieves which amassed $1200.00. At age ten, the youngest actress to win a Best Supporting Actress Oscar. Was Michael Jackson's first girlfriend. Once married to tennis great John McEnroe. Named after the great pianist Art Tatum.
Major Awards: Oscar, DDA, GG

O'Neil, Barbara

1940-(BSA) *All This, and Heaven Too*
  Winner: Jane Darwell, *The Grapes of Wrath*
- Born 7/17/1910 in St. Louis, MO.
  Died 9/3/80 of natural causes.
- Ellen O'Hara, Scarlett's mother in *Gone with the Wind*
- Her family was high society and she graduated from Sarah Lawrence College. For two years she was an artist-in-residence at the University of Denver. Once married to playwright director Josh Logan whom she met at The Cape Cod University Players.

Among her actor classmates were Henry Fonda and James Stewart.

Osment, Haley Joel

1999-(BSA) *The Sixth Sense*
  Winner: Michael Caine, *The Cider House Rules*
- Born 4/10/88 in Los Angeles, CA.
- Cole Sear in nominated role.
- He started acting at age four and is a straight A student with hopes of attending Yale. Runs cross country for his high school. Has pet lizards. Youngest actor to win an MTV award. Made his first film appearance in *Forrest Gump*. Stacked up his car in 2006 and broke his ribs and shoulder and received numerous lacerations.
Major Awards: KCFCC, Saturn, Las Vegas FC

O'Toole, Peter

1962-(BA) *Lawrence of Arabia*
  Winner: Gregory Peck, *To Kill a Mockingbird*
1964-(BA) *Becket*
  Winner: Rex Harrison, *My Fair Lady*
1968-(BA) *The Lion in Winter*
  Winner: Cliff Robertson, *Charly*
1969-(BA) *Goodbye, Mr. Chips*
  Winner: John Wayne, *True Grit*
1972-(BA) *The Ruling Class*
  Winner: Marlon Brando, *The Godfather*
1980-(BA) *The Stunt Man*
  Winner: Robert DeNiro, *Raging Bull*
1982-(BA) *My Favorite Year*
  Winner: Ben Kingsley, *Gandhi*

Peter O'Toole in *Lawrence of Arabia*.

2003-Honorary Oscar
2006-(BA) *Venus*
> Winner: Forest Whitaker, *The Last King of Scotland*
▦ Born 8/2/32 in Connemara, County Galway, Ireland.
〰 T.E. Lawrence in *Lawrence of Arabia*
✎ Quit school at age 14. Went to a parochial school where the nuns beat him to correct his left-handedness. Spent two years in the Royal Navy as a decoder and signalman. His father was a nomadic bookie whose nickname was Captain Paddy. Attended RADA on a scholarship. Only one of a few actors to be nominated twice for the same role in two different movies, Henry II in *Becket* and *The Lion in Winter*. Had to have surgery on his intestine and stomach because of his heavy drinking. Likes to wear green socks. As they say life isn't fair. O'Toole broke the tie he had with Richard Burton: he has knocked on Oscar's door eight times and Oscar has yet to answer.
Major Awards: Oscar, GG, CA, NBR, BAFTA, Emmy, NSFC, DDA

Owen, Clive

2004-(BSA) *Closer*
> Winner: Morgan Freeman, *Million Dollar Baby*
▦ Born 10/3/64 in Keresley, Coventry, Warwickshire, England.
〰 Title role in *King Arthur*
✎ His father, a country/western singer abandoned the family when he was three. After high school he panhandled and went on the dole. Graduated from the Royal Academy of Dramatic Arts. Got his big break by doing BMW commercials. He was voted Best Dressed Male in 2006 by *Gentleman's Quarterley*.
Major Awards: SAG, GG, BAFTA, NBR, NYFC, BFCC

Ouspenskaya, Maria

1936-(BSA) *Dodsworth*
> Winner: Gale Sondegaard, *Anthony Adverse*
1939-(BA) *Love Affair*
> Winner: Hattie McDaniel, *Gone with the Wind*
▦ Born 7/29/1876 in Tula, Russia. Died 12/13/49 due to smoke inhalation after a lit cigarette set her sofa on fire, which led to a stroke.
〰 Maleva the gypsy fortune-teller in *The Wolf Man*
✎ She studied as an opera singer in Warsaw and Moscow. Fled Communist Russia with the Moscow Art Theater, which toured Europe and America. Formed her own acting school. Her students were Stella Adler, Lee Strasberg, and John Garfield.

Pacino, Al

1972-(BSA) *The Godfather*
> Winner: Joel Grey, *Cabaret*
1973-(BA) *Serpico*
> Winner: Jack Lemmon, *Save the Tiger*
1974-(BA) *The Godfather, Part II*
> Winner: Art Carney, *Harry and Tonto*
1975-(BA) *Dog Day Afternoon*
> Winner: Jack Nicholson, *One Flew Over the Cuckoo's Nest*
1979-(BA) *... And Justice For All*
> Winner: Dustin Hoffman, *Kramer vs. Kramer*
1990-(BSA) *Dick Tracy*
> Winner: Joe Pesci, *Goodfellas*
1992-(BSA) *Glengary Glen Ross*
> Winner: Gene Hackman, *Unforgiven*
1992-(BA) *Scent Of A Woman*
▦ Born 4/25/40 in South Bronx, NY.
〰 Michael Corleone in *The Godfather Trilogies* (#11 on AFI's Villain List), Frank Serpico in *Serpico*, (#40 on AFI's Hero List), Tony Camonte in *Scarface* (#47 on AFI's Villain List).
✎ His father was born in Corleone, Sicily. He worked as an usher at Carnegie Hall. Dropped out of school in his junior year. Studied acting under Lee Strasberg. Once worked as a switchboard operator. Kicked a two-pack-a-day smoking habit. He loves the opera and Shakespeare. He has never been married. He achieved the rare Triple Crown, and he is the only actor to win an Oscar, Tony, Obie, and Emmy.

Major Awards: Oscar, Emmy, Tony, Obie, DDA, NBR, GG, LAFC, NSFC, SAG, CBD, BAFTA, Cannes, AFI Life Achievement

Page, Geraldine

1953-(BSA) *Hondo*
   Winner: Donna Reed, *From Here to Eternity*
1961-(BA) *Summer and Smoke*
   Winner: Sophia Loren, *Two Women*
1962-(BA) *Sweet Bird of Youth*
   Winner: Anne Bancroft, *The Miracle Worker*
1966-(BSA) *You're A Big Boy Now*
   Winner: Sandy Dennis, *Who's Afraid of Virginia Woolf?*
1972-(BSA) *Pete 'n' Tille*
   Winner: Eileen Heckart, *Butterflies Are Free*
1978-(BA) *Interiors*
   Winner: Jane Fonda, *Coming Home*
1984-(BSA) *The Pope of Greenwich Village*
   Winner: Dame Peggy Ashcroft, *A Passage to India*
1985-(BA) *The Trip to Bountiful*
▪ Born 11/22/24 in Kirksville, MO. Died 6/13/87 of a heart attack.
〰 Mrs. Carrie Watts in Oscar'd role.
🔖 She won a scholarship to the Chicago Academy of Fine Arts. Originally wanted to be a writer, painter and pianist. Married to actor Rip Torn until her death 24 years later. Had twin boys. She was an acting teacher at the Actors Studio, Ahmanson Theater, and Pelican Theater. She was nominated four times for a Tony Award and never won.
Major Awards: Emmy, NBR, GG, BAFTA, BSFC, ISA

Palance, Jack

1952-(BSA) *Sudden Fear*
   Winner: Anthony Quinn, *Viva Zapata!*
1953-(BSA) *Shane*
   Winner: Frank Sinatra, *From Here to Eternity*
1991-(BSA) *City Slickers*

▪ Born *Vladimir Palahnuik* on 2/18/19 in Lattimer Mines, PA. Died 11/10/06 of natural causes.
〰 Curly Washburn in Oscar'd role.
🔖 Son of a coal miner. He was a professional boxer with wins in 15 bouts, 12 by knock-outs. Worked as a soda jerk, cook, waiter, and lifeguard. He was a pilot in WW II. Due to a plane crash, he had to have plastic surgery, and he received the Purple Heart, Good Conduct, and Victory Medals. Attended the University of North Carolina. He was an artist and poet and spoke six languages fluently: Ukrainian, Russian, English, French, Spanish, and Italian. Will be remembered forever for his one-arm push-up on Oscar night at age 72.
Major Awards: Emmy, Oscar, NBR, GG, BAFTA, WOF

Paltrow, Gwyneth

1998-(BA) *Shakespeare in Love*
▪ Born 9/27/72 in Los Angeles, CA
〰 Viola De Lesseps in Oscar'd role.
🔖 Her mother is actress Blythe Danner. Attended the University of California one year, and then dropped out. Once engaged to actor Brad Pitt. She can speak Spanish and is a vegetarian. She has been on a macrobiotic diet for years. When dating Ben Affleck she gave him $20,000 for his birthday. Her godfather is Stephen Spielberg. Keeps her Oscar in her closet, says it creeps her out.
Major Awards: Oscar, GG, MTV, SAG

Palminteri, Chazz

1994-(BSA) *Bullets over Broadway*
   Winner: Martin Landau, *Ed Wood*
▪ Born *Calogero Lorenzo Palminteri* on 5/15/51 in The Bronx, NY.
〰 Sonny, the gangster, in *A Bronx Tale*
🔖 Attended Bronx College, He was once a bouncer and doorman. Wrote the play *A Bronx Tale* , which sold out for four straight months in New York. It

is an autobiographical account of his tough days as a youth growing up in the Bronx. Turned down over a million dollars for the rights. Robert DeNiro backed the movie. He had a cancerous tumor removed from his neck in 1997.
Major Awards: NBR, ISA, Sundance

Paquin, Anna

1993-(BSA) *The Piano*
▪ Born 7/24/82 in Winnepeg, Manitoba, Canada
✎ Rogue in the *X-Men*
♀ Although born in Canada she grew up in New Zealand. When her parents divorced she, her mother, and her sister moved to Los Angeles. She's a vegetarian, is into photography, and plays the cello and piano. Graduated from Columbia University. She also enjoys alternative music and her favorite color is green. First actress from New Zealand to win an Oscar. Speaks French fluently and likes to knit, ski, and swim.
Major Awards: LAFC

Parker, Eleanor

1950-(BA) *Caged*
   Winner: Judy Holliday, *Born Yesterday*
1951-(BA) *Detective Story*
   Winner: Vivienne Leigh, *A Streetcar Named Desire*
1955-(BA) *Interrupted Melody*
   Winner: Anna Magnani, *The Rose Tattoo*
▪ Born 6/26/22 in Cedarville, OH.
✎ Marie Allen in *Caged*
♀ Started her acting career at age ten. A talent agent discovered her in the audience while she was attending a show at the Pasadena Playhouse. Signed with Warner Bros. at age 18. Starred in the TV series *Bracken's World* in the late '60s. After a ten-year absence from film returned triumphantly as Lady Amberly in *The Kent Chronicles*.
Major Awards: WOF, VFF

Parks, Larry

1946-(BA) *The Jolson Story*
   Winner: Frederic March, *The Best Years of Our Lives*
▪ Born: 12/13/14 in Olathe, KS. Died 4/13/75 of a heart attack.
✎ Al Jolson in nominated role.
♀ Graduated from the University of Illinois. Once was an usher at Carnegie Hall. He was the only actor named by the House Un-American Activities Committee. He testified he was once a member of the Communist party, and his admission killed his career, as he was blacklisted forever.

Parsons, Estelle

1967-(BSA) *Bonnie and Clyde*
1968-(BSA) *Rachel, Rachel*
   Winner: Ruth Gordon, *Rosemary's Baby*
▪ Born 11/20/27 in Lynn, MO.
✎ Blanche Barrow in *Bonnie and Clyde*
♀ Originally wanted to be an attorney and attended Boston University Law School. She once was a writer and producer of TV's *Today Show*. Has taught acting at Yale and Columbia. She is now Artistic Director for the Actors Studio. Nominated four times for a Tony and has never won.
Major Awards: Obie, Laurel

Pavan, Marisa

1955-(BSA) *The Rose Tattoo*
   Winner: Jo Van Fleet, *East of Eden*
▪ Born 6/19/32 in Cagliari, Sardinia, Italy.
✎ Rosa Delle Rose in nominated role.
♀ Her twin sister is actress Pier Angeli. She attended Torquado College before coming to the U.S. Had a hit record in 1974 in France that was written by famed songwriter Burt Bacharach. She was married to French film star Jean-Pierre Aumont for 45 years until his death in 2001.
Major Awards: GG

Paxinou, Katina

1943-(BSA) *For Whom the Bell Tolls*
▩ Born *Ekaterini Constantopoules* on 12/17/1900 in Piraeus, Athens, Greece. Died 2/22/73 of cancer.
🖋 Originally set out to be an opera singer. Was performing in England when WW II broke out. She was unable to return to her home and landed in the U.S. Years later she returned home and was the founder of the Greek Royal Theater. First actor from Greece to win an Oscar. Considered the greatest Greek actress of the twentieth century.
Major Awards: GG, WOF

Paymer, David

1992-(BSA) *Mr. Saturday Night*
 Winner: Gene Hackman, *Unforgiven*
▩ Born 8/30/54 in Oceanside, Long Island, NY.
🖋 Stan Young in nominated role
🖋 Paymer graduated from the University of Michigan, majoring in acting and psychology. His mother had to escape to the U.S. because of the Nazi invasion in Belgium. He was an acting teacher at the Film Actors' Workshop. Wrote and performed standup comedy acts at The Improv and Comedy Store. To date has appeared in over 70 movies.
Major Awards: NBR, FFCC, Online FC

Peck, Gregory

1945-(BA) *The Keys of the Kingdom*
 Winner: Ray Milland, *The Lost Weekend*
1946-(BA) *The Yearling*
 Winner: Frederic March, *The Best Years of Our Lives*
1947-(BA) *Gentleman's Agreement*
 Winner: Ronald Coleman, *A Double Life*
1949-(BA) *12 O'Clock High*
 Winner: Broderick Crawford, *All the King's Men*
1962-(BA) *To Kill a Mockingbird*
▩ Born Eldred Gregory Peck on 4/5/16 in La Jolla, CA. Died 6/12/03 of natural causes

Gregory Peck in *To Kill a Mockingbird.*

🖋 Atticus Finch in Oscar'd role (#1 on AFI's Hero List)
🖋 Was a carnival barker, tour guide and catalog model. Graduated from San Diego State in pre-med. Barred from the military when WW II broke out due to a spinal injury incurred while on his college rowing team. Chairman of the American Cancer Society, American Film Institute, and the Academy of Motion Picture Arts and Sciences. First native Californian to win an Oscar. Considered running for governor of California against Ronald Reagan in 1970. Suffered a great loss when his son Jonathon committed suicide. Hated his name "Eldred."
Major Awards: Jean Hersholt Humanitarian, AFI Life Achievement, Medal of Freedom, GGWFF, GG, CB DeMille, SAGLA, Cannes, NYFC, NBR, César, DDA, BIFF, WOF

Penn, Sean

1995-(BA) *Dead Man Walking*
 Winner: Nicholas Cage, *Leaving Las Vegas*

1999-(BA) *Sweet and Lowdown*
  Winner: Kevin Spacey, *American Beauty*
2001-(BA) *I Am Sam*
  Winner: Denzel Washington, *Training Day*
2003-(BA) *Mystic River*
▦ Born 8/17/60 in Santa Monica, CA.
✍ Jimmy Markum in Oscar'd role
✎ Saying acting is in his blood would not be an understatement—his father was a director and his mother an actress. His house burned down in 1993 during the Malibu fires. Until he kicked his habit he was smoking four packs of cigarettes a day. His volatile temper got him thrown in the slammer for over a month after he slugged an extra. Once married to pop diva Madonna.
Major Awards: Oscar, Cannes, GG, NBR, LAFC , VFF, BIFF, BSFC, KCFCC

Perez, Rosie

1993-(BSA) *Fearless*
  Winner: Anna Paquin, *The Piano*
▦ Born 9/6/64 in Brooklyn, NY.
✍ Carla Rodrigo in nominated role.
✎ Before she was a teenager she assaulted a woman and was placed in a group home. She was a dancer for *Soul Train*. Hired as a choreographer for music videos. She worked with Bobby Brown and Diana Ross. She practices Kung-Fu. Once arrested for disorderly conduct in Manhattan. She has a twin sister Carmine.
Major Awards: LAFC, BIFF, BSFC

Perkins, Anthony

1956-(BSA) *Friendly Persuasion*
  Winner: Anthony Quinn, *Lust for Life*
▦ Born 9/6/64 in New York, NY. Died 9/12/92 of pneumonia as a result of AIDS.
✍ Norman Bates in *Pycho* (#2 on AFI's Villain List)
✎ Started acting at age 15. Attended Rollins College where one of his classmates was Fred (Mr.) Rogers. He never graduated but years later received an Honorary degree. The *National Enquirer* illegally obtained his blood sample and tested it for AIDS. He found out about his positive results by reading the article.
Major Awards: Cannes, GG, WOF

Perrine, Valerie

1974-(BA) *Lenny*
  Winner: Ellen Burstyn, *Alice Doesn't Live Here Anymore*
▦ Born 9/3/43 in Galveston, TX.
✍ Honey in nominated role.
✎ She grew up an Army brat. Her father was a Lt. Colonel and she spent her childhood in Japan. She attended the University of Arizona wanting to be a psychologist. For a while she worked as a topless showgirl in Las Vegas. She has never been married, although she was engaged to a gun dealer who was accidentally killed by a ricocheted bullet.
Major Awards: NBR, NYFC, Cannes, BAFTA

Pesci, Joe

1980-(BSA) *Raging Bull*
  Winner: Timothy Hutton, *Ordinary People*
1990-(BSA) *Goodfellas*
▦ Born 2/9/43 in Newark, NJ
✍ Tommy DeVito in Oscar'd role.
✎ Started acting on stage at age five. Once played guitar for Joey D and the Starlighters. Cut a few records in the '60s under the name Joe Richie. Pesci means "fish" in Italian. Close personal friends with George Carlin and Robert DeNiro. He was managing a restaurant when Martin Scorsese called him for the role of Jake LaMotta's brother in *Raging Bull*.
Major Awards: Oscar, NBR, NYFC, NSFC, GG, BAFTA, BSFC, KCFCC, LAFC

Peters, Susan

1942-(BSA) *Random Harvest*
  Winner: Teresa Wright, *Mrs. Miniver*
▦ Born *Suzanne Carnahan* on 7/3/21 in Spokane, WA. Died 10/23/52 of self-imposed starvation.

Her father died in an auto accident when she was seven. The fates were cruel to her. In a freak hunting accident her rifle discharged sending a bullet through her spine. This paralyzed her and she was wheelchair-bound the rest of her short life. In constant pain and battling kidney problems and pneumonia, she lost her will to live.

Major Awards: WOF

Pfeiffer, Michelle

1988-(BSA) *Dangerous Liaisons*
Winner: Geena Davis, *The Accidental Tourist*
1989-(BA) *The Fabulous Baker Boys*
Winner: Jessica Tandy, *Driving Miss Daisy*
1992-(BA) *Love Field*
Winner: Emma Thompson, *Howard's End*
Born 4/29/58 in Santa Ana, CA.
Madame Marie de Tourvel in *Dangerous Liaisons*
She won the Miss Los Angeles and Orange County beauty pageants. Once worked as a grocery cashier and court reporter. Voted the Best Dressed Movie Star in 1997. She adopted a baby girl without the baggage of a husband. Turned down the role of Clarice Starling in *The Silence of the Lambs.*

Major Awards: NBR, NYFC, NSFC, GG, BAFTA, LAFC, BIFF, KCFCC, WFCA, WOF

Phoenix, Joaquin

2000-(BSA) *Gladiator*
Winner: Benicio Del Toro, *Traffic*
2005-(BA) *Walk the Line*
Winner: Philip Seymour Hoffman, *Capote*
Born Joaquin Rafael Bottom on 10/28/74 in San Juan, Puerto Rico.
Johnny Cash in nominated role
His parents were missionaries and migrant fruit pickers traveling through Mexico and Central and South America. He dropped out of high school in the ninth grade. Brother to River, Rain, Liberty, and Summer. Called 911 when his brother River overdosed. He is a strict vegetarian and a spokesman for PETA. Speaks Spanish fluently. When in grade school he was called Leaf because no one could pronounce Joaquin.

Major Awards: NBR, GG

Phoenix, River

1988-(BSA) *Running on Empty*
Winner: Kevin Kline, *A Fish Called Wanda*
Born *River Jude Bottom* on 8/23/70 in Madras, OR. Died 10/3/93 of heart failure due to a drug overdose.
Young Indiana Jones in *The Last Crusade*
He was literally born in a cabin. He started his acting career at age ten. Played the guitar and formed a band called Aleka's Attic—he was the lead singer and songwriter. He was at Johnny Depp's Viper Club when he overdosed. He was also a strict vegetarian and a PETA member. He and Joaquin are the only brothers ever nominated.

Major Awards: NBR, NSFC, VFF, ISA

Pickford, Mary

1928/29-(BA) *Coquette*
1975-Honorary Oscar
Born Gladys Marie Smith on 4/8/1893 in Toronto, Ontario, Canada. Died 5/29/79 of a cerebral hemorrhage.
America's Sweetheart
Her father died when she was five. Her stage mother pushed her into acting as "Baby Gladys." When she was 16 she was offered a movie contract. By age 24 she was earning $10,000 a week in 1916, an astronomical sum at that time. Formed United Artists with Charlie Chaplin, D.W. Griffith, and Douglas Fairbanks. First movie star to place her hand and foot prints at Grauman's Chinese Theater.

Major Awards: WOF

Pidgeon, Walter

1942-(BA) *Mrs. Miniver*
Winner: James Cagney, *Yankee Doodle Dandy*

1943-(BA) *Madame Curie*
    Winner: Paul Lukas, *Watch on the Rhine*
■ Born 9/23/1897 in St. John, New Brunswick, Canada. Died 9/25/84 of a series of strokes.
🎬 Dr. Edward Morbius in *The Forbidden Planet*
🔍 He was wounded in WW I and spent 17 months in a hospital. After his release, he shipped off to the states and made his film debut in 1925. His first wife Muriel died in childbirth. He was president of the Screen Actors Guild for five years.
Major Awards: SAG, Venice FF, WOF

Pitt, Brad

1995-(BSA) *12 Monkeys*
    Winner: Kevin Spacey, *The Usual Suspects*
■ Born 12/18/63 in Shawnee, OK
🎬 J.D. the ruthless hitchhiker in *Thelma & Louise*
🔍 He is two credit hours short of graduating from the University of Missouri. He was majoring in journalism. Once in his early years he was so poor he lived out of his car. Cast in *Thelma & Louise* after a producer saw him in a Levi's TV commercial. He has had LASIK eye surgery and his teeth capped. Ironically, he tore his Achilles tendon playing the role of Achilles in *Troy*. Banned from China because of his role in *Seven Years in Tibet*. Once married to actress Jennifer Aniston and presently seen everywhere with Angelina Jolie and their brood.
Major Awards: GG, Western Heritage, PC

Plowright, Dame Joan

1992-(BSA) *Enchanted April*
    Winner: Marisa Tomei, *My Cousin Vinny*
■ Born 10/28/29 in Briggs, No. Lincolnshire, England.
🎬 Mrs. Fisher in nominated role
🔍 Married to Sir Laurence Olivier for 29 years. Awarded Commander of the British Empire in 1970. Member of the Royal Academy of Dramatic Arts. Appointed Dame Commander by the Queen in 2004. She is a master at foreign accents,
Major Awards: GG, Tony, WFCA

Poitier, Sir Sidney

1958-(BA) *The Defiant Ones*
    Winner: David Niven, *Separate Tables*
1963-(BA) *Lilies of the Field*
2001-Honorary Oscar
■ Born 2/20/27 in Miami, FL.
🎬 Virgil Tibbs in *The Heat of the Night*, (#19 on AFI's Hero List), Mark Thackeray in *To Sir with Love*
🔍 Grew up dirt poor on a tomato farm on Cat Island in the Bahamas. Dropped out of school at age 13 to help his family. Did a hitch in the Army and was discharged in 1945. Auditioned and was turned down flat at the American Negro Theater in Harlem because of his Bahamian accent, but he overcame his thick accent and six months later got the job. First black male to receive a Best Actor Oscar. He is an early riser and exercises every day. Speaks Russian fluently. Knighted by the Queen in 1974.
Major Awards: Oscar, SAG Life Achievement, CBD, GG, AFI Life Achievement, NBR, BAFTA, WOF

Sidney Poitier with Stanley Adams in *Lilies of the Field*.

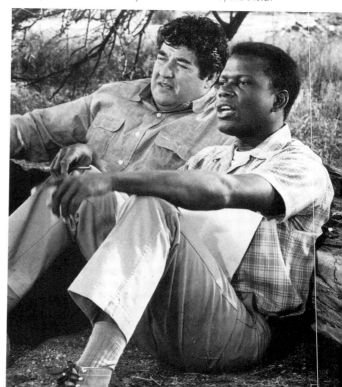

Pollard, Michael J.

1967-(BSA) *Bonnie and Clyde*
   Winner: George Kennedy, *Cool Hand Luke*
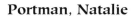 Born *Michael Pollack* on 5/30/39 in
   Passaic, NJ.
C.W. Moss in nominated role.
He was almost cast as Jerome Krebs, Maynard
Kreb's offbeat cousin on TV's *Dobie Gillis Show*. The
star, Bob Denver was about to be drafted and Plan B
was to introduce the cousin. However Denver's health
problems got him classified 4-F, and the cousin's part
was written out. Got a part of a 14-year-old on TV's
Star Trek when he was, in reality, 30 years old!
Major Awards: BAFTA

Myrna Loy and William Powell in *The Thin Man*.

Portman, Natalie

2004-(BSA) *Closer*
   Winner: Cate Blanchett, *The Aviator*
Born 6/9/81 in Jerusalem, Israel.
Queen Amidala in *The Phantom Menace*
Her father's a doctor and her mother an artist,
who also acts as her agent. She was a straight-A
student in high school and graduated from Harvard
in 2003. She has been training in ballet and tap
dancing since she was four. Discovered by an agent
in a pizza parlor at age 11. Is a vegetarian. Speaks
Hebrew fluently and reads French and Japanese.
Major Awards: GG, NBR, SDFC

Postlewaite, Pete

1993-(BSA) *In the Name of the Father*
   Winner: Tommy Lee Jones, *The Fugitive*
Born 2/7/45 in Warrington, Cheshire, England.
Roland Tembo in *The Lost World, Jurassic Park*
Graduated from college and was a drama teacher.
He followed his heart and ended up in The Royal
Shakespeare Company. Once taught at a Catholic
girls' convent. Initially his father was embarrassed
that he became an actor. Appointed Officer of the
British Empire in 2004. Steven Spielberg called
him "the best actor in the world."
Major Awards: NBR

Powell, William

1934-(BA) *The Thin Man*
   Winner: Clark Gable, *It Happened One Night*
1936-(BA) *My Man Godfrey*
   Winner: Paul Muni, *The Life of Louis Pasteur*
1947-(BA) *Life with Father*
   Winner: Ronald Coleman, *A Double Life*
Born 7/29/1892 in Pittsburgh, PA. Died
   3/5/84 of cardiac arrest.
Nick Charles in *The Thin Man*
Made his Broadway debut in 1912. He was engaged to Jean Harlow at the time of her death.
He paid for her $30,000 funeral. Myrna Loy sums
him up best: "He was a brilliant actor, a delightful
companion, a great friend, and above all a true
gentleman." His son committed suicide by stabbing
himself to death while taking a shower.
Major Awards: NYFC, WOF

Preston, Robert

1982-(BSA) *Victor/Victoria*
   Winner: Louis Gossett Jr., *An Officer and a
   Gentleman*
Born *Robert Preston Meservey* on 6/8/1918 in
   Newton Highlands, MA. Died 3/21/87 of
   lung cancer.

Professor Harold Hill in *The Music Man*

He was a talented musician, adept in playing the piano and several other instruments on a concert level. A talent scout changed his last name to his middle, saying that no one could pronounce his real name. Served in the Army Air Corps in WW II. Although a favorite of famed director Cecil B. DeMille, he couldn't stand him.

Major Awards: Tony (2), NSFC, NBR, LAFC, Western Heritage

Quaid, Randy

1973-(BSA) *The Last Detail*
　　Winner: John Houseman, *The Paper Chase*

Born 10/1/50 in Houston, TX.

Cousin Eddie Johnson in *National Lampoon's Vacation* series

Majored in Drama at the University of Houston. Left for Hollywood, where he worked as a janitor. Big break came when Peter Bogdanovich cast him in *The Last Picture Show* while he was still in college. His high school baseball coach was major leaguer Chuck Knoblauch's father. He has been nominated for three Emmys. Brother to actor Dennis Quaid.

Major Awards: GG.WOF

Quayle, Sir Anthony

1969-(BSA) *Anne of the Thousand Days*
　　Winner: Gig Young, *They Shoot Horses, Don't They?*

Born 9/7/13 in Ainsdale Southport Sefon Merseyside, England. Died 10/20/89 of liver cancer.

Cardinal Wolsey in nominated role.

Debuted on stage at age 18. He was a major during WW II in the Royal Artillery. Graduate of RADA. Appointed Commander of the British Empire in 1952. Knighted by the Queen in 1985. Wrote two best-selling novels *Eight Hours From England* and *On Such a Night*.

Major Awards: Emmy

Quinn, Anthony

★ 1952-(BSA) *Viva Zapata!*
★ 1956-(BSA) *Lust For Life*
1957-(BA) *Wild Is the Wind*
　　Winner: Alec Guinness, *The Bridge on the River Kwai*
1964-(BA) *Zorba the Greek*
　　Winner: Rex Harrison, *My Fair Lady*

Born 4/21/15 in Chihahau, Mexico. Died 6/3/2001 of pneumonia and throat cancer.

Title role *Zorba the Greek*

He is of Irish-Mexican parentage, not Greek as is often believed. His parents fled the country when the Mexican Revolution broke out—he was hidden in a coal wagon and nearly smothered. Married to Cecil B. DeMille's daughter Katharine for 30 years. Fathered 13 children with various women. Studied architecture with Frank Lloyd Wright. He was a sparring partner for world heavyweight champion Primo Carnera, and he played the sax in Aimee' Semple McPherson's Temple Band. He was a serious painter and sculptor. He appeared with more Oscar-winning actors than anyone else, 46 in total. He was awarded an Oscar with the shortest time on screen for an actor (7 minutes, 57 seconds) in *Lust for Life*. First actor from Mexico to win an Oscar.

Major Awards: Oscar, NBR, CBD, GG, WOF

Queen Latifah

2002-(BSA) *Chicago*
　　Winner: Catherine Zeta-Jones, *Chicago*

Born *Dana Elaine Owens* on 3/18/70 in Newark, NJ.

Queen of the Rap artists

Once worked at a Burger King. Led her high school girl's basketball team to two state championships. Her brother, a policeman, died in an accident on the motorcycle she had bought for him as a present. Once arrested for assaulting a photographer, carrying a concealed weapon, and marijuana possession.

Major Awards: BCFC, SAG, Grammy, WOF

Quinlan, Kathleen

1995-(BSA) *Apollo 13*
    Winner: Mira Sorvino, *Mighty Aphrodite*
▓ Born 11/19/54 in Pasadena. CA.
🖋 Lynn Holt on *Family Law*
🔍 She was a championship diver on her swim team and a gymnast. Big break came when George Lucas plucked her out of her high school class for a role in *American Graffiti*. She has a clause in her contract that stipulates she can't work past 6:00 p.m. so that she can be home with her family.
Major Awards: Blockbuster

Rainer, Luise

1936-(BA) *The Great Ziegfield*
1937-(BA) *The Good Earth*
▓ Born 1/12/1910 in Dusseldorf, Germany.
🖋 O-Lan in *The Good Earth*
🔍 British citizen for 65 years. Along with her parents fled Germany when Hitler came into power. Once married to writer Clifford Odets. During WW II she toured Europe boosting morale for the troops. Only made nine movies. She is the first actor to win two Oscars in consecutive years. First actress to be nominated twice, to win twice, and to win two Oscars before the age of 30. Also the first actress from Germany to win an Oscar.
Major Awards: Oscar, NYFC, WOF

Rains, Claude

1939-(BSA) *Mr. Smith Goes to Washington*
    Winner: Thomas Mitchell, *Stagecoach*
1943-(BSA) *Casablanca*
    Winner: Charles Coburn, *The More the Merrier*
1944-(BSA) *Mr. Skeffington*
    Winner: Barry Fitzgerald, *Going My Way*
1946-(BSA) *Notorious*
    Winner: Harold Russell, *The Best Years of Our Lives*
▓ Born 11/10/1910 in London, England.
    Died 5/30/67 of an intestinal hemorrhage.
🖋 Captain Louis Renault in *Casablanca*
🔍 Made stage debut at age 11. He taught classes at RADA, and one of his students was a young Laurence Olivier. Fought with the Scottish Regiment during WW I, where he was made semi-blind in one eye due to a gas attack. Married six times. First actor to receive a million dollars for one movie, *Caesar and Cleopatra*.
Major Awards: Tony, WOF

Rambeau, Marjorie

1940-(BSA) *Primrose Path*
    Winner: Jane Darwell, *The Grapes of Wrath*
1953-(BSA) *Torch Song*
    Winner: Donna Reed, *From Here to Eternity*
▓ Born 7/15/1889 in San Francisco, CA.
    Died 7/6/70 of natural causes.
🖋 Mamie Adams in *Primrose Path*
🔍 Survivor of the great San Francisco earthquake of 1906. She made her stage debut at the age of 12. An under-appreciated actress, she was known for her scene-stealing prowess. She usually played floozy, haggard, hard-luck dames. Her career spanned 40 years.
Major Awards: NBR, WOF

Ramsey, Anne

1987-(BSA) *Throw Momma from the Train*
    Winner: Olympia Dukakis, *Moonstruck*
▓ Born Anne Mobley on 9/1/29 in Omaha, NE.
    Died 8/11/88 of throat cancer.
🖋 Momma (Mrs. Lift) in titled role
🔍 Graduated from Bennington College. Founded the Philadelphia Theater of Living Arts. Her ancestors on her mother's side were original Pilgrims. Although suffering from throat cancer and having her part of her jaw and tongue removed, she still completed *Throw Momma from the Train*. Died three months after receiving her Oscar nomination.
Major Awards: Saturn Award

Rathbone, Basil

1936-(BSA) *Romeo and Juliet*
    Winner: Walter Brennan, *Come and Get It*
1938-(BSA) *If I Were a King*
    Winner: Walter Brennan, *Kentucky*
▪ Born 6/13/1892 in Johannesburg, South
    Africa. Died 7/21/67 of a heart attack.
🎞 Sherlock Holmes role in 15 movies, and
    Sir Guy of Gisbourne in *The Adventures of
    Robin Hood*
🔍 He was a descendant of King Henry lV on his
mother's side. He was a captain during WW I, serving
in the Liverpool Scottish Regiment and received the
Military Cross for bravery. It was common knowledge
that he was the best fencer in Hollywood. Be that as
it may, he only won one on-screen sword fight.
Major Awards: Tony, WOF

Rea, Stephen

1992-(BA) *The Crying Game*
    Winner: Al Pacino, *Scent of a Woman*
▪ Born *Graham Rea* on 10/31/46 in Belfast,
    Northern Ireland.
🎞 Fergus in nominated role.
🔍 Born of Protestant parents in war-racked Belfast.
Studied acting at the Abbey Theater. He is married to
the former Irish Republican Army bomber, Dolores
Price. Founded the Field Day Theater Company
in 1980. Now resides in Dublin, Ireland.
Major Awards: NBR, NSFC, OCC

Redford, Robert

1973-(BA) *The Sting*
    Winner: Jack Lemmon, *Save the Tiger*
1980-(Best Director) *Ordinary People*
1994-(BD) *Quiz Show*
1994-(BP) *Quiz Show*
2001-Honorary Oscar
▪ Born 8/18/37 in Santa Monica, CA.
🎞 Sundance Kid in *Butch Cassidy and the
    Sundance Kid*

🔍 Received a baseball scholarship as a pitcher for
the University of Colorado. He was booted when
he was caught drinking. One of his teammates was
future Dodgers pitcher Don Drysdale. He was a
cartoonist for his high school newspaper. Art was
his first love, and he left for Europe and studied
painting in Paris and Florence. He is a superb athlete
and enjoys snow and water skiing, boating, tennis,
hunting, fishing and has his own pilot's license.
He is the founder of the Sundance Film Festival.
Received an honorary Doctorate of Letters from
Bard College.
Major Awards: Oscar, BAFTA, DG, GG, CBD,
NBR, SAGLA, BW, DDA, KCFCC

Redgrave, Lynne

1966-(BA) *Georgy Girl*
    Winner: Elizabeth Taylor, *Who's Afraid of
    Virginia Woolf?*
1998-(BSA) *Gods and Monsters*
    Winner: Judi Dench, *Shakespeare in Love*
▪ Born 3/8/43 in London, England.
🎞 Georgy Parkin in titled role.
🔍 Daughter of Sir Michael Redgrave. She was
confined to a wheelchair until she was six due to
an acute case of anemia. She was made Officer of
the Order of the British Empire by the Queen. In
only the second time sisters vied for an Oscar, she
and Vanessa were both nominated, although neither
won. Olivia de Havilland and Joan Fontaine were
the first in 1941—Joan won.
Major Awards: GG, NYFC, ISA, KCFCC

Redgrave, Sir Michael

1947-(BA) *Mourning Becomes Electra*
    Winner: Ronald Coleman, *A Double Life*
▪ Born 3/20/1908 in Bristol, Glouchestershire,
    England. Died 3/21/85 of Parkinson's Disease.
🎞 Orin Mannon in nominated role.
🔍 Graduated from Cambridge. Father of Lynne
and Vanessa. Once was a journalist and teacher,
schoolmaster at Cranleigh High School. Appointed

Commander of the British Empire in 1952 and knighted by the Queen in 1959. He produced, directed, and wrote many hit plays.
Major Awards: NBR, Cannes

Redgrave, Vanessa

1966-(BA) *Morgan!*
  Winner: Elizabeth Taylor, *Who's Afraid of Virginia Woolf?*
1968-(BA) *Isadora*
  Winner: Katharine Hepburn, *The Lion in Winter*
1971-(BA) *Mary, Queen Of Scots*
  Winner: Jane Fonda, *Klute*
1977-(BSA) *Julia*
1984-(BA) *The Bostonians*
  Winner: Sally Field, *Places in the Heart*
1992-(BSA) *Howard's End*
  Winner: Marisa Tomei, *My Cousin Vinny*
▦ Born 1/30/37 in London, England.
❦ Title role in *Julia*
❧ Only person to win a BSA Oscar for a title role. Daughter of Michael and sister of Lynne. Won the Triple Crown of acting: Oscar, Tony, Emmy. She is a self-professed communist and is vehemently anti-American. First actor to win the Cannes twice. Nominated 13 times for a Golden Globe, winning twice.
Major Awards: Oscar, Tony, Emmy, Obie, NSFC, LAFC, GG, NYFC, Cannes, VFF, SAG, DDA, KCFCC

Redman, Joyce

1963-(BSA) *Tom Jones*
  Winner: Margaret Rutherford, *The V.I.P.s*
1965-(BSA) *Othello*
  Winner: Shelley Winters, *A Patch of Blue*
▦ Born 1918 in County Mayo, Ireland
❦ Mrs. Waters in *Tom Jones*
❧ She was home schooled and educated by private governesses. Graduated from the Royal Academy of Dramatic Arts. Once owned her own island off the coast of Ireland. *Tom Jones* is the only movie in which three actresses were nominated for a BSA.

Reed, Donna

1953-(BSA) *From Here to Eternity*
▦ Born *Donna Belle Mullenger* on 1/27/21 in Denison, IA. Died 1/14/86 of pancreatic cancer.
❦ Mary Hatch Bailey in *It's a Wonderful Life*. Her eponymous TV show.
❧ She was raised on a farm. She was elected Campus Queen at Los Angeles City College. The true All-American girl, she was, however, a staunch anti-nuclear and anti-war activist. She sued the producers of *Dallas* for breach of contract and won a million dollars. She was nominated for an Emmy four times for her role on *The Donna Reed Show* and never won.
Major Awards: Oscar, GG, WOF

Reilly, John C.

2002-(BSA) *Chicago*
  Winner: Chris Cooper, *Adaptation*
▦ Born 5/24/65 in Chicago, IL.
❦ Amos Hart in nominated role
❧ Has five brothers and sisters. Graduated from DePaul University. Hit the stage at age five at the Goodman School of Drama. Member of the famed Steppenwolf Theater. Did all of his own singing in *Chicago*. An animal rights advocate, he quit the movie *Manderlay* when they killed a donkey while filming
Major Awards: BCFC, FFCC, LVFC, SAG

Remick, Lee

1962-(BA) *Days of Wine and Roses*
  Winner: Anne Bancroft, *The Miracle Worker*
▦ Born 12/14/35 in Quincy, MA. Died 7/2/91 of kidney and liver cancer.
❦ Kirsten Arnesen in nominated role.
❧ Graduated from Barnard College. Started career as a dancer. She was set to replace a chronically late

Marilyn Monroe in her last movie *Something's Got to Give*, but co-star Dean Martin nixed it, and the movie was scrapped. Nominated for an Emmy six times.
Major Awards: GG, CA, Laurel, BAFTA, WFCA, WOF

Revere, Anne

1943-(BSA) *The Song of Bernadette*
  Winner: Katina Paxinou, *For Whom the Bell Tolls*
1945-(BSA) *National Velvet*
1947-(BSA) *Gentleman's Agreement*
  Winner: Celeste Holm, *Gentleman's Agreement*
▪ Born 6/25/1903 in New York, NY.
  Died 12/18/90 of pneumonia.
▥ Mrs. Brown in Oscar'd role.
🔍 Graduated from Wellesley College. In 1951 she was grilled by the House Un-American Activities Committee. She took the Fifth Amendment and was blacklisted for 20 years. She always claimed she was framed. She was a distant relative to Revolutionary War hero Paul Revere. Served as the treasurer of the Screen Actors Guild.
Major Awards: Oscar, Tony

Reynolds, Burt

1997-(BSA) *Boogie Nights*
  Winner: Robin Williams, *Good Will Hunting*
▪ Born 2/11/36 in Waycross, GA.
▥ Lewis Medlock in *Deliverance*, Paul Crewe in *The Longest Yard*
🔍 Graduated from Florida State. Played football there on a scholarship and was an All-Conference running back. He was drafted by the Baltimore Colts, but a knee injury ended his career. He is part Cherokee. First actor to host *The Johnny Carson Show*. He was No. 1 at the box office from 1978–1982. Appeared in the centerfold of *Cosmopolitan* magazine in 1972. Had romances with Sally Field, Dinah Shore, and Inger Stevens. Turned down the role of Jack Nicholson in *Terms of Endearment* and said it was the worse mistake he ever made.

Major Awards: Emmy, FFC, GG, CFC, PC (5), LAFC, NSFC, NYFC, WOF

Reynolds, Debbie

1964-(BA) *The Unsinkable Molly Brown*
  Winner: Julie Andrews, *Mary Poppins*
▪ Born Mary Frances Reynolds on 4/1/32 in El Paso, TX.
▥ Molly Brown in titled role. Once married to singer Eddie Fisher until Elizabeth Taylor stepped into the picture.
🔍 Once wanted to be a teacher. Won 48 merit badges in the Girl Scouts. Won Miss Burbank beauty contest, which launched her career at Warner Bros. Jack Warner named her Debbie and then dropped her contract. Has a huge collection of movie memorabilia and once had a museum in Las Vegas. Her daughter is actress Carrie Fisher. Recorded the song of the year in 1957, "Tammy."
Major Awards: NBR, WOF

Richards, Beah

1967-(BSA) *Guess Who's Coming To Dinner*
  Winner: Estelle Parsons, *Bonnie and Clyde*
▪ Born *Beulah Richards* on 7/12/20 in Vicksburg, MS. Died 9/14/2000 of emphysema.
▥ Mrs. Prentice in nominated role.
🔍 Her father was a Baptist minister and her mother a seamstress. She graduated from Dillard University. She made her Broadway debut in 1955. Besides being an actress she was a playwright, novelist, and poet. She has authored three books. Received an Emmy two days before she died.
Major Awards: Emmy (2)

Richardson, Miranda

1992-(BSA) *Damage*
  Winner: Marisa Tomei, *My Cousin Vinny*
1994-(BA) *Tom and Viv*
  Winner: Jessica Lange, *Blue Sky*

▦ Born 3/3/58 in Southport, Lancashire, England

⚡ Ingrid Fleming in *Damage*

✎ She wanted to join the Old Vick so badly she dropped out of high school. She once had ambitions to be a veterinarian. She was a stage manager for the Library Theater. In the '70s she was considered a trendsetter when she started wearing toe rings. She is basically a loner who enjoys gardening, music, and drawing.

Major Awards: GG, NBR, NYFC, BAFTA

Richardson, Sir Ralph

1949-(BSA) *The Heiress*
  Winner: Dean Jagger, *12 O'Clock High*
1984-(BSA) Greystoke: *The Legend of Tarzan, Lord of the Apes*
  Winner: Haing S. Ngor, *The Killing Fields*
▦ Born 12/19/1902 in Cheltenham, Glouchestershire, England. Died 10/10/83 of a stroke.
⚡ Supreme Being in *Time Bandits*
✎ Once worked as an office boy in an insurance company. Inherited 500 English pounds, which enabled him to enroll at Brighton School. His Catholic mother deserted his Quaker father and he lived with her. His hobby was collecting vintage motorcycles. He was knighted by the Queen in 1947.

Major Awards: NBR, NYFC, Cannes, OCC, BAFTA

Ritter, Thelma

1950-(BSA) *All About Eve*
  Winner: Josephine Hull, *Harvey*
1951-(BSA) *The Mating Season*
  Winner: Kim Hunter, *A Streetcar Named Desire*
1952-(BSA) *With a Song in My Heart*
  Winner: Gloria Grahame, *The Bad and the Beautiful*
1953-(BSA) *Pick Up on South Street*
  Winner: Donna Reed, *From Here to Eternity*
1959-(BSA) *Pillow Talk*
  Winner: Shelley Winters, *The Diary of Anne Frank*

1962-(BSA) *Birdman Of Alcatraz*
  Winner: Patty Duke, *The Miracle Worker*
▦ Born 2/14/1905 in Brooklyn, NY.
  Died 2/5/69 of a heart attack.
⚡ Birdie the wisecracking assistant to Bette Davis in *All About Eve*
✎ She was a child prodigy, starting to perform and recite long passages at age eight. Her bit part in *Miracle on 34th Street* caught the attention of Darryl F. Zanuck and it landed her a contract with 20th Century Fox. Once won a set of encyclopedias on the radio quiz show *Information Please*. She is the most nominated actress who never received an Oscar.

Major Awards: Tony

Robards, Jason

1976-(BSA) *All the President's Men*
1977-(BSA) *Julia*
1980-(BSA) *Melvin and Howard*
  Winner: Timothy Hutton, *Ordinary People*
▦ Born 7/26/22 in Chicago, IL.
  Died 12/26/2000 of lung cancer.
⚡ Newspaper editor Ben Bradlee in *All the President's* Men.
✎ Debuted in school play, acting the part of a rear end of a cow. In WW II he was a radioman and was present at the bombing of Pearl Harbor. Later he was awarded the Navy Cross for valor. Distraught after losing a movie part, he was involved in a horrible near-fatal auto accident, and he ended up facially disfigured and requiring five surgeries. He is the most nominated actor for a Tony Award, eight times. Once married to actress Lauren Bacall. He was the 11th actor to win the Triple Crown.

Major Awards: Oscar, Tony, Emmy, Obie, LAFC, NYFC, NSFC, Cannes, NBR, BSFC, KCFCC

Robbins, Tim

1995-(BD) *Dead Man Walking*
2003-(BSA) *Mystic River*
▦ Born 10/16/58 in West Covina, CA

🍴 Andy Dufresne in *The Shawshank Redemption*

🥄 Played hockey on the Stuyvesant, NY high school team and was booted off for fighting. His dad was a member of the folk music band The Highwaymen. Graduated from UCLA with honors. At 6'5" he is the tallest actor to ever win an Oscar. He has been partnered with actress Susan Sarandon for 18 years and they have two children. He is a big fan of the New York Mets and the Rangers.

Major Awards: Oscar, Cannes, SAG, BSFC, NBR, VFF, BIFF

Roberts, Eric

1985-(BSA) *Runaway Train*
Winner: Don Ameche, *Cocoon*

◻ Born 4/18/56 in Biloxi, MS.

🍴 Buck in nominated role.

🥄 Before stardom he appeared in the soap opera *Another World*. In 1981 he was almost killed in an auto accident. He was in a coma for three days and his ring finger was permanently disfigured. Brother to actress Julia Roberts. His success prompted Julia to go to Hollywood. He was the fifth actor to portray Dr. Who.

Major Awards: BSFC, GS

Roberts, Julia

1989-(BSA) *Steel Magnolias*
Winner: Brenda Fricker, *My Left Foot*
1990-(BA) *Pretty Woman*
Winner: Kathy Bates, *Misery*
2000-(BA) *Erin Brockovich*

◻ Born 10/28/67 in Smyna, GA.

🍴 Erin Brockovich in title role (#31 on AFI's Hero List)

🥄 She originally wanted to be a veterinarian and journalist. Played the clarinet in her high school band. Once worked as a shoe salesman and ice cream scooper. Owns a 50-acre ranch in Taos, NM. Has been romantically linked to Keifer Sutherland, Liam Neeson, and Daniel-Day Lewis. Knitting is her hobby. She's the highest paid actress in Hollywood history, reportedly making $20 million per movie.

Won *The Peoples Choice Awards* ten times.

Major Awards: Oscar, PC, SAG, NBR, LAFC, BAFTA, GG

Roberts, Rachel

1963-(BA) *This Sporting Life*
Winner: Patricia Neal, *Hud*

◻ Born 9/20/27 in Llanelli, Carmarthenshire, Wales, England. Died 11/26/80 of suicide from an overdose of barbiturates.

🍴 Mrs. Hammond in nominated role.

🥄 Graduated from RADA. Once married to actor Rex Harrison. Kept a diary up to the day she committed suicide. As if overdosing on drugs wasn't enough, she also swallowed lye and an alkali substance, which is what really killed her.

Major Awards: BAFTA (3)

Robertson, Cliff

1968-(BA) *Charly*

◻ Born 9/9/25 in La Jolla, CA.

🍴 Title role as JFK in *PT 109*

🥄 Enlisted in the Merchant Marines during WW II at age 16. His ship was bombed by the Japanese and he was reported killed in action. After service he was a journalist and radio announcer. He was personally picked by John F. Kennedy to portray him in *PT 109*. In 1965 he reported seeing a UFO. He is a sailplane pilot and has a vintage German Messerschmitt.

Major Awards: Oscar, Emmy, NBR, WOF

Robinson, Edward G.

Honorary Oscar

◻ Born *Emmanuel Goldenberg* on 12/12/1893 in Bucharest, Romania. Died 1/26/73 of cancer.

🍴 Enrico Bandello in *Little Caesar* (#38 on AFI's Villain List)

🥄 Set foot in New York's East Side at age ten. His parents wanted him to be a lawyer or rabbi. He once

Edward G. Robinson in *Little Ceasar*.

owned the largest private art collection in the U.S. before he had to sell it off in a divorce settlement. Featured on a 33-cent Commemorative postage stamp. He was fluent in seven different languages. In real life he was a quiet, reserved, private man who was liked by everyone, a great contrast to the image he portrayed on the screen.
Major Awards: Cannes, SAG, WOF

Robson, Dame Flora

1946-(BSA) *Saratoga Trunk*
    Winner: Anne Baxter, *The Razor's Edge*
▨ Born 3/28/1902 in South Shields, Durham, England. Died 7/7/84 of cancer.
〰 Queen Elizabeth I in *The Sea Hawk*
⚲ Graduated from RADA and won the prestigious Bronze Medal for Acting. Made her stage debut in 1921 and retired 48 years later. Appointed Commander of the British Empire in 1952. Knighted Dame Commander in 1960. She was never married and never had any children. One of the greats of the British stage.

Robson, May

1932/33-(BA) *Lady for a Day*
    Winner: Katharine Hepburn, *Morning Glory*
▨ Born *Mary Jeanette Robinson* on 4/19/1858 in Melbourne, Victoria, Australia. Died 10/20/42 of natural causes.
〰 Apple Annie in nominated role.
⚲ She was educated in Belgium, France and England. She married at age 16 and moved to the U.S. She was widowed at age 20. She supported herself and her three children as a dressmaker and jewelry designer before stumbling into acting. For 65 years until Gloria Stuart in *Titanic* she was the oldest actress to be nominated for an Oscar. Born in 1858, she was the earliest born actor to receive an Oscar nomination.

Rogers, Ginger

1940-(BA) *Kitty Foyle*
▨ Born *Virginia Katharine McMath* on 7/16/1911 in Independence, MO. Died 4/25/95 of congestive heart failure.
〰 Kitty Foyle in title role. Dancing partner with Fred Astaire in ten movies.
⚲ Her father died when she was 11. Appeared in vaudeville at age 14. Won Texas State Charleston dancing contest in 1927. Her mother was one of the first female sergeants in the Marines. She was a life-long Republican and a Christian Scientist. She had many hobbies—she was a painter, sculptor, fisherman, skeet shooter, and near champion tennis player. She was the highest-paid actor in 1942. Lucille Ball was her distant cousin.
Major Awards: Oscar, BIFF, WOF

Rollins, Howard E. Jr.

1981-(BSA) *Ragtime*
    Winner: Sir John Gielgud, *Arthur*
▨ Born 10/17/50 in Baltimore, MD. Died 12/8/96 of complications of lymphoma.
〰 Coalhouse Walker in nominated role and Virgil Tibbs in TV's *In the Heat of the Night*.

❦ Graduated from Towson State College. Once nominated for an Emmy in daytime soaper *Another World*. Voted in *Screen World* as one of the most promising young actors of 1981. Battled a chronic drug habit for years. Carol O'Connor, who played the sheriff in *In the Heat of the Night*, saved Harold's job on several occasions when he didn't show up for work.

Rooney, Mickey

1938-Honorary Oscar
1939-(BA) *Babes in Arms*
　　Winner: Robert Donat, *Goodbye, Mr. Chips*
1943-(BA) *The Human Comedy*
　　Winner: Paul Lukas, *Watch on the Rhine*
1956-(BSA) *The Bold and the Brave*
　　Winner: Anthony Quinn, *Lust for Life*
1979-(BSA) *The Black Stallion*
　　Winner: Melvyn Douglas, *Being There*
1982-Honorary Oscar
▣ Born *Joe Yule Jr.* on 9/23/20 in Brooklyn, NY
✎ Andy Hardy role and many memorable performances throughout his long distinguished career.
❦ Made his vaudeville debut at age 15 months. At 5'3" he was the Pacific Southwest Junior Singles Champion in tennis, and he once beat tennis great Bill Tilden in five straight sets. Loves golfing and the ponies. Composed a symphony called *Melodante* in 1941. He was drafted in WW II. He has married eight times. Ava Gardner was his first wife. One story has it that Walt Disney named his famed mouse after him. Holds the record for the longest career in the movies at 80 years, from 1926 to 2006 . . . and beyond.
Major Awards: Emmy, GG, WOF

Ross, Diana

1972-(BA) *Lady Sings the Blues*
　　Winner: Liza Minnelli, *Cabaret*
▣ Born 3/26/44 in Detroit, MI
✎ Lead singer for the Supremes. Billie Holiday in nominated role.

❦ Started as a singer in the choir at a Baptist church. Declared by the *Guinness Book of World Records* as the most successful female singer of all time. Had 18 No. 1 hits. Arrested in 2002 for driving under the influence. Enjoys skiing and tennis. Her first child was fathered by Motown mogul Barry Gordy. Elected to the Rock and Roll Hall of Fame. *Billboard* magazine named her the Female Entertainer of the Century. Nominated for 12 Grammys but only won once.
Major Awards: Tony, GG, Grammy, WOF

Ross, Katharine

1967-(BSA) *The Graduate*
　　Winner: Estelle Parsons, *Bonnie and Clyde*
▣ Born 1/29/40 in Hollywood, CA
✎ Etta Place in *Butch Cassidy and the Sundance Kid*
❦ Began career at age 17 in the Actors Studio. Oscar winning actress Simone Signoret recommended her to director Mike Nichols for her role of Elaine Robinson in *The Graduate*. She is a successful author of many books for children and has been happily married to actor Sam Elliot for 22 years.
Major Awards: BAFTA, GG, Laurel

Roth, Tim

1995-(BSA) *Rob Roy*
　　Winner: Kevin Spacey, *The Usual Suspects*
▣ Born *Timothy Smith* on 5/14/61 in London, England.
✎ Archibald Cunningham in nominated role.
❦ His mother was a teacher and landscape artist, and his father was a journalist who changed their last name. He once studied to be a sculptor and artist. Lifelong buddies with actor Gary Oldham. Has five tattoos representing events in his life. Tends bar in his neighborhood pub from time to time.
Major Awards: BAFTA, BIFF, KCFCC

Rowlands, Gena

1974-(BA) *A Woman Under the Influence*
  Winner: Ellen Burstyn, *Alice Doesn't Live Here Anymore*
1980-(BA) *Gloria*
  Winner: Sissy Spacek, *Coal Miner's Daughter*
▪ Born 6/19/30 in Cambria, WI.
▥ Mabel Longhetti in *A Women Under the Influence*
♜ Attended the University of Wisconsin. Her father was a state assemblyman. Met and married legendary film director and actor John Cassavettes while in college. Starred in syndicated TV series *Top Secret USA* in the '50s. Nominated seven times for an Emmy and won four times.
Major Awards: Emmy, NBR, GG, BIFF, BSFC, KCFCC, Sundance

Ruehl, Mercedes

1991-(BSA) *The Fisher King*
▪ Born 2/28/48 in Queens, NY.
▥ Anne Napolitano in Oscar'd role.
♜ Her father was a FBI agent. Graduated from New Rochelle College in 1969. Married Ed Ruehl in the same year. She was recently reunited with her son Chris whom she had given up for adoption when she was 28. Worked for Baltimore Gas & Electric before hitting the stage. Divorced after 33 years of marriage and five children.
Major Awards: Tony, Obie, LAFC, GG, NSFC, BSFC, Saturn

Rush, Geoffrey

1996-(BA) *Shine*
1998-(BSA) *Shakespeare In Love*
  Winner: James Coburn, *Affliction*
2000-(BA) *Quills*
  Winner: Russell Crowe, *Gladiator*
▪ Born 7/6/51 in Toowoomba, Queensland, Australia.
▥ David Helfgott in Oscar'd role.

♜ Graduated from the University of Queensland with a degree in arts. The university awarded him an Honorary Doctorate in Letters and he was Alumnus of the Year in 1998. Studied acting in France before returning to Australia as a director. Once roomed with actor Mel Gibson while in college. Due to his hectic schedule and calamitous events in his life, he had a nervous breakdown in 1992. He is married and has two children.
Major Awards: Oscar, NYFC, LAFC, GG, SAG, BAFTA, BSFC, Emmy, KCFCC

Russell, Harold

1946-(BSA) *The Best Years of Our Lives*
1946-Honorary Oscar
▪ Born 1/14/14 in North Sidney, Nova Scotia, Canada. Died 1/29/2002 of a heart attack.
▥ Homer Parrish in Oscar'd role.
♜ Lost his hands in a training accident during WW II when dynamite exploded. Graduated from Boston College at the encouragement of director Billy Wyler. Only actor to win two Oscars for the same role. He founded the AMVETS and was its national leader for years. Had to sell his Oscar in 1992 to pay for his wife's hospital bills. It went for $66,500. The annual Presidential Award to people with disabilities is called the Harold Russell Award.
Major Awards: Oscar, GG, WOF

Russell, Rosalind

1942-(BA) *My Sister Eileen*
  Winner: Greer Garson, *Mrs. Miniver*
1946-(BA) *Sister Kenny*
  Winner: Olivia de Havilland, *To Each His Own*
1947-(BA) *Mourning Becomes Electra*
  Winner: Loretta Young, *The Farmer's Daughter*
1958-(BA) *Auntie Mame*
  Winner: Susan Hayward, *I Want To Live*
▪ Born 6/4/1907 in Waterbury, CT. Died 11/28/76 of breast cancer.
▥ Auntie Mame in title role.

Rosalind Russell in *Auntie Mame*.

Her mother was a fashion editor and her father was a lawyer. They named her after the steamship S.S. Rosalind. She spearheaded many charity drives in Hollywood and was awarded the Jean Hersholt Humanitarian Award in 1972. In 1957 she wrote the screenplay for the movie *Unguarded Moment*. Her film career was cut short after she was stricken with crippling arthritis.

Major Awards: Tony, GG (5), Jean Hersholt, WOF

Rutherford, Dame Margaret

1963-(BSA) *The V.I.P.s*
- Born 5/11/1892 in Balham, London, England. Died 5/22/72 of pneumonia.
- Mrs. Marple in Agatha Christie's novels turned into movies

Her mother died when she was three, and she was raised by her two aunts. Her father killed her grandfather and she took her mother's maiden name. Attended the Old Vic. Made her film debut when she was 44. Married when she was 52 and Oscar'd when she was 74. Awarded the OBE in 1961 and made Dame of the British Empire in 1967. Agatha Christie dedicated her novel *Mirror Cracked* to her out of admiration.

Major Awards: Oscar, GG, NBR

Ryan, Robert

1947-(BSA) *Crossfire*
   Winner: Edmund Gwenn, *Miracle on 34th Street*
- Born 11/11/1909 in Chicago, IL. Died 7/11/73 of lung cancer.
- Bill "Stoker" Thompson in *The Set-Up*

Attended Dartmouth and held the heavyweight boxing championship for four years. Won the school playwright award in 1931. His fraternity brother was Nelson Rockefeller. Enlisted in the Marines during WW II. He was an avid ACLU supporter. Donated time and money in founding the UCLA Theater Group. When he moved out of his apartment at the Dakota in New York he sold it to John Lennon and Yoko Ono.

Major Awards: NBR, NSFC, KCFCC

Ryder, Winona

1993-(BSA) *The Age of Innocence*
  Winner: Anna Paquin, *The Piano*
1994-(BA) *Little Women*
  Winner: Jessica Lange, *Blue Sky*
◼ Born *Winona Horowitz* on 10/29/71 in Winona, MN.
🖋 Jo March in *Little Women*, shoplifting
🔍 Grew up in a commune in California with no running water or electricity. Her godfather was LSD promoter and philosopher Dr. Timothy Leary. Poet Alan Ginsberg is a close friend of the family. She was nabbed and convicted of grand larceny in 2002 and sentenced to 480 hours of community service work and three years probation. She is a pack-a-day smoker. Changed her last name to Ryder after singer Mitch Ryder.
Major Awards: NBR, GG, KCFCC, WOF

Saint, Eva Marie

★ 1954-(BSA) *On the Waterfront*
◼ Born 7/4/24 in Newark, NJ
🖋 Edie Doyle in Oscar'd role.
🔍 Graduated from Bowling Green State University and started her career in radio, television, and then Broadway. Beat out TV's *Bewitched* star Elizabeth Montgomery for the lead role in *On the Waterfront*. Her old alma mater dedicated the school's drama theater in her name, and she has two stars on the Hollywood WOF—one for the movies and one for television.
Major Awards: Oscar, Emmy, WOF

Sanders, George

★ 1950-(BSA) *All About Eve*
◼ Born 7/3/1906 in St. Petersburg, Russia. Committed suicide on 4/25/72.
🖋 The acerbic Addison DeWitt in Oscar'd role.
🔍 Once worked in a textile mill, as a tobacco salesman, and as a writer for an advertising agency. He was enticed into acting by the agency's secretary one

Greer Garson. His brother was actor Tom Conway. Married to Zsa Zsa and Magda Gabor. His final written message was "Dear world I'm leaving, I am bored. I feel I have lived long enough. I am leaving you with your worries in this sweet cesspool, good luck."
Major Awards: Oscar, NBR, WOF

Sarandon, Chris

1975-(BSA) *Dog Day Afternoon*
  Winner: George Burns, *The Sunshine Boys*
◼ Born 7/24/42 in Beckley, WV
🖋 The vampire, Jerry Dandridge in *Fright Night*
🔍 Singer in the band The Teen Tones, the warm-up band for Bobby Darin. Graduated from the University of West Virginia Magna Cum Laude and got his Masters at Catholic University. Once married to actress Susan Sarandon. Portrayed doctors in the TV medical series *ER*, *The Practice*, and *Chicago Hope*.

Sarandon, Susan

1981-(BA) *Atlantic City*
  Winner: Katharine Hepburn, *On Golden Pond*
1991-(BA) *Thelma & Louise*
  Winner: Jodie Foster, *The Silence of the Lambs*
1992-(BA) *Lorenzo's Oil*
  Winner: Emma Thompson, *Howard's End*
1994-(BA) *The Client*
  Winner: Jessica Lange, *Blue Sky*
★ 1995-(BA) *Dead Man Walking*
◼ Born Susan Tomalin on 10/4/46 in New York, NY.
🖋 Louise in title role (#24 on AFI's Hero List)
🔍 Graduated from Catholic University. Met husband Chris Sarandon there, and they were married for 12 years. Partnered with actor Tim Robbins and they have two children. First actress to win an Oscar playing a nun. She is a goodwill ambassador for UNICEF. Carried the Olympic Flag in the 2006 opening ceremonies. Keeps her Oscar in the bathroom as does Emma Thompson.
Major Awards: OSCAR, CA, NBR, SAG, BAFTA, BSFC, DDA, VFF, KCFCC, WOF

Savalas, Telly

1962-(BSA) *Birdman of Alcatraz*
Winner: Ed Begley, *Sweet Bird of Youth*

◾ Born *Aristoteles Savalas* on 1/22/22 in Garden City, NJ: Died 1/22/94 of bladder cancer.

✦ Theo Kojak in TV's detective series *Kojak*. "Who loves you baby . . ."

✎ Served on the battlefront in WW II and was wounded in action. He would never talk about his war experiences. Graduated from Columbia University. Once was an executive for ABC and won a Peabody Award. He was an avid golfer, swimmer, and poker player. He won many tournaments in Vegas. Spoke Greek fluently and had a fear of flying.

Major Awards: Emmy, Peabody, GG, WOF

Scarwid, Diana

1980-(BSA) *Inside Moves*
Winner: Mary Steenburgen, *Melvin and Howard*

◾ Born 8/27/55 in Savannah, GA.

✦ Louise in nominated role.

✎ Graduated from the American Academy for Dramatic Arts. She has taken an active role in the Georgia Theater, Film Actors Workshop, and the Shakespeare Conservatory. She was listed as one of the ten most promising actors of 1980. After she was nominated for her Oscar she became the first person to be a winner for a Razzie in the same year for playing Christina Crawford in *Mommie Dearest*.

Major Award: Razzie

Scheider, Roy

1971-(BSA) *The French Connection*
Winner: Ben Johnson, *The Last Picture Show*
1979-(BA) *All That Jazz*
Winner: Dustin Hoffman, *Kramer vs. Kramer*

◾ Born 11/10/32 in Orange, NJ.

✦ Chief Martin Brody in *Jaws*

✎ Excelled in baseball while in school. Fought in the Golden Gloves as a teenager where his nose was broken on several occasions. He did a hitch in the Air Force. Graduated from Franklin Marshall College. He was originally cast as Michael in *The Deer Hunter*, but had to pass due to a previous commitment. Recently underwent a bone marrow transplant to treat cancer of the blood cells.

Major Awards: Western Heritage

Schell, Maximilian

★ 1961-(BA) *Judgement at Nuremberg*
1975-(BA) *The Man in the Glass Booth*
Winner: Jack Nicholson, *One Flew Over the Cuckoo's Nest*
1977-(BSA) *Julia*
Winner: Jason Robards, *Julia*

◾ Born 12/8/30 in Austria, Vienna.

✦ Hans Rolfe, the defense attorney in Oscar'd role.

✎ Fled with his parents to Switzerland to avoid Nazi occupation. Attended the Universities of Zurich, Basel, and Munich. Nominated for producing, writing, and directing. Oscar nominated for best foreign film *The Pedestrian*. His great-grandfather was friends with Richard Wagner and Franz Liszt. He is the godfather to actress Angelina Jolie.

Major Awards: Oscar, GG, NYFC

Schildkraut, Joseph

★ 1937-(BSA) *The Life of Emile Zola*

◾ Born 3/22/1896 in Vienna, Austria. Died 1/21/64 of a heart attack.

✦ Captain Alfred Dreyfus in Oscar'd role

✎ Toured the U.S. with his actor father in 1910. He was a star of the Berlin stage before the Nazi regime took over Germany. Studied at the Academy of Dramatic Arts. He was the first actor from Austria to win an Oscar. A true professional in every sense of the word. While filming a *Twilight Zone* episode, his wife of 29 years died, but he refused to mourn her death until taping was finished.

Major Awards: Oscar, NBR, WOF

Scofield, Paul

★ 1966-(BA) *A Man for All Seasons*
1994-(BSA) *Quiz Show*
   Winner: Martin Landau, *Ed Wood*
◾ Born 1/21/22 in Hurstpierpoint, West Sussex, England.
〰 Sir Thomas Moore in Oscar'd role.
⚲ Educated at the Vardean School for Boys and made his stage debut at age 14. Won the Triple Crown of Acting. Made CBE in 1956. Declined knighthood three times, saying he didn't like the sound of "Sir Paul." Only one of eight actors to win both the Tony and Oscar for the same role on stage and film. First English actor invited to Russia since their revolution in 1917.
Major Awards: Oscar, Tony, Emmy, NBR, GG, NYFC, BAFTA, KCFCC

Scott, George C.

1959-(BSA) *Anatomy of a Murder*
   Winner: Hugh Griffith, *Ben-Hur*
1961-(BSA) *The Hustler*
   Winner: George Chakiris, *West Side Story*
★ 1970-(BA) *Patton*
1971-(BA) *The Hospital*
   Winner: Gene Hackman, *The French Connection*
◾ Born 10/18/27 in Wise, VA. Died 9/22/99 of a abdominal aortic aneurism.
〰 General George Patton in title role.
⚲ His mother died when he was eight. Spent four years in the Marines. Studied journalism at the University of Missouri. First actor to refuse an Oscar, stating the ceremony was nothing but a meat parade. On Oscar night, he stayed home watching a hockey game. He was a heavy drinker and an expert chess player. Nominated five times for a Tony, but never won.
Major Awards: Oscar, Emmy, NBR, NSFC, Obie, GG, NYFC, KCFCC

Scott-Thomas, Kristin

1996-(BA) *The English Patient*
   Winner: Frances McDormand, *Fargo*
◾ Born 5/24/60 in Redruth, Cornwall, England.
〰 Katharine Clifton in nominated role.
⚲ Her father and stepfather were both pilots and both were killed in flying accidents. She left England for Paris where she was an au pair, and she speaks French fluently. She was awarded France's highest civilian award, the Legion of Honor. In 2003 Queen Elizabeth made her an Officer of the British Empire.
Major Awards: NBR, BAFTA, SAG

Scott, Martha

1940-(BA) *Our Town*
   Winner: Ginger Rogers, *Kitty Foyle*
◾ Born 9/22/1912 in Jamesport, MO.
   Died 5/28/2003 of natural causes.
⚲ Graduated from the University of Michigan majoring in Drama. *Our Town* was her first movie. Played in Shakespeare at the 1933 Chicago World's Fair. She was a third cousin to President William McKinley. Founded the Plumstead Playhouse in NY with Henry Fonda and Robert Ryan. She had a relatively short film career but worked steadily in television.
Major Awards: WOF

Segal, George

1966-(BSA) *Who's Afraid of Virginia Woolf?*
   Winner: Walter Matthau, *The Fortune Cookie*
◾ Born 2/13/34 in Great Neck, Long Island, NY
〰 Nick in nominated role.
⚲ Graduated from Columbia University. Did a stint in the army and while there formed his own band called Corp. Bruno's Sad Sack Six. Worked as a janitor, usher, and jazz musician before breaking into films. He is an accomplished banjo player and also plays the trombone. Has made over 100 TV appearances.
Major Awards: GG, KCFCC

Sellers, Peter

1960-(Best Short Subject) *Running, Jumping, &
Standing Still*
1964-(BA) *Dr. Strangelove, Or: How I Learned to
Stop Worrying and Love the Bomb*
Winner: Rex Harrison, *My Fair Lady*
1979-(BA) *Being There*
Winner: Dustin Hoffman, *Kramer vs. Kramer*
■ Born *Richard Sellers* on 9/8/1925 in Southsea,
England. Died 7/24/80 of a heart attack.
✹ Inspector Clouseau in the *Pink Panther*
❦ His parents were stage comedians where he per-
formed as a child. Joined the Royal Air Force during
WW II where he was camp entertainer. Appointed
Commander of the British Empire in 1966. First
male to appear on the cover of *Playboy* in 1964. He
was a vegetarian, vice president of the London Judo
Society, and an auto enthusiast who owned 62 cars.
A workaholic and perfectionist, he had four heart
attacks. Married four times.
Major Awards: BAFTA, NBR, GG

Sevigny, Chloe

1999-(BA) *Boys Don't Cry*
Winner: Angelina Jolie, *Boys Don't Cry*
■ Born 11/18/74 in Springfield, MA.
✹ Lana Tisdel in nominated role.
❦ She shaved her head for graduation. She was
discovered on the streets of New York by a fashion
editor for *Sassy* magazine. Modeled for *H & M* and
was a spokesman for *MAC* cosmetics. She selects
movies based on scripts and content, not money. She
once turned down $500,000 for a movie because of its
script. She is a direct descendant of the 17th century
French aristocrat, the Marquise de Sevigne.
Major Awards: NSFC, LAFC, ISA

Shariff, Omar

1962-(BSA) *Lawrence of Arabia*
Winner: Ed Begley, *Sweet Bird of Youth*
■ Born *Michael Shalhoub* on 4/10/32 in Alexan-
dria, Egypt.

✹ Dr. Zhivago in title role.
❦ He is of Lebanese and Syrian descent. Majored
in math and physics at the Cairo Victory College.
Has the distinction of being the first actor to be
filmed kissing in an Arabic movie, *The Blazing Sun*.
Fluent in English, Greek, Arabic, and French. He
is a Master and World Class Bridge player who
has authored several books on the game. Once
did a Stolichnaya vodka TV commercial because
everybody thought he was Russian.
Major Awards: GG, César, VFF

Shaw, Robert

1966-(BSA) *A Man for All Seasons*
Winner: Walter Matthau, *The Fortune Cookie*
■ Born 8/9/27 in Westhoughton, Lancashire,
England. Died 8/28/78 of a heart attack.
✹ The crusty old sailor Captain Quint in *Jaws*
❦ His father was an alcoholic and committed suicide
when he was 12. Graduated from RADA. Although in
lot of his films he played the heavy, and he was, in fact,
a gifted writer who wrote several prize-winning novels
and plays, most notably *The Man in the Glass Booth*,
for which he was nominated for a Tony. Fathered
ten children by three wives. He had a lifelong battle
with the bottle.
Major Awards: NBR, KCFCC, WOF

Shearer, Norma

★ 1929/30-(BA) *The Divorcée*
1929/30-(BA) *Their Own Desire*
1930/31-(BA) *A Free Soul*
Winner: Marie Dressler, *Min and Bill*
1934-(BA) *The Barretts of Wimpole Street*
Winner: Claudette Colbert, *It Happened
One Night*
1936-(BA) *Romeo and Juliet*
Winner: Luise Rainer, *The Great Ziegfeld*
1938-(BA) *Marie Antoinette*
Winner: Bette Davis, *Jezebel*
■ Born 8/10/1902 in Montreal, Quebec, Canada.
Died 6/12/83 of pneumonia.
✹ First Queen of MGM

🖋 She was a beauty pageant winner at age 14. Billed in 1930 as the First Lady of the Screen. Married to Hollywood Boy Wonder Irving Thalberg. Her brother, Douglas, won 12 Oscars as head sound director at MGM. Her sister Athole was married to director Howard Hawks. At the height of her career she was making $6,000 a week. Married a ski instructor 20 years her junior in 1942 and retired.

Major Awards: Oscar, VFF, WOF

Shepard, Sam

1983-(BSA) *The Right Stuff*
  Winner: Jack Nicholson, *Terms of Endearment*
■ Born *Sam Rogers* on 11/5/43 in
  Fort Sheridan, IL.
🖋 Chuck Yeager in nominated role.
🖋 The actor, director, writer, and playwright grew up an Army Brat. Wrote 30 plays before the age of 30. Has won to date 11 Obies. He plays the drums, has a fear of flying, and suffers from stage fright. Only actor to win a Pulitzer Prize for the play *The Buried Child*. Wrote songs with Bob Dylan. Has been with actress Jessica Lange since 1982.

Major Awards: Pulitzer Prize, Obie

Shire, Talia

1974-(BSA) *The Godfather, Part II*
  Winner: Ingrid Bergman, *Murder on the Orient Express*
1976-(BA) *Rocky*
  Winner: Faye Dunaway, *Network*
■ Born *Talia Coppola* on 4/25/46 in Lake Success, Long Island, NY.
🖋 Connie Corleone in *The Godfather* series
🖋 Graduated from Yale Drama School. Sister to movie director Francis Ford Coppola. Aunt to actors Nicholas Cage and Sofia Coppola. Once married to composer David Shire. Ironically her father Carmine was a composer as well. After filming *Rocky* together she developed a life-long friendship with actor Bert Young. She and her brother were

the first siblings to be nominated for Oscars in two different categories in the same year.

Major Awards: NBR, NYFC

Shirley, Anne

1937-(BSA) *Stella Dallas*
  Winner: Alice Brady, *In Old Chicago*
■ Born *Dawn Evelyn Paris* on 4/17/1918 in New York, NY. Died 7/4/93 of lung cancer.
🖋 Laurel Dallas in nominated role.
🖋 Made film debut at age four in 1922. She was originally billed as Dawn O'Day. Kept that name until she made the movie *Anne of Green Gables* in 1934. After filming she adopted the name of the lead character in the movie, Anne Shirley. Retired in 1944 at the ripe old age of 26 after being in movies for 22 years. Once married to actor John Payne.

Major Awards: WOF

Shue, Elizabeth

1995-(BA) *Leaving Las Vegas*
  Winner: Susan Sarandon, *Dead Man Walking*
■ Born 10/6/63 in Wilmington, DE.
🖋 Sera in nominated role.
🖋 Her parents divorced when she was in the fourth grade. She was a renegade in high school drinking heavily and smoking pot, however she was on the honor role and was a state finalist in gymnastics. She was the Burger King Girl in their '80s TV commercials. Attended Wellesley and graduated from Harvard 15 years after she dropped out to pursue her career.

Major Awards: NSFC, LAFC, ISA

Sidney, Sylvia

1973-(BSA) *Summer Wishes, Winter Dreams*
  Winner: Tatum O'Neal, *Paper Moon*
■ Born *Sophia Kosow* on 8/8/10 in the Bronx, NY. Died 7/1/99 of throat cancer
🖋 Mrs. Pritchett in nominated role.

Her parents divorced at birth. Made acting debut at age 15. Nominated for an Oscar 17 years after she retired from the movies. Wrote two books on her favorite hobby, needlepoint. Once married to Random House president, author, and game show panelist Bennett Cerf and to actor Luther Adler. First actress to appear in an outdoor Technicolor movie, *Trail of the Lonesome Pine*.
Major Awards: NBR, GG, KCFCC, WOF

Signoret, Simone

★ 1959-(BA) *Room at the Top*
1965-(BA) *Ship of Fools*
   Winner: Julie Christie, *Darling*
Born *Henriette Charlotte Simone Kaminker* on 3/25/21 in Weisbaden, Germany. Died 9/13/85 of Pancreatic Cancer.
Alice Aisgill in Oscar'd role.
Her family split up during WW II. Her father fled to England because of his Jewish ancestry and became an interpreter for the United Nations. She supported her mother and siblings during the Nazi occupation. Married to actor-singer Yves Montand. They were close friends with Marilyn Monroe and Arthur Miller. Fluent in English, French, and German. First actress to win an Oscar for a non-American film.

Major Awards: Emmy, NBR, Cannes, BAFTA, César, DDA, BIFF

Simmons, Jean

1948-(BSA) *Hamlet*
   Winner: Clair Trevor, *Key Largo*
1969-(BA) *The Happy Ending*
   Winner: Maggie Smith, *The Prime of Miss Jean Brodie*
Born 1/31/29 in Crouch Hill, London, England.
Julie Maragon in *The Big Country*
Made her screen debut when she was 14. Once married to actor Stuart Granger and currently married to director Richard Brooks. In the '50s she sued Howard Hughes over a contract dispute and won a $250,000 settlement. She is a naturalized U.S. citizen. Suffered from depression and became dependant on alcohol for a brief period in the '80s.
Major Awards: Emmy, NBR, GG, VFF

Sinatra, Frank

1945-Special Oscar, *The House I Live In*
★ 1953-(BSA) *From Here to Eternity*

Frank Sinatra (far right) in *From Here to Eternity*.

1955-(BA) *The Man with the Golden Arm*
  Winner: Ernest Borgnine, *Marty*
▪ Born 12/12/1915 in Hoboken, NJ.
  Died 5/14/98 of heart and kidney disease
  and bladder cancer.
Ole Blue Eyes, Chairman of the Board
Tried to enlist four times in the Army during
WW II but was declared 4F because of a perforated
eardrum. Because of his sudden mood changes he
was thought to be bi-polar. He was an accomplished
painter. Once was saved from drowning by actor
Brad Dexter. Notorious womanizer, chain smoker,
and pro drinker. Due to hemorrhaged vocal chords
he was flat broke in the early '50s and was bailed
out by future wife Ava Gardner. He, along with the
rest of the Rat Pack, were banned from Marilyn
Monroe's funeral by Joe DiMaggio. He was true
to his epitaph; he did it his way.
Major Awards: Oscar, GG, Grammy, J. Hersholt,
Peabody, SAGLA, WOF

Sinise, Gary

1994-(BSA) *Forrest Gump*
  Winner: Martin Landau, *Ed Wood*
▪ Born 3/17/55 in Blue Island, IL.
Lt. Dan in nominated role.
He was considered a wild man in high school.
Plays the bass guitar and sings in his band Bon-
soir Boys. Original co-founder of the Steppenwolf
Theater in the basement of his church. Now it is
located in an eight-million-dollar theater complex.
Received an honorary degree from Amherst College.
Founded the charity Operation Iraqi Children in
2004.
Major Awards: Emmy, CA, NBR, Obie,
CFC, SAG

Skala, Lilia

1963-(BSA) *Lilies of the Field*
  Winner: Margaret-Rutherford, *The V.I.P.s*
▪ Born 11/28/1896 in Vienna, Austria.
  Died 12/18/94 of natural causes.

Maria, Mother Superior in nominated role.
After college she was Austria's first female archi-
tect. Worked for Max Rienhardt's theater prior to
WW II. Her Jewish husband was arrested by the
Nazis. She bribed a guard and he was released.
He fled the country and was joined later by Lilia
and the children. Once worked for the New York
Transit Authority and after *Lilies of the Field* always
made her living acting.
Major Awards: Western Heritage

Smith, Dame Maggie

1965-(BSA) *Othello*
  Winner: Shelley Winters, *A Patch of Blue*
★ 1969-(BA) *The Prime of Miss Jean Brodie*
1972-(BA) *Travels with My Aunt*
  Winner: Liza Minnelli, *Cabaret*
★ 1978-(BSA) *California Suite*
1986-(BSA) *A Room with a View*
  Winner: Dianne Wiest, *Hannah and Her Sisters*
2001-(BSA) *Gosford Park*
  Winner: Jennifer Connelly, *A Beautiful Mind*
▪ Born 12/28/34 in Ilford, Essex, England.
Miss Jean Brodie in Oscar'd role.
Educated at the Oxford Repertory Theater. Her
father was a pathologist at Oxford University and
her twin brothers were architects. Close friends with
Sir Laurence Olivier and Dame Judi Dench. She
was appointed Commander of the British Empire by
the Queen in 1970 and Dame Commander in 1990.
Thirteenth winner of the Triple Crown of Acting.
Ranked the tenth best British actress ever.
Major Awards: Oscar, Tony, Emmy, OCC, GG,
BAFTA, NBR, SAG, KCFCC

Smith, Will

2001-(BA) *Ali*
  Winner: Denzel Washington, *Training Day*
2006-(BA) *The Pursuit of Happiness*
  Winner: Forest Whitaker, *The Last King of
  Scotland*
▪ Born 9/25/68 in Philadelphia, PA.

✐ Agent J in *Men In Black*

⚲ His parents owned a refrigeration company. Turned down scholarships to Harvard and MIT to be a rapper, and he has won a Grammy. Achieved stardom as The Fresh Prince on the TV sitcom. Blew through a million bucks in one year. Has since toned down his spending habits. Speaks Spanish fluently. First hip-hop artist to be nominated for an Oscar. Turned down the role of Neo in *The Matrix*, which he said was one of his biggest mistakes.

Major Awards: Grammy, PC, César

Snodgrass, Carrie

1970-(BA) *Diary of a Mad Housewife*
    Winner: Glenda Jackson, *Women in Love*
▥ Born 10/27/46 in Park Ridge, IL.
    Died 4/1/2004 of heart and liver failure.
✐ Tina Balser in nominated role
⚲ Graduated from Northern Illinois University. Received prestigious outstanding graduate award from Chicago's Goodman Theater. Dropped out of the movies for six years for a relationship with rocker Neil Young. Their son Zeke has cerebral palsey.

Major Awards: GG

Sondergaard, Gale

★ 1936-(BSA) *Anthony Adverse*
1946-(BSA) *Anna and the King of Siam*
    Winner: Anne Baxter, *The Razor's Edge*
▥ Born 2/15/1899 in Litchfield, MN.
    Died 8/14/85 of cerebral vascular thrombosis.
✐ Sinister Mrs. Hammond in *The Letter*
⚲ Graduated from the University of Minnesota. Married director Herbert Biberman and followed him to Hollywood. She was pursued by director Mervyn LeRoy for her role in *Anthony Adverse* and won the first Oscar for a supporting role for actresses. Turned down the role of the Wicked Witch in *The Wizard of Oz*. During the Red Scare of the '50s she and her husband were blacklisted.

Major Awards: Oscar

Sorvino, Mira

★ 1995-(BSA) *Mighty Aphrodite*
▥ Born 9/28/67 in Tenafly, NJ.
✐ Linda Ash in Oscar'd role.
⚲ Her father is veteran actor and opera singer Paul Sorvino. He discouraged her from getting into acting. She was an accomplished ballerina at age 12. Graduated from Harvard magna cum laude majoring in Chinese, and her thesis won the Harvard Hoopes Award for writing. Member of the jury on the Cannes Film festival in 1997. She is fluent in French and Mandarin Chinese.

Major Awards: GG, NBR, NYFC

Sothern, Ann

1987-(BSA) *The Whales of August*
    Winner: Olympia Dukakis, *Moonstruck*
▥ Born *Harriette Lake* on 1/22/1909 in Valley City, ND. Died 3/15/2001 of heart failure.
✐ Susie MacNamara on '50s TV series *Private Secretary*
⚲ Started career as an extra in 1934's *Kid Millions* with Eddie Cantor. Her mother was a concert singer and her grandfather, Simon Lake, invented the modern submarine. She sang with Artie Shaw, published several songs, and recorded two albums. Her sister Bonnie wrote "Sandman" and "I've Got Your Number." First to portray a working woman on TV. Nominated for four Emmys.

Major Awards: GG, WOF

Spacek, Sissy

1976-(BA) *Carrie*
    Winner: Faye Dunaway, *Network*
★ 1980-(BA) *Coal Miner's Daughter*
1982-(BA) *Missing*
    Winner: Meryl Streep, *Sophie's Choice*
1984-(BA) *The River*
    Winner: Sallie Field, *Places in the Heart*
1986-(BA) *Crimes of the Heart*
    Winner: Marlee Matlin, *Children of a Lesser God*

2001-(BA) *In the Bedroom*
    Winner: Halle Berry, *Monster's Ball*
▦ Born 12/25/49 in Quitman, TX.
✄ Loretta Lynn in Oscar'd role.
♞ She was a full-blown tomboy as a young girl however she was a majorette and elected homecoming queen at Quitman High. Her brother Robbie died of leukemia at age 18. That's when she decided life was too short to spend four years in college. She then moved to New York at the urging of actor cousin Rip Torn and was tutored by Lee Strasberg. Released a country/western album in 1983. Sang and played guitar in *Coal Miner's Daughter*. She was nominated for a Grammy for her rendition of the title song.
Major Awards: Oscar, NYFC, NBR, NSFC, LAFC, GG, DD, ISA, KCFCC

Spacey, Kevin

★ 1995-(BSA) *The Usual Suspects*
★ 1999-(BA) *American Beauty*
▦ Born *Kevin Spacey Fowler* 7/26/59 in South Orange, NJ.
✄ Verbal Kent in the Usual Suspects (#48 on AFI's Villain List)
♞ Quite the handful as a teen—he burned down his sister's tree house and was sent to Northridge Military Academy. There he was promptly thrown out for bashing a fellow cadet. Eventually graduated from Chatsworth High School as co-valedictorian with Mare Willingham. Val Kilmer was also a classmate and studied with him at Juilliard. Once auditioned for the *Gong Show* and was given the boot as the producers said he wasn't talented enough. He dedicated his BSA Oscar to Jack Lemmon who was his idol and role model.
Major Awards: Oscar, Tony, NBR, NYFC, SAG, BAFTA, BSFC, KCFCC, Sundance, WOF

Stack, Robert

1956-(BSA) *Written on the Wind*
    Winner: Anthony Quinn, *Lust for Life*
▦ Born 1/13/1919 in Los Angeles, CA.

Died 5/14/2003 of a heart attack.
✄ Eliot Ness in '50s TV series *The Untouchables*
♞ His parents divorced when he was one and his mother moved to Europe. He was a veteran of WW II and won the Victory Medal, Asiatic-Pacific and American Campaign Medals. He was an expert rifle and pistol man. He was National Skeet Shooting champion in 1937. He spoke French and Italian fluently. Spencer Tracy and Clark Gable took him hunting and fishing on a regular basis when he was a kid.
Major Awards: Emmy, WOF

Stallone, Sylvester

1976-(BA) *Rocky*
    Winner: Peter Finch, *Network*
1976-(Best Original Screenplay) *Rocky*
▦ Born 7/6/46 IN New York, NY
✄ *Rocky* in title role (#7 on AFI's Hero List), Rambo
♞ During birth forceps caused permanent paralysis of the left side of his face. Raised in Hell's Kitchen, he was expelled from 11 schools in 14 years. His classmates voted him most likely to be electrocuted. He was destitute and cleaning lion cages when he wrote the screenplay for *Rocky*. He turned down $300,000 and instead took a percentage of the gate and a starring role. The shrewd move made him an instant millionaire and an overnight star. He likes to paint and is an avid weight lifter and heath nut. He was the third actor nominated for acting and writing in the same movie. He is in very good company—with Charlie Chaplin and Orson Welles.
Major Awards: PC, César, DDA, KCFCC, PC, WOF

Stamp, Terence

1962-(BSA) *Billy Budd*
    Winner: Ed Begley, *Sweet Bird of Youth*
▦ Born 7/22/39 in Stepney, London, England.
✄ General Zod *in Superman II*
♞ His dad was a tugboat captain. He won a scholarship to prestigious Webber-Douglas Drama Acad-

emy. Once courted actress Julie Christie. Peter Ustinov was his guide and mentor. Left the movies for ten years and went to India on a soul-searching sabbatical after breaking up with his longtime girl-friend, supermodel Jean Shrimpton.
Major Awards: Cannes, GG

Stanley, Kim

1964-(BA) *Séance on a Wet Afternoon*
  Winner: Julie Andrews, *Mary Poppins*
1982-(BSA) *Frances*
  Winner: Jessica Lange, *Tootsie*
▪ Born *Patricia Reid* on 2/11/25 in Tularosa, NM. Died 8/20/2001 of uterine cancer.
🖉 Myra Savage in *Séance on a Wet Afternoon*
🔍 Graduated from the University of Texas with a degree in psychology. Searching for a career in acting she went to New York with only $21 in her pocket. She made ends meet working as a model and waitress. Studied under Lee Strasberg at the Actors Studio. Mainly a stage actress, she only made three movies. Suffered a nervous breakdown and left films for a teaching career at the University of New Mexico.
Major Awards: Emmy, NBR, NYFC

Stanwyck, Barbara

1937-(BA) *Stella Dallas*
  Winner: Luise Rainer, *The Good Earth*
1941-(BA) *Ball of Fire*
  Winner: Joan Fontaine, *Suspicion*
1944-(BA) *Double Indemnity*
  Winner: Ingrid Bergman, *Gaslight*
1948-(BA) *Sorry, Wrong Number*
  Winner: Jane Wyman, *Johnny Belinda*
1981-Honorary Oscar
▪ Born *Ruby Stevens* on 7/16/1907 in Brooklyn, NY. Died 1/20/1990 of congestive heart failure.
🖉 Victoria Barkley in TV western series *The Big Valley*, Phyllis Dietrichson in *Double Indemnity* (#8 on AFI's Villain List)
🔍 She was orphaned at age four after her mother was knocked off a trolley by a drunk. She worked as a secretary and chorus girl in the Zeigfield Fol-

John Boles and Barbara Stanwyck in *Stella Dallas.*

lies. She was the highest paid actress in 1944 at $400,000. She was married to actor Robert Taylor. She was tutor and mentor to William Holden. She was beaten and robbed in a home invasion in 1981. When she died she had no funeral but was cremated, and her ashes were scattered to the wind.
Major Awards: Emmy (3), LAFC, SAGLA, CBD, AFI Life Achievement, VFF, WOF

Stapleton, Maureen

1958-(BSA) *Lonely Hearts*
  Winner: Wendy Hiller, *Separate Tables*
1970-(BSA) *Airport*
  Winner: Helen Hayes, *Airport*
1978-(BSA) *Interiors*
  Winner: Maggie Smith, *California Suite*
★ 1981-(BSA) *Reds*
▪ Born 6/21/25 in Troy, NY. Died 3/13/06 of chronic pulmonary disease.
🖉 Emma Goldman in Oscar'd role
🔍 Graduated from the Actors Studio. Once was a waitress and model. She modeled for burlesque paintings for artists Reginald Marsh and Raphael Soyer. Has a fear of flying, didn't travel on trains and hated elevators. She became the tenth actor to

win the Triple Crown of acting. Nominated for an Emmy seven times.

Major Awards: Oscar, Emmy, Tony, LAFC, GG, BAFTA, NSFC, NYFC

Staunton, Imelda

2004-(BA) *Vera Drake*
  Winner: Hilary Swank, *Million Dollar Baby*
▦ Born1/9/56 in London, England.
𝄞 Vera Drake in title role
𝄞 Once planned on being a nun and attended the LaSainte Union Convent. Graduated from RADA. Has won three Laurence Olivier awards. Her idols are Bette Davis, Vivien Leigh, and Angelou Maya. She hates any celebrity who accepts gifts stating, "It is just ridiculous, give it to the people who need it." She was appointed Officer of the British Empire by the Queen in 2006.

Major Awards: NSFC, BAFTA, NYFC, SAG

Steenburgen, Mary

★ 1980-(BSA) *Melvin and Howard*
▦ Born 2/8/53 in Newport, AR.
𝄞 Clara Clayton in *Back to the Future III*
𝄞 Graduated from Hendrix College. Worked in a bookstore and was a waitress. A staunch democrat, she campaigned for Bill Clinton and was a frequent visitor to the White House. Fulfilled a promise to teach acting at her high school alma mater to the parents of Theo Leopoulos who was killed in an auto accident. Divorced from Malcom McDowell, and married to actor Ted Danson.

Major Awards: Oscar, NTFC, NSFC, LAFC, GG, KCFCC, NYFC, BSFC

Steiger, Rod

1954-(BSA) *On the Waterfront*
  Winner: Edmond O'Brien, *The Barefoot Contessa*
1965-(BA) *The Pawnbroker*
  Winner: Lee Marvin, *Cat Ballou*

★ 1967-(BA) *In the Heat of the Night*
▦ Born 4/14/25 in Westhampton, NY
  Died 7/9/2002 of kidney failure and pneumonia.
𝄞 Sheriff Bill Gillespie in Oscar'd role.
𝄞 Dropped out of high school and enlisted in the U.S. Navy. He was stationed on a destroyer as a torpedo man in the Pacific during WW II. He used the GI Bill to enroll at the Actors Studio in NY. Originated the role of Marty on TV and gained wide recognition in Hollywood. Suffered severe bouts of depression when his career temporarily tanked and sought psychiatric counseling.

Major Awards: Oscar, NYFC, NSFC, GG, BAFTA, BIFF, KCFCC, WOF

Stephenson, James

1940-(BSA) *The Letter*
  Winner: Walter Brennan, *The Westener*
▦ Born 4/14/1889 in Selby, Yorkshire, England. Died 7/29/41 of a massive heart attack.
𝄞 Attorney Howard Joyce in nominated role.
𝄞 He was a long-time British stage actor. He got his big break at age 49 and made his film debut when director William Wyler ignored studio brass and hired him for a part in *The Letter*. He was the original Philo Vance. With his career in full swing he bowed out at the young age of 53.

Sterling, Jan

1954-(BSA) *The High and the Mighty*
  Winner: Eva Marie Saint, *On the Waterfront*
▦ Born *Jane Sterling Adriance* on 4/3/21 in NY, NY. Died 3/26/2004 of several strokes.
𝄞 Sally McKee in nominated role.
𝄞 After her mother divorced and remarried, the family moved to Europe. There she received her education through private tutors in London and Paris. She was a descendant of presidents John Adams and John Quincy Adams. She was the original Billie Dawn in stage production of *Born Yesterday*. Married to actor Paul Douglas.

Major Awards: NBR, GG, WOF

Stewart, James

1939-(BA) *Mr. Smith Goes to Washington*
    Winner: Robert Donat, *Goodbye, Mr. Chips*
★ 1940-(BA) *The Philadelphia Story*
1946-(BA) *It's a Wonderful Life*
    Winner: Frederic March, *The Best Years of Our Lives*
1950-(BA) *Harvey*
    Winner: Jose Ferrer, *Cyrano de Bergerac*
1959-(BA) *Anatomy of a Murder*
    Winner: Charlton Heston, *Ben-Hur*
1984-Honorary Oscar
▥ Born 5/20/1908 in Indiana, PA.
    Died 7/2/97 of a pulmonary embolism.
✎ Jeff Smith, *Mr. Smith Goes to Washington* (#11 on AFI's Hero List); George Bailey, *It's a Wonderful Life* (#9 on AFI's Hero List); and many more.
⚲ Graduated from Princeton majoring in architecture. Enlisted in the Air Force during WW II. Flew 20 bombing missions in the European theater. Won the Air Medal, Distinguished Flying Cross, Croix de Guerre, and seven Battle Stars. His son Ron was killed in Vietnam. Played the accordion. His best friend was Henry Fonda—they once roomed together and got into a fistfight over politics. Fonda won, but they remained lifelong friends. Voted Third Greatest Movie actor of all time by *Entertainment Weekly*. Over 10,000 people attended his funeral.

James Stewart (right) in *It's a Wonderful Life.*

Once proposed to Olivia de Havilland, but she turned him down.
Major Awards: Oscar, GG, NYFC, NBR, SAGLA, CBD, Kennedy Center, AFI Life Achievement, BIFF, VFF, WOF

Stockwell, Dean

1988-(BSA) *Married to the Mob*
    Winner: Kevin Kline, *A Fish Called Wanda*
▥ Born 3/5/36 in Hollywood, CA.
✎ Admiral Albert Calaricci
⚲ He made his movie debut at age eight. Brother to actor Guy Stockwell. His father sang the part of the prince in Disney's *Snow White and the Seven Dwarves.* Dropped out of the movies for six years to protest how studios treated actors. Inspired the title for rocker Neil Young's 1970 album *After the Gold Rush.* Only actor to win two awards at the Cannes Film Festival.
Major Awards: Cannes (2), GG, NYFC, NSFC, KCFCC, WOF

Stone, Lewis

1928/29-(BA) *The Patriot*
    Winner: Warner Baxter, *In Old Arizona*
▥ Born 11/15/1879 in Worcester, MA.
    Died 9/12/53 of a heart attack.
✎ Judge James Hardy in the *Andy Hardy* series
⚲ He was prematurely grey at age 20. Fought in the cavalry in the Spanish American War and was a major during WW I. Holds the record for the longest contract with MGM at 29 years and over 200 films. Died when chasing teen vandals out of his prized garden after having a massive heart attack.
Major Awards: WOF

Stone, Sharon

1995-(BA) *Casino*
    Winner: Susan Sarandon, *Dead Man Walking*
▥ Born 3/10/58 in Meadville, PA.
✎ Catherine Trammel in *Basic Instinct*

🔑 Graduated from Edinboro University with a degree in Creative Writing. Has an IQ of 154. Won the Miss Pennsylvania beauty pageant. Posed nude for *Playboy* at the age of 32. Once was a successful model for the Ford Agency. Is fluent in Italian. Hugh fundraiser for fighting AIDS. Sharon has her share of health problems—she had a brain aneurysm and has continual back problems. She is allergic to caffeine and is asthmatic and a diabetic.
Major Awards: GG, Emmy, WFCA, WOF

Straight, Beatrice

★ 1976-(BSA) *Network*
▪ Born 8/2/1914 in Old Westbury, NY.
   Died 4/7/2001 of pneumonia.
🎞 Louise Schumacher in Oscar'd role
🔑 Her father was a banker and worked with JP Morgan. Her brother was the youngest person (16) to be a licensed airplane pilot in England. She was educated in Devonshire, England. Mainly a stage actor, she made her debut at age 20. Cousin to Gloria Vanderbuilt. Her Oscar-winning role only lasted 5 minutes and 40 seconds, the shortest time on screen ever.
Major Awards: Oscar, Tony

Strasberg, Lee

1974-(BSA) *The Godfather, Part II*
   Winner: Robert DeNiro, *The Godfather, Part II*
▪ Born Israel Lee Strasberg on 11/17/1901 in Budanov, Ukraine. Died 2/17/82 of a heart attack.
🎞 Hyman Roth in nominated role.
🔑 Director, actor and teacher. He was the director of the famed Actors Studio for years. He was a strong proponent of the Method Acting system pioneered by Stanislavski and Stella Adler. Had many protégés—among them Marlon Brando, Robert DeNiro, Al Pacino, Montgomery Clift, James Dean, and Marilyn Monroe. Marilyn Monroe was so grateful for his kindness that in her final will she gave him total control of her estate, which earns millions.
Major Awards: VFF, WOF

Strathairn, David

2005-(BA) *Good Night and Good Luck*
   Winner: Philip Seymour Hoffman, *Capote*
▪ Born 1/26/49 in San Francisco, CA.
🎞 Edward R. Morrow in nominated role.
🔑 Graduated from Williams College. His father was a teacher as is his brother. He traveled to Florida with his grandfather but on the way the grandfather died. Once in Florida he enrolled in Ringling Bros. Clown College where he got his start traveling across the country with the circus. During the summers he would hitchhike, crisscrossing the country working in local theaters.
Major Awards: VFF, ISA

Strauss, Robert

1953-(BSA) *Stalag 17*
   Winner: Frank Sinatra, *From Here to Eternity*
▪ Born 11/8/1913 in New York, NY.
   Died 2/20/75 of a paralytic stroke.
🎞 Animal Stosh in nominated role
🔑 His high school classmates voted him the Wittiest and Most Likely to Succeed. His father was a theater costume designer. He once worked as a salesman, singing waiter, and busboy. In the early '70s he was almost totally incapacitated by a stroke, which eventually took his life.

Streep, Meryl

1978-(BSA) *The Deer Hunter*
   Winner: Maggie Smith, *California Suite*
★ 1979-(BSA) *Kramer vs. Kramer*
1981-(BA) *The French Lieutenant's Woman*
   Winner: Katharine Hepburn, *On Golden Pond*
★ 1982-(BA) *Sophie's Choice*
1983-(BA) *Silkwood*
   Winner: Shirley MacLaine, *Terms of Endearment*
1985-(BA) *Out of Africa*
   Winner: Geraldine Page, *The Trip to Bountiful*
1987-(BA) *Ironwood*
   Winner: Cher, *Moonstruck*

1988-(BA) *A Cry in the Wilderness*
  Winner: Jodie Foster, *The Accused*
1990-(BA) *Postcards from the Edge*
  Winner: Kathy Bates, *Misery*
1995-(BA) *The Bridges of Madison County*
  Winner: Susan Sarandon, *Dead Man Walking*
1998-(BA) *One True Thing*
  Winner: Gwyneth Paltrow, *Shakespeare in Love*
1999-(BA) *Music of the Heart*
  Winner: Hilary Swank, *Boys Don't Cry*
2002-(BSA) *Adaptation*
  Winner: Catherine Zeta Jones, *Chicago*
2006-(BSA) *The Devil Wears Prada*
  Winner: Jennifer Hudson, *Dreamgirls*
  Born 6/22/49 in Summit, NJ.
  Joanna Kramer and Sofia in Oscar'd roles (#47 on AFI's Hero List), as Karen Silkwood in *Silkwood*
  Originally studied to be an opera singer. She was a cheerleader and homecoming queen. Graduated from Vassar and attended Yale Drama School. Known as a perfectionist and a master of any accent and dialect. Learned to play the violin in eight weeks by practicing six hours a day. Considered among her peers as the greatest living actress. She has a deviated septum. Nominated an unprecedented 19 times for a Golden Globe, and holds the record for the most Oscar nominations at 14.
Major Awards: Oscar, Emmy, NBR (3), LAFC (4), NYFC (3) NSFC (3), Cannes, Obie, GG (5), SAG, AFI Life Achievement, BAFTA, César, BIFF, BSFC, DDA, KCFCC, PC, Australian FI, WFCA, WOF

Meryl Streep and Kevin Kline in *Sophie's Choice*.

Streisand, Barbra

★ 1968-(BA) *Funny Girl*
1973-(BA) *The Way We Were*
  Winner: Glenda Jackson, *A Touch of Class*
★ 1977-(Best Original Song) *A Star Is Born*
1991-(Best Producer/Picture) *Prince of Tides*
1997-(Best Original Song) *The Mirror Has Two Faces*
  Born 4/24/42 in Brooklyn, NY.
  Singer extraordinaire, Fanny Brice in *Funny Girl*
  Graduated with Neil Diamond. Once worked as a switchboard operator. Got her big break when she won a talent contest in Greenwich Village. First person to win an Emmy, Oscar, Tony, and Grammy. She has sold over 68 million records—13 multi-platinum, 28 platinum, and 47 gold. First woman to direct, write, produce, and sing in a feature film, *Yentl*. Has the record for the highest grossing single concert at 14.6 million. Once married to Elliot Gould and currently married to James Brolin. Saying she is multi-talented would be an understatement. One of the rare few to win the Superfecta of acting.
Major Awards: Oscar, Tony, Grammy, Emmy (3), CB DeMille, GG, PC, AFI Life Achievement, DDA, WOF

Stuart, Gloria

1997-(BSA) *Titanic*
  Winner: Kim Basinger, *L.A. Confidential*
  Born 7/4/10 in Santa Monica, CA
  Rose Dawson Calvert in nominated role.
  Attended the University of California at Berkeley. Had a reputation as a wild child and flapper during the Roaring '20s. She was a founding member of the Screen Actors Guild. She is a strong environmentalist. Quit the screen for several years to paint, and her paintings were exhibited in major art galleries here and abroad. Oldest person ever nominated for an Oscar at age 87. By her own candid admission she is a proponent of free love and devoted to masturbation.
Major Awards: SAG, KCFCC, WOF

Sullavan, Margaret

1938-(BA) *Three Comrades*
   Winner: Bette Davis, *Jezebel*
▪ Born *Margaret Brooke* on 5/16/1911 in Norfolk, VA. Died 1/1/60 of a suicide by barbiturate overdose.
▨ Klara Novak in *Little Shop Around the Corner*
⚲ Her parents were wealthy, and she was educated in elite private schools. Married to Henry Fonda (two months), director William Wyler, and super agent Leland Hayward. She retired at the age of 32. She started to go progressively deaf. Two of her three children were in mental institutions, and her daughter Bridget also committed suicide.
Major Awards: NYFC, WOF

Suzman, Janet

1971-(BA) *Nicholas and Alexandra*
   Winner: Jane Fonda, *Klute*
▪ Born 2/9/39 in Johannesburg, South Africa.
▨ Empress Alexandra in nominated role.
⚲ Graduated from Witwatersand University. She was adamantly against apartheid and was politically active against the government policy. This caused her to leave the country in 1959. She was mainly a stage actress and over her career received rave reviews for her Shakespearian roles. She has received honorary degrees from the Universities of Warwick and Leicester.

Swanson, Gloria

1927/28-(BA) *Sadie Thompson*
   Winner: Janet Gaynor, *Seventh Heaven*
1929/30-(BA) *The Trespasser*
   Winner: Norma Shearer, *The Divorcée*
1950-(BA) *Sunset Boulevard*
   Winner: Judy Holliday, *Born Yesterday*
▪ Born *Gloria Svensson* on 3/27/1897 in Chicago, IL. Died 4/4/83 of natural causes.
▨ Norma Desmond in *Sunset Boulevard*
⚲ She was an army brat and attended school in San Juan, Puerto Rico. She was married seven times. Her

Gloria Swanson in *Sunset Boulevard*.

first husband was Wallace Beery for a total of three weeks. She was one of the highest paid actresses during the '20s and it is reported that she spent over eight million during that period. Carried on a clandestine love affair with Senator Joseph Kennedy. During one of their trysts aboard his yacht, young JFK walked in on them. He was so distraught he jumped overboard and had to be saved by the crew. Took up sculpting in her 70s and had many of her works exhibited in New York galleries.
Major Awards: GG, NBR, WOF

Swank, Hilary

★ 1999-(BA) *Boys Don't Cry*
★ 2004-(BA) *Million Dollar Baby*
▪ Born 7/30/74 in Lincoln, NE.
✎ Maggie Fitzgerald in *Million Dollar Baby*
✦ Appeared in her first play at age nine and was a professional at age 16. Competed in the Junior Olympics in swimming and placed fifth in the state of Washington in all-around gymnastics. When her parents separated she and her mother moved to L.A. They were so destitute they lived in their car. She attended Santa Monica College and is a vegetarian. She is the only woman to win an Oscar portraying a boxer. She is two for two in Oscar nominations and wins—joining Vivien Leigh, Helen Hayes, Sally Field, and Louise Rainer.
Major Awards: LAFC, NBR, NSFC, NYFC, SAG, BSFC, ISA, KCFCC, GG, WOF

Tamblyn, Russ

1957-(BSA) *Peyton Place*
    Winner: Red Buttons, *Sayonara*
▪ Born 12/30/34 in Los Angeles, CA.
✎ Riff, the gang leader in *West Side Story*
✦ Studied dancing and gymnastics from the age of six. Discovered by actor Lloyd Bridges at the age of ten. Multi-talented, he won the plumb role of Norman Page in *Peyton Place*. His daughter Amber stars in the TV series *Joan of Arcadia*. He currently manages her career and coaches choreography in his spare time.
Major Awards: GG

Tamiroff, Akim

1936-(BSA) *The General Dies at Dawn*
    Winner: Walter Brennan, *Come and Get It*
1943-(BSA) *For Whom the Bell Tolls*
    Winner: Charles Coburn, *The More the Merrier*
▪ Born 10/29/1899 in Tibilisi, Georgia.
    Died 9/17/72 of cancer.
✎ Pablo in *For Whom the Bell Tolls*

✦ Graduated from Moscow University and was a mainstay at the Moscow Theater. Traveled throughout Europe in the Russian acting troupe. Arrived in the U.S. and, tiring of the travel, he decided to stay. He once offered to take elocution lessons to rid himself of his heavy Russian accent. He was informed by Hollywood brass that if he did he wouldn't find any more work.
Major Awards: GG, WOF

Tandy, Jessica

★ 1989-(BA) *Driving Miss Daisy*
1991-(BSA) *Fried Green Tomatoes*
    Winner: Mercedes Ruehl, *The Fisher King*
▪ Born 6/7/1909 in London, England.
    Died 9/11/94 of ovarian cancer.
✎ Miss Daisy Werthan in Oscar'd role.
✦ Made her acting debut at age 16 and her stage debut at age 21. Once married to actor Jack Hawkins. She was the original Blanche Dubois on Broadway and won a Tony. However she lost the screen role to Vivien Leigh because the producers thought she was too short. Married to actor Hume Cronyn for 52 years. They collaborated on many projects and were dubbed America's First Couple of the Theater. She achieved the Triple Crown of Acting in 1989. She was the oldest at age 80 yrs, 9 months to win the Best Actress Oscar.
Major Awards: Oscar, Tony (4), Obie, GG, BAFTA, BIFF, DDA, Emmy, KCFCC, WFCA, WOF

Taylor, Dame Elizabeth

1957-(BA) *Raintree County*
    Winner: Joanne Woodward, *The Three Faces of Eve*
1958-(BA) *Cat on a Hot Tin Roof*
    Winner: Susan Hayward, *I Want To Live!*
1959-(BA) *Suddenly Last Summer*
    Winner: Simone Signoret, *Room at the Top*
★ 1960-(BA) *Butterfield 8*
★ 1966-(BA) *Who's Afraid of Virginia Woolf?*
▪ Born 2/27/32 in Hampstead, London, England.

Elizabeth Taylor and Richard Burton
in *Who's Afraid of Virginia Woolf?*

🖋 Many roles, most notably Virginia Woolf—
and her many high-profile marriages
🔍 Her parents were American art dealers and left England at the outbreak of WW II. Made her screen debut at age ten. Has appeared on the cover of *People* magazine 14 times and *Life* ten times. First actress to make a million dollars for one movie (*Cleopatra*). Has been married eight times—to Michael Todd, Conrad Hilton Jr., Eddie Fisher, Richard Burton, and Senator John Warner. Has dodged the grim reaper many times and has suffered health problems over the years, including a brain tumor, a broken back (four times), heart failure, and a rare staphylococcus pneumonia (she is the only known survivor). She has an explosive temper and likes Jack Daniels. Made Dame Commander by the Queen in 1999. Married Richard Burton twice.
Major Awards: Oscar, GG, NBR, NYFC, CB DeMille, BAFTA, SAG, Jean Hersholt Humanitarian, AFI Life Achievement, BIFF, DDA, KCFCC, WFCA, SAGLA, WOF

Temple, Shirley

1934-Honorary Oscar
▪ Born 4/23/28 in Santa Monica, CA.

🖋 Once a national institution with golden curly locks. At age five she could do it all, dance, sing, and act.
🔍 Started in the movies at age three. She was a box office champ three straight years 1936–38. She made her first million at age ten. Youngest person to make the cover of *Time* magazine (April, 1936). J. Edgar Hover made her an honorary G-Man, the Texas Rangers made her an honorary captain, and the American Legion made her an honorary colonel. Her mother Gertrude always did her curls, exactly 56. Married Charles Black after divorcing John Agar. She was ambassador to Ghana and Czechoslovakia. Youngest person to be awarded an Oscar—at age six.
Major Awards: NBR, LA, SAGLA, WOF

Theron, Charlize

★ 2003-(BA) *Monster*
2005-(BA) *North Country*
    Winner: Reese Witherspoon, *Walk the Line*
▪ Born 8/7/75 in Benoni, Gauteng, South Africa.
🖋 Aileen Wuornos in Oscar'd role
🔍 She worked as a model at age 14. She was a ballet dancer for the Joffrey Ballet until she injured her knee. At age 15 her mother was attacked by her father, and her mother shot and killed him. She was acquitted. Second Oscar winner to appear nude in *Playboy* in May, 1999 (Kim Basinger was the first). First language was Afrikaans and learned to speak English by watching soap operas. First African to win an Oscar. Gained 30 pounds for her role in *Monster*.
Major Awards: NBR, NSFC, GG, BIFF, ISA, SAG, WOF

Thompson, Emma

★ 1992-(BA) *Howard's End*
1993-(BA) *The Remains of the Day*
    Winner: Holly Hunter, *The Piano*
1993-(BSA) *In the Name of the Father*
    Winner: Anna Paquin, *The Piano*
1995-(BA) *Sense and Sensibility*
    Winner: Susan Sarandon, *Dead Man Walking*

★ 1995-(Best Writer)) *Sense and Sensibility*

■ Born 4/15/59 in Paddington, London, England.

〃 Margaret Schlegal in Oscar'd role.

🔍 Graduated from Cambridge. Once wanted to be a standup comedian and worked with the Monte Python group. She is the only person to win Oscars in both acting and writing. One of only ten persons nominated for BA and BSA in two different movies in the same years. Once married to actor director Kenneth Branagh. Speaks French and Spanish fluently. She keeps her two Oscars in her bath room as does Susan Sarandon.

Major Awards: Oscar, NBR, NTFC, NSFC, LAFC, GG, BAFTA, Emmy, BSFC, DDA, KCFCC, VFF, WGA

Thornton, Billy Bob

1996-(BA) *Sling Blade*
    Winner: Geoffrey Rush, *Shine*
★ 1996-(Best Writer) *Sling Blade*
1998-(BSA) *A Simple Plan*
    Winner: James Coburn, *Affliction*
■ Born 8/4/55 in Alpine, AR.

〃 Carl Childers in *Sling Blade*

🔍 His family was so poor that they had no electricity and used an outhouse. His mother was a psychic and predicted he would once work with Burt Reynolds, which he did on *Evening Shade*. He played the drums in his own band, Tres Hombres, and opened for Hank Williams, Jr. Before his success he was so destitute that he was hospitalized for a near heart attack because of malnutrition. His cousins are pro wrestlers Terry and Dory Funk, Jr. Has a morbid fear of antique furniture and hates flying. Married five times, once to Angelina Jolie.

Major Awards: Oscar, NBR, LAFC, Saturn, BSFC, ISA, KCFCC, WGA, WOF

Thurman, Uma

1994-(BSA) *Pulp Fiction*
    Winner: Dianne Wiest, *Bullets over Broadway*

■ Born 4/29/70 in Boston, MA.

〃 The Bride in the *Kill Bill* series

🔍 Her father is a professor of Asian religion at Columbia University and the first Westener to become a Tibetan Buddist monk. The Dali Lama was a frequent visitor and she was named after a Hindu god. Her mother was once married to LSD guru Dr. Timothy Leary. She was introduced to Leary by Salvador Dali. She dropped out of school at age 16 and moved to New York where she got a modeling job. She is six feet tall and wears size 11 shoes. Her uncle is a concert cellist. Married to actor Gary Oldman and now married to Ethan Hawke.

Major Awards: GG, Saturn

Tibbett, Lawrence

1929/30-(BA) *The Rogue Song*
    Winner: George Arliss, *Disraeli*
■ Born 11/16/1896 in Bakersfield, CA. Died 7/15/60 of complications following surgery.

〃 Metropolitan Opera singer

🔍 His father was the county sheriff and was fatally shot by cattle rustlers when he was six. Blessed with a great voice, he sang at the Metropolitan Opera House for 28 years. Only one of six actors to receive an Oscar nomination in their first movie appearance, he being the first. Featured on a 32-cent stamp in 1997. After a night of drinking he stumbled and fell on his TV set, driving bone fragments into his skull, which killed him when they couldn't save him in surgery.

Major Awards: WOF

Tierney, Gene

1945-(BA) *Leave Her to Heaven*
    Winner: Joan Crawford, *Mildred Pierce*
■ Born 11/19/20 in Brooklyn, NY. Died 11/6/91 of emphysema.

〃 Laura Hunt in title role *Laura*.

🔍 She was educated in Switzerland. Discovered by movie mogul Darryl F. Zanuck. Once married to fashion designer Oleg Cassini. Her daughter was born retarded because she had caught measles on a USO tour. Spoke French fluently. Received electro-shock therapy for treatment of depression. Had many love affairs, most notably with Tyrone Power, Prince Aly Khan, and President John F. Kennedy.

Major Awards: WOF

Tilly, Jennifer

1994-(BSA) *Bullets over Broadway*
    Winner: Dianne Wiest, *Bullets over Broadway*
▪ Born *Jennifer Chan* on 9/16/58 in Harber City, CA.
✎ Olive Neal in nominated role, voice of Tiffany in the *Child's Play* kitsch horror films.
✎ Financed her education at Stephans College in Missouri by winning writing competitions. She is a real fashion hound, owning over 400 pairs of shoes. Meg Tilly is her sister. She is half Chinese. She is an expert poker player, becoming the first celebrity to win the World Series of Poker (WSOP) Ladies Only Texas Hold'em championship. She earned the coveted WSOP Bracelet, beating out over 600 other women.

Major Awards: Fantafestival

Tilly, Meg

1985-(BSA) *Agnes of God*
    Winner: Anjelica Huston, *Prizzi's Honor*
▪ Born *Margaret Chan* on 2/14/60 in Texada, British Columbia, Canada.
✎ Sister Agnes in nominated role.
✎ Changed her surname to her mother's maiden name when she divorced. Raised in British Columbia, Canada. Started dancing lessons at age 12. Earned a scholarship to New York Ballet school and was in involved with the Connecticut Ballet. Her dancing career ended when she suffered a serious back injury. That steered her into acting. Sister to Jennifer Tilly. Had a child out of wedlock with British actor Colin Firth. Retired from films in 1995 to raise her children.

Major Awards: GG

Todd, Richard

1949-(BA) *The Hasty Heart*
    Winner: Broderick Crawford, *All the King's Men*
▪ Born 6/11/19 in Dublin, Ireland.
✎ Cpl. Lachie MacLachlan in nominated role.
✎ Spent his childhood years in India where his father was an army physician. Co-founded the Dundee Repertory Theater in England. He was an officer and decorated paratrooper in WW II, one of the first to parachute into France on D-Day. Suffered a tragic loss with the suicide of his son. In 1970 he founded the Triumph Theater Production Company and toured the world putting on various plays.

Major Awards: GG

Tomei, Marisa

★ 1992-(BSA) *My Cousin Vinny*
2001-(BSA) *In the Bedroom*
    Winner: Jennifer Connelly, *A Beautiful Mind*
▪ Born 12/4/64 in Brooklyn, NY.
✎ Mona Lisa Vito in Oscar'd role.
✎ Her father was a lawyer and her mother a teacher. She attended Boston University and dropped out after one year. Starred on the daytime soaps *As the World Turns* and *One Life to Live*. She has dual citizenship between America and Italy. She is a smoker. Subject of an urban legend: on awards night, Jack Palance read her name by mistake, instead of the real Oscar winner, and it would have been to embarrassing to correct. But that's just a myth.

Major Awards: Oscar

Tomlin, Lily

1975-(BSA) *Nashville*
    Winner: Lee Grant, *Shampoo*
▪ Born 9/1/39 in Detroit, MI.
✎ Ernestine, the phone operator in TV's *Laugh In*
✎ Her family moved from the hills of Kentucky to Detroit. She was a pre-med student at Wayne State University. She dropped out to study under mime master Paul Curtis. Once worked as a waitress

at a Howard Johnson's on Broadway. Has been in a 30-year relationship with another woman, Jane Wagner. Years back bought W.C. Fields's Hollywood mansion for the bargain price of $500,000.
Major Awards: Grammy, Emmy (4), Tony, NYFC, NSFC, BIFF, KCFCC, VFF, WFCA

Tone, Franchot

1935-(BA) *Mutiny on the Bounty*
   Winner: Victor McLaglen, *The Informer*
▦ Born 2/27/05 in Niagara Falls, NY.
   Died 9/18/68 of lung cancer.
🖋 Roger Byam in nominated role.
☿ Always suave and debonair, he was educated at Rennes University in France and graduated Phi Beta Kappa from Cornell University. He was married four times, his first wife being Joan Crawford. He was involved in a brutal barroom brawl with actor Tom Neal over some off-color remarks to his third wife, Barbara Payton. Franchot suffered a crushed cheekbone, broken nose, and brain injury—Neal was once a Notre Dame boxing champion and later a convicted murderer.
Major Awards: WOF

Topol

1971-(BA) *Fiddler on the Roof*
   Winner: Gene Hackman, *The French Connection*
▦ Born *Chaim Topal* on 9/9/35 in Tel Aviv, Palestine.
🖋 Tevye, the milkman in nominated role.
☿ Served in the Israeli Army and was on active duty when he was nominated. The army gave him permission to attend the ceremony. He played *Tevye* over 400 times before landing the role for the film version. Since then he reprised the role over 2000 times all over the world. His best friend Ghandi Ze'evi, a minister in the Israeli government, was murdered by a Palestinian terrorist in 2001.
Major Awards: GG, DDA

Torn, Rip

1983-(BSA) *Cross Creek*
   Winner: Jack Nicholson, *Terms of Endearment*
▦ Born *Elmore Torn* on 2/6/31 in Temple TX.
🖋 Arthur on HBO's *The Larry Sanders Show*
☿ Graduated from Texas A&M in animal husbandry. Married to actress Geraldine Page for 25 years and is first cousin to Sissy Spacek. After college he hitchhiked to Hollywood and ended up in New York. He studied under Lee Strasberg at the Actors Studio and took dancing lessons from Martha Graham, all the while washing dishes at a New York bistro. Won a hefty defamation suit ($475,000) against Dennis Hopper for his remarks on the *Jay Leno Show* in 1994. Lifetime member of Sigma Chi fraternity.
Major Awards: Emmy, Obie, BW

Tracy, Lee

1964-(BSA) *The Best Man*
   Winner: Peter Ustinov, *Topkapi*
▦ Born 4/14/1898 in Atlanta, GA.
   Died 10/18/68 of cancer.
🖋 Art Hockstader in nominated role.
☿ Graduated from Union College in New York. Before making his stage debut he worked for the railroad. His career went into a major tailspin while filming *Viva Villa* in Mexico: after a heavy night of boozing he urinated on a passing military parade. This created a major international incident and he was promptly fired.
Major Awards: WO

Tracy, Spencer

1936-(BA) *San Francisco*
   Winner: Paul Muni, *The Story of Louis Pasteur*
★ 1937-(BA) *Captains Courageous*
★ 1938-(BA) *Boys Town*
1950-(BA) *Father of the Bride*
   Winner: Jose Ferrer, *Cyrano de Bergerac*
1955-(BA) *Bad Day at Black Rock*
   Winner: Ernest Borgnine, *Marty*

1958-(BA) *The Old Man and the Sea*
    Winner: David Niven, *Separate Tables*
1960-(BA) *Inherit the Wind*
    Winner: Burt Lancaster, *Elmer Gantry*
1961-(BA) *Judgement at Nuremberg*
    Winner: Maximilian Schell, *Judgement at Nuremberg*
1967-(BA) *Guess Who's Coming To Dinner*
    Winner: Rod Steiger, *In the Heat of the Night*
▪ Born 4/5/1900 in Milwaukee, WI.
    Died 6/10/67 of diabetes and heart failure.
🎖 Many memorable roles: Father Flanagan
    (#42 on AFI's Hero List), Manuel Fidello in
    Captains Courageous, and many more.
🔍 Attended Marquette Academy to become a priest.
He and his childhood buddy, Pat O'Brian, enlisted
in the Navy during WW I. Married actress Louise
Treadwell in 1923. Their son John was born deaf.
Unhappy, he had a lifelong relationship with actress
Katharine Hepburn although, being a devout Catho-
lic, he never divorced. He had a life-time battle with
the bottle and suffered from insomnia. When the
pressures of Hollywood ganged up on him he would
head to Milwaukee and burrow into his old watering
holes and wouldn't be seen for weeks. George M.
Cohan once stated that he was the best actor ever.
Lifelong friends with Humphrey Bogart and was at
his bedside when he died. AFI's #9 Greatest Actor.
First actor to win back-to-back Oscars.
Major Awards: Oscar, Cannes, GG, BAFTA,
NBR, WOF

Travers, Henry

1942-(BSA) *Mrs. Miniver*
    Winner: Van Heflin, *Johnny Eager*
▪ Born *Travers Haegewrty* on 3/5/1874 in
    Berwick-Upon Tweed, Northumberland,
    England. Died 10/18/65 of arteriosclerosis.
🎖 Clarence Oddbody, the wingless angel,
    in *It's a Wonderful Life*
🔍 Started out on the British stage. After WW
I he jumped on a ship and headed for America.
There he starred on Broadway until Hollywood
beckoned in 1933. He didn't make his film debut

until he was 59. Played kindly, goodhearted, and
befuddled gentlemen throughout his career. Many
of his movies where he was a character actor, at the
time, were huge box office successes. Retired from
the screen in 1949.

Travolta, John

1977-(BA) *Saturday Night Fever*
    Winner: Richard Dreyfuss, *The Goodbye Girl*
1994-(BA) *Pulp Fiction*
    Winner: Tom Hanks, *Forrest Gump*
▪ Born 2/18/54 in Englewood, NJ.
🎖 Tony Manero in *Saturday Night Fever*
🔍 Dropped out of high school when he was 16.
Moved to New York and did TV commercials.
Landed the part of Vinnie Barbarino in *Welcome Back,
Kotter*. Holds the record for the most appearances
on the cover of *Rolling Stone* magazine. Also the first
male in 100 years to appear on the cover of *McCall's*
magazine. Started taking flying lessons at age 16,
and now has his own jet. Once was a Catholic but
has been a member of the Church of Scientology
for 20 years. He is a junk food junkie.
Major Awards: GG, LAFC, NBR, GGWFF,
DDA, WOF

Trevor, Claire

1937-(BSA) *Dead End*
    Winner: Alice Brady, *In Old Chicago*
★ 1948-(BSA) *Key Largo*
1954-(BSA) *The High and the Mighty*
    Winner: Eva Marie Saint, *On the Waterfront*
▪ Born *Claire Wemlinger* on 3/8/1910 in New
    York, NY. Died 4/18/2000 of respiratory
    ailments.
🎖 Gaye Dawn in Oscar'd role
🔍 Her father was born in Paris and lost his business during the Depression. Her mother was born
in Ireland. She attended Columbia. From there she
graduated to Vitaphone shorts. Really was noticed
after starring in *Stagecoach* with John Wayne in 1939.
Her son Charles Dunsmoore died in a plane crash

in 1978. Her other son, Donald Bren, is reportedly a billionaire and survives her.
Major Awards: Oscar, Emmy, WOF

Troisi, Massino

1995-(BA) *The Postman*
   Winner: Nicholas Cage, *Leaving Las Vegas*
▪ Born 2/19/53 in San Giorgio Cremano, Naples, Italy. Died 6/4/94 of a heart attack.
✎ Mario Ruoppolo in nominated role.
✎ Got into the acting business at age 15. By the time he was 17 he had founded his own acting troupe, La Smorfia. As a child he suffered many bouts of rheumatic fever, and this contributed to his severe heart condition. His doctor begged him to get treatment—he brushed him off and died 12 hours after the *The Postman* was completed.
Major Awards: VFF, DDA

Tully, Tom

1954-(BSA) *The Caine Mutiny*
   Winner: Edmond O'Brien, *The Barefoot Contessa*
▪ Born 8/21/1908 in Durango, CO. Died 4/27/82 of cancer.
✎ Commander DeVriess in nominated role.
✎ Enrolled at the Naval Academy. The tough academic requirements prompted him to quit and enlist in the real Navy. A life-changing affliction hit him while entertaining the troops with Bob Hope in Vietnam. He contracted a worm that causes elephantiasis that cut off the circulation in his leg, which led to amputation. Surgical complications resulted in deafness and pleuritis. During all of this he was diagnosed with cancer. He literally gave his life for his country.
Major Awards: WOF

Turner, Kathleen

1986-(BA) *Peggy Sue Got Married*
   Winner: Marlee Matlin, *Children of a Lesser God*
▪ Born 6/19/54 in Springfield, MO.
✎ Joan Wilder in *Romancing the Stone*
✎ Her father was a prisoner of war in WW II and later a foreign diplomat. She spent her childhood years in Cuba, Venezuela, and Canada and went to high school in London. Graduated from the University of Maryland. Starred in the daytime soap opera *The Doctors* for two years. She does her own stunt work and once broke her nose filming *V.I. Warshawski*. Suffers from rheumatoid arthritis. Speaks Spanish fluently.
Major Awards: GG, LAFC, NBR

Turner, Lana

1957-(BA) *Peyton Place*
   Winner: Joanne Woodward, *The Three Faces of Eve*
▪ Born *Julia Frances Turner* on 2/8/21 in Wallace, ID. Died 6/29/95 of throat cancer.
✎ The Sweater Girl, WW II Pinup Girl
✎ Her father was murdered during a robbery when she was eight. Her mother and family moved to California. She made her movie debut when she was 17. Contrary to legend she was discovered by a Hollywood reporter, not in Schwab's Drug Store but in Currie's Ice Cream Parlor across from her high school. She was married eight times. She carried on an abusive relationship with gangster Johnny Stompanato. When she refused to take him to the Oscar ceremony he went ballistic. He was savagely beating her when her daughter Cheryl snapped, grabbed a kitchen knife, and stabbed him to death. Cheryl was later acquitted.
Major Awards: WOF

Tyrrell, Susan

1972-(BSA) *Fat City*
   Winner: Eileen Hackert, *Butterflies Are Free*
▪ Born 3/18/45 in San Francisco, CA.
✎ Oma in nominated role.
✎ Her father was an agent for the William Morris Agency. She made her Broadway debut at age 17.

In 1991 she wrote and performed the one-woman show "My Rotten Life." In 2000 she contracted a near-fatal illness. As a result of a rare blood disease, essential thrombocythermia, she had to have both of her legs amputated below the knee. A real gutsy trooper, she still performs, writes, and paints.
Major Awards: Saturn Award

Tyson, Cicely

1972-(BA) *Sounder*
  Winner: Liza Minnelli, *Cabaret*
▪ Born 12/19/33 in New York, NY.
▨ Title role in *The Autobiography of Miss Jane Pittman*
♦ She grew up in Harlem. Her parents were very religious and haled from the Caribbean island Nevis. She worked as a secretary and model. She was married to jazz great Miles Davis by mayor of Atlanta Andrew Young at the house of best man Bill Cosby. She was the first female African-American to win an Emmy. Nominated seven times for an Emmy. Co-founder of the Harlem Dance Theater.
Major Awards: CA, Emmy (3), NBR, NSFC, KCFCC, WFCA, WOF

Ullmann, Liv

1972-(BA) *The Emigrants*
  Winner: Liza Minnelli, *Cabaret*
1976-(BA) *Face to Face*
  Winner: Faye Dunaway, *Network*
▪ Born 12/16/38 in Tokyo, Japan.
▨ Kristina in *The Emigrants*
♦ Her father was a traveling Norwegian engineer. As a child she lived in Japan, Canada, Norway, and the U.S. Made her stage debut at age 19 in Norway. Made ten films for her mentor and companion for five years, Ingmar Bergman. Long-time goodwill ambassador for UNICEF. Awarded Knight and Commander of the Order of St. Olav, a great honor in Norway rarely bestowed upon civilians. Jurist at the Cannes Film Festival.
Major Awards: GG, LAFC, NBR (3), NSFC (3), NYFC (3), BW, Guldbagge (Sweden's Oscar), Goya, VFF, DDA, WFCA

Umeki, Miyoshi

★ 1957-(BSA) *Sayonara*
▪ Born 4/3/29 in Otaru, Hokkaido, Japan

Miyoshi Umeki with Marlon Brando and Red Buttons in *Sayonara*.

🖋 Katsumi in Oscar'd role.

🔍 Started out as a nightclub singer and dancer. First Asian to win an Oscar. Appeared on the cover of *Time* magazine in 1958. She starred in the TV sitcom as dependable housekeeper Mrs. Livingston in *The Courtship of Eddie's Father*. She operated a dance studio in Hollywood for 20 years. She retired to Hawaii and later to a small town in Missouri to be near her son.

Major Awards: Oscar

Ure, Mary

1960-(BSA) *Sons and Lovers*
   Winner: Shirley Jones, *Elmer Gantry*

🔲 Born 2/18/33 in Glasgow, Scotland, UK. Died 4/3/75 of an accidental overdose of whiskey and tranquillizers.

🖋 Clara Dawes in nominated role.

🔍 She was 22 when she starred in her first movie. Had an affair with a married John Osbourne, who she eventually married, and with actor Robert Shaw who she also married. Shaw was a notorious drinker and philanderer. He got his ex-wife and Mary pregnant at the same time, while he was having an affair with his secretary. This, along with a career setback, put her over the edge tragically at age 42.

Ustinov, Sir Peter

1951-(BSA) *Quo Vadis*
   Winner: Karl Malden, *A Streetcar Named Desire*
★ 1960-(BSA) *Spartacus*
★ 1964-(BSA) *Topkapi*
1968-(BW) *Hot Millions*

🔲 Born 4/16/21 in London, England. Died 3/28/2004 of heart failure.

🖋 Lentulus Batiatus in *Spartacus*

🔍 His grandfather was an officer in the Russian Army who refused the Czar's request to convert to the Orthodox religion and was exiled to England. He was one-quarter Ethiopian on his father's side. During WW II he was aide to Lt. Col. David Niven. Produced his first play at age 21. He was fluent in English, French, German, Italian, Russian, Spanish,

Turkish, and Greek. The Queen made him Commander of the British Empire in 1975 and knighted him in 1990. He was a goodwill ambassador for UNICEF for 36 years and was Chancellor at the University of Durham for 12 years.

Major Awards: Oscar, Emmy, BIFF, GG

Vaccaro, Brenda

1975-(BSA) *Jacqueline Susann's Once Is Not Enough*
   Winner: Lee Grant, *Shampoo*

🔲 Born 11/18/39 in Brooklyn, NY.

🖋 Linda Riggs in nominated role.

🔍 Raised in Dallas, TX. She made her first professional appearance at age 12 and debuted on Broadway ten years later. Studied acting at the Neighborhood Playhouse under acting maestro Sanford Misner. She has been married four times. She was Michael Douglas's constant companion for six years. Starred in the TV series *Dear Detective* in 1979 and *Paper Dolls* in 1984.

Major Awards: GG, Emmy

Van Fleet, Jo

★ 1955-(BSA) *East of Eden*

🔲 Born 2/23/38 in San Mateo, CA. Died 11/19/92 of respiratory failure.

🖋 Kate in Oscar'd role.

🔍 Attended the University of the Pacific. Moved to New York and studied acting under the tutelage of Sanford Misner, Lee Strasberg, and Elia Kazan at the Actors Studio and the Neighborhood Playhouse. Didn't make her Broadway debut until she was 40. One of the few actors to win an Oscar in a film debut.

Major Awards: Oscar, Tony, WOF

Varsi, Diane

1957-(BSA) *Peyton Place*
   Winner: Miyoshi Umeki, *Sayonara*

🔲 Born 2/23/38 in San Mateo, CA. Died 11/19/92 of respiratory failure.

🖋 Allison MacKenzie in nominated role

Once worked as an apple picker, waitress, and factory worker. She then hooked up with a band and played the drums and sang. One of the few actresses to be nominated in her first film. After three more movies with 20th Century Fox she became disenchanted and unhappy in Hollywood and walked out on her contract. After that she couldn't get work for another seven years. She suffered from Lyme's Disease.

Major Awards: GG

Vaughn, Robert

1959-(BSA) *The Young Philadelphians*
   Winner: Hugh Griffith, *Ben-Hur*
- Born 11/22/32 in New York, NY.
- Napoleon Solo in TV's *The Man From U.N.C.L.E.*
- His parents were show biz people. His dad was a radio actor and his mother a stage actor. He is probably one of the most educated actors in Hollywood. He graduated from L.A. City College, got his Master's at L.A. State College, and earned his Doctorate at USC in Communications. The California Democratic Party wanted him to run for governor against Ronald Reagan, but he refused. Good friends with Robert F. Kennedy. Last living actor of *The Magnificent Seven*. OK, trivia geeks: What does U.N.C.L.E. stand for? United Network Command for Law Enforcement.

Major Awards: Emmy, WOF

Voight, Jon

1969-(BA) *Midnight Cowboy*
   Winner: John Wayne, *True Grit*
★ 1978-(BA) *Coming Home*
1985-(BA) *Runaway Train*
   Winner: William Hurt, *Kiss of the Spider Woman*
2001-(BSA) *Ali*
   Winner: Jim Broadbent, *Iris*
- Born 12/29/38 in Yonkers, NY.
- Joe Buck in *Midnight Cowboy*
- His father was a Czechoslovakian pro golfer. He graduated from Catholic University majoring

in art. His two brothers are very successful as well. Wes, better known as Chip Taylor, wrote the smash song "Wild Thing" for The Troggs, and brother Barry is a professor of volcanology at Penn State. Made his Broadway debut in 1965 in *The Sound of Music* singing "I am 16." Father to actress Angelina Jolie. He is 6'4" tall. He is a goodwill ambassador for Indian Rights especially the Hopi Indians.

Major Awards: Oscar, BAFTA, Cannes, GG (3), LAFC, NBR, NSFC, NYFC

Von Stroheim, Erich

1950-(BSA) *Sunset Boulevard*
   Winner: George Sanders, *All About Eve*
- Born 9/22/1885 in Vienna, Austria.
   Died 5/12/57 of cancer.
- Max Von Mayerling in nominated role.
- He served briefly in the Prussian Army and was a supervisor in his father's straw-hat factory. Emigrated to the U.S. before WW I. Joined the Calvary and fought against Pancho Villa. He was assistant to D.W. Griffith. Has the distinction of filming the longest movie, *Greed*, which lasted close to seven hours. It was eventually cut to 100 minutes. Due to his extravagant spending and intransigent attitude, MGM canned him. He was awarded the French Legion of Honor in 1956.

Major Awards: WOF, BAFTA

Von Sydow, Max

1988-(BA) *Pelle The Conqueror*
   Winner: Dustin Hoffman, *Rain Man*
- Born 4/10/29 in Lund, Skane, Ian, Sweden.
- Father Merrin in *The Exorcist*
- His father was an ethnologist. He did a stint in the Swedish Army. Studied at Stockholm's Royal dramatic Theater. Made 13 movies with famed director Ingmar Bergman. Only actor to play an exorcist, Lucifer in *Needful Things*, and Jesus in *The Greatest Story Ever Told* despite being a confirmed atheist. His favorite movie is *Runaway Train*.

Major Awards: Guldbagge (3) (Sweden's Oscar), KCFCC, VFF, BW, Australian FI

Wahlberg, Mark

2006-(BSA) *The Departed*
   Winner: Alan Arkin, *Little Miss Sunshine*
◻ Born 6/5/71 in Dorchester, MA.
▧ As Markie Mark and the Funkie Bunch
⚲ Dropped out of high school at age 14. He was a delinquent and was tossed in the calaboose 50 days for assault. His brother Donnie was a member of New Kids on the Block. He called in some favors and got himself a recording contract, and thus the Funky Bunch was born. His pugnacious nature led to the band's collapse—and that's when he got into acting.
Major Awards: BSFC, NBR, NSFC

Walken, Christopher

★ 1978-(BSA) *The Deer Hunter*
2002-(BSA) *Catch Me if You Can*
   Winner: Chris Cooper, *Adaptation*
◻ Born 3/31/43 in Queens, NY.
▧ Nikanor (Nick) Chevotarevich in Oscar'd role
⚲ His father was a baker. At age 15, he became a lion tamer in the circus. He studied acting and dancing at Hofstra University. He was George Lucas's second choice to play Han Solo in *Star Wars.* He doesn't like going fast in cars, hates handguns, and loves movies with zombies. He puts a dance step in all of his movies. He is heterochromatic, that is one eye is blue and the other hazel.
Major Awards: BAFTA, NSFC, NYFC, SAG, WOF

Walters, Julie

1983-(BA) *Educating Rita*
   Winner: Shirley MacLaine, *Terms of Endearment*
2000-(BSA) *Billy Elliot*
   Winner: Marcia Gay Harden, *Pollack*
◻ Born 2/22/50 in Birmingham, West Midlands, England.
▧ Rita in the title role

⚲ Started out studying to be a nurse, but, despite her parent's objections, switched to acting. Took two years off to care for her daughter who had contracted leukemia, which thankfully went into remission. Frequent guest on *The Tonight Show* with Johnny Carson. She has been nominated for a BAFTA award eleven times, winning five times. She was made Officer of the British Empire in 1999.
Major Awards: BAFTA, GG

Watanabe, Ken

2003-(BSA) *The Last Samurai*
   Winner: Tim Robbins, *Mystic River*
◻ Born 10/21/59 in Koide, Nigata, Japan.
▧ Katsomoto in nominated role.
⚲ His mother taught education and his father was a calligrapher. He collapsed while filming a movie in Canada. He was diagnosed with leukemia and was in and out of hospitals for over two years before the cancer went into remission. "Watanabe" means "modesty" in Japanese. Gained 20 pounds for his role in *The Last Samurai*. Follows the Busido code in his everyday life—honor, pride, and discipline. Sixth Asian actor to be nominated.
Major Awards: Blue Ribbon

Warden, Jack

1975-(BSA) *Shampoo*
   Winner: George Burns, *The Sunshine Boys*
1978-(BSA) *Heaven Can Wait*
   Winner: Christopher Walken, *The Deer Hunter*
◻ Born *John Lebzelter* on 9/18/20 in Newark, NJ. Died 7/19/06 of heart and kidney failure.
▧ Dr. William Dedham in *Donovan's Reef*
⚲ He was expelled from high school for constantly fighting. He then became a prizefighter. He fought under the name Johnny Costello in the welterweight division. Quit the ring and became a bouncer. From 1938 to 1941 he was in the Navy, then the merchant marines, and finally the Army. He was a paratrooper and platoon sergeant, and fought in the Battle of the Bulge. Decided to get into acting when he was in the hospital recovering from a shattered leg during

a jump in WW II. In the '70s, he starred in his own TV series *Crazy Like a Fox*.

Major Awards: Emmy, Obie

Warner, H.B.

1937-(BSA) *Lost Horizon*
  Winner: Joseph Schildkraut, *The Life of Emile Zola*

▦ Born *Henry Byron Warner* on 10/26/1875 London, England. Died 12/21/58 of natural causes.

✐ Mr. Emil Gower, the pharmacist in *It's a Wonderful Life*

✎ He came from an acting family going back five generations. Took drama and acting lessons in Paris and Italy. H.B. liked to live it up—on the set of *King of Kings*, cast as Jesus Christ, he was sitting in full costume reading a racing form, sipping on a bottle of liquor, and lighting a cigarette. A shutterbug snapped a shot and ran off. C.B. DeMille chided H.B. He arose from his chair, transformed into character, and proclaimed, "Do you realize who you are talking to?"

Major Awards: WOF

Warren, Lesley Ann

1982-(BSA) *Victor/Victoria*
  Winner: Jessica Lange, *Tootsie*

▦ Born 8/16/46 in New York, NY.

✐ Norma Cassady in nominated role.

✎ Her father changed his surname from Warrenoff. Her father was a realtor and her mother a nightclub singer. She made her Broadway stage debut at age 16. She wanted to be a ballerina but switched to acting. She was the youngest actor ever accepted at the famed Actors Studio in New York. Was a regular on TV's *Mission Impossible* as Dana Lambert and more recently as Sofie Bremmer on TV's *Desperate Housewives*.

Major Awards: GG

Washington, Denzel

1987-(BSA) *Cry Freedom*
  Winner: Sean Connery, *The Untouchables*

★ 1989-(BSA) *Glory*

1992-(BA) *Malcom X*
  Winner: Al Pacino, *Scent of a Woman*

1999-(BA) *The Hurricane*
  Winner: Kevin Spacey, *American Beauty*

★ 2001-(BA) *Training Day*

▦ Born 12/28/54 in Mt. Vernon, NY.

✐ Alonzo Harris in *Training Day*

✎ His father was a minister and his mother a beautician. Graduated from Fordham University. Once wanted to be a doctor. Voted by *People* magazine as one of the 50 Most Beautiful people in the world. First African-American to win two Oscars. During a visit to Brooks Army Medical Center in Texas, he heard they needed another wing to house the families of wounded soldiers. Without hesitating, he wrote out a check on the spot for the full amount to pay for it.

Major Awards: Oscar, AFI, GG, LAFC, NYFC, BIFF, BSFC, KCFCC

Denzel Washington in *Training Day*.

Waters, Ethel

1949-(BSA) *Pinky*
  Winner: Mercedes McCambridge, *All the King's Men*
- Born 10/31/1896 in Chester, PA.
  Died 9/1/77 of heart disease.
- Aunt Dicey in nominated role.
- She was the child of a teenage rape victim and grew up an orphan in the slums of Philadelphia. Made her singing debut in 1917 on the black vaudeville circuit. She was the first African-American on radio and the second black actress to be nominated for an Oscar. Became a born-again Christian at a Billy Graham Crusade in the '50s. Irving Berlin wrote the song "Suppertime" specifically for her to sing on Broadway.

Waterston, Sam

1984-(BA) *The Killing Fields*
  Winner: F. Murray Abraham, *Amadeus*
- Born 11/15/40 in Cambridge, MA.
- Sidney Schanberg, *NY Times* reporter, in nominated role
- Made his stage debut at age ten in the play *Antigone*, directed by his father. Graduated from Yale University. Also received honorary Doctorate from the University of the South. He is the official spokesman for TD Waterhouse. Once lived in a house previously owned by famed writer James Thurber. Nominated six times for an Emmy. Starred on TV's incredibly popular *Law and Order* as ADA Jack McCoy.
Major Awards: Emmy, GG, SAG

Watson, Emily

1996-(BA) *Breaking the Waves*
  Winner: Frances McDormand, *Fargo*
1998-(BA) *Hilary and Jackie*
  Winner: Gwyneth Paltrow, *Shakespeare in Love*
- Born 1/14/67 in Islington, London, England.
- Jacqueline du Pre' in title role

- Her dad was an architect and her mother a professor with a Ph.D. in English. Graduated from Bristol University with a degree in English. She was turned down numerous times applying for the London Drama School. After three years working as a waitress and secretary she was finally accepted. She sponsors the English soccer team Arsenal.
Major Awards: LAFC, NSFC, NYFC, SAG

Watson, Lucile

1943-(BSA) *Watch on the Rhine*
  Winner: Katina Paxinou, *For Whom the Bell Tolls*
- Born 5/27/1879 in Quebec, Canada.
  Died 6/24/62 of a heart attack.
- Fanny Farrelly in nominated role.
- She was educated in a convent. Studied acting in the Gay '90s at the American Academy of the Dramatic Arts. Married playwright Louis Shipman. She mainly was a studio actor. Starred in one of the earliest TV productions in 1948 on Philco Television Playhouse. Didn't make her film debut until she was 55.

Watts, Naomi

2003-(BA) *21 Grams*
  Winner: Charlize Theron, *Monster*
- Born 9/28/68 in Shorem, Sussex, England.
- Ann Darrow in *King Kong*
- Although born in England, she was raised in Australia. She was a high school dropout. Her father Peter was the sound engineer for *Pink Floyd*. He died when she was seven. Her best friend is actress Nicole Kidman. They once roomed together. She is a vegetarian and her favorite vegetable is baked beans. She likes to watch soccer, boxing, and tennis. She was selected, in 2002 by *Empire* magazine, as Australia's Woman of the Year.
Major Awards: Saturn, LAFC, NBA, NSFC, ISA, VFF

Wayne, John

1949-(BA) *The Sands of Iwo Jima*
   Winner: Broderick Crawford, *All the King's Men*
1960-(BP) *The Alamo*
★ 1969-(BA) *True Grit*
▪ Born *Marion Robert Morrison* on 5/26/1907 in Winterset, IO. Died 6/11/79 of lung and stomach cancer.
〆 Rooster Cogburn, *True Grit* (#36 on AFI's Hero List); Ethan Edwards, *The Searchers;* Sean Thornton, *The Quiet Man;* and many other memorable roles.
⚲ His dad was a pharmacist and moved to California because of a lung ailment. Attended USC on a football scholarship, narrowly missing an appointment to Annapolis. His favorite drink was sauza tequila. Enjoyed playing poker, bridge, and chess. Featured on 25-cent and 37-cent stamps. Long-time friend of director John Ford and actor Ward Bond (Bond was Wayne's Best Man). John Wayne was just as tough in real life as he was on the screen. One night in Vegas Frank Sinatra was having a party in the room below his. After repeated complaints, Wayne went down to the room. A muscular bodyguard came

John Wayne in *True Grit*.

to the door. Wayne said to knock off the racket, and the bodyguard said, "Nobody talks to Mr. Sinatra like that." Without hesitation, Wayne knocked the guy out. Holds record for most leading roles, 142. He hated the name Marion, saying it sounded too feminine. He had a dog named Duke and when he was walking past the neighborhood firehouse the firefighters started calling him Duke and the nickname stuck for the rest of his life.
Major Awards: Oscar, GG, CB DeMille, Congressional Medal of Freedom, BW, PC, WOF

Weaver, Sigourney

1986-(BA) *Aliens*
   Winner: Marlee Matlin, *Children of a Lesser God*
1988-(BA) *Gorillas in the Mist*
   Winner: Jodie Foster, *The Accused*
1988-(BSA) *Working Girl*
   Winner: Geena Davis, *The Accidental Tourist*
▪ Born 10/8/49 in New York, NY.
〆 Ripley in *Aliens*
⚲ Her father was a producer for NBC. She was brought up in a world of privilege raised by nannies and maids. Graduated from Stanford and Yale Drama School. After school she went to Israel and spent time in a kibbutz. She speaks French and German fluently. Only one of ten actors to be nominated for both Supporting and Lead Oscars in the same year. Has a morbid fear of elevators.
Major Awards: Saturn, BAFTA, GG, WOF

Webb, Clifton

1944-(BSA) *Laura*
   Winner: Barry Fitzgerald, *Going My Way*
1946-(BSA) *The Razor's Edge*
   Winner: Harold Russell, *The Best Years of Our Lives*
1948-(BA) *Sitting Party*
   Winner: Laurence Olivier, *Hamlet*
▪ Born *Webb Parmallee Hollenbeck* on 11/11/1889 in Indianapolis, IN. Died 10/13/66 of a heart attack.

Waldo Lydecker in *Laura*

He was trained as a dancer, painter, and musician. Gave a one-man art show at the age of 14 and was considered a prodigy. Sang for the Boston Opera House at the age of 17. By 19 he was a professional dancer in New York. He introduced the Irving Berlin classic song "Easter Parade" on Broadway. He was inseparable from his mother who lived with him until she died. He kept his gay lifestyle a secret for years.

Major Awards: GG, WOF

Weisz, Rachel

★ 2005-(BSA) *The Constant Gardner*

Born 3/7/71 in London, England.

Evelyn Carnahan in the *Mummy* series

Her mother is a psychoanalyst and her father a Hungarian inventor who came up with the oxygen respirator and a machine that detects land mines. Began modeling at age 14. Graduated from Cambridge University where she was a well-known radical feminist. Drives a vintage Jaguar.

Major Awards: GG, SAG

Weld, Tuesday

1977-(BSA) *Looking for Mr. Goodbar*
 Winner: Vanessa Redgrave, *Julia*

Born *Susan Ker Weld* on 8/27/43 in New York, NY.

Katharine Dunn in nominated role.

As a child actress she supported her whole family. The pressure was too much. She suffered a nervous breakdown at age nine, alcoholism at age ten, was sexually active at age twelve, and attempted suicide at age thirteen. She starred in her first movie at age thirteen. Through therapy, she eventually overcame her problems and was class valedictorian. Turned down the role of Bonnie Parker in *Bonnie and Clyde*. Once married to actor Dudley Moore.

Major Awards: GG

Welles, Orson

1941-(BA) *Citizen Kane*
 Winner: Gary Cooper, *Sergeant York*
1941-(BP) *Citizen Kane*
1941-(BD) *Citizen Kane*
★ 1941-(Best Original Screenplay) *Citizen Kane*
1942-(BP) *The Magnificent Ambersons*
1970-Honorary Oscar

Born 5/6/15 in Kenosha, WI. Died 10/10/85 of a heart attack.

Charles Foster Kane in nominated role (# 37 on AFI's Villain List); Harry Lime in *The Third Man*; the voice of the original *War of the Worlds* radio broadcast; pitchman for Gallo Wines.

His dad was an inventor and his mother a concert pianist. She died when he was nine. He was a child prodigy gifted as a magician, pianist, and painter. Traveled to Ireland, England, Morocco and in Spain where he was a bullfighter at age 21. Only one of six actors to be nominated in their first screen role. He was a world, class trencherman and weighed over 350 pounds. Once ate 18 hotdogs at a sitting. His typical dinner was two steaks with all the trimmings and a pint of scotch.

Orson Welles in *Citizen Kane.*

Major Awards: Oscar, NBR, Cannes (3), LAFC, Peabody, AFI Award, Radio Hall of Fame, DGA, D.W. Griffith, BIFF, DDA, LAFC, VFF, WOF

Werner, Oskar

1965-(BA) *Ship of Fools*
  Winner: Lee Marvin, *Cat Ballou*
▨ Born *Oskar Josef Bschliessmayer* on 11/13/22 in Vienna, Austria. Died 10/23/84 of a heart attack.
✔ Dr. Schumann in nominated role.
✎ Starred in Vienna's famed Burgtheater and was considered Austria's greatest actor. Drafted into the German Army. Sent to officer's training school against his objections. He pretended to be incompetent and eventually deserted. He was a lifelong pacifist, and knew well of the Nazi's evil intent. He was also a lifelong friend of French director Francois Truffaut.
Major Awards: NYFC, GG

Whitaker, Forest

★ 2006-(BA) *The Last King of Scotland*
▨ Born 7/15/61 in Longview, TX.
✎ Received a football scholarship to USC. Once enrolled, he changed his priorities and studied opera and drama. He has an amblyopic eye since birth and is a vegetarian. Besides being an actor he is a producer and director. Started Spirit Dance Entertainment Production Company. He is well respected and liked among his Hollywood peers.
Major Awards: BSFC, Cannes, Emmy, LAFC, NBR, NSFC, NYFC

Whiteley, Jon

1953-Honorary Oscar
▨ Born 02/19/45 in Monymusk, Scotland, UK.
✔ Outstanding Juvenile Actor in the role of Harry in *The Little Kidnappers*

✎ After a short film career and at the urging of his parents he focused on an education. He graduated from Oxford University and went on to get his doctoral thesis in French Art. In 1973 he was appointed Assistant Curator at Christ Church Picture Gallery at Oxford. He has been Assistant Keeper at Ashmolean Museum since 1978. He teaches at Oxford from time to time. He speaks French fluently. He has also written several books on French Art.

Whitman, Stuart

1961-(BA) *The Mark*
  Winner: Maximilian Schell, *Judgement at Nuremberg*
▨ Born 2/1/26 in San Francisco, CA.
✔ Paul Regret in *The Commancheros*
✎ After high school he enlisted in the Army Corps of Engineers. The three years he was in the service he boxed in the Light-Heavy division winning all of his 32 bouts. Starred in the TV western *Cimmarron Strip*. He amassed a 100-million-dollar fortune investing mainly in real estate, securities, cattle, and horses.
Major Awards: Bronze Wrangler, WOF

Whitmore, James

1949-(BSA) *Battleground*
  Winner: Dean Jagger, *12 O'Clock High*
1975-(BA) *Give 'em Hell Harry*
  Winner: Jack Nicholson, *One Flew Over the Cuckoo's Nest*
▨ Born 10/1/21 in White Plains, NY.
✔ Brooks Hatlen in *The Shawshank Redemption*
✎ Graduated from Yale on a football scholarship. Co-founded the Yale radio station. Member of the infamous Skull & Bones Club, whose present and past members include Presidents George Bush Sr. & Jr., William F. Buckley, John Kerry and President William Taft. He was an officer in the Marines during WW II. Starred with First Lady Nancy Reagan in the movie *The Next Voice You Hear*.
Major Awards: GG, Tony, Emmy, WOF

Whitty, Dame May

1937-(BSA) *Night Must Fall*
  Winner: Alice Brady, *In Old Chicago*
1942-(BSA) *Mrs. Miniver*
  Winner: Teresa Wright, *Mrs. Miniver*
▣ Born 6/19/1865 in Liverpool, England.
  Died 5/29/48 of cancer.
🖉 Lady Beldon in nominated role.
🔍 Made stage debut at age 17. Performed on the British stage for 25 years. Entertained the troops during WW I, and the Queen named her Dame Commander. She was 50 before she made her first movie. She never retired. She acted up until the final shots on *The Sign of the Ram* and passed away shortly after at age 82.
Major Awards: NBR

Widmark, Richard

1947-(BSA) *Kiss of Death*
  Winner: Edmund Gwenn, *Miracle on 34th Street*
▣ Born 12/26/1914 in Sunrise, MN.
🖉 Tommy Udo, the pychotic killer in nominated role.
🔍 He was president of his senior class. Graduated from Lake Forrest College in Chicago, and he initially wanted to be a lawyer. He tried to enlist in the army during WW II but was rejected because of a perforated eardrum. Made Broadway debut at age 18. Gave up a successful career in radio for a job in Hollywood. His daughter Anne was married to L.A. Dodger's pitcher Sandy Koufax. It is mazing that this great actor was nominated only once during his career.
Major Awards: GG, Bronze Wrangler, LAFC, NBR, WOF

Wiest, Diane

★ 1986-(BSA) *Hannah and Her Sisters*
1989-(BSA) *Parenthood*
  Winner: Brenda Fricker, *My Left Foot*

★ 1994-(BSA) *Bullets Over Broadway*
▣ Born 3/28/48 in Kansas City, MO.
🖉 Helen Sinclair in *Bullets Over Broadway*
🔍 Originally wanted to be a ballerina. Attended Maryland University. She was an army brat. Her father was pilot and her mother a nurse. She lived in several countries including Germany. Dropped out of college and toured with the American Shakespeare Company and traveled all over the world, including Russia.
Major Awards: NBR, Obie, Emmy, NYFC, NSFC, SAG, LAFC, GG, BSFC, ISA, KCFCC, Sundance

Wild, Jack

1968-(BSA) *Oliver!*
  Winner: Jack Albertson, *The Subject Was Roses*
▣ Born 9/30/52 in Royton, Lancashire, England. Died 3/1/06 of tongue and throat cancer.
🖉 The Artful Dodger in nominated role.
🔍 He was discovered by singer Phil Collins's mother who was a talent scout. Used his Artful Dodger role as a segue into the hit TV series *HR Pufunstuf*. Released three successful albums during the early '70s. Underwent oral surgery to remove cancer in July 2004. Part of his tongue and vocal cords had to be removed.

Wilde, Cornell

1945-(BA) *A Song To Remember*
  Winner: Ray Milland, *The Lost Weekend*
▣ Born 10/13/1915 in New York, NY.
  Died 10/16/89 of leukemia.
🖉 The Man in *The Naked Prey*
🔍 Graduated from high school at age 14 and graduated from New York City College in only three years. Turned down a medical scholarship and went overseas to travel in Europe. He was a commercial artist, salesman, and Boy Scout counselor. A natural athlete, he was selected for the 1936 Olympic

Fencing Team, but he turned them down to pursue an acting career. He was fluent in Hungarian, French, German, English, Italian, and Russian.
Major Awards: WOF

Wilder, Gene

1968-(BSA) *The Producers*
Winner: Jack Albertson, *The Subject Was Roses*
★ 1974-(BW) *Young Frankenstein*
■ Born *Jerome Silberman* on 6/11/33 in Milwaukee, WI.
🖊 Leo Bloom in nominated role.
🔍 Graduated from the University of Iowa. He did a two-year hitch in the Army. He was married to comedian Gilda Radner of Saturday Night Live fame. She died of ovarian cancer. Later he himself was treated for a cancerous lymphoma and underwent chemotherapy. He has made a full recovery. He is a lifelong friend of Mel Brooks. He not only wrote, directed, and starred in *The World's Greatest Lover*, he even wrote a song for the movie.
Major Awards: Emmy

Wilkinson, Tom

2001-(BA) *In the Bedroom*
Winner: Denzel Washington, *Training Day*
■ Born 12/12/48 in Leeds, West Yorkshire, England.
🖊 Matt Fowler in nominated role
🔍 His family was impoverished and moved to Canada when he was a child. Moved back to England five years later and graduated from the University of Kent in Canterbury majoring in English. He was awarded an honorary Doctor of Letters in 2001. Also graduated from RADA and landed a job the very next day. He was made an Officer of the British Empire by the Queen in 2005.
Major Awards: BAFTA, NYFC, SAG, ISA, Sundance

Williams, Cara

1958-(BSA) *The Defiant Ones*
Winner: Wendy Hiller, *Separate Tables*
■ Born Bernice Kamiat on 6/29/25 in Brooklyn, NY.
🖊 The Woman in nominated role
🔍 Her father left the family when she was a child and they moved to Los Angeles. Her first job was as an impressionist of movie stars in cartoons. With her great comedic timing she was touted as the next Lucille Ball. She had her own TV show in 1964. She was married to actor John Drew Barrymore and had a son John Blyth. She now is an interior designer and a championship poker player.

Williams, Michelle

2005-(BSA) *Brokeback Mountain*
Winner: Rachel Weisz, *The Constant Gardner*
■ Born 9/9/80 in Kalispell, MT.
🖊 Alma in nominated role
🔍 She was home schooled and after testing she graduated from high school at age 15. Loves reading and collecting rare books and has a first edition of F. Scott Fitzgerald's *The Great Gatsby*. Her partner and fiancé is Heath Ledger with whom she has a daughter. At age 16 won a stock futures trading contest by taking $10,000 and turning it into $100,000.
Major Awards: Phoenix Film Critics Society

Williams, Robin

1987-(BSA) *Good Morning Vietnam*
Winner: Michael Douglas, *Wall Street*
1989-(BA) *Dead Poets Society*
Winner: Daniel Day Lewis, *My Left Foot*
1991-(BA) *The Fisher King*
Winner: Anthony Hopkins, *The Silence of the Lambs*
★ 1997-(BSA) *Good Will Hunting*
■ Born 7/21/51 in Chicago, IL.
🖊 As a standup comedian

Graduated from Claremont Men's College, where he played soccer, and from Julliard. His classmate was actor Christopher Reeve whom he later helped with his medical bills when Reeves was paralyzed. He is a lifelong Democrat. Enjoys paintball and cycling, riding about a 100 miles a week. His classmates in high school voted him Funniest but Least Likely to Succeed. Co-owns the Rubicon Restaurant in San Francisco with Francis Ford Coppola and Robert DeNiro.
Major Awards: Saturn, Oscar, Emmy, Grammy, NBR, Cable Ace, GG, CBD, Saturn, SAG, PC, WOF

Wills, Chill

1960-(BSA) *The Alamo*
   Winner: Peter Ustinov, *Spartacus*
Born 7/18/1903 in Seagoville, TX.
   Died 12/15/78 of cancer.
Drago in *McLintock*
His parents named him Chill because he was born on the hottest day in Texas history. He started out as a musician at the age of 12. Toured the vaudeville circuit and tent shows with his own band, The Avalon Boys, where he sang bass. His over-the-top self-promotion when he was nominated might well have cost him the award. He did the voice of Francis the Talking Mule.
Major Awards: WOF

Winfield, Paul

1972-(BA) *Sounder*
   Winner: Marlon Brando, *The Godfather*
Born 5/22/41 in Los Angeles, CA.
   Died 3/7/2004 of a heart attack.
Nathan Lee Morgan in nominated role.
Began his acting career at the University of Portland on a scholarship. Continued his education at Stanford, Los Angeles City College, and the University of California—eventually graduating from UCLA. Shared a lifelong partnership with architect and set designer Charles Gillan. His cousin is ac-

tor William Marshall known for his *Blackula* role. First and only person to win the Speech and Drama Teachers Association award three years in a row.
Major Awards: Emmy

Winfrey, Oprah

1985-(BSA) *The Color Purple*
   Winner: Anjelica Huston, *Prizzi's Honor*
Born 1/29/54 in Koscius, MS.
Her world famous *Oprah Winfrey Show*
Born into horrid poverty she didn't get her first pair of shoes until she was six. Her mother and father never married. She was raised by her grandmother. She was sexually abused by a cousin and ran away from home when she was 13. She won the Miss Black Tennessee Pageant. Graduated from Tennessee State University. She was the first black news anchor-woman in Nashville. She is the only woman in TV history to own and produce her own show. She is the first African-American to be named to the Forbes Billionaire List. Has her own magazine *O*. The greatest role model for African-American females in America, period!
Major Awards: Emmy, Peabody, PC

Winger, Debra

1982-(BA) *An Officer and a Gentleman*
   Winner: Meryl Streep, *Sophie's Choice*
1983-(BA) *Terms of Endearment*
   Winner: Shirley MacLaine, *Terms of Endearment*
1993-(BA) *Shadowlands*
   Winner: Holly Hunter, *The Piano*
Born 5/16/55 in Cleveland Heights, OH.
Paula Pokrifki in *An Officer and a Gentleman*
She dropped out of high school and moved into a kibbutz in Israel. She lived there for two years and was in the Israeli army for three months. Returned to the States where she was a costumed tour guide at Magic Mountain. While in her troll suit she had an accident and was in a coma. After her recovery she turned to acting. Once married to actor Tim

Hutton and has been linked to Nick Nolte and Senator Robert Kerry. Retired from acting in 2001.
Major Awards: NSFC

Winningham, Mare

1995-(BSA) *Georgia*
    Winner: Mira Sorvino, *Mighty Aphrodite*
▨ Born 5/16/59 in Phoenix, AZ.
〆 *Georgia* in title role
⚲ Made her TV debut on the *Gong Show*. She sang and played the guitar the Beatles song "Here, There and Everywhere." She wasn't gonged—the audience and panel adored her. She co-starred in her high school production of *The Sound of Music* with Kevin Spacey. They were also co-valedictorians. Her other classmate was Val Kilmer who she dated for five years. Suffered a tragic loss when her son committed suicide in 2005.
Major Awards: Emmy, ISA

Winslet, Kate

1995-(BSA) *Sense And Sensibility*
    Winner: Miro Sorvino, *Mighty Aphrodite*
1997-(BA) *Titanic*
    Winner: Helen Hunt, *As Good As It Gets*
2001-(BSA) *Iris*
    Winner: Jennifer Connelly, *A Beautiful Mind*
2004-(BA) *Eternal Sunshine of the Spotless Mind*
    Winner: Hilary Swank, *Million Dollar Baby*
2006-(BA) *Little Children*
    Winner: Helen Mirren, *The Queen*
▨ Born 10/5/75 in Reading, Berkshire, England.
〆 Rose DeWitt Bukater in *Titanic*
⚲ Hails from a family of actors going back generations. Made first TV appearance at age 11. She was overweight in high school, and her nickname was Blubber. She has since lost 50 pounds. Wears size 11 shoes. She recorded a hit song, which made the top ten in England. Only twice have two actors been nominated for playing the same role in the same film—she and Gloria Stewart in *Titanic*, and

she and Judi Dench in *Iris*. She is the only actress to be nominated five times before the age of 31.
Major Awards: SAG, LAFC, BAFTA

Winter, Vincent

★ 1954-Honorary Oscar
▨ Born 12/29/47 in Aberdeenshire, Scotland, UK. Died 11/2/98 of a heart attack.
〆 Outstanding juvenile role as Davy in *The Little Kidnappers*
⚲ He did several more movies, and then he moved to Australia. There he did extensive work on the stage and took on various other movie related tasks. He was a production designer, production manager, first assistant director, supervisor manager, and associate producer.

Winters, Shelly

1951-(BA) *A Place in the Sun*
    Winner: Vivien Leigh, *A Streecar Named Desire*
★ 1959-(BSA) *The Diary of Anne Frank*
★ 1965-(BSA) *A Patch of Blue*
1972-(BSA) *The Poseidon Adventure*
    Winner: Eileen Heckart, *Butterflies Are Free*
▨ Born *Shirley Schrift* on 8/18/20 in East St. Louis, MO. Died 1/14/06 of heart failure.
〆 Belle Rosen in *The Poseidon Adventure*
⚲ Her family was so poor that she was selling magazine subscriptions at age nine. In her early years she studied under Charles Laughton and enrolled at the Actors Studio. Made her Broadway debut in 1940. She once roomed with Marilyn Monroe. She donated her Oscar for *The Diary of Anne Frank* to the Anne Frank Museum. Wrote two tell-all biographies which described her dalliances with some leading Hollywood men, among them Burt Lancaster, William Holden, Marlon Brando, Clark Gable, and Errol Flynn. Played Roseanne Barr's mother Nana Mary on the TV show *Roseanne*.
Major Awards: Oscar, Emmy, GG, DDA, KCFCC, VFF, WOF

Witherspoon, Reese

★ 2005-(BA) *Walk the Line*

▪ Born 3/22/76 in Baton Rouge, LA.

〽 June Carter in nominated role.

🔍 She was a gymnast and cheerleader. Started modeling at age seven. Grew up in Weisbaden, West Germany. Her father was an Army surgeon and Lt. Colonel who was stationed there. Her mother was a Ph.D. nurse. She attended Stanford University. Her distant relative, John Witherspoon, was one of the signers of the Declaration of Independence. She collects antique linens. The name Reese is her mother's maiden name.

Major Awards: GG, NSFC, NYFC, SAG, BAFTA, BSFC, KCFCC, PC

Wood, Natalie

1955-(BSA) *Rebel Without a Cause*
   Winner: Jo Van Fleet, *East of Eden*
1961-(BSA) *Splendor in the Grass*
   Winner: Sophia Loren, *Two Women*
1963-(BA) *Love With the Proper Stranger*
   Winner: Patricia Neal, *Hud*

▪ Born *Natalia Zakharenko* on 7/30/38 in San Francisco, CA. Died 11/29/81 in a mysterious drowning accident.

〽 Maria in *West Side Story*

🔍 Her parents emigrated from Russia and could barely speak English. She failed her first screen test but bounced back to win the role of little Susan Walker in *Miracle on 34th Street.* She dated Elvis Presley in the '50s and wanted to get married, but Elvis's mother didn't like her. She must have had a premonition of her death because she always had a crippling fear of water. Her pallbearers were Frank Sinatra, Rock Hudson, Laurence Olivier, Elia Kazan, Gregory Peck, David Niven, and Fred Astaire. Married twice to Robert Wagner.

Major Awards: GG, GGWFF, WOF

Wood, Peggy

1965-(BSA) *The Sound of Music*
   Winner: Shelley Winters, *A Patch of Blue*

▪ Born 2/9/1892 in Brooklyn, NY.
   Died 3/18/78 of a stroke.

〽 Mother Abbess in nominated role.

🔍 She was a gifted soprano on stage and in the opera. She was a member of the intellectual circuit and a frequent lunch attendee at the infamous Algonquin Round Table where she often joined in with the rapier wit of the likes of Dorothy Parker, Alexander Wolcott, Robert Benchley, George S. Kaufman, and Edna Ferber.

Woodard, Alfre

1983-(BSA) *Cross Creek*
   Winner: Linda Hunt, *The Year of Living Dangerously*

▪ Born 11/8/52 in Tulsa, OK.

〽 Geechee in nominated role.

🔍 She was named by her grandmother who had a dream in which she saw the name Alfre written in golden letters. Attended a parochial school where she was encouraged by a wise nun to pursue an acting career. She was a cheerleader and a track star. Graduated from Boston University. She was nominated 11 times for an Emmy and has won four. Holds the record for winning the most prime-time Emmys by an African-American.

Major Awards: CA, Emmy, SAG, ISA, WFCA

Woods, James

1986-(BA) *Salvador*
   Winner: Paul Newman, *The Color of Money*
1996-(BSA) *The Ghosts of Mississippi*
   Winner: Cuba Gooding Jr., *Jerry Maguire*

▪ Born 4/18/47 in Vernal, Utah.

〽 Richard Boyle in *Salvador*

🔍 He was the son of an Army Intelligence officer who was constantly moving. He once lived in Guam.

Graduated from high school at the top of his class. Received a scholarship to MIT but dropped out to pursue an acting career. Reportedly has an IQ of 180, is a Mensa member, and scored a 1579 on his SAT test. He is a reserve police officer for LAPD. He loves photography, cooking, playing poker, and golf.

Major Awards: GG, Emmy, Obie, ISA, KCFCC, WOF

Woodward, Joanne

★ 1957-(BA) *The Three Faces of Eve*
1968-(BA) *Rachel, Rachel*
   Winner: Katharine Hepburn, *The Lion in Winter*
1973-(BA) *Summer Wishes, Winter Dreams*
   Winner: Glenda Jackson, *A Touch of Class*
1990-(BA) *Mr. and Mrs. Bridge*
   Winner: Kathy Bates, *Misery*
▨ Born 2/27/30 in Thomasville, GA.
🖊 Eve White, Eve Black, and Jane in title role.
🖋 Graduated from Louisiana State University. Won several Georgia beauty pageants. She was once engaged to writer and novelist Gore Vidal. Married to Paul Newman for 48 years. She and Paul are the first married couple to win Best Actor Oscars. Made her own dress for Oscar night. She loves horseback riding, ballet, jazz, and poetry. She and Paul donate heavily to children with terminal illnesses and life-threatening diseases.

Major Awards: Oscar, Emmy, Cannes, NBR, NYFC, BAFTA, SAGLA, GG, KCFCC, SAG, WOF

Woolley, Monty

1942-(BA) *The Pied Piper*
   Winner: James Cagney, *Yankee Doodle Dandy*
1944-(BSA) *Since You Went Away*
   Winner: Barry Fitzgerald, *Going My Way*
▨ Born 8/17/1888 in New York, NY.
   Died 5/16/63 of kidney and heart failure.
🖊 Sheridan Whitesides in *The Man Who Came to Dinner*
🖋 Graduated from Yale. His classmate and best friend was Cole Porter. He was president of the Yale Drama Club. He was an intelligence officer in the Army during WW I serving in the Mexican Border campaign. He taught English at Yale for 18 years and two of his prized students were novelist Thornton Wilder and Steven Vincent Benét. Cole Porter got him into the movies and he played himself in Porter's bio-pic *Night and Day*.

Major Awards: WOF

Wright, Teresa

1941-(BSA) *The Little Foxes*
   Winner: Mary Astor, *The Great Lie*
1942-(BA) *The Pride of the Yankees*
   Winner: Greer Garson, *Mrs. Miniver*
★ 1942-(BSA) *Mrs. Miniver*
▨ Born *Muriel Teresa Wright* in Manhattan, NY. Died 3/6/2005 of a heart attack.
🖊 Elenor Twitchell in *The Pride of the Yankees*
🖋 She made her Broadway debut in 1938. The only actress to be nominated in her first three movie appearances. She is one of ten actors to be nominated for both supporting and lead awards in the same year. She was making $5,000 a week when she protested the workings of the studio system. Sam Goldwyn fired her but she was so adamant in her conviction it never even fazed her. She used her middle name because there was another actress by the name of Muriel Wright.

Major Awards: Oscar, NBR, WOF

Wycherly, Margaret

1941-(BSA) *Sergeant York*
   Winner: Mary Astor, *The Great Lie*
▨ Born 10/26/1881 in London, England. Died 6/6/56 of natural causes.
🖊 Mother York in nominated role
🖋 She was primarily a stage actor and didn't make her film debut until she was 34. Stole the show

from star Bela Lugosi in the 1929 remake of *The 13th Chair*. She is really only remembered for two of her roles—which were totally opposite of each other: the solid backwoods mother to Gary Cooper in *Sergeant York* and James Cagney's malevolent mother in *White Heat*.

Wyman, Jane

1946-(BA) *The Yearling*
    Winner: Olivia de Havilland, *To Each His Own*
★ 1948-(BA) *Johnny Belinda*
1951-(BA) *The Blue Veil*
    Winner: Vivian Leigh, *A Streetcar Named Desire*
1954-(BA) *The Magnificent Obsession*
    Winner: Grace Kelley, *The Country Girl*
▦ Born *Sarah Jane Fulks* on 1/4/14 in
    St. Joseph, MO.
⩗ Belinda McDonald in Oscar'd role.
⚲ Started out as a radio singer, chorus girl, and switchboard operator. Attended the University of Missouri. Married to future president Ronald Reagan from 1940 to 1948. Divorced him after falling for co-star Lew Ayres. Her best friends were Barbara Stanwyck, Loretta Young, and Agnes Moorehead. Mother to Maureen Reagan. She is a convert to Roman Catholicism. She would never talk about Ronald Reagan, but always voted for him and attended his funeral. Starred in '80s TV series *Falcon Crest*.
Major Awards: Oscar, GG, WOF

Wynn, Ed

1959-(BSA) *The Diary of Anne Frank*
    Winner: Hugh Griffith, *Ben-Hur*
▦ Born *Isaiah Edwin Leopold* on 11/9/1886 in
    Philadelphia, PA. Died 6/19/66 of cancer.
⩗ The Perfect Fool, Albert Dussel in nominated
    role
⚲ Started on the vaudeville circuit and performed in the *Zeigfeld Follies*. Got into well-publicized feud with W.C. Fields in the teens over an actors strike. After his career stalled he broke into films at the urging of his son Keenan. He was originally picked

to be the wizard in *The Wizard of Oz*; however, he felt the part was too small for an actor of his stature? Duh. He was the first actor to receive a TV Emmy award.
Major Awards: Emmy, WOF

Wynyard, Diana

1932/33, (BA) *Cavalcade*
    Winner: Katharine Hepburn, *Morning Glory*
▦ Born *Dorothy Cox* on 1/16/1906 in London,
    England. Died 5/13/64 of kidney failure.
⩗ Jane Maryott in nominated role.
⚲ Debuted on the London stage in 1925. She was signed by MGM in 1932. One of her frequent co-stars was John Barrymore. Married to Oscar winning-director Carol Reed. Nominated in her very first film. Took a 20-year hiatus from the movies to return to the London stage. Made her last film appearance in *Islands in the Sun* in 1957.

York, Susannah

1969, (BSA) *They Shoot Horses, Don't They?*
    Winner: Goldie Hawn, *Cactus Flower*
▦ Born *Susannah Fletcher* on 1/9/41 in London,
    England.
⩗ Alice in nominated role.
⚲ Graduated from RADA. Studied pantomime. She has written two successful children's books, in *Search of Unicorns* and *Lark's Castle*. She raised some Hollywood eyebrows when she partook in a risqué lesbian love scene in Robert Aldrich's *The Killing of Sister George*. She is fluent in French. She has served on the Cannes jury.
Major Awards: Cannes, BAFTA

Young, Burt

1976-(BSA) *Rocky*
    Winner: Jason Robards, *All the President's Men*
▦ Born Jerry DeLouise on 4/30/40 in New
    York, NY.

🍴 Paulie in nominated role.

🔍 Joined the Marines out of high school. Worked as a carpet layer and cleaner, salesman, truck driver, and prizefighter. Learned his trade from Lee Strasberg at the Actors Studio. Wrote, directed, and starred in a one-man show *SOS*. Wrote the first teleplay for the hit TV series *Baretta*. Once submitted a short story, "Sicilian Love Potion," to *Playboy* but it was turned down.

Young, Gig

1951-(BSA) *Come Fill the Cup*
 Winner: Karl Malden, *A Streetcar Named Desire*
1958-(BSA) *Teacher's Pet*
 Winner: Burl Ives, *The Big Country*
★ 1969-(BSA) *They Shoot Horses, Don't They?*
▪ Born *Byron Barr* on 11/4/1913 in St. Cloud, MN. Died 10/19/78 of a self-inflected gun shot.
🍴 Dr. Hugo Pine in *Teacher's Pet*
🔍 After high school received a scholarship to the Pasadena Playhouse. Called into the Coast Guard during WW II. There was another actor with the same name so he changed his to Gig Young from a character he played in the movie *The Gay Sisters*. He was once married to TV series *Bewitched* star Elizabeth Montgomery. Emotionally devastated because he could never get top billing, he became an alcoholic. Three weeks after he married his fifth wife he shot her, then himself. A tragic ending for a great actor.
Major Awards: GG, KCFCC, WOF

Young, Loretta

★ 1947-(BA) *The Farmer's Daughter*
1949-(BA) *Come to the Stable*
 Winner: Olivia de Havilland, *The Heiress*
▪ Born *Gretchen Young* on 1/6/1913 in Salt Lake, UT. Died 8/12/2000 of ovarian cancer.
🍴 Herself in her TV series *Letters to Loretta*

🔍 Made her first screen appearance when she was four. Her father left her mother and her three sisters when she was five, and she never saw him again. She entered a convent when she was 14. During the filming of *The Call of the Wild* she and her co-star, a married Clark Gable, had a love child. They kept it a secret for years and it wasn't until much later that her daughter found out who her real father was. Won a settlement against NBC for $600,000 when they unlawfully aired her program overseas. Nominated eight times for an Emmy.
Major Awards: Oscar, Emmy, GG, WFCA, WOF

Young, Roland

1937-(BSA) *Topper*
 Winner: Joseph Schildkraut, *The Life of Emile Zola*
▪ Born 11/11/1887 in London, England. Died 6/5/53 of natural causes.
🍴 Cosmo Topper in nominated role.
🔍 Educated at Sherbone College and London University. Attended RADA. Made his Broadway debut when he was 25. Served in the Army during WW I. He was cast as the first Dr. Watson in the 1922 silent version of *Sherlock Holmes*. Holmes was played by the great John Barrymore.
Major Awards: WOF

Zellweger, Renée

2001-(BA) *Bridget Jones's Diary*
 Winner: Halle Berry, *Monster's Ball*
2002-(BA) *Chicago*
 Winner: Nicole Kidman, *The Hours*
★ 2003-(BSA) *Cold Mountain*
▪ Born 4/25/69 in Katy, TX.
🍴 Ruby Thewes in Oscar'd role.
🔍 She was a high school cheerleader. Her father is Swiss, and her mother is Norwegian. While awaiting stardom she worked as a cocktail waitress in a strip club to make ends meet. Dated Jim Carey—he

gave her a $200,000 friendship ring. For the part in *Chicago* she took voice and dancing lessons for ten grueling months to achieve professional authenticity for the movie. Married to country western singer Kenny Chesney.

Major Awards: BAFTA, NBR, SAG, PC, WOF

Zeta-Jones, Catherine

★ 2002-(BSA) *Chicago*

Born 11/25/69 in Swansea, West Glamorgan, Wales, UK.

Velma Kelly in Oscar'd role.

She was singing and dancing at age ten. Became a star in the British TV series *The Darling Buds of May*. She is the spokeswoman for T-Mobile and Elizabeth Arden. Recorded several songs that reached the top 75 on the British music chart. Married to actor Michael Douglas and both have the same birth dates. Speaks Welsh fluently. Had a breathing disorder as a child and had to undergo a tracheotomy—she still bears the scar.

Major Awards: Oscar, BAFTA, SAG

ACADEMY AWARD WINNERS BY YEAR

1927–28 Academy Awards

Best Picture
Wings
Seventh Heaven
The Racket

Best Actor
Emil Jannings, *The Last Command* and *The Way of All Flesh*
Charles Chaplin, *The Circus*
Richard Barthelmess, *The Noose* and *The Patent Leather Kid*

Best Actress
Janet Gaynor, *Seventh Heaven, Street Angel* and *Sunrise*
Louise Dresser, *A Ship Comes In*
Gloria Swanson, *Sadie Thompson*

1928–29 Academy Awards

Best Picture
The Broadway Melody
Alibi
Hollywood Revue
In Old Arizona
The Patriot

Best Actor
Warner Baxter, *In Old Arizona*
George Bancroft, *Thunderbolt*
Chester Morris, *Alibi*
Paul Muni, *The Valiant*
Lewis Stone, *The Patriot*

Best Actress
Mary Pickford, *Coquette*
Betty Compson, *The Barker*
Jeanne Eagels, *The Letter*
Corinne Griffith, *The Divine Lady*
Bessie Love, *The Broadway Melody*
Ruth Chatterton, *Madame X*

1929–1930 Academy Awards

Best Picture
All Quiet on the Western Front
The Big House
Disraeli
The Divorcée
The Love Parade

Best Actor
George Arliss, *Disraeli*
George Arliss, *The Green Goddess*
Wallace Beery, *The Big House*
Maurice Chevalier, *The Big Pond* and *The Love Parade*
Ronald Colman, *Bulldog Drummond* and *Condemned*
Lawrence Tibbett, *The Rogue Song*

Best Actress
Norma Shearer, The Divorcée
Ruth Chatterton, *Sarah and Son*
Greta Garbo, *Anna Christie* and *Romance*
Nancy Carroll, *The Devil's Holiday*
Norma Shearer, *Their Own Desire*
Gloria Swanson, *The Trespasser*

1930–31 Academy Awards

Best Picture
Cimarron
East Lynne
The Front Page
Skippy
Trader Horn

Best Actor
Lionel Barrymore, *A Free Soul*
Jackie Cooper, *Skippy*
Richard Dix, *Cimarron*
Fredric March, *The Royal Family of Broadway*
Adolphe Menjou, *The Front Page*

Best Actress

Marie Dressler, *Min and Bill*
Marlene Dietrich, *Morocco*
Irene Dunne, *Cimarron*
Ann Harding, *Holiday*
Norma Shearer, *A Free Soul*

1931–32 Academy Awards

Best Picture

Grand Hotel
Bad Girl
The Champ
Five Star Final
Arrowsmith
One Hour with You
Shanghai Express
The Smiling Lieutenant

Best Actor * (tie)

Wallace Beery * *The Champ*
Fredric March * *Dr. Jekyll and Mr. Hyde*
Alfred Lunt, *The Guardsman*

Best Actress

Helen Hayes, *The Sin of Madelon Claudet*
Lynn Fontanne, *The Guardsman*
Marie Dressler, *Emma*

1932–33 Academy Awards

Best Picture

Cavalcade
A Farewell to Arms
42nd Street
I Am a Fugitive from a Chain Gang
Lady for a Day
Little Women
The Private Life of Henry VIII
She Done Him Wrong
Smilin' Through
State Fair

Best Actor

**Charles Laughton, *The Private Life of
   Henry VIII***

Leslie Howard, *Berkeley Square*
Paul Muni, *I Am a Fugitive From a Chain Gang*

Best Actress

Katharine Hepburn, *Morning Glory*
May Robson, *Lady for a Day*
Diana Wynyard, *Cavalcade*

1934 Academy Awards

Best Picture

It Happened One Night
Cleopatra
Flirtation Walk
The Gay Divorcée
Here Comes the Navy
The House of Rothschild
Imitation of Life
The Barretts of Wimpole Street
One Night of Love
The Thin Man
Viva Villa!
The White Parade

Best Actor

Clark Gable, *It Happened One Night*
Frank Morgan, *The Affairs of Cellini*
William Powell, *The Thin Man*

Best Actress

Claudette Colbert, *It Happened One Night*
Bette Davis, *Of Human Bondage*
Grace Moore, *One Night of Love*
Norma Shearer, *The Barretts of Wimpole Street*

1935 Academy Awards

Best Picture

Mutiny on the Bounty
Broadway Melody of 1936
Captain Blood
David Copperfield
The Informer
Les Misérables
The Lives of a Bengal Lancer
A Midsummer Night's Dream

Alice Adams
Naughty Marietta
Ruggles of Red Gap
Top Hat

Best Actor

Victor McLaglen, *The Informer*
Charles Laughton, *Mutiny on the Bounty*
Clark Gable, *Mutiny on the Bounty*
Paul Muni, *Black Fury*
Franchot Tone, *Mutiny on the Bounty*

Best Actress

Bette Davis, *Dangerous*
Claudette Colbert, *Private Worlds*
Elisabeth Bergner, *Escape Me Never*
Katharine Hepburn, *Alice Adams*
Miriam Hopkins, *Becky Sharp*
Merle Oberon, *The Dark Angel*

1936 Academy Awards

Best Picture

The Great Ziegfeld
Dodsworth
Anthony Adverse
Libeled Lady
Mr. Deeds Goes to Town
Romeo and Juliet
San Francisco
The Story of Louis Pasteur
A Tale of Two Cities
Three Smart Girls

Best Actor

Paul Muni, *The Story of Louis Pasteur*
Walter Huston, *Dodsworth*
Gary Cooper, *Mr. Deeds Goes to Town*
William Powell, *My Man Godfrey*
Spencer Tracy, *San Francisco*

Best Actress

Luise Rainer, *The Great Ziegfeld*
Gladys George, *Valiant Is the Word for Carrie*
Carole Lombard, *My Man Godfrey*
Irene Dunne, *Theodora Goes Wild*
Norma Shearer, *Romeo and Juliet*

Best Supporting Actor

Walter Brennan, *Come and Get It*
Mischa Auer, *My Man Godfrey*
Stuart Erwin, *Pigskin Parade*
Basil Rathbone, *Romeo and Juliet*
Akim Tamiroff, *The General Died at Dawn*

Best Supporting Actress

Gale Sondergaard, *Anthony Adverse*
Alice Brady, *My Man Godfrey*
Bonita Granville, *These Three*
Maria Ouspenskaya, *Dodsworth*
Beulah Bondi, *The Gorgeous Hussy*

1937 Academy Awards

Best Picture

The Life of Emile Zola
Captains Courageous
Dead End
The Good Earth
In Old Chicago
The Awful Truth
Lost Horizon
One Hundred Men and a Girl
Stage Door
A Star Is Born

Best Actor

Spencer Tracy, *Captains Courageous*
Fredric March, *A Star Is Born*
Robert Montgomery, *Night Must Fall*
Paul Muni, *The Life of Emile Zola*
Charles Boyer, *Conquest*

Best Actress

Luise Rainer, *The Good Earth*
Greta Garbo, *Camille*
Janet Gaynor, *A Star Is Born*
Irene Dunne, *The Awful Truth*
Barbara Stanwyck, *Stella Dallas*

Best Supporting Actor

Joseph Schildkraut, *The Life of Emile Zola*
Thomas Mitchell, *The Hurricane*
Ralph Bellamy, *The Awful Truth*
H. B. Warner, *Lost Horizon*
Roland Young, *Topper*

Best Supporting Actress

Alice Brady, *In Old Chicago*
Andrea Leeds, *Stage Door*
Anne Shirley, *Stella Dallas*
Claire Trevor, *Dead End*
Dame May Whitty, *Night Must Fall*

1938 Academy Awards

Best Picture

You Can't Take It With You
Alexander's Ragtime Band
Boys Town
The Citadel
Four Daughters
Grand Illusion
Jezebel
Pygmalion
Test Pilot
The Adventures of Robin Hood

Best Actor

Spencer Tracy, *Boys Town*
James Cagney, *Angels with Dirty Faces*
Robert Donat, *The Citadel*
Leslie Howard, *Pygmalion*
Charles Boyer, *Algiers*

Best Actress

Bette Davis, *Jezebel*
Fay Bainter, *White Banners*
Wendy Hiller, *Pygmalion*
Norma Shearer, *Marie Antoinette*
Margaret Sullavan, *Three Comrades*

Best Supporting Actor

Walter Brennan, *Kentucky*
John Garfield, *Four Daughters*
Gene Lockhart, *Algiers*
Robert Morley, *Marie Antoinette*
Basil Rathbone, *If I Were King*

Best Supporting Actress

Fay Bainter, *Jezebel*
Beulah Bondi, *Of Human Hearts*
Billie Burke, *Merrily We Live*
Spring Byington, *You Can't Take it with You*
Miliza Korjus, *The Great Waltz*

1939 Academy Awards

Best Picture

Gone with the Wind
Dark Victory
Goodbye, Mr. Chips
Love Affair
Mr. Smith Goes to Washington
Ninotchka
Of Mice and Men
Stagecoach
The Wizard of Oz
Wuthering Heights

Best Actor

Robert Donat, *Goodbye, Mr. Chips*
Clark Gable, *Gone with the Wind*
Laurence Olivier, *Wuthering Heights*
Mickey Rooney, *Babes in Arms*
James Stewart, *Mr. Smith Goes to Washington*

Best Actress,

Vivien Leigh, *Gone with the Wind*
Irene Dunne, *Love Affair*
Greta Garbo, *Ninotchka*
Greer Garson, *Goodbye, Mr. Chips*
Bette Davis, *Dark Victory*

Best Supporting Actor

Thomas Mitchell, *Stagecoach*
Harry Carey, *Mr. Smith Goes to Washington*
Brian Donlevy, *Beau Geste*
Brian Aherne, *Juarez*
Claude Rains, *Mr. Smith Goes to Washington*

Best Supporting Actress

Hattie McDaniel, *Gone with the Wind*
Geraldine Fitzgerald, *Wuthering Heights*
Olivia de Havilland, *Gone with the Wind*
Edna May Oliver, *Drums Along the Mohawk*
Maria Ouspenskaya, *Love Affair*

1940 Academy Awards

Best Picture

Rebecca
Foreign Correspondent
The Grapes of Wrath

The Great Dictator
Kitty Foyle
The Letter
The Long Voyage Home
Our Town
The Philadelphia Story
All This, and Heaven Too

Best Actor,

James Stewart, *The Philadelphia Story*
Henry Fonda, *The Grapes of Wrath*
Raymond Massey, *Abe Lincoln in Illinois*
Laurence Olivier, *Rebecca*
Charles Chaplin, *The Great Dictator*

Best Actress,

Ginger Rogers, *Kitty Foyle*
Joan Fontaine, *Rebecca*
Katharine Hepburn, *The Philadelphia Story*
Bette Davis, *The Letter*
Martha Scott, *Our Town*

Best Supporting Actor

Walter Brennan, *The Westerner*
Albert Basserman, *Foreign Correspondent*
William Gargan, *They Knew What They Wanted*
Jack Oakie, *The Great Dictator*
James Stephenson, *The Letter*

Best Supporting Actress

Jane Darwell, *The Grapes of Wrath*
Judith Anderson, *Rebecca*
Ruth Hussey, *The Philadelphia Story*
Barbara O'Neil, *All This, and Heaven Too*
Marjorie Rambeau, *Primrose Path*

1941 Academy Awards

Best Picture

How Green Was My Valley
Citizen Kane
Here Comes Mr. Jordan
Hold Back the Dawn
Blossoms in the Dust
The Little Foxes
The Maltese Falcon
One Foot in Heaven
Sergeant York
Suspicion

Best Actor

Gary Cooper, *Sergeant York*
Cary Grant, *Penny Serenade*
Walter Huston, *All That Money Can Buy*
Robert Montgomery, *Here Comes Mr. Jordan*
Orson Welles, *Citizen Kane*

Best Actress

Joan Fontaine, *Suspicion*
Olivia de Havilland, *Hold Back the Dawn*
Bette Davis, *The Little Foxes*
Greer Garson, *Blossoms in the Dust*
Barbara Stanwyck, *Ball of Fire*

Best Supporting Actor

Donald Crisp, *How Green Was My Valley*
Charles Coburn, *The Devil and Miss Jones*
Walter Brennan, *Sergeant York*
James Gleason, *Here Comes Mr. Jordan*
Sydney Greenstreet, *The Maltese Falcon*

Best Supporting Actress

Mary Astor, *The Great Lie*
Sarah Allgood, *How Green Was My Valley*
Patricia Collinge, *The Little Foxes*
Teresa Wright, *The Little Foxes*
Margaret Wycherly, *Sergeant York*

1942 Academy Awards

Best Picture

Mrs. Miniver
Kings Row
The Magnificent Ambersons
The Invaders
The Pied Piper
The Pride of the Yankees
Random Harvest
The Talk of the Town
Wake Island
Yankee Doodle Dandy

Best Actor

James Cagney, *Yankee Doodle Dandy*
Ronald Colman, *Random Harvest*
Gary Cooper, *The Pride of the Yankees*
Walter Pidgeon, *Mrs. Miniver*
Monty Woolley, *The Pied Piper*

Best Actress

Greer Garson, *Mrs. Miniver*
Bette Davis, *Now, Voyager*
Teresa Wright, *The Pride of the Yankees*
Katharine Hepburn, *Woman of the Year*
Rosalind Russell, *My Sister Eileen*

Best Supporting Actor

Van Heflin, *Johnny Eager*
William Bendix, *Wake Island*
Henry Travers, *Mrs. Miniver*
Walter Huston, *Yankee Doodle Dandy*
Frank Morgan, *Tortilla Flat*

Best Supporting Actress

Teresa Wright, *Mrs. Miniver*
Gladys Cooper, *Now, Voyager*
Agnes Moorehead, *The Magnificent Ambersons*
Susan Peters, *Random Harvest*
Dame May Whitty, *Mrs. Miniver*

1943 Academy Awards

Best Picture

Casablanca
For Whom the Bell Tolls
Heaven Can Wait
The Human Comedy
In Which We Serve
Madame Curie
The More the Merrier
The Ox-Bow Incident
The Song of Bernadette
Watch on the Rhine

Best Actor

Paul Lukas, *Watch on the Rhine*
Gary Cooper, *For Whom the Bell Tolls*
Humphrey Bogart, *Casablanca*
Walter Pidgeon, *Madame Curie*
Mickey Rooney, *The Human Comedy*

Best Actress

Jennifer Jones, *The Song of Bernadette*
Ingrid Bergman, *For Whom the Bell Tolls*
Joan Fontaine, *The Constant Nymph*
Greer Garson, *Madame Curie*
Jean Arthur, *The More the Merrier*

Best Supporting Actor

Charles Coburn, *The More the Merrier*
Charles Bickford, *The Song of Bernadette*
J. Carrol Naish, *Sahara*
Claude Rains, *Casablanca*
Akim Tamiroff, *For Whom the Bell Tolls*

Best Supporting Actress

Katina Paxinou, *For Whom the Bell Tolls*
Paulette Goddard, *So Proudly We Hail!*
Gladys Cooper, *The Song of Bernadette*
Anne Revere, *The Song of Bernadette*
Lucile Watson, *Watch on the Rhine*

1944 Academy Awards

Best Picture

Going My Way
Gaslight
Double Indemnity
Since You Went Away
Wilson

Best Actor

Bing Crosby, *Going My Way*
Charles Boyer, *Gaslight*
Barry Fitzgerald, *Going My Way*
Cary Grant, *None but the Lonely Heart*
Alexander Knox, *Wilson*

Best Actress

Ingrid Bergman, *Gaslight*
Claudette Colbert, *Since You Went Away*
Bette Davis, *Mr. Skeffington*
Greer Garson, *Mrs. Parkington*
Barbara Stanwyck, *Double Indemnity*

Best Supporting Actor

Barry Fitzgerald, *Going My Way*
Hume Cronyn, *The Seventh Cross*
Claude Rains, *Mr. Skeffington*
Clifton Webb, *Laura*
Monty Woolley, *Since You Went Away*

Best Supporting Actress

Ethel Barrymore, *None but the Lonely Heart*
Jennifer Jones, *Since You Went Away*
Angela Lansbury, *Gaslight*
Aline MacMahon, *Dragon Seed*
Agnes Moorehead, *Mrs. Parkington*

1945 Academy Awards

Best Picture
The Lost Weekend
The Bells of St. Mary's
Anchors Aweigh
Mildred Pierce
Spellbound

Best Actor
Ray Milland, *The Lost Weekend*
Gene Kelly, *Anchors Aweigh*
Bing Crosby, *The Bells of St. Mary's*
Gregory Peck, *The Keys of the Kingdom*
Cornel Wilde, *A Song to Remember*

Best Actress
Joan Crawford, *Mildred Pierce*
Ingrid Bergman, *The Bells of St. Mary's*
Greer Garson, *The Valley of Decision*
Jennifer Jones, *Love Letters*
Gene Tierney, *Leave Her to Heaven*

Best Supporting Actor
James Dunn, *A Tree Grows in Brooklyn*
John Dall, *The Corn Is Green*
Michael Chekhov, *Spellbound*
Robert Mitchum, *G. I. Joe*
J. Carrol Naish, *A Medal for Benny*

Best Supporting Actress
Anne Revere, *National Velvet*
Ann Blyth, *Mildred Pierce*
Angela Lansbury, *The Picture of Dorian Gray*
Joan Loring, *The Corn Is Green*
Eve Arden, *Mildred Pierce*

1946 Academy Awards

Best Picture
The Best Years of Our Lives
Henry V
It's a Wonderful Life
The Razor's Edge
The Yearling

Best Actor
Fredric March, *The Best Years of Our Lives*
Laurence Olivier, *Henry V*

Larry Parks, *The Jolson Story*
Gregory Peck, *The Yearling*
James Stewart, *It's a Wonderful Life*

Best Actress
Olivia de Havilland, *To Each His Own*
Celia Johnson, *Brief Encounter*
Jennifer Jones, *Duel in the Sun*
Rosalind Russell, *Sister Kenny*
Jane Wyman, *The Yearling*

Best Supporting Actor
Harold Russell, *The Best Years of Our Lives*
William Demarest, *The Jolson Story*
Claude Rains, *Notorious*
Charles Coburn, *The Green Years*
Clifton Webb, *The Razor's Edge*

Best Supporting Actress
Anne Baxter, *The Razor's Edge*
Ethel Barrymore, *The Spiral Staircase*
Lillian Gish, *Duel in the Sun*
Flora Robson, *Saratoga Trunk*
Gale Sondergaard, *Anna and the King of Siam*

1947 Academy Awards

Best Picture
Gentleman's Agreement
Crossfire
The Bishop's Wife
Great Expectations
Miracle on 34th Street

Best Actor
Ronald Colman, *A Double Life*
John Garfield, *Body and Soul*
Gregory Peck, *Gentleman's Agreement*
William Powell, *Life with Father*
Michael Redgrave, *Mourning Becomes Electra*

Best Actress
Loretta Young, *The Farmer's Daughter*
Susan Hayward, *Smash Up—The Story of a Woman*
Dorothy McGuire, *Gentleman's Agreement*
Rosalind Russell, *Mourning Becomes Electra*
Joan Crawford, *Possessed*

Best Supporting Actor

Edmund Gwenn, *Miracle on 34th Street*
Thomas Gomez, *Ride the Pink Horse*
Charles Bickford, *The Farmer's Daughter*
Robert Ryan, *Crossfire*
Richard Widmark, *Kiss of Death*

Best Supporting Actress

Celeste Holm, *Gentleman's Agreement*
Gloria Grahame, *Crossfire*
Ethel Barrymore, *The Paradine Case*
Marjorie Main, *The Egg and I*
Anne Revere, *Gentleman's Agreement*

1948 Academy Awards

Best Picture

Hamlet
Johnny Belinda
The Red Shoes
The Snake Pit
The Treasure of the Sierra Madre

Best Actor

Laurence Olivier, *Hamlet*
Montgomery Clift, *The Search*
Dan Dailey, *When My Baby Smiles at Me*
Lew Ayres, *Johnny Belinda*
Clifton Webb, *Sitting Pretty*

Best Actress

Jane Wyman, *Johnny Belinda*
Olivia de Havilland, *The Snake Pit*
Irene Dunne, *I Remember Mama*
Barbara Stanwyck, *Sorry, Wrong Number*
Ingrid Bergman, *Joan of Arc*

Best Supporting Actor

Walter Huston, *The Treasure of the Sierra Madre*
José Ferrer, *Joan of Arc*
Oscar Homolka, *I Remember Mama*
Charles Bickford, *Johnny Belinda*
Cecil Kellaway, *The Luck of the Irish*

Best Supporting Actress

Claire Trevor, *Key Largo*
Ellen Corby, *I Remember Mama*

Agnes Moorehead, *Johnny Belinda*
Jean Simmons, *Hamlet*
Barbara Bel Geddes, *I Remember Mama*

1949 Academy Awards

Best Picture

All the King's Men
Battleground
The Heiress
A Letter to Three Wives
Twelve O'Clock High

Best Actor

Broderick Crawford, *All the King's Men*
Kirk Douglas, *Champion*
Gregory Peck, *Twelve O'Clock High*
Richard Todd, *The Hasty Heart*
John Wayne, *Sands of Iwo Jima*

Best Actress

Olivia de Havilland, *The Heiress*
Jeanne Crain, *Pinky*
Susan Hayward, *My Foolish Heart*
Deborah Kerr, *Edward, My Son*
Loretta Young, *Come to the Stable*

Best Supporting Actor

Dean Jagger, *Twelve O'Clock High*
John Ireland, *All the King's Men*
Arthur Kennedy, *Champion*
Ralph Richardson, *The Heiress*
James Whitmore, *Battleground*

Best Supporting Actress

Mercedes McCambridge, *All the King's Men*
Celeste Holm, *Come to the Stable*
Elsa Lanchester, *Come to the Stable*
Ethel Barrymore, *Pinky*
Ethel Waters, *Pinky*

1950 Academy Awards

Best Picture

All About Eve
Born Yesterday

Father of the Bride
King Solomon's Mines
Sunset Boulevard

Best Actor

José Ferrer, *Cyrano de Bergerac*
Louis Calhern, *The Magnificent Yankee*
William Holden, *Sunset Boulevard*
James Stewart, *Harvey*
Spencer Tracy, *Father of the Bride*

Best Actress

Judy Holliday, *Born Yesterday*
Bette Davis, *All About Eve*
Anne Baxter, *All About Eve*
Eleanor Parker, *Caged*
Gloria Swanson, *Sunset Boulevard*

Best Supporting Actor

George Sanders, *All About Eve*
Edmund Gwenn, *Mister 880*
Sam Jaffe, *The Asphalt Jungle*
Jeff Chandler, *Broken Arrow*
Erich von Stroheim, *Sunset Boulevard*

Best Supporting Actress

Josephine Hull, *Harvey*
Celeste Holm, *All About Eve*
Hope Emerson, *Caged*
Nancy Olson, *Sunset Boulevard*
Thelma Ritter, *All About Eve*

1951 Academy Awards

Best Picture

An American in Paris
Decision Before Dawn
A Place in the Sun
Quo Vadis
A Streetcar Named Desire

Best Actor

Humphrey Bogart, *The African Queen*
Marlon Brando, *A Streetcar Named Desire*
Montgomery Clift, *A Place in the Sun*
Arthur Kennedy, *Bright Victory*
Fredric March, *Death of a Salesman*

Best Actress

Vivien Leigh, *A Streetcar Named Desire*
Katharine Hepburn, *The African Queen*
Eleanor Parker, *Detective Story*
Shelley Winters, *A Place in the Sun*
Jane Wyman, *The Blue Veil*

Best Supporting Actor

Karl Malden, *A Streetcar Named Desire*
Leo Genn, *Quo Vadis*
Kevin McCarthy, *Death of a Salesman*
Peter Ustinov, *Quo Vadis*
Gig Young, *Come Fill the Cup*

Best Supporting Actress,

Kim Hunter, *A Streetcar Named Desire*
Mildred Dunnock, *Death of a Salesman*
Lee Grant, *Detective Story*
Joan Blondell, *The Blue Veil*
Thelma Ritter, *The Mating Season*

1952 Academy Awards

Best Picture

The Greatest Show on Earth
High Noon
Ivanhoe
Moulin Rouge
The Quiet Man

Best Actor

Gary Cooper, *High Noon*
Marlon Brando, *Viva Zapata!*
Kirk Douglas, *The Bad and the Beautiful*
José Ferrer, *Moulin Rouge*
Alec Guinness, *The Lavender Hill Mob*

Best Actress

Shirley Booth, *Come Back, Little Sheba*
Joan Crawford, *Sudden Fear*
Bette Davis, *The Star*
Julie Harris, *The Member of the Wedding*
Susan Hayward, *With a Song in My Heart*

Best Supporting Actor

Anthony Quinn, *Viva Zapata!*
Arthur Hunnicutt, *The Big Sky*
Victor McLaglen, *The Quiet Man*

Jack Palance, *Sudden Fear*
Richard Burton, *My Cousin Rachel*

Best Supporting Actress
Gloria Grahame, *The Bad and the Beautiful*
Jean Hagen, *Singin' in the Rain*
Colette Marchand, *Moulin Rouge*
Terry Moore, *Come Back, Little Sheba*
Thelma Ritter, *With a Song in My Heart*

1953 Academy Awards

Best Picture
From Here to Eternity
Julius Caesar
The Robe
Roman Holiday
Shane

Best Actor
William Holden, *Stalag 17*
Richard Burton, *The Robe*
Montgomery Clift, *From Here to Eternity*
Marlon Brando, *Julius Caesar*
Burt Lancaster, *From Here to Eternity*

Best Actress
Audrey Hepburn, *Roman Holiday*
Ava Gardner, *Mogambo*
Leslie Caron, *Lili*
Deborah Kerr, *From Here to Eternity*
Maggie McNamara, *The Moon Is Blue*

Best Supporting Actor
Frank Sinatra, *From Here to Eternity*
Brandon de Wilde, *Shane*
Jack Palance, *Shane*
Eddie Albert, *Roman Holiday*
Robert Strauss, *Stalag 17*

Best Supporting Actress
Donna Reed, *From Here to Eternity*
Geraldine Page, *Hondo*
Marjorie Rambeau, *Torch Song*
Grace Kelly, *Mogambo*
Thelma Ritter, *Pickup on South Street*

1954 Academy Awards

Best Picture
On the Waterfront
The Country Girl
The Caine Mutiny
Seven Brides for Seven Brothers
Three Coins in the Fountain

Best Actor
Marlon Brando, *On the Waterfront*
Humphrey Bogart, *The Caine Mutiny*
Bing Crosby, *The Country Girl*
James Mason, *A Star Is Born*
Dan O'Herlihy, *Adventures of Robinson Crusoe*

Best Actress
Grace Kelly, *The Country Girl*
Judy Garland, *A Star Is Born*
Audrey Hepburn, *Sabrina*
Dorothy Dandridge, *Carmen Jones*
Jane Wyman, *Magnificent Obsession*

Best Supporting Actor
Edmond O'Brien, *The Barefoot Contessa*
Karl Malden, *On the Waterfront*
Lee J. Cobb, *On the Waterfront*
Rod Steiger, *On the Waterfront*
Tom Tully, *The Caine Mutiny*

Best Supporting Actress
Eva Maria Saint, *On the Waterfront*
Katy Jurado, *Broken Lance*
Nina Foch, *Executive Suite*
Jan Sterling, *The High and the Mighty*
Claire Trevor, *The High and the Mighty*

1955 Academy Awards

Best Picture
Marty
Love Is a Many Splendored Thing
Mister Roberts
Picnic, Fred Kohlmar
The Rose Tattoo

Best Actor
Ernest Borgnine, *Marty*
James Cagney, *Love Me or Leave Me*

James Dean, *East of Eden*
Frank Sinatra, *The Man with the Golden Arm*
Spencer Tracy, *Bad Day at Black Rock*

Best Actress

Anna Magnani, *The Rose Tattoo*
Katharine Hepburn, *Summertime*
Jennifer Jones, *Love Is a Many Splendored Thing*
Susan Hayward, *I'll Cry Tomorrow*
Eleanor Parker, *Interrupted Melody*

Best Supporting Actor

Jack Lemmon, *Mister Roberts*
Arthur Kennedy, *Trial*
Joe Mantell, *Marty*
Sal Mineo, *Rebel Without a Cause*
Arthur O'Connell, *Picnic*

Best Supporting Actress

Jo Van Fleet, *East of Eden*
Betsy Blair, *Marty*
Peggy Lee, *Pete Kelly's Blues*
Marisa Pavan, *The Rose Tattoo*
Natalie Wood, *Rebel Without a Cause*

1956 Academy Awards

Best Picture

Around the World in 80 Days
Friendly Persuasion
Giant
The King and I
The Ten Commandments

Best Actor

Yul Brynner, *The King and I*
James Dean, *Giant*
Kirk Douglas, *Lust for Life*
Rock Hudson, *Giant*
Sir Laurence Olivier, *Richard III*

Best Actress

Ingrid Bergman, *Anastasia*
Carroll Baker, *Baby Doll*
Katharine Hepburn, *The Rainmaker*
Nancy Kelly, *The Bad Seed*
Deborah Kerr, *The King and I*

Best Supporting Actor

Anthony Quinn, *Lust for Life*
Anthony Perkins, *Friendly Persuasion*
Don Murray, *Bus Stop*
Mickey Rooney, *The Bold and the Brave*
Robert Stack, *Written on the Wind*

Best Supporting Actress

Dorothy Malone, *Written on the Wind*
Eileen Heckart, *The Bad Seed*
Mercedes McCambridge, *Giant*
Patty McCormack, *The Bad Seed*
Mildred Dunnock, *Baby Doll*

1957 Academy Awards

Best Picture

The Bridge on the River Kwai
Peyton Place
Sayonara
12 Angry Men
Witness for the Prosecution

Best Actor

Alec Guinness, *The Bridge on the River Kwai*
Anthony Franciosa, *A Hatful of Rain*
Marlon Brando, *Sayonara*
Charles Laughton, *Witness for the Prosecution*
Anthony Quinn, *Wild Is the Wind*

Best Actress

Joanne Woodward, *The Three Faces of Eve*
Anna Magnani, *Wild Is the Wind*
Elizabeth Taylor, *Raintree County*
Lana Turner, *Peyton Place*
Deborah Kerr, *Heaven Knows, Mr. Allison*

Best Supporting Actor

Red Buttons, *Sayonara*
Vittorio de Sica, *A Farewell to Arms*
Sessue Hayakawa, *The Bridge on the River Kwai*
Arthur Kennedy, *Peyton Place*
Russ Tamblyn, *Peyton Place*

Best Supporting Actress

Miyoshi Umeki, *Sayonara*
Elsa Lanchester, *Witness for the Prosecution*
Hope Lange, *Peyton Place*

Carolyn Jones, *The Bachelor Party*
Diane Varsi, *Peyton Place*

1958 Academy Awards

Best Picture
***Gigi*, Arthur Freed**
Cat on a Hot Tin Roof
The Defiant Ones
Auntie Mame
Separate Tables

Best Actor
David Niven, *Separate Tables*
Paul Newman, *Cat on a Hot Tin Roof*
Tony Curtis, *The Defiant Ones*
Sidney Poitier, *The Defiant Ones*
Spencer Tracy, *The Old Man and the Sea*

Best Actress
Susan Hayward, *I Want to Live!*
Deborah Kerr, *Separate Tables*
Shirley MacLaine, *Some Came Running*
Rosalind Russell, *Auntie Mame*
Elizabeth Taylor, *Cat on a Hot Tin Roof*

Best Supporting Actor
Burl Ives, *The Big Country*
Lee J. Cobb, *The Brothers Karamazov*
Theodore Bikel, *The Defiant Ones*
Arthur Kennedy, *Some Came Running*
Gig Young, *Teacher's Pet*

Best Supporting Actress
Wendy Hiller, *Separate Tables*
Peggy Cass, *Auntie Mame*
Martha Hyer, *Some Came Running*
Maureen Stapleton, *Lonelyhearts*
Cara Williams, *The Defiant Ones*

1959 Academy Awards

Best Picture
Ben-Hur
Anatomy of a Murder
The Diary of Anne Frank

The Nun's Story
Room at the Top

Best Actor
Charlton Heston, *Ben-Hur*
Laurence Harvey, *Room at the Top*
Jack Lemmon, *Some Like It Hot*
Paul Muni, *The Last Angry Man*
James Stewart, *Anatomy of a Murder*

Best Actress
Simone Signoret, *Room at the Top*
Audrey Hepburn, *The Nun's Story*
Katharine Hepburn, *Suddenly, Last Summer*
Doris Day, *Pillow Talk*
Elizabeth Taylor, *Suddenly, Last Summer*

Best Supporting Actor
Hugh Griffith, *Ben-Hur*
Arthur O'Connell, *Anatomy of a Murder*
George C. Scott, *Anatomy of a Murder*
Robert Vaughn, *The Young Philadelphians*
Ed Wynn, *The Diary of Anne Frank*

Best Supporting Actress
Shelley Winters, *The Diary of Anne Frank*
Susan Kohner, *Imitation of Life*
Juanita Moore, *Imitation of Life*
Thelma Ritter, *Pillow Talk*
Hermione Baddeley, *Room at the Top*

1960 Academy Awards

Best Picture
***The Apartment*, Billy Wilder**
The Alamo
Elmer Gantry
Sons and Lovers
The Sundowners

Best Actor
Burt Lancaster, *Elmer Gantry*
Trevor Howard, *Sons and Lovers*
Jack Lemmon, *The Apartment*
Laurence Olivier, *The Entertainer*
Spencer Tracy, *Inherit the Wind*

Best Actress

Elizabeth Taylor, *Butterfield 8*
Deborah Kerr, *The Sundowners*
Shirley MacLaine, *The Apartment*
Melina Mercouri, *Never on Sunday*
Greer Garson, *Sunrise at Campobello*

Best Supporting Actor

Peter Ustinov, *Spartacus*
Jack Kruschen, *The Apartment*
Sal Mineo, *Exodus*
Peter Falk, *Murder, Inc.*
Chill Wills, *The Alamo*

Best Supporting Actress

Shirley Jones, *Elmer Gantry*
Glynis Johns, *The Sundowners*
Shirley Knight, *The Dark at the Top of the Stairs*
Janet Leigh, *Psycho*
Mary Ure, *Sons and Lovers*

1961 Academy Awards

Best Picture,

West Side Story
The Guns of Navarone
The Hustler, Robert Rossen
Judgment at Nuremberg
Fanny

Best Actor

Maximilian Schell, *Judgment at Nuremberg*
Paul Newman, *The Hustler*
Charles Boyer, *Fanny*
Spencer Tracy, *Judgment at Nuremberg*
Stuart Whitman, *The Mark*

Best Actress

Sophia Loren, *Two Women*
Piper Laurie, *The Hustler*
Audrey Hepburn, *Breakfast at Tiffany's*
Geraldine Page, *Summer and Smoke*
Natalie Wood, *Splendor in the Grass*

Best Supporting Actor

George Chakiris, *West Side Story*
Montgomery Clift, *Judgment at Nuremberg*
Peter Falk, *Pocketful of Miracles*

Jackie Gleason, *The Hustler*
George C. Scott, *The Hustler*

Best Supporting Actress

Rita Moreno, *West Side Story*
Judy Garland, *Judgment at Nuremberg*
Lotte Lenya, *The Roman Spring of Mrs. Stone*
Una Merkel, *Summer and Smoke*
Fay Bainter, *The Children's Hour*

1962 Academy Awards

Best Picture

Lawrence of Arabia
The Longest Day
Meredith Wilson's the Music Man
Mutiny on the Bounty
To Kill a Mockingbird

Best Actor

Gregory Peck, *To Kill a Mockingbird*
Jack Lemmon, *Days of Wine and Roses*
Marcello Mastroianni, *Divorce—Italian Style*
Peter O'Toole, *Lawrence of Arabia*
Burt Lancaster, *Birdman of Alcatraz*

Best Actress

Anne Bancroft, *The Miracle Worker*
Bette Davis, *What Ever Happened to Baby Jane?*
Katharine Hepburn, *Long Day's Journey Into Night*
Geraldine Page, *Sweet Bird of Youth*
Lee Remick, *Days of Wine and Roses*

Best Supporting Actor

Ed Begley, *Sweet Bird of Youth*
Victor Buono, *What Ever Happened to Baby Jane?*
Telly Savalas, *Birdman of Alcatraz*
Omar Sharif, *Lawrence of Arabia*
Terence Stamp, *Billy Budd*

Best Supporting Actress

Patty Duke, *The Miracle Worker*
Mary Badham, *To Kill a Mockingbird*
Shirley Knight, *Sweet Bird of Youth*
Angela Lansbury, *The Manchurian Candidate*
Thelma Ritter, *Birdman of Alcatraz*

1963 Academy Awards

Best Picture
Tom Jones
Cleopatra
How the West Was Won
Lilies of the Field
America, America

Best Actor
Sidney Poitier, *Lilies of the Field*
Richard Harris, *This Sporting Life*
Rex Harrison, *Cleopatra*
Paul Newman, *Hud*
Albert Finney, *Tom Jones*

Best Actress,
Patricia Neal, *Hud*
Shirley MacLaine, *Irma La Douce*
Leslie Caron, *The L-Shaped Room*
Rachel Roberts, *This Sporting Life*
Natalie Wood, *Love With the Proper Stranger*

Best Supporting Actor
Melvyn Douglas, *Hud*
Bobby Darin, *Captain Newman, M.D.*
Nick Adams, *Twilight of Honor*
Hugh Griffith, *Tom Jones*
John Huston, *The Cardinal*

Best Supporting Actress
Margaret Rutherford, *The V.I.P.s*
Dame Edith Evans, *Tom Jones*
Joyce Redman, *Tom Jones*
Diane Cilento, *Tom Jones*
Lilia Skala, *Lilies of the Field*

1964 Academy Awards

Best Picture
My Fair Lady
Dr. Strangelove or: How I Learned to Stop Worrying and Love the Bomb
Mary Poppins
Becket
Zorba the Greek

Best Actor
Rex Harrison, *My Fair Lady*
Richard Burton, *Becket*
Peter O'Toole, *Becket*
Anthony Quinn, *Zorba the Greek*
Peter Sellers, *Dr. Strangelove or: How I Learned to Stop Worrying and Love the Bomb*

Best Actress
Julie Andrews, *Mary Poppins*
Anne Bancroft, *The Pumpkin Eater*
Sophia Loren, *Marriage Italian Style*
Debbie Reynolds, *The Unsinkable Molly Brown*
Kim Stanley, *Seance on a Wet Afternoon*

Best Supporting Actor
Peter Ustinov, *Topkapi*
Stanley Holloway, *My Fair Lady*
Edmond O'Brien, *Seven Days in May*
Lee Tracy, *The Best Man*
John Gielgud, *Becket*

Best Supporting Actress
Lila Kedrova, *Zorba the Greek*
Dame Edith Evans, *The Chalk Garden*
Grayson Hall, *The Night of the Iguana*
Gladys Cooper, *My Fair Lady*
Agnes Moorehead, *Hush . . . Hush, Sweet Charlotte*

1965 Academy Awards

Best Picture
The Sound of Music
Doctor Zhivago
Ship of Fools
Darling
A Thousand Clowns

Best Actor
Lee Marvin, *Cat Ballou*
Richard Burton, *The Spy Who Came in From the Cold*
Laurence Olivier, *Othello*
Rod Steiger, *The Pawnbroker*
Oskar Werner, *Ship of Fools*

Best Actress

    Julie Christie, *Darling*

Julie Andrews, *The Sound of Music*

Samantha Eggar, *The Collector*

Elizabeth Hartman, *A Patch of Blue*

Simone Signoret, *Ship of Fools*

Best Supporting Actor

    Martin Balsam, *A Thousand Clowns*

Ian Bannen, *The Flight of the Phoenix*

Tom Courtenay, *Doctor Zhivago*

Michael Dunn, *Ship of Fools*

Frank Finlay, *Othello*

Best Supporting Actress

    Shelley Winters, *A Patch of Blue*

Joyce Redman, *Othello*

Maggie Smith, *Othello*

Ruth Gordon, *Inside Daisy Clover*

Peggy Wood, *The Sound of Music*

1966 Academy Awards

Best Picture

    A Man for All Seasons

Alfie

The Russians Are Coming, The Russians Are Coming

The Sand Pebbles

Who's Afraid of Virginia Woolf?

Best Actor

    Paul Scofield, *A Man for All Seasons*

Richard Burton, *Who's Afraid of Virginia Woolf?*

Michael Caine, *Alfie*

Steve McQueen, *The Sand Pebbles*

Alan Arkin, *The Russians Are Coming The Russians Are Coming*

Best Actress

    Elizabeth Taylor, *Who's Afraid of Virginia Woolf?*

Ida Kaminska, *The Shop on Main Street*

Lynn Redgrave, *Georgy Girl*

Vanessa Redgrave, *Morgan!*

Anouk Aimée, *A Man and a Woman*

Best Supporting Actor

    Walter Matthau, *The Fortune Cookie*

James Mason, *Georgy Girl*

Mako, *The Sand Pebbles*

George Segal, *Who's Afraid of Virginia Woolf?*

Robert Shaw, *A Man for All Seasons*

Best Supporting Actress

    Sandy Dennis, *Who's Afraid of Virginia Woolf?*

Wendy Hiller, *A Man for All Seasons*

Jocelyne Lagarde, *Hawaii*

Vivien Merchant, *Alfie*

Geraldine Page, *You're a Big Boy Now*

1967 Academy Awards

Best Picture

    In the Heat of the Night

Doctor Dolittle

The Graduate

Guess Who's Coming to Dinner

Bonnie and Clyde

Best Actor

    Rod Steiger, *In the Heat of the Night*

Dustin Hoffman, *The Graduate*

Paul Newman, *Cool Hand Luke*

Warren Beatty, *Bonnie and Clyde*

Spencer Tracy, *Guess Who's Coming to Dinner*

Best Actress

    Katharine Hepburn, *Guess Who's Coming to Dinner*

Faye Dunaway, *Bonnie and Clyde*

Dame Edith Evans, *The Whisperers*

Audrey Hepburn, *Wait Until Dark*

Anne Bancroft, *The Graduate*

Best Supporting Actor

    George Kennedy, *Cool Hand Luke*

Gene Hackman, *Bonnie and Clyde*

Cecil Kellaway, *Guess Who's Coming to Dinner*

John Cassavetes, *The Dirty Dozen*

Michael J. Pollard, *Bonnie and Clyde*

Best Supporting Actress

    Estelle Parsons, *Bonnie and Clyde*

Mildred Natwick, *Barefoot in the Park*

Carol Channing, *Thoroughly Modern Millie*
Beah Richards, *Guess Who's Coming to Dinner*
Katharine Ross, *The Graduate*

1968 Academy Awards

Best Picture

Oliver!
The Lion in Winter
Funny Girl,
Rachel, Rachel
Romeo and Juliet

Best Actor

Cliff Robertson, *Charly*
Alan Bates, *The Fixer*
Ron Moody, *Oliver!*
Peter O'Toole, *The Lion in Winter*
Alan Arkin, *The Heart Is a Lonely Hunter*

Best Actress (tie)

Katharine Hepburn, *The Lion in Winter*
Barbra Streisand, *Funny Girl*
Vanessa Redgrave, *Isadora*
Patricia Neal, *The Subject Was Roses*
Joanne Woodward, *Rachel, Rachel*

Best Supporting Actor

Jack Albertson, *The Subject Was Roses*
Seymour Cassel, *Faces*
Daniel Massey, *Star!*
Jack Wild, *Oliver!*
Gene Wilder, *The Producers*

Best Supporting Actress

Ruth Gordon, *Rosemary's Baby*
Lynn Carlin, *Faces*
Sondra Locke, *The Heart Is a Lonely Hunter*
Kay Medford, *Funny Girl*
Estelle Parsons, *Rachel, Rachel*

1969 Academy Awards

Best Picture

Midnight Cowboy
Butch Cassidy and the Sundance Kid

Hello, Dolly!
Anne of the Thousand Days
Z

Best Actor

John Wayne, *True Grit*
Dustin Hoffman, *Midnight Cowboy*
Peter O'Toole, *Goodbye, Mr. Chips*
Jon Voight, *Midnight Cowboy*
Richard Burton, *Anne of the Thousand Days*

Best Actress

Maggie Smith, *The Prime of Miss Jean Brodie*
Jane Fonda, *They Shoot Horses, Don't They?*
Liza Minnelli, *The Sterile Cuckoo*
Jean Simmons, *The Happy Ending*
Genevieve Bujold, *Anne of the Thousand Days*

Best Supporting Actor

Gig Young, *They Shoot Horses, Don't They?*
Elliott Gould, *Bob & Carol & Ted & Alice*
Jack Nicholson, *Easy Rider*
Anthony Quayle, *Anne of the Thousand Days*
Rupert Crosse, *The Reivers*

Best Supporting Actor

Goldie Hawn, *Cactus Flower*
Dyan Cannon, *Bob & Carol & Ted & Alice*
Catherine Burns, *Last Summer*
Sylvia Miles, *Midnight Cowboy*
Susannah York, *They Shoot Horses, Don't They*

1970 Academy Awards

Best Picture

Patton
Five Easy Pieces
Love Story
*M*A*S*H*
Airport

Best Actor

George C. Scott, *Patton*
James Earl Jones, *The Great White Hope*
Jack Nicholson, *Five Easy Pieces*
Ryan O'Neal, *Love Story*
Melvyn Douglas, *I Never Sang for My Father*

Best Actress

Glenda Jackson, *Women in Love*
Jane Alexander, *The Great White Hope*
Ali MacGraw, *Love Story*
Sarah Miles, *Ryan's Daughter*
Carrie Snodgress, *Diary of a Mad Housewife*

Best Supporting Actor

John Mills, *Ryan's Daughter*
Chief Dan George, *Little Big Man*
Gene Hackman, *I Never Sang for My Father*
John Marley, *Love Story*
Richard Castellano, *Lovers and Other Strangers*

Best Supporting Actress

Helen Hayes, *Airport*
Lee Grant, *The Landlord*
Karen Black, *Five Easy Pieces*
Sally Kellerman, *M*A*S*H*
Maureen Stapleton, *Airport*

1971 Academy Awards

Best Picture

The French Connection
Fiddler on the Roof
A Clockwork Orange
The Last Picture Show
Nicholas and Alexandra

Best Actor

Gene Hackman, *The French Connection*
Peter Finch, *Sunday Bloody Sunday*
Walter Matthau, *Kotch*
George C. Scott, *The Hospital*
Topol, *Fiddler on the Roof*

Best Actress

Jane Fonda, *Klute*
Julie Christie, *McCabe & Mrs. Miller*
Glenda Jackson, *Sunday Bloody Sunday*
Vanessa Redgrave, *Mary, Queen of Scots*
Janet Suzman, *Nicholas and Alexandra*

Best Supporting Actor

Ben Johnson, *The Last Picture Show*
Leonard Frey, *Fiddler on the Roof*

Richard Jaeckel, *Sometimes a Great Notion*
Jeff Bridges, *The Last Picture Show*
Roy Scheider, *The French Connection*

Best Supporting Actress

Cloris Leachman, *The Last Picture Show*
Barbara Harris, *Who Is Harry Kellerman and Why Is He Saying Those Terrible Things About Me?*
Ellen Burstyn, *The Last Picture Show*
Margaret Leighton, *The Go-Between*
Ann-Margret, *Carnal Knowledge*

1972 Academy Awards

Best Picture

The Godfather
Deliverance
The Emigrants
Cabaret,
Sounder

Best Actor

Marlon Brando, *The Godfather*
Michael Caine, *Sleuth*
Laurence Olivier, *Sleuth*
Peter O'Toole, *The Ruling Class*
Paul Winfield, *Sounder*

Best Actress

Liza Minnelli, *Cabaret*
Diana Ross, *Lady Sings the Blues*
Maggie Smith, *Travels With My Aunt*
Cicely Tyson, *Sounder*
Liv Ullman, *The Emigrants*

Best Supporting Actor

Joel Grey, *Cabaret*
James Caan, *The Godfather*
Robert Duvall, *The Godfather*
Eddie Albert, *The Heartbreak Kid*
Al Pacino, *The Godfather*

Best Supporting Actress

Eileen Heckart, *Butterflies Are Free*
Jeannie Berlin, *The Heartbreak Kid*
Geraldine Page, *Pete 'n' Tillie*
Susan Tyrrell, *Fat City*
Shelley Winters, *The Poseidon Adventure*

1973 Academy Awards

Best Picture

The Sting
Cries and Whispers
The Exorcist
American Graffiti
A Touch of Class

Best Actor

Jack Lemmon, *Save the Tiger*
Marlon Brando, *Last Tango in Paris*
Jack Nicholson, *The Last Detail*
Al Pacino, *Serpico*
Robert Redford, *The Sting*

Best Actress

Glenda Jackson, *A Touch of Class*
Ellen Burstyn, *The Exorcist*
Marsha Mason, *Cinderella Liberty*
Barbra Streisand, *The Way We Were*
Joanne Woodward, *Summer Wishes, Winter Dreams*

Best Supporting Actor

John Houseman, *The Paper Chase*
Jack Gilford, *Save the Tiger*
Vincent Gardenia, *Bang the Drum Slowly*
Jason Miller, *The Exorcist*
Randy Quaid, *The Last Detail*

Best Supporting Actress

Tatum O'Neal, *Paper Moon*
Candy Clark, *American Graffiti*
Madeline Kahn, *Paper Moon*
Linda Blair, *The Exorcist*
Sylvia Sidney, *Summer Wishes, Winter Dreams*

1974 Academy Awards

Best Picture

The Godfather, Part II
The Conversation
Chinatown
Lenny
The Towering Inferno

Best Actor

Art Carney, *Harry and Tonto*
Albert Finney, *Murder on the Orient Express*
Dustin Hoffman, *Lenny*
Jack Nicholson, *Chinatown*
Al Pacino, *The Godfather, Part II*

Best Actress

Ellen Burstyn, *Alice Doesn't Live Here Anymore*
Diahann Carroll, *Claudine*
Faye Dunaway, *Chinatown*
Valerie Perrine, *Lenny*
Gena Rowlands, *A Woman Under the Influence*

Best Supporting Actor

Robert De Niro, *The Godfather, Part II*
Jeff Bridges, *Thunderbolt and Lightfoot*
Fred Astaire, *The Towering Inferno*
Michael V. Gazzo, *The Godfather Part II*
Lee Strasberg, *The Godfather, Part II*

Best Supporting Actress

Ingrid Bergman, *Murder on the Orient Express*
Valentina Cortese, *Day for Night*
Madeline Kahn, *Blazing Saddles*
Diane Ladd, *Alice Doesn't Live Here Anymore*
Talia Shire, *The Godfather, Part II*

1975 Academy Awards

Best Picture

One Flew Over the Cuckoo's Nest
Dog Day Afternoon
Jaws
Nashville
Barry Lyndon

Best Actor

Jack Nicholson, *One Flew Over the Cuckoo's Nest*
Walter Matthau, *The Sunshine Boys*
Al Pacino, *Dog Day Afternoon*
Maximilian Schell, *The Man in the Glass Booth*
James Whitmore, *Give 'em Hell, Harry!*

Best Actress

Louise Fletcher, *One Flew Over the Cuckoo's Nest*
Isabelle Adjani, *The Story of Adele H*
Glenda Jackson, *Hedda*
Carol Kane, *Hester Street*
Ann-Margret, *Tommy*

Best Supporting Actor

George Burns, *The Sunshine Boys*
Brad Dourif, *One Flew Over the Cuckoo's Nest*
Burgess Meredith, *The Day of the Locust*
Chris Sarandon, *Dog Day Afternoon*
Jack Warden, *Shampoo*

Best Supporting Actress

Lee Grant, *Shampoo*
Ronee Blakley, *Nashville*
Sylvia Miles, *Farewell, My Lovely*
Lily Tomlin, *Nashville*
Brenda Vaccaro, *Jacqueline Susann's Once Is Not Enough*

1976 Academy Awards

Best Picture,

Rocky
Bound for Glory
Network
All the President's Men
Taxi Driver

Best Actor

Peter Finch, *Network*
Robert De Niro, *Taxi Driver*
Giancarlo Giannini, *Seven Beauties*
William Holden, *Network*
Sylvester Stallone, *Rocky*

Best Actress

Faye Dunaway, *Network*
Marie-Christine Barrault, *Cousin, Cousine*
Talia Shire, *Rocky*
Sissy Spacek, *Carrie*
Liv Ullman, *Face to Face*

Best Supporting Actor

Jason Robards, *All the President's Men*
Burgess Meredith, *Rocky*

Laurence Olivier, *Marathon Man*
Ned Beatty, *Network*
Burt Young, *Rocky*

Best Supporting Actress

Beatrice Straight, *Network*
Jodie Foster, *Taxi Driver*
Lee Grant, *Voyage of the Damned*
Piper Laurie, *Carrie*
Jane Alexander, *All the President's Men*

1977 Academy Awards

Best Picture

Annie Hall
The Goodbye Girl
Julia
Star Wars
The Turning Point

Best Actor

Richard Dreyfuss, *The Goodbye Girl*
Richard Burton, *Equus*
Woody Allen, *Annie Hall*
Marcello Mastroianni, *A Special Day*
John Travolta, *Saturday Night Fever*

Best Actress

Diane Keaton, *Annie Hall*
Jane Fonda, *Julia*
Anne Bancroft, *The Turning Point*
Shirley MacLaine, *The Turning Point*
Marsha Mason, *The Goodbye Girl*

Best Supporting Actor

Jason Robards, *Julia*
Peter Firth, *Equus*
Alec Guinness, *Star Wars*
Mikhail Baryshnikov, *The Turning Point*
Maximilian Schell, *Julia*

Best Supporting Actress

Vanessa Redgrave, *Julia*
Quinn Cummings, *The Goodbye Girl*
Melinda Dillon, *Close Encounters of the Third Kind*
Leslie Browne, *The Turning Point*
Tuesday Weld, *Looking for Mr. Goodbar*

1978 Academy Awards

Best Picture
The Deer Hunter
Coming Home
Heaven Can Wait
Midnight Express
An Unmarried Woman

Best Actor
Jon Voight, *Coming Home*
Gary Busey, *The Buddy Holly Story*
Robert De Niro, *The Deer Hunter*
Laurence Olivier, *The Boys From Brazil*
Warren Beatty, *Heaven Can Wait*

Best Actress
Jane Fonda, *Coming Home*
Ellen Burstyn, *Same Time, Next Year*
Jill Clayburgh, *An Unmarried Woman*
Ingrid Bergman, *Autumn Sonata*
Geraldine Page, *Interiors*

Best Supporting Actor
Christopher Walken, *The Deer Hunter*
Richard Farnsworth, *Comes a Horseman*
John Hurt, *Midnight Express*
Bruce Dern, *Coming Home*
Jack Warden, *Heaven Can Wait*

Best Supporting Actress
Maggie Smith, *California Suite*
Penelope Milford, *Coming Home*
Dyan Cannon, *Heaven Can Wait*
Maureen Stapleton, *Interiors*
Meryl Streep, *The Deer Hunter*

1979 Academy Awards

Best Picture
Kramer vs. Kramer
Apocalypse Now
Breaking Away
All That Jazz
Norma Rae

Best Actor
Dustin Hoffman, *Kramer vs. Kramer*
Jack Lemmon, *The China Syndrome*

Al Pacino, *. . . And Justice for All*
Roy Scheider, *All That Jazz*
Peter Sellers, *Being There*

Best Actress
Sally Field, *Norma Rae*
Jill Clayburgh, *Starting Over*
Jane Fonda, *The China Syndrome*
Marsha Mason, *Chapter Two*
Bette Midler, *The Rose*

Best Supporting Actor
Melvyn Douglas, *Being There*
Robert Duvall, *Apocalypse Now*
Frederic Forrest, *The Rose*
Justin Henry, *Kramer vs. Kramer*
Mickey Rooney, *The Black Stallion*

Best Supporting Actress
Meryl Streep, *Kramer vs. Kramer*
Barbara Barrie, *Breaking Away*
Candice Bergen, *Starting Over*
Mariel Hemingway, *Manhattan*
Jane Alexander, *Kramer vs. Kramer*

1980 Academy Awards

Best Picture
Ordinary People
The Elephant Man
Coal Miner's Daughter
Raging Bull
Tess

Best Actor
Robert De Niro, *Raging Bull*
Robert Duvall, *The Great Santini*
John Hurt, *The Elephant Man*
Jack Lemmon, *Tribute*
Peter O'Toole, *The Stunt Man*

Best Actress
Sissy Spacek, *Coal Miner's Daughter*
Goldie Hawn, *Private Benjamin*
Mary Tyler Moore, *Ordinary People*
Gena Rowlands, *Gloria*
Ellen Burstyn, *Resurrection*

Best Supporting Actor

Timothy Hutton, *Ordinary People*
Judd Hirsch, *Ordinary People*
Michael O'Keefe, *The Great Santini*
Joe Pesci, *Raging Bull*
Jason Robards, *Melvin and Howard*

Best Supporting Actress

Mary Steenburgen, *Melvin and Howard*
Eva Le Gallienne, *Resurrection*
Cathy Moriarty, *Raging Bull*
Diana Scarwid, *Inside Moves*
Eileen Brennan, *Private Benjamin*

1981 Academy Awards

Best Picture

Chariots of Fire
Atlantic City
On Golden Pond
Raiders of the Lost Ark
Reds

Best Actor

Henry Fonda, *On Golden Pond*
Warren Beatty, *Reds*
Burt Lancaster, *Atlantic City*
Dudley Moore, *Arthur*
Paul Newman, *Absence of Malice*

Best Actress

Katharine Hepburn, *On Golden Pond*
Diane Keaton, *Reds*
Marsha Mason, *Only When I Laugh*
Susan Sarandon, *Atlantic City*
Meryl Streep, *The French Lieutenant's Woman*

Best Supporting Actor

John Gielgud, *Arthur*
James Coco, *Only When I Laugh*
Ian Holm, *Chariots of Fire*
Jack Nicholson, *Reds*
Howard E. Rollins, Jr., *Ragtime*

Best Supporting Actress

Maureen Stapleton, *Reds*
Jane Fonda, *On Golden Pond*
Joan Hackett, *Only When I Laugh*

Elizabeth McGovern, *Ragtime*
Melinda Dillon, *Absence of Malice*

1982 Academy Awards

Best Picture

Gandhi
E.T. the Extra-Terrestrial
Missing
Tootsie
The Verdict

Best Actor

Ben Kingsley, *Gandhi*
Dustin Hoffman, *Tootsie*
Jack Lemmon, *Missing*
Paul Newman, *The Verdict*
Peter O'Toole, *My Favorite Year*

Best Actress

Meryl Streep, *Sophie's Choice*
Jessica Lange, *Frances*
Sissy Spacek, *Missing*
Julie Andrews, *Victor/Victoria*
Debra Winger, *An Officer and a Gentleman*

Best Supporting Actor

Louis Gossett, Jr., *An Officer and a Gentleman*
Charles Durning, *The Best Little Whorehouse in Texas*
John Lithgow, *The World According to Garp*
James Mason, *The Verdict*
Robert Preston, *Victor/Victoria*

Best Supporting Actress,

Jessica Lange, *Tootsie*
Teri Garr, *Tootsie*
Glenn Close, *The World According to Garp*
Kim Stanley, *Frances*
Lesley Ann Warren, *Victor/Victoria*

1983 Academy Awards

Best Picture

Terms of Endearment
The Dresser

The Right Stuff
Tender Mercies
The Big Chill

Best Actor

Robert Duvall, *Tender Mercies*
Tom Conti, *Reuben, Reuben*
Tom Courtenay, *The Dresser*
Michael Caine, *Educating Rita*
Albert Finney, *The Dresser*

Best Actress

Shirley MacLaine, *Terms of Endearment*
Jane Alexander, *Testament*
Meryl Streep, *Silkwood*
Julie Walters, *Educating Rita*
Debra Winger, *Terms of Endearment*

Best Supporting Actor

Jack Nicholson, *Terms of Endearment*
John Lithgow, *Terms of Endearment*
Charles Durning, *To Be or Not to Be*
Sam Shepard, *The Right Stuff*
Rip Torn, *Cross Creek*

Best Supporting Actress

Linda Hunt, *The Year of Living Dangerously*
Glenn Close, *The Big Chill*
Cher, *Silkwood*
Amy Irving, *Yentl*
Alfre Woodard, *Cross Creek*

1984 Academy Awards

Best Picture

Amadeus
The Killing Fields
A Passage to India
Places in the Heart
A Soldier's Story

Best Actor

F. Murray Abraham, *Amadeus*
Jeff Bridges, *Starman*
Albert Finney, *Under the Volcano*
Tom Hulce, *Amadeus*
Sam Waterston, *The Killing Fields*

Best Actress

Sally Field, *Places in the Heart*
Judy Davis, *A Passage to India*
Jessica Lange, *Country*
Vanessa Redgrave, *The Bostonians*
Sissy Spacek, *The River*

Best Supporting Actor

Haing S. Ngor, *The Killing Fields*
John Malkovich, *Places in the Heart*
Noriyuki "Pat" Morita, *The Karate Kid*
Adolph Caesar, *A Soldier's Story*
Ralph Richardson, *Greystoke: The Legend of Tarzan, Lord of the Apes*

Best Supporting Actress

Peggy Ashcroft, *A Passage to India*
Glenn Close, *The Natural*
Lindsay Crouse, *Places in the Heart*
Christine Lahti, *Swing Shift*
Geraldine Page, *The Pope of Greenwich Village*

1985 Academy Awards

Best Picture

Out of Africa
Kiss of the Spider Woman
The Color Purple
Prizzi's Honor
Witness

Best Actor

William Hurt, *Kiss of the Spider Woman*
James Garner, *Murphy's Romance*
Harrison Ford, *Witness*
Jack Nicholson, *Prizzi's Honor*
Jon Voight, *Runaway Train*

Best Actress

Geraldine Page, *The Trip to Bountiful*
Whoopi Goldberg, *The Color Purple*
Jessica Lange, *Sweet Dreams*
Anne Bancroft, *Agnes of God*
Meryl Streep, *Out of Africa*

Best Supporting Actor

Don Ameche, *Cocoon*
Klaus Maria Brandauer, *Out of Africa*
William Hickey, *Prizzi's Honor*

Robert Loggia, *Jagged Edge*
Eric Roberts, *Runaway Train*

Best Supporting Actress

Anjelica Huston, *Prizzi's Honor*
Margaret Avery, *The Color Purple*
Amy Madigan, *Twice in a Lifetime*
Meg Tilly, *Agnes of God*
Oprah Winfrey, *The Color Purple*

1986 Academy Awards

Best Picture

Platoon
Hannah and Her Sisters
The Mission
Children of a Lesser God
A Room with a View

Best Actor

Paul Newman, *The Color of Money*
Bob Hoskins, *Mona Lisa*
William Hurt, *Children of a Lesser God*
Dexter Gordon, *'Round Midnight*
James Woods, *Salvador*

Best Actress

Marlee Matlin, *Children of a Lesser God*
Jane Fonda, *The Morning After*
Sissy Spacek, *Crimes of the Heart*
Kathleen Turner, *Peggy Sue Got Married*
Sigourney Weaver, *Aliens*

Best Supporting Actor

Michael Caine, *Hannah and Her Sisters*
Tom Berenger, *Platoon*
Willem Dafoe, *Platoon*
Denholm Elliott, *A Room With a View*
Dennis Hopper, *Hoosiers*

Best Supporting Actress

Dianne Wiest, *Hannah and Her Sisters*
Piper Laurie, *Children of a Lesser God*
Mary Elizabeth Mastrantonio, *The Color of Money*
Maggie Smith, *A Room With a View*
Tess Harper, *Crimes of the Heart*

1987 Academy Awards

Best Picture

The Last Emperor
Fatal Attraction
Hope and Glory
Broadcast News
Moonstruck

Best Actor

Michael Douglas, *Wall Street*
William Hurt, *Broadcast News*
Marcello Mastroianni, *Dark Eyes*
Jack Nicholson, *Ironweed*
Robin Williams, *Good Morning, Vietnam*

Best Actress

Cher, *Moonstruck*
Glenn Close, *Fatal Attraction*
Holly Hunter, *Broadcast News*
Sally Kirkland, *Anna*
Meryl Streep, *Ironweed*

Best Supporting Actor

Sean Connery, *The Untouchables*
Albert Brooks, *Broadcast News*
Morgan Freeman, *Street Smart*
Vincent Gardenia, *Moonstruck*
Denzel Washington, *Cry Freedom*

Best Supporting Actress

Olympia Dukakis, *Moonstruck*
Anne Archer, *Fatal Attraction*
Norma Aleandro, *Gaby—A True Story*
Anne Ramsey, *Throw Momma From the Train*
Ann Sothern, *The Whales of August*

1988 Academy Awards

Best Picture

Rain Man
Dangerous Liaisons
Mississippi Burning
The Accidental Tourist
Working Girl

Best Actor

Dustin Hoffman, *Rain Man*
Tom Hanks, *Big*

Gene Hackman, *Mississippi Burning*

Edward James Olmos, *Stand and Deliver*

Max von Sydow, *Pelle the Conqueror*

Best Actress

Jodie Foster, *The Accused*

Glenn Close, *Dangerous Liaisons*

Melanie Griffith, *Working Girl*

Meryl Streep, *A Cry in the Dark*

Sigourney Weaver, *Gorillas in the Mist*

Best Supporting Actor

Kevin Kline, *A Fish Called Wanda*

Alec Guinness, *Little Dorrit*

Martin Landau, *Tucker: The Man and His Dream*

River Phoenix, *Running on Empty*

Dean Stockwell, *Married to the Mob*

Best Supporting Actress

Geena Davis, *The Accidental Tourist*

Joan Cusack, *Working Girl*

Frances McDormand, *Mississippi Burning*

Michelle Pfeiffer, *Dangerous Liaisons*

Sigourney Weaver, *Working Girl*

1989 Academy Awards

Best Picture

Driving Miss Daisy

Dead Poets Society

Born on the Fourth of July

Field of Dreams

My Left Foot

Best Actor

Daniel Day-Lewis, *My Left Foot*

Tom Cruise, *Born on the Fourth of July*

Kenneth Branagh, *Henry V*

Morgan Freeman, *Driving Miss Daisy*

Robin Williams, *Dead Poets Society*

Best Actress

Jessica Tandy, *Driving Miss Daisy*

Pauline Collins, *Shirley Valentine*

Jessica Lange, *Music Box*

Michelle Pfeiffer, *The Fabulous Baker Boys*

Isabelle Adjani, *Camille Claudel*

Best Supporting Actor

Denzel Washington, *Glory*

Dan Aykroyd, *Driving Miss Daisy*

Marlon Brando, *A Dry White Season*

Martin Landau, *Crimes and Misdemeanors*

Danny Aiello, *Do the Right Thing*

Best Supporting Actress

Brenda Fricker, *My Left Foot*

Anjelica Huston, *Enemies, A Love Story*

Lena Olin, *Enemies, A Love Story*

Julia Roberts, *Steel Magnolias*

Dianne Wiest, *Parenthood*

1990 Academy Awards

Best Picture

Dances with Wolves

Awakenings

Ghost

The Godfather, Part III

GoodFellas

Best Actor

Jeremy Irons, *Reversal of Fortune*

Robert De Niro, *Awakenings*

Gérard Depardieu, *Cyrano de Bergerac*

Richard Harris, *The Field*

Kevin Costner, *Dances with Wolves*

Best Actress

Kathy Bates, *Misery*

Anjelica Huston, *The Grifters*

Julia Roberts, *Pretty Woman*

Meryl Streep, *Postcards From the Edge*

Joanne Woodward, *Mr. and Mrs. Bridge*

Best Supporting Actor

Joe Pesci, *GoodFellas*

Andy Garcia, *The Godfather, Part III*

Graham Greene, *Dances with Wolves*

Al Pacino, *Dick Tracy*

Bruce Davison, *Longtime Companion*

Best Supporting Actress

Whoopi Goldberg, *Ghost*

Lorraine Bracco, *GoodFellas*

Annette Bening, *The Grifters*

Diane Ladd, *Wild at Heart*
Mary McDonnell, *Dances with Wolves*

1991 Academy Awards

Best Picture
The Silence of the Lambs
Bugsy
JFK
The Prince of Tides
Beauty and the Beast

Best Actor
Anthony Hopkins, *The Silence of the Lambs*
Robert De Niro, *Cape Fear*
Warren Beatty, *Bugsy*
Nick Nolte, *The Prince of Tides*
Robin Williams, *The Fisher King*

Best Actress
Jodie Foster, *The Silence of the Lambs*
Laura Dern, *Rambling Rose*
Geena Davis, *Thelma & Louise*
Bette Midler, *For the Boys*
Susan Sarandon, *Thelma & Louise*

Best Supporting Actor
Jack Palance, *City Slickers*
Harvey Keitel, *Bugsy*
Ben Kingsley, *Bugsy*
Michael Lerner, *Barton Fink*
Tommy Lee Jones, *JFK*

Best Supporting Actress
Mercedes Ruehl, *The Fisher King*
Juliette Lewis, *Cape Fear*
Kate Nelligan, *The Prince of Tides*
Diane Ladd, *Rambling Rose*
Jessica Tandy, Fried Green Tomatoes

1992 Academy Awards

Best Picture
Unforgiven
A Few Good Men
Howards End
Scent of a Woman
The Crying Game

Best Actor
Al Pacino, *Scent of a Woman*
Clint Eastwood, *Unforgiven*
Robert Downey, Jr., *Chaplin*
Stephen Rea, *The Crying Game*
Denzel Washington, *Malcolm X*

Best Actress
Emma Thompson, *Howards End*
Mary McDonnell, *Passion Fish*
Michelle Pfeiffer, *Love Field*
Susan Sarandon, *Lorenzo's Oil*
Catherine Deneuve, *Indochine*

Best Supporting Actor
Gene Hackman, *Unforgiven*
Jaye Davidson, *The Crying Game*
Jack Nicholson, *A Few Good Men*
Al Pacino, *Glengarry Glen Ross*
David Paymer, *Mr. Saturday Night*

Best Supporting Actress
Marisa Tomei, *My Cousin Vinny*
Joan Plowright, *Enchanted April*
Vanessa Redgrave, *Howards End*
Miranda Richardson, *Damage*
Judy Davis, *Husbands and Wives*

1993 Academy Awards

Best Picture
Schindler's List
In the Name of the Father
The Piano
The Remains of the Day
The Fugitive

Best Actor
Tom Hanks, *Philadelphia*
Laurence Fishburne, *What's Love Got to Do With It*
Daniel Day-Lewis, *In the Name of the Father*
Anthony Hopkins, *The Remains of the Day*
Liam Neeson, *Schindler's List*

Best Actress

Holly Hunter, *The Piano*
Stockard Channing, *Six Degrees of Separation*
Angela Bassett, *What's Love Got to Do With It*
Emma Thompson, *The Remains of the Day*
Debra Winger, *Shadowlands*

Best Supporting Actor

Tommy Lee Jones, *The Fugitive*
Ralph Fiennes, *Schindler's List*
Leonardo DiCaprio, *What's Eating Gilbert Grape*
John Malkovich, *In the Line of Fire*
Pete Postlethwaite, *In the Name of the Father*

Best Supporting Actress

Anna Paquin, *The Piano*
Holly Hunter, *The Firm*
Rosie Perez, *Fearless*
Winona Ryder, *The Age of Innocence*
Emma Thompson, *In the Name of the Father*

1994 Academy Awards

Best Picture

Forrest Gump
Four Weddings and a Funeral
Pulp Fiction
Quiz Show
The Shawshank Redemption

Best Actor

Tom Hanks, *Forrest Gump*
Morgan Freeman, *The Shawshank Redemption*
Nigel Hawthorne, *The Madness of King George*
Paul Newman, *Nobody's Fool*
John Travolta, *Pulp Fiction*

Best Actress

Jessica Lange, *Blue Sky*
Jodie Foster, *Nell*
Miranda Richardson, *Tom and Viv*
Winona Ryder, *Little Women*
Susan Sarandon, *The Client*

Best Supporting Actor

Martin Landau, *Ed Wood*
Samuel L. Jackson, *Pulp Fiction*

Chazz Palminteri, *Bullets Over Broadway*
Paul Scofield, *Quiz Show*
Gary Sinise, *Forrest Gump*

Best Supporting Actress

Dianne Wiest, *Bullets Over Broadway*
Helen Mirren, *The Madness of King George*
Uma Thurman, *Pulp Fiction*
Jennifer Tilly, *Bullets Over Broadway*
Rosemary Harris, *Tom and Viv*

1995 Academy Awards

Best Picture

Braveheart
Babe
Apollo 13
The Postman
Sense and Sensibility

Best Actor

Nicolas Cage, *Leaving Las Vegas*
Richard Dreyfuss, *Mr. Holland's Opus*
Anthony Hopkins, *Nixon*
Sean Penn, *Dead Man Walking*
Massimo Troisi, *The Postman (Il Postino)*

Best Actress

Susan Sarandon, *Dead Man Walking*
Elisabeth Shue, *Leaving Las Vegas*
Sharon Stone, *Casino*
Meryl Streep, *The Bridges of Madison County*
Emma Thompson, *Sense and Sensibility*

Best Supporting Actor

Kevin Spacey, *The Usual Suspects*
Ed Harris, *Apollo 13*
Brad Pitt, *12 Monkeys*
Tim Roth, *Rob Roy*
James Cromwell, *Babe*

Best Supporting Actress

Mira Sorvino, *Mighty Aphrodite*
Kathleen Quinlan, *Apollo 13*
Joan Allen, *Nixon*
Mare Winningham, *Georgia*
Kate Winslet, *Sense and Sensibility*

1996 Academy Awards

Best Picture

The English Patient
Fargo
Jerry Maguire
Secrets and Lies
Shine, Jane Scott

Best Actor

Geoffrey Rush, *Shine*
Tom Cruise, *Jerry Maguire*
Ralph Fiennes, *The English Patient*
Woody Harrelson, *The People vs. Larry Flynt*
Billy Bob Thornton, *Sling Blade*

Best Actress

Frances McDormand, *Fargo*
Brenda Blethyn, *Secrets and Lies*
Diane Keaton, *Marvin's Room*
Kristen Scott Thomas, *The English Patient*
Emily Watson, *Breaking the Waves*

Best Supporting Actor

Cuba Gooding, Jr., *Jerry Maguire*
William H. Macy, *Fargo*
Armin Mueller-Stahl, *Shine*
Edward Norton, *Primal Fear*
James Woods, *Ghosts of Mississippi*

Best Supporting Actress

Juliette Binoche, *The English Patient*
Joan Allen, *The Crucible*
Lauren Bacall, *The Mirror Has Two Faces*
Barbara Hershey, *The Portrait of a Lady*
Marianne Jean-Baptiste, *Secrets and Lies*

1997 Academy Awards

Best Picture

Titanic
The Full Monty
Good Will Hunting
L.A. Confidential
As Good as It Gets

Beat Actor

Jack Nicholson, *As Good as It Gets*
Robert Duvall, *The Apostle*

Peter Fonda, *Ulee's Gold*
Dustin Hoffman, *Wag the Dog*
Matt Damon, *Good Will Hunting*

Best Actress

Helen Hunt, *As Good as It Gets*
Julie Christie, *Afterglow*
Judi Dench, *Mrs. Brown*
Helena Bonham Carter, *The Wings of the Dove*
Kate Winslet, *Titanic*

Best Supporting Actor

Robin Williams, *Good Will Hunting*
Anthony Hopkins, *Amistad*
Greg Kinnear, *As Good as It Gets*
Burt Reynolds, *Boogie Nights*
Robert Forster, *Jackie Brown*

Best Supporting Actress

Kim Basinger, *L.A. Confidential*
Joan Cusack, *In & Out*
Minnie Driver, *Good Will Hunting*
Julianne Moore, *Boogie Nights*
Gloria Stuart, *Titanic*

1998 Academy Awards

Best Picture

Shakespeare in Love
Life Is Beautiful
Saving Private Ryan
Elizabeth
The Thin Red Line

Best Actor

Roberto Benigni, *Life Is Beautiful*
Tom Hanks, *Saving Private Ryan*
Ian McKellen, *Gods and Monsters*
Nick Nolte, *Affliction*
Edward Norton, *American History X*

Best Actress

Gwyneth Paltrow, *Shakespeare in Love*
Fernanda Montenegro, *Central Station*
Cate Blanchett, *Elizabeth*
Meryl Streep, *One True Thing*
Emily Watson, *Hilary and Jackie*

Best Supporting Actor

James Coburn, *Affliction*
Robert Duvall, *A Civil Action*
Ed Harris, *The Truman Show*
Geoffrey Rush, *Shakespeare in Love*
Billy Bob Thornton, *A Simple Plan*

Best Supporting Actress

Judi Dench, *Shakespeare in Love*
Brenda Blethyn, *Little Voice*
Kathy Bates, *Primary Colors*
Rachel Griffiths, *Hilary and Jackie*
Lynn Redgrave, *Gods and Monsters*

1999 Academy Awards

Best Picture

American Beauty
The Cider House Rules
The Green Mile
The Insider
The Sixth Sense

Best Actor

Kevin Spacey, *American Beauty*
Richard Farnsworth, *The Straight Story*
Sean Penn, *Sweet and Lowdown*
Russell Crowe, *The Insider*
Denzel Washington, *The Hurricane*

Best Actress

Hilary Swank, *Boys Don't Cry*
Janet McTeer, *Tumbleweeds*
Julianne Moore, *The End of the Affair*
Meryl Streep, *Music of the Heart*
Annette Bening, *American Beauty*

Best Supporting Actor

Michael Caine, *The Cider House Rules*
Tom Cruise, *Magnolia*
Michael Clarke Duncan, *The Green Mile*
Jude Law, *The Talented Mr. Ripley*
Haley Joel Osment, *The Sixth Sense*

Best Supporting Actress

Angelina Jolie, *Girl, Interrupted*
Toni Collette, *The Sixth Sense*
Catherine Keener, *Being John Malkovich*

Samantha Morton, *Sweet and Lowdown*
Chloë Sevigny, *Boys Don't Cry*

2000 Academy Awards

Best Picture

Gladiator
Crouching Tiger, Hidden Dragon
Erin Brockovich
Chocolat
Traffic

Best Actor

Russell Crowe, *Gladiator*
Javier Bardem, *Before Night Falls*
Tom Hanks, *Cast Away*
Ed Harris, *Pollock*
Geoffrey Rush, *Quills*

Best Actress

Julia Roberts, *Erin Brockovich*
Juliette Binoche, *Chocolat*
Ellen Burstyn, *Requiem for a Dream*
Laura Linney, *You Can Count on Me*
Joan Allen, *The Contender*

Best Supporting Actor

Benicio Del Toro, *Traffic*
Willem Dafoe, *Shadow of the Vampire*
Jeff Bridges, *The Contender*
Albert Finney, *Erin Brockovich*
Joaquin Phoenix, *Gladiator*

Best Supporting Actress

Marcia Gay Harden, *Pollock*
Judi Dench, *Chocolat*
Kate Hudson, *Almost Famous*
Frances McDormand, *Almost Famous*
Julie Walters, *Billy Elliot*

2001 Academy Awards

Best Picture

A Beautiful Mind
Gosford Park
In the Bedroom

The Lord of the Rings: The Fellowship of the Ring
Moulin Rouge

Best Actor

Denzel Washington, *Training Day*
Sean Penn, *I Am Sam*
Will Smith, *Ali*
Russell Crowe, *A Beautiful Mind*
Tom Wilkinson, *In the Bedroom*

Best Actress

Halle Berry, *Monster's Ball*
Judi Dench, *Iris*
Nicole Kidman, *Moulin Rouge*
Sissy Spacek, *In the Bedroom*
Renée Zellweger, *Bridget Jones's Diary*

Best Supporting Actor

Jim Broadbent, *Iris*
Ethan Hawke, *Training Day*
Ben Kingsley, *Sexy Beast*
Ian McKellen, *The Lord of the Rings: The Fellowship of the Ring*
Jon Voight, *Ali*

Best Supporting Actress

Jennifer Connelly, *A Beautiful Mind*
Helen Mirren, *Gosford Park*
Maggie Smith, *Gosford Park*
Marisa Tomei, *In the Bedroom*
Kate Winslet, *Iris*

2002 Academy Awards

Best Picture

Chicago
Gangs of New York
The Hours
The Lord of the Rings: The Two Towers
The Pianist

Best Actor

Adrien Brody, *The Pianist*
Nicolas Cage, *Adaptation*
Michael Caine, *The Quiet American*
Daniel Day-Lewis, *Gangs of New York*
Jack Nicholson, *About Schmidt*

Best Actress

Nicole Kidman, *The Hours*
Salma Hayek, *Frida*
Diane Lane, *Unfaithful*
Julianne Moore, *Far From Heaven*
Renée Zellweger, *Chicago*

Best Supporting Actor

Chris Cooper, *Adaptation*
Ed Harris, *The Hours*
Paul Newman, *The Road to Perdition*
John C. Reilly, *Chicago*
Christopher Walken, *Catch Me if You Can*

Best Supporting Actress

Catherine Zeta-Jones, *Chicago*
Julianne Moore, *The Hours*
Queen Latifah, *Chicago*
Meryl Streep, *Adaptation*
Kathy Bates, *About Schmidt*

2003 Academy Awards

Best Picture

The Lord of the Rings: The Return of the King
Lost in Translation
Master and Commander: The Far Side of the World
Mystic River
Seabiscuit

Best Actor

Sean Penn, *Mystic River*
Ben Kingsley, *House of Sand and Fog*
Jude Law, *Cold Mountain*
Bill Murray, *Lost in Translation*
Johnny Depp, *Pirates of the Caribbean: The Curse of the Black Pearl*

Best Actress

Charlize Theron, *Monster*
Diane Keaton, *Something's Gotta Give*
Samantha Morton, *In America*
Keisha Castle-Hughes, *Whale Rider*
Naomi Watts, *21 Grams*

Best Supporting Actor

Tim Robbins, *Mystic River*
Benicio Del Toro, *21 Grams*

Djimon Hounsou, *In America*
Alec Baldwin, *The Cooler*
Ken Watanabe, *The Last Samurai*

Best Supporting Actress
Renée Zellweger, *Cold Mountain*
Patricia Clarkson, *Pieces of April*
Marcia Gay Harden, *Mystic River*
Holly Hunter, *Thirteen*
Shohreh Aghdashloo, *House of Sand and Fog*

2004 Academy Awards

Best Picture
Million Dollar Baby
Finding Neverland
The Aviator
Ray
Sideways

Best Actor
Jamie Foxx, *Ray*
Johnny Depp, *Finding Neverland*
Leonardo DiCaprio, *The Aviator*
Clint Eastwood, *Million Dollar Baby*
Don Cheadle, *Hotel Rwanda*

Best Actress
Hilary Swank, *Million Dollar Baby*
Catalina Sandino Moreno, *Maria Full of Grace*
Imelda Staunton, *Vera Drake*
Annette Bening, *Being Julia*
Kate Winslet, *Eternal Sunshine of the Spotless Mind*

Best Supporting Actor
Morgan Freeman, *Million Dollar Baby*
Thomas Haden Church, *Sideways*
Jamie Foxx, *Collateral*
Alan Alda, *The Aviator*
Clive Owen, *Closer*

Best Supporting Actress
Cate Blanchett, *The Aviator*
Laura Linney, *Kinsey*
Virginia Madsen, *Sideways*
Sophie Okonedo, *Hotel Rwanda*
Natalie Portman, *Closer*

2005 Academy Awards

Best Picture
Crash
Capote
Brokeback Mountain
Good Night, and Good Luck
Munich

Best Actor
Philip Seymour Hoffman *Capote*
Terrence Howard, *Hustle & Flow*
Heath Ledger, *Brokeback Mountain*
Joaquin Phoenix, *Walk the Line*
David Strathairn, *Good Night, and Good Luck*

Best Actress
Reese Witherspoon, *Walk the Line*
Felicity Huffman, *Transamerica*
Keira Knightley, *Pride & Prejudice*
Charlize Theron, *North Country*
Judi Dench, *Mrs. Henderson Presents*

Best Supporting Actor
George Clooney, *Syriana*
Matt Dillon, *Crash*
Paul Giamatti, *Cinderella Man*
Jake Gyllenhaal, *Brokeback Mountain*
William Hurt, *A History of Violence*

Best Supporting Actress
Rachel Weisz, *The Constant Gardener*
Catherine Keener, *Capote*
Frances McDormand, *North Country*
Amy Adams, *Junebug*
Michelle Williams, *Brokeback Mountain*

2006 Academy Awards Nominations

Best Picture
The Departed
Babel
Letters from Iwo Jima
Little Miss Sunshine
The Queen

Best Actor

Forest Whitaker, *The Last King of Scotland*
Ryan Gosling, *Half Nelson*
Peter O'Toole, *Venus*
Will Smith, *The Pursuit of Happyness*
Leonardo DiCaprio, *Blood Diamond*

Best Actress

Helen Mirren, *The Queen*
Judi Dench, *Notes on a Scandal*
Penélope Cruz, *Volver*
Meryl Streep, *The Devil Wears Prada*
Kate Winslet, *Little Children*

Best Supporting Actor

Alan Arkin, *Little Miss Sunshine*
Jackie Earle Haley, *Little Children*
Djimon Hounsou, *Blood Diamond*
Eddie Murphy, *Dreamgirls*
Mark Wahlberg, *The Departed*

Best Supporting Actress,

Jennifer Hudson, *Dreamgirls*
Cate Blanchett, *Notes on a Scandal*
Abigail Breslin, *Little Miss Sunshine*
Adriana Barraza, *Babel*
Rinko Kikuchi, *Babel*

OSCAR, EMMY, TONY & GRAMMY WINNERS

These are the four major awards in American show business. The Oscar is bestowed to the best actor in the movies. The Tony is awarded to the best actor on Broadway—that is a live performance onstage. The Emmy is awarded to the best actor in the television industry. Finally, the Grammy is awarded to the best artist in the music industry. Only seven thespians have won all four (*Superfecta*) and another 16 have won the *Triple Crown*. The following is a list of those exceptional performers.

Superfecta

1. **John Gielgud**
   - Oscar: 1981, Best Supporting Actor, *Arthur*
   - Emmy: 1991, Best Actor in a Special, *Summer's Lease*
   - Tony: 1961, Best Director, *Big Fish, Little Fish*
   - Grammy: 1979, Best Spoken Word Drama, *Ages of Man*

2. **Whoopi Goldberg**
   - Oscar: 1991, Best Supporting Actress, *Ghost*
   - Emmy: 2002, Outstanding Special, *Beyond Tara, The Extraordinary Life of Hattie McDaniel*
   - Tony: 2002, Best Producer of a Musical, *Thoroughly Modern Millie*
   - Grammy: 1985, Best Comedy Recording, Whoopi Goldberg, *Original Broadway Show Recording*

3. **Helen Hayes**
   - Oscar: 1931/32, Best Actress, *The Sin of Madelon Claudet*
     1970, Best Supporting Actress, *Airport*
   - Emmy: 1953, Best Actress
   - Tony: 1947, Best Actress, *Happy Birthday*
     1958, Best Actress, *Time Remembered*
     1980, Lifetime Achievement Award

   - Grammy: 1976, Best Spoken Word, *Great American Documents*

4. **Audrey Hepburn**
   - Oscar: 1953, Best Actress, *Roman Holiday*
   - Emmy: 1993, Special Outstanding Achievement, *Gardens of the World with Audrey Hepburn*
   - Tony: 1954, Best Actress, *Ondine*
     1968, Lifetime Achievement
   - Grammy: 1993, Best Spoken Word, *Audrey Hepburn's Enchanted Tales*

5. **Liza Minnelli**
   - Oscar: 1972, Best Actress, *Cabaret*
   - Emmy: 1973, Best Single Performance, *Singer Presents Liza with a 'Z*
   - Tony: 1965, Best Actress, *Flora, The Red Menace*
     1974, Special Award
     1978, Best Actress, *The Act*
   - Grammy: 1990, Special Merit Legend Award

6. **Rita Moreno**
   - Oscar: 1961, Best Supporting Actress, *West Side Story*
   - Emmy: 1977, Best Supporting Actress, *The Muppet Show*
     1978, Best Supporting Actress, *The Rockford Files*
   - Tony: 1975, Best Supporting Actress, *The Ritz*
   - Grammy: 1972, Best Recording for Children, *The Electric Company*

7. **Barbra Streisand**
   - Oscar: 1968, Best Actress, *Funny Girl*
     1977, Best Song, *A Star Is Born*
   - Emmy: 1965, Outstanding Individual Achievement, *My Name Is Barbra*
     1995, Outstanding Individual Performance, *Barbra Streisand: The Concert*

1995, Outstanding Variety Special, *Barbra Streisand: The Concert*
2001, Outstanding Individual Performance, *Timeless: Live in Concert*
- Tony: 1970, Star of the Decade
- Grammy: 1963, Best Vocal Performance, Album of the Year, *The Barbra Streisand Album*
1964, Best Score, *Funny Girl*
1964, Best Vocal Performance, *People*
1965, Best Vocal Performance, *My Name Is Barbra*
1977, Best Vocal Performance, Song of the Year, *Evergreen*
1980, Best Performance By a Duo, *Guilty* (Barry Gibb)
1986, Best Vocal Performance, *The Broadway Album*
1995, *Lifetime Achievement Award*

Triple Crown

8. Jack Albertson
- Oscar: 1965, Best Supporting Actor, *The Subject Was Roses*
- Emmy: 1975, Outstanding Performance, *Cher Variety Show*
1976, Outstanding Lead Actor, *Chico and the Man*
- Tony: 1965, Outstanding Supporting Actor, *The Subject Was Roses*

9. Anne Bancroft
- Oscar: 1962, Best Actress, *The Miracle Worker*
- Emmy: 1969, Outstanding Lead Actress, *The Women in the Life of a Man*
- Tony: 1957, Best Actress, *Two for the Seesaw*
1959, Best Actress, *The Miracle Worker*

10. Ingrid Bergman
- Oscar: 1944, Best Actress, *Gaslight*
1956, Best Actress, *Anastasia*

1974, Best Supporting Actress, *Murder on the Orient Express*
- Emmy: 1959, Best Actress, *The Turn of the Screw*
1981, Best Actress, *A Woman Named Golda*
- Tony: 1946, Best Actress, *Joan of Lorraine*

11. Shirley Booth
- Oscar: 1952, Best Actress, *Come Back, Little Sheba*
- Emmy: 1961, Outstanding Lead Actress in a Comedy, *Hazel*
1962, Outstanding Lead Actress in a Comedy, *Hazel*
- Tony: 1948, Best Actress, *Goodbye My Fancy*
1949, Best Actress, *Come Back, Little Sheba*
1952, Best Actress, *The Time of the Cuckoo*

12. Melvyn Douglas
- Oscar: 1963, Best Supporting Actor, *Hud*
1979, Best Supporting Actor, *Being There*
- Emmy: 1967, Outstanding Lead Actor, *Do Not Go Gentle into that Night*
- Tony: 1959, Best Actor, *The Best Man*

13. Henry Fonda
- Oscar: 1981, Best Actor, *On Golden Pond*
- Tony: 1947, Best Actor, *Mister Roberts*
- Grammy: 1976, Best Spoken Word, *Great American Documents*

14. Eileen Heckart
- Oscar: 1972, Best Actress, *Butterflies Are Free*
- Emmy: 1992, Best Guest Performance, *Love and War*
- Tony: 2000, *Excellence in the Theater*

15. Jeremy Irons
- Oscar: 1990, Best Actor, *Reversal of Fortune*
- Tony: 1984, Best Actor, *The Real Thing*
- Emmy: 1997, Best Actor, Outstanding Voiceover, *The Great War and the Shaping of the 20th Century, Voice of Siegfried Sassoon*

16. **Thomas Mitchell**
    - Oscar: 1939, Best Supporting Actor, *Stagecoach*
    - Emmy: 1952, Best Actor in unspecified role
    - Tony: 1952, Best Actor, *Hazel Flagg*

17. **Al Pacino**
    - Oscar: 1992, Best Actor, *Scent of a Woman*
    - Emmy: 2004, Best Actor, *Angels in America*
    - Tony: 1969, Best Supporting Actor, *Does a Tiger Wear a Necktie?*
    1977, Best Actor, *The Basic Training of Pavlo Hummel*

18. **Vanessa Redgrave**
    - Oscar: 1977, Best Actress, *Julia*
    - Emmy: 1980, Best Actress, *Playing for Time*
    2000, Best Supporting Actress: *If These Walls Could Talk*
    - Tony: 2003, Best Actress, *Long Day's Journey into Night*

9. **Jason Robards**
    - Oscar: 1976, Best Supporting Actor, *All the President's Men*
    1977, Best Supporting Actor, *Julia*
    - Emmy: 1987, Best Actor in a TV Movie, *Inherit the Wind*
    - Tony: 1958, Best Actor, *The Disenchanted*

20. **Paul Scofield**
    - Oscar: 1966, Best Actor, *A Man for All Seasons*

    - Emmy: 1968, Best Actor, *Male of the Species*
    - Tony: 1961, Best Actor, *A Man for All Seasons*

21. **Maggie Smith**
    - Oscar: 1969, Best Actress, *The Prime of Miss Jean Brodie*
    1978, Best Supporting Actress, *California Suite*
    - Emmy: 2003, Best Actress, *My House in Umbria*
    - Tony: 1990, Best Actress, *Lettuce & Loveage*

22. **Maureen Stapleton**
    - Oscar: 1981, Best Supporting Actress, *Reds*
    - Emmy: 1967, Outstanding Lead Performance, *Among the Paths of Eden*
    - Tony: 1950, Best Actress, *The Rose Tattoo*
    1970, Best Actress, *The Gingerbread Lady*

23. **Jessica Tandy**
    - Oscar: 1989, Best Actress, *Driving Miss Daisy*
    - Emmy: 1987, Best Actress in a TV Movie, *Foxfire*
    - Tony: 1947, Best Actress, *A Streetcar Named Desire*
    1977, Best Actress, *The Gin Game*
    1982, Best Actress, *Foxfire*

OSCAR TRIVIA AND MORE...

Most Oscar Wins:
Katharine Hepburn, 4 Oscars

Most Nominated Performers:
Meryl Streep, 14
Katharine Hepburn, 12
Jack Nicholson, 12
Laurence Olivier, 10
Peter O'Toole, 8 (Honorary Oscar), 2003)
Richard Burton, 7
Deborah Kerr, 6 (Honorary Oscar, 1994)
Thelma Ritter, 6

Most Nominated Performer Without Winning an Oscar:
Peter O'Toole, 8

Most Oscars Won by Individuals:
Walt Disney, 24 (63 nominations)
Edith Head, 8 (35 nominations, Costume Design)

Most Oscars Won in One Year:
1953, Walt Disney, 4 (Feature, Cartoon, Short Subject, Two-Reel Short)
1960, Billy Wilder, 3
1973, Marvin Hamlisch, 3

Performers Receiving Oscars for Best Actor and Best Supporting Actor:
Helen Hayes
Jack Lemmon
Jessica Lange
Ingrid Bergman
Robert DeNiro
Gene Hackman
Maggie Smith
Jack Nicholson
Denzel Washington
Meryl Streep
Kevin Spacey

Most Oscars Won By Directors:
John Ford, 4
Frank Capra, 3
William Wyler, 3 + (Honorary Oscar)
Billy Wilder, 2 + (Honorary Oscar)

Most Nominated Directors:
William Wyler, 12
Billy Wilder, 8

Only Actors To Be Nominated as a Producer, Director, Actor, and Screenwriter in Same Year:
Orson Welles, *Citizen Kane*, 1941
Warren Beatty, *Heaven Can Wait*, 1978
Warren Beatty, *Reds*, 1981

Only Actors to Win Consecutive Oscars:
Luise Rainer (1936/37)
Spencer Tracy (1937/38)
Katharine Hepburn (1967/68)
Jason Robards (1976/77)
Tom Hanks (1993/94)

Only Actors Nominated for Two Oscars in Same Year:
Sigourney Weaver, 1988
Emma Thompson, 1993
Julianne Moore, 2002

Only Actors to be Nominated over Five Decades:
Laurence Olivier (Consecutive Decades)
Jack Nicholson (Consecutive Decades)
Paul Newman
Katharine Hepburn

The Most Consecutive Years Being Nominated for an Oscar:
5, Bette Davis and Greer Garson

Only Performer to be Nominated for an Oscar, Tony, and Emmy for the Same Role:

Jose Ferrer, *Cyrano de Bergerac*

Only Actors to be Nominated for Playing the Same Character in the Same Film:

Kate Winslet as Young Rose Bukater and Gloria Stuart as Old Rose Bukater in *Titanic*

Kate Winslet and Judi Dench as Iris Murdock in *Iris*

Only Actors Nominated Twice for Playing the Same Role in Two Different Movies:

Bing Crosby as Father O'Malley, 1944, *Going My Way*, and 1945, *The Bells of St. Mary's*

Paul Newman as Fast Eddy Felson, 1961, *The Hustler* and 1986, *The Color of Money*

Peter O'Toole as King Henry II, 1964, *Becket* and 1968, *The Lion in Winter*

Al Pacino as Michael Corleone, 1972, *The Godfather* and 1974, *The Godfather, Part II*

Only Actors to Win Oscars for Best Supporting and Best Acting Roles:

Dame Maggie Smith 1969, 1978
Denzel Washington 1989, 2001
Gene Hackman 1971, 1992
Helen Hayes 1931/32, 1970
Ingrid Berman 1944, 1965, 1974
Jack Lemmon 1955, 1973
Jack Nicholson 1975, 1983, 1997
Jessica Lange 1982, 1994
Kevin Spacey 1995, 1999
Meryl Streep 1979, 1982
Robert DeNiro 1974, 1980

Only Actor to Win an Oscar for Playing an Oscar Loser:

Maggie Smith, *California Suite*

Only Actor Nominated for Playing a Real-Life Oscar Winner:

Robert Downey as Charley Chaplin in *Chaplin*

Only Actor to Win an Oscar for Playing the Opposite Sex:

Linda Hunt, 1983, *The Year of Living Dangerously*

Only Actor Nominated Twice (Best Actor and Supporting Actor) for the Same Performance:

Barry Fitzgerald, *Going My Way

Only Actor to Win Oscars for the Same Performance:

Harold Russell, 1944, *The Best Years of Our Lives* (BSA and Honorary)

Only Actors to Direct Themselves to a Best Actor Oscar:

Laurence Olivier, 1948, *Hamlet*
Roberto Benigni, 1998, *Life Is Beautiful*

Only Actors to win an Oscar for the least amount of minutes on the screen

Anthony Quinn, 1956, *Lust for Life*, 9 minutes

Dame Judi Dench, 1998, *Shakespeare in Love*, 8 minutes

Longest Time Between Actor Oscar Wins:

Helen Hayes, 38 years, 4 months, 1931/32 (BA) *The Sin of Madelon Claudet* and 1970 (BSA) *Airport*

Longest Time Between Oscar Nominations:

Jack Palance, 38 years, 1953 (BSA) *Shane* and 1991 (BSA) *City Slickers*

Performer with the Most Movies Made Before Winning an Oscar:

John Wayne, 160 films

Performer with the Longest Film Career:

80 years, Mickey Rooney, First film 1926, *Not to be Trusted*; Last Film to Date 2006, *Night at the Museum *Indicates win.*

Shortest Time on Screen to Win an Oscar:

Actress: Beatrice Straight, *Network*, 5 minutes and 40 seconds.

Actor: Anthony Quinn, *Lust for Life*, 7 minutes and 57 seconds.

Most Nominations Before an Oscar Win:

Geraldine Page, 8 nominations

Only Three-Generation Oscar-Winning Families:

The Hustons

Walter Huston (BSA) 1948, *The Treasure of the Sierra Madre*

John Huston (BD) 1948, *The Treasure of the Sierra Madre*

Angelica Huston (BSA) 1985, *Prizzi's Honor*

The Coppolas

Carmine Coppola (BDS), *The Godfather*

Francis Coppola (BD), *The Godfather*

Sofia Coppola (BOSP), *Lost in Translation*

Only Brother and Sister to Win Oscars:

Lionel Barrymore (BA) 1930, *A Free Soul*

Ethel Barrymore (BSA) 1944, *None but the Lonely Heart*

Only Sisters to Have Competed Against Each Other for Oscars:

1941, *Joan Fontaine, *Suspicion*

1941, Olivia de Havilland, *Hold Back the Dawn*

1966, Vanessa Redgrave, *Morgan!*

1966, Lynne Redgrave, *Georgy Girl*

Only Sisters to Win Oscars:

Joan Fontaine, 1941 (BA) *Suspicion*

Olivia de Havilland 1946 (BA) *To Each His Own*, 1949 (BA) *The Heiress*

Only Actors to Win an Oscar in a Foreign Language Film:

Sofia Loren, 1961, *Two Women*

Roberto Benigni, 1998, *Life Is Beautiful*

Only Actor to Win an Oscar Posthumously:

Peter Finch, 1975, *Network*

Only Six Actors Receiving Posthumous Oscar Nominations:

Jeanne Eagles, Peter Finch, James Dean, Spencer Tracy, Ralph Richardson, and Massimo Troisi

Only Actor to get Two Posthumous Nominations:

James Dean, 1955, *East of Eden* and 1956, *Giant*

Only Oscar Winner to be Murdered:

Haing S. Ngor. He was gunned down in his front yard by gang members because he refused to give up a gold locket with his wife's picture who was allowed to die in childbirth by the Khmer Rouge soldiers in Cambodia.

Only Oscar Winners to Commit Suicide:

Gig Young and George Sanders

Only Oscar Winner to have a Lobotomy:

Warner Baxter

Father and Daughters who have been nominated for Oscars (*indicates win)

Henry Fonda, 1981, *On Golden Pond* and Jane Fonda, 1971 *Klute*, 1978, *Coming Home*

Jon Voight, 1978, *Coming Home* and Angelina Jolie, 1999, *Girl, Interrupted*

John Huston, 1948 (BD) *The Treasure of the Sierra Madre* and Angelica Huston (BSA) *Prizzi's Honor*

Sir Michael Redgrave, 1940 (BA) *Mourning Becomes Electra* and Lynne Redgrave, *Georgy Girl* and Vanessa Redgrave, *Julia*

Sir John Mills, 1970 (BSA) *Ryan's Daughter* and Haley Mills, 1960, Honorary Oscar

Bruce Dern, 1978 (BSA) *Coming Home* and Laura Dern, 1991 (BA) *Rambling Rose*

Ryan O'Neal, 1979 (BSA) *Love Story* and Tatum O'Neal (BSA) *Paper Moon*

Only Mother and Daughter to be Nominated for Oscars:

Liza Minnelli and Judy Garland
Dianne Ladd and Laura Dern

Only Father and Sons to be Nominated for Oscars:

Walter Huston and John Huston
Raymond Massey and Daniel Massey
Henry Fonda and Peter Fonda
Kirk Douglas and Michael Douglas

First Husband and Wife to be Nominated in the Same Movie:

1931/32, *The Guardsman*, Alfred Lunt and
Lynn Fontanne

Only Husband and Wife Who Have Won Oscars:

Laurence Olivier and Vivien Leigh
Paul Newman and Joanne Woodward

Only Oscar Winner with Parents who Received Oscars:

Liza Minnelli, her mother Judy Garland
(1939), and director father Vincent Minnelli

Only Actors to Refuse Oscars:

George C. Scott, 1970, *Patton*
Marlon Brando, 1972, *The Godfather*

Only Actors to Tie for Best Acting Oscars:

1931, Fredric March, *Dr. Jekyll and Mr. Hyde*,
Wallace Beery, *The Champ*
1969, Katharine Hepburn, *The Lion in Winter*,
Barbra Streisand, *Funny Girl*

Shortest Actor to be Nominated:

Michael Dunn (BSA*)* *Ship of Fools*. He was
3'6" tall and the only midget honored.

Tallest Actor to be Nominated:

James Cromwell 1995 (BSA) *Babe*.
He is 6'7" tall.

Tallest Actress to be Nominated:

Hope Emerson 1950 (BSA) *Caged*.
She was 6'3" tall.

Heaviest Actor to be Nominated

Sydney Greenstreet 1941 (BSA) *Casablanca*.
Tipped the scales at over 350 pounds, although
later in their careers Oscar nominees Orson
Welles and Marlon Brando were well over
300 pounds.

Heaviest Actress to be Nominated

Jocelyn Lagarde 1966 (BSA) Hawaii.
She tipped the scales over 400 pounds.

First Performer to be Nominated for an Oscar in a Film Debut:

Lawrence Tibbett, 1936 (BA) *The Rogue Song*

First Performer to Win an Oscar in a Film Debut:

Gale Sondergaard 1936 (BSA) *Anthony Adverse*

First Black Actress to Be Nominated and Win a Best Supporting Oscar:

Hattie McDaniel 1939 (BSA) *Gone With the Wind*

First Black Actress to be Nominated for a Best Acting Oscar:

Dorothy Dandridge, 1954, *Carmen Jones*

First Black Actress to Win a Best Acting Oscar:

Halle Berry, 2001, *Monster's Ball*

First Black Actor to Receive an Oscar:

James Baskette, 1947, Honorary Oscar for
Song of the South

First Black Actor to be Nominated and Win an Oscar:

Sidney Poitier, 1963, *Lilies of the Field*

First Black Actor to be Nominated for Best Supporting Actor:

Rupert Crosse, 1969, *The Reivers*

First Black Actor to Win a Best Supporting Oscar:

Denzel Washington, 1989, *Glory*

The Age Factor

Youngest Actor to Receive an Oscar:

Shirley Temple, 1934, Honorary Oscar. She was 6 years, 10 months old.

Youngest Actor to be Nominated for an Oscar:

Justin Henry, 1979 (BSA) *Kramer vs. Kramer*. He was 8 years, 10 months.

Youngest Actor to be Nominated for a Best Actor Oscar:

Jackie Cooper, 1930/31 (BA) *Skippy*. He was 9 years, 1 month old.

Youngest Actor to Win a Best Supporting Oscar:

Timothy Hutton, 1981 (BSA) *Ordinary People*. He was 20 years, 7 months.

Youngest Actor to Win a Best Actor Oscar:

Adrien Brody, 2003 (BA) *The Pianist*. He was 29 years, 11 months.

Youngest Actress to be Nominated and Win a Best Supporting Oscar:

Tatum O'Neal, 1973 (BSA) *Paper Moon*. She was 10 years, 3 months.

Youngest Actress to be Nominated for a Best Actor Oscar:

Keisha Castle-Hughes, 2003 (BA) *Whale Rider*. She was 13 years, 10 months.

Youngest Actress to Win a Best Acting Oscar:

Marlee Matlin, 1986 (BA) *Children of a Lesser God*. She was 21 years, 7 months.

Oldest Actress to be Nominated for a Best Supporting Oscar:

Gloria Stuart, 1997 (BSA) *Titanic*. She was 87 years, 7 months.

Oldest Actress to Win a Best Supporting Oscar:

Dame Peggy Ashcroft (BSA*) A Passage to India*. She was 77 years, 3 months.

Oldest Actress to Win a Best Actor Oscar:

Jessica Tandy, 1989 (BA) *Driving Miss Daisy*. She was 80 years, 9 months.

Oldest Actor to be Nominated in a Leading Role:

Richard Farnsworth, 1999 (BA) *The Straight Story*. He was 79 years, 167 days old.

Oldest Actor to be Nominated for a Best Supporting Oscar:

Sir Ralph Richardson, 1984 (BSA) *Greystoke: The Legend of Tarzan, Lord of the Apes*. He was 82 years, 1 month old.

Oldest Actor to Win a Best Supporting Oscar:

George Burns, 1978 (BSA) *The Sunshine Boys*. He was 80 years, 2 months.

Oldest Actor to Win a Best Actor Oscar:

Henry Fonda, 1981 (BA) *On Golden Pond*. He was 76 years, 9 months.

Miscellaneous

Most Nominated Actors in the Same Movie: (*Signifies Oscar Winner)

The Longest Day
Eddie Albert
Richard Burton
Red Buttons*
Sean Connery*
Frank Finlay
Henry Fonda*
Leo Genn
Alexander Knox
Sal Mineo
Robert Mitchum
Edmond O'Brien*
Robert Ryan
George Segal
Rod Steiger*
Lee Strasberg
Richard Todd
Stuart Whitman
John Wayne*

Most Actors Nominated with the Same Last Name:

Dudley Moore
Grace Moore
Juanita Moore
Julianne Moore
Mary Tyler Moore
Terry Moore

Famous Actors Who Never Received an Acting Nomination

Alan Ladd
Ann Sheridan
Bela Lugosi
Ben Gazzara
Betty Grable
Boris Karloff
Charles Bronson
Christopher Plummer
Dan Duryea
Dana Andrews
Danny Kaye

Dean Martin
Dick Powell
Dirk Bogarde
Donald Sutherland
Dorothy Lamour
Douglas Fairbanks, Jr.
Edward G. Robinson
Eli Wallach
Elisha Cook Jr.
Erroll Flynn
Everett Sloane
Frances Farmer
Fred MacMurray
George Peppard
George Raft
Glen Ford
Heddy Lamarr
Herbert Marshall
Ida Lupino
Jacqueline Bisset
Jane Russell
Jane Wyatt
Jean Harlow
Jeffrey Hunter
Jerry Lewis
Joan Bennett
Joel McCrea
John Barrymore
John Carradine
John Payne
Joseph Cotton
Kim Novak
Lloyd Bridges
Louis Jourdan
Lucille Ball
Mae West
Malcom McDowell
Margot Kidder
Marilyn Monroe
Maureen O'Hara
Mel Gibson
Myrna Loy
Neville Brand
Oliver Reed
Peter Lorre
Randolph Scott
Raymond Burr

Richard Attenborough
Richard Crenna
Richard Gere
Rita Hayworth
Robert Cummings
Robert Morley
Robert Taylor
Robert Wagner
Robert Walker
Robert Young
Roddy McDowell

Sterling Hayden
Tallulah Bankhead
Tyrone Power
Van Johnson
Veronica Lake
Victor Mature
Vincent Price
W.C. Fields
Warren Oates
Yvonne de Carlo
Zero Mostel

BIBLIOGRAPHY

Anderson, Christopher P., *The Book of People*, Perigee Books, 1981

Aylesworth, Thomas G. and John Bowan, *World Almanac Who's Who of Film*, Bison Book Corporation, 1987

Bergan, Ronald, *A–Z Movie Directors*, Proteus Books, 1982

Bona, Damien and Mason Wiley, *Inside Oscar*, Balentine Books, 1986

Connors, Michael, Beth Fhaner, and Kelly Cross, *Video Hound All Movie Guide and Stargazer*, Visible Ink Press, 1996

Dale, Steve and Matthew Daniels, *Movie Trivia Mania*, Publications International, Beekman House, 1984

Davidson, Bill; *The Real and the Unreal*, Lancer Books, 1961

Fredrik, Natalie and Auriel, Douglas, *History of the Academy Awards*, Price, Stern, Sloan Publishers, 1971

Gordon, Lester, *Let's Go To The Movies!*, Santa Monica Press, 1992

Harkness, John, *Academy Awards Handbook*, Pinnacle Books, 1994

Hirsch, Phil; *Hollywood Uncensored*, Pyramid Books, 1969

Hirschhorn, Joel; *Rating the Movie Stars*, Beekman House, 1993

Katz, Ephraim; *The Film Encyclopedia*, Perigee Books, 1979

Kinn, Gail and Jim Piazza, *The Academy Awards*, Black Dog & Leventhal Publishing, 2002

Lamparski, Richard, *Whatever Became Of...Vol. I*, Ace Books, 1970

Lamparski, Richard; *Whatever Became Of... Vol. III*, Ace Books, 1973

Likeness, George; *The Oscar People: From Wings to My Fair Lady*, The Wayside Press, 1965

Lloyd, Ann and David Robinson, *The Illustrated History of the Cinema*, Orbis Book Publishing, 1986

Lloyd, Ann and Graham Fuller, *The Illustrated Who's Who of the Cinema*, Portland House, 1983

Lucaire, Ed, *Celebrity Book of Lists*, Stein & Day Publishers, 1984

Lucaire, Ed, *Celebrity Trivia*, Warner Books, 1980

Maltin, Leonard; *TV Movies and Video Guide*, Penguin Putnam Inc., 1969

Michael, Paul, *The Academy Awards: A Pictorial History*, Crown Publishing, 1975

Miller, Frank, *Movies We Love*, Turner Publishing, 1996

Monaco, James, *The Encyclopedia of Film*, Perigee Books, 1991

Morgan, Rubin and George Perry, *The Book of Film Biographies*, Fromm International Publishing Corporation, 1997

People's Almanac, Cader Books, 2003

Picard, Roy, *Oscar Stars A to Z*, Headline Books, 1996

Podrazik, Walter, *TV & Movie Facts*, Better Way Books, 1985

Robertson, Patrick, *Movie Facts and Feats*, Sterling Publication, 1980

Rovin, Jeff, *The Book of Movie List*, Signet Books, 1979

Sackett, Susan, *The Hollywood Reporter Book of Box Office Hits*, Billboard Books, 1990

Shale, Richard, *Unger Reference Index of Academy Awards*, Ungar Publishing, 1978

Steinberg, Cobbett; *Reel Facts*, First Vintage Books, 1992

Stewart, Joseph, *Famous Movie Stars & Directors*, Santa Monica Press, 1993

Symons, Mitchell, *That Book of Perfectly Useless Information*, Harper Entertainment, 2004

Worth, Fred, and David Strass, *Hollywood Trivia*, Warner Books, 1981

Internet Resources

Academy of Motion Pictures Arts and Sciences (oscars.org)

Academy of Television Arts and Sciences (emmys.com)

American Film Institute (AFI.com)

American Theater Wing (tonyawards.com)

Cannes Film Festival (festival-cannes.com)

Guide to the Film Stars (filmbug.com)

Hollywood Stories (hollywoodstories.com)

International Movie Data Base (imdb.com)

Johnny's Movie Site (madbeast.com)

New York Times (movie2nyt5imes.com)

Obie Site (villagevoice.com/obies)

The Oscar Site (theoscarsite.com)

Wikipedia On Line (wikipedia.com)

Yahoo Movies (movies.yahoo.com)